Compiler Construction

C.A.R. Hoare, Series Editor

ARNOLD, A., *Finite Transition Systems*
BACKHOUSE, R.C., *Program Construction and Verification*
BACKHOUSE, R.C., *Syntax of Programming Languages*
DEBAKKER, J.W., *Mathematical Theory of Program Correctness*
BARR, M. and WELLS, C., *Category Theory for Computing Science*
BEN-ARI, M., *Principles of Concurrent and Distributed Programming*
BEN-ARI, M., *Mathematical Logic for Computer Science*
BIRD, R. and WADLER, P., *Introduction to Functional Programming*
BORNAT, R., *Programming from First Principles*
BOVET, D.P. and CRESCENZI, P., *Introduction to the Theory of Complexity*
BUSTARD, D., ELDER, J. and WELSH, J., *Concurrent Program Structures*
CLARK, K. and McCABE, F.G., *Micro-Prolog: Programming in Logic*
DAHL, O.-J., *Verifiable Programming*
DROMEY, R.G., *How to Solve It by Computer*
DUNCAN, E., *Microprocessor Programming and Software Development*
ELDER, J., *Construction of Data Processing Software*
ELLIOTT, R.J. and HOARE, C.A.R. (eds), *Scientific Applications of Multiprocessors*
FREEMAN, T.L. and PHILLIPS, R.C., *Parallel Numerical Algorithms*
GOLDSCHLAGER, L. and LISTER, A., *Computer Science: A modern introduction (2nd edn)*
GORDON, M.J.C., *Programming Language Theory and Its Implementation*
GRAY, P.M.D., KULKARNI, K.G. and PATON, N.W., *Object-oriented Databases*
HAYES, I. (ed.), *Specification Case Studies (2nd edn)*
HEHNER, E.C.R., *The Logic of Programming*
HENDERSON, P., *Functional Programming: Application and implementation*
HOARE, C.A.R., *Communicating Sequential Processes*
HOARE, C.A.R. and GORDON, M.J.C. (eds), *Mechanized Reasoning and Hardware Design*
HOARE, C.A.R. and JONES, C.B. (eds), *Essays in Computing Science*
HOARE, C.A.R. and SHEPHERDSON, J.C. (eds), *Mechanical Logic and Programming Languages*
HUGHES, J.G., *Database Technology: A software engineering approach*
HUGHES, J.G., *Object-oriented Databases*
INMOS LTD, *Occam 2 Reference Manual*
JACKSON, M.A., *System Development*
JOHNSTON, H., *Learning to Program*
JONES, C.B., *Systematic Software Development Using VDM (2nd edn)*
JONES, C.B. and SHAW, R.C.F. (eds), *Case Studies in Systematic Software Development*
JONES, G., *Programming in Occam*
JONES, G. and GOLDSMITH, M., *Programming in Occam 2*
JONES, N.D., GOMARD, C.K. and SESTOFT, P., *Partial Evaluation and Automatic Program Generation*
JOSEPH, M., PRASAD, V.R. and NATARAJAN, N., *A Multiprocessor Operating System*
KALDEWAIJ, A., *Programming: The derivation of algorithms*
KING, P.J.B., *Computer and Communications Systems Performance Modelling*
LALEMENT, R., *Computation as Logic*
LEW, A., *Computer Science: A mathematical introduction*
McCABE, F.G., *Logic and Objects*
McCABE, F.G., *High-level Programmer's Guide to the 68000*
MEYER, B., *Introduction to the Theory of Programming Languages*
MEYER, B., *Object-oriented Software Construction*
MILNER, R., *Communication and Concurrency*
MITCHELL, R., *Abstract Data Types and Modula 2*
MORGAN, C., *Programming from Specifications*
PEYTON JONES, S.L., *The Implementation of Functional Programming Languages*
PEYTON JONES, S. and LESTER, D., *Implementing Functional Languages*
POMBERGER, G., *Software Engineering and Modula-2*
POTTER, B., SINCLAIR, J. and TILL, D., *An Introduction to Formal Specification and Z*
REYNOLDS, J.C., *The Craft of Programming*

Compiler Construction
A Recursive Descent Model

John Elder

Queen's University of Belfast
Northern Ireland

Prentice Hall

New York   London   Toronto   Sydney   Tokyo   Singapore

First published 1994 by
Prentice Hall International (UK) Limited
Campus 400, Maylands Avenue
Hemel Hempstead
Hertfordshire, HP2 7EZ
A division of
Simon & Schuster International Group

Printed and bound in Great Britain at the
University Press, Cambridge

Library of Congress Cataloging-in-Publication Data

Elder, John, 1949–
    Compiler construction: a recursive descent model / John Elder
        p.   cm. – (Prentice Hall international series in computer
science)
    Includes bibliographical references and index.
    ISBN 0-13-291139-6
    1. Compilers (Computer programs)   I. Title.   II. Series.
QA76.76.C65E43   1994
005.4′53–dc20
                                                          93-49801
                                                              CIP

British Library Cataloguing in Publication Data

A catalogue record for this book is available from
the British Library

ISBN 0-13-291139-6

---

1 2 3 4 5   98 97 96 95 94

Contents

Preface

Any reader who has programmed a computer in a high-level programming language will be aware that compilers are an essential part of a modern computer system— without them all programming would have to be done at the machine language level. Until I saw my first compiler from the inside, during a graduate course given by Jim Welsh at Belfast in 1972, the translation of Fortran and Pascal programs into machine code had been a complete mystery to me and a source of much wonderment. Later I undertook the implementation of a Pascal subset as a project supervised by Jim. It was indeed a fortunate choice as it led to me becoming one of a generation of software developers in Belfast who produced a wide range of compilers for Pascal-based programming languages.

What impressed me in particular about the first compiler to whose inner workings I was exposed, the famous Belfast Pascal compiler for the ICL 1900 series machines, was the clarity of its design and the elegance of its programming. Many compiler writers who read that compiler or subsequent compilers based on it were equally impressed and strove to incorporate the same qualities in their own products. When Jim Welsh and Atholl Hay published their model implementation of Standard Pascal as a book, 'literate programming' took on a new meaning. Demonstrating and teaching those qualities of clarity and elegance to students and enabling them to appreciate that compilers can be objects of programming beauty are sources of much personal satisfaction.

Aims of the book

The aim of this book is to describe the principles and techniques involved in compiler design and construction for languages in the Pascal family and to illustrate the use of many of them within an actual compiler. Some compiler textbooks concentrate on providing an in-depth theoretical knowledge of the subject for the reader, while others are devoted to descriptions of the implementations of particular compilers. In contrast, this book attempts to blend theoretical knowledge with practical experience by taking a pragmatic approach to compiler design and implementation. It presents a restricted amount of theory and techniques, but quite sufficient to enable the development of compilers for procedural languages such as Pascal and Modula-2.

Each aspect of compiler design treated is, as far as possible, related to the practical study of a complete, working, compiler which is developed as a running theme throughout the book and its text is included in the book. This model compiler implements a practical programming language that includes many of the features of Modula-2. It is written in Modula-2 and its modular design makes its structure and detail easy to construct and equally easy to read by anyone with a knowledge of Pascal or a similar language. The design is based upon a technique known as recursive descent analysis, a commonly used method for compilation and generally accepted to be one of the best methods. It is also one which can be readily employed in the development of other types of software.

This study is intended to help the readers to understand the workings of the compilers they use, and thereby enable them to use them a little better. Hopefully, it may even lead some readers to become compiler writers themselves! However, the compiler design and construction techniques described herein are applicable to a very wide range of text processing and language processing software and, together with the experience gained from working with the model compiler, should enable the reader to tackle, with confidence, a wide range of applications.

A secondary, but nonetheless important, objective is to provide an opportunity (perhaps the first for some readers) to study a large-scale program in some detail, and to observe the standards of structuring and documentation used therein. As such it is also an example of the application of sound software engineering principles and techniques, something which is not always demonstrated in compiler textbooks!

The case study compiler

The language translated by the model compiler is a Modula-2 subset, named *Model*, that features scalar and array data-types as well as a wide range of statements, including procedures, case-statements and for-statements. The target computer is a hypothetical register-based machine, known as the *Target*. However, its architecture has been designed to be representative of that of many modern computers. A consequence of choosing a hypothetical computer as the target machine is that it enables much of the intricate and obscuring detail of code generation to be avoided and a complete code generator of manageable size and complexity may be developed. An appendix contains a complete listing of a simulator for the Target machine, thereby making it possible to execute the object programs produced by the compiler.

The compiler runs on any Apple Macintosh and, with slight modifications of implementation-defined features which are, however, isolated to one or two modules, will run on any machine for which a Modula-2 compiler is available. Although the appendices contain the complete compiler text, the source text of both the compiler and the Target simulator may be obtained by contacting the author at Department of

Computer Science, The Queen's University of Belfast, Belfast BT7 1NN, Northern Ireland, United Kingdom.

Intended readership

This book is suitable for undergraduate and graduate students of computer science and information technology. The development and text of a complete compiler may appeal to professional software engineers and language implementors. The practical approach which has been adopted makes it useful also for self-study as there are numerous references given to other books and papers giving more detailed information as well as extensive exercises.

The background required is competence in a high-level programming language such as Pascal, Modula-2 or C and previous attendance at a course on data structures. Although it is used to implement the model compiler, it is not essential to have any previous knowledge of Modula-2. Indeed, it can be learned easily by reading the program fragments in the text and the compiler module listings in the appendices.

Structure of the book

Chapter 1 is an introduction to various types of compilers and discusses the decomposition of a typical compiler into its various component parts.

Chapter 2 introduces the Model language, the Target machine and the Model compiler. Chapter 3 examines the interface between the compiler and its users and in Chapter 4 we construct a source handler for the Model compiler, which will handle the input of the programs to be compiled and the production of their listings.

Chapter 5 develops the basic structuring of the compiler into an analyzer and a code generator and the further subdivision of the analyzer into lexical, syntax and semantic analyzers.

Chapter 6 introduces notations for defining the grammars of context-free programming languages, and some transformations which enable the manipulation of grammars into forms suitable for use in parsing algorithms.

Chapter 7 concentrates on lexical analysis and shows how a scanner can be constructed systematically from the lexical definition of the symbols of a language.

Chapter 8 studies syntax analysis in more detail. It looks at top-down analysis and recursive descent parsing in particular, and contrasts them with bottom-up analysis techniques.

Chapter 9 constructs a working recursive descent parser for Model by deriving a set of rules for the systematic translation of the syntax rules of such a language into equivalent parsing routines.

Chapter 10 examines the problems of handling input programs which are syntactically incorrect and develops a technique for the systematic introduction of error recovery actions into the parsing routines.

Chapter 11 presents a range of possible structures and searching algorithms for the tables used to record information about the objects, such as identifiers and labels, declared in a program. Chapter 12 examines the information that must be recorded for such objects. It also discusses the implementation of type checking actions and introduces methods for recovery from contextual errors, such as type incompatibilities and violations of the scope rules, that may occur in an input program.

Chapter 13 applies the methods and techniques developed in Chapters 11 and 12 to the construction of a working semantic analyzer for Model, by enrichment of the syntax analyzer with the required semantic actions.

Chapter 14 examines the interface between the analyzer and the code generator and defines it in terms of the operation of a hypothetical stack-based computer.

Chapter 15 looks at the various forms of object code that may be generated by a compiler—absolute machine code, relocatable code and interpretive code.

Chapter 16 defines possible machine representations of the values of the range of data-types which occur in Pascal-like languages. Chapter 17 develops this treatment of the run-time representation of source programs by discussing storage allocation and the representation of procedures, functions and their parameters.

Chapter 18 shows how machine code is generated and is a detailed examination of the generation process, illustrated by the construction of the complete code generator for the Model compiler.

Chapter 19 completes the book by considering the generation of run-time error checking code and the provision of meaningful, source-related, run-time error diagnostic facilities.

Exercises

With just a few exceptions, all the chapters end with a set of exercises. Some of these are pen and paper exercises that reinforce the material of the chapter, while others involve the programming of modifications to the Model compiler or its extension with additional language features.

Acknowledgements

Much, indeed almost all, of what I know about compilation is a result of my association with Jim Welsh that began in 1973 when he acted as my project supervisor. I soon came to realize that he was not just a superb compiler writer but also a creator of programs that were always of great elegance. Unfortunately other commitments made it impossible for him to become involved in the writing of this book but he has allowed much material of his to be used in various ways. In particular, some passages of this book have been based directly on corresponding parts of the compiler section in *Structured System Programming*, an outstanding book on software development written by Jim with Mike McKeag. They appear with Jim's permission and I wish to record my thanks to him for his encouragement and assistance.

Most of the contents of the book have been presented to various classes of final-year students at the Queen's University of Belfast and they have been responsible for discovering errors both in the material and in the Model compiler. Most of the exercises have been tried out on them, either as programming assignments or as examination questions! Sean McKeever has always been a willing source of advice and assistance. Queen's University must also be thanked for their excellent computing facilities on which the software was developed and this book was produced. Finally, my thanks to Helen Martin at Prentice Hall International for tolerating my failure to meet deadlines.

Belfast   John Elder
August 1993

Chapter 1

Introduction

1.1 What is a compiler?

A *compiler* is a computer program which accepts as input the text of a program expressed in a given programming language (known as the *source program*) and produces as output an equivalent machine code program (known as the *object program*). This object program may then be executed on its own data to produce results of some form. The *compilation/execution cycle* for a given source program is shown in Figure 1.1.

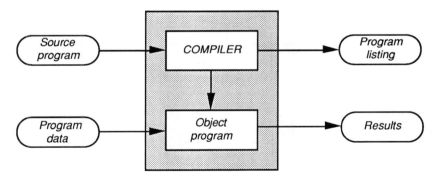

Figure 1.1 *Compile/execute cycle (1)*

This diagram implies that the compiler and the complete object program which it produces coexist within the computer's main memory. We refer to such an scheme as *in-memory compilation* and, whenever it can be employed, it is extremely efficient since it minimizes the overheads involved in proceeding from compilation of the source program to execution of the corresponding object program, and also in proceeding from the compilation of one source program to the next if both programs are expressed in the same programming language.

In general, however, compilers are written to output the object program which they produce to some secondary memory medium such as a disk file. When compilation of a source program is complete the compiler may be deleted from the computer's main memory and a utility program, known as a *loader*, is then invoked to copy the object program from the secondary memory medium into the main memory ready for execution. The compile/execute cycle is then as shown in Figure 1.2.

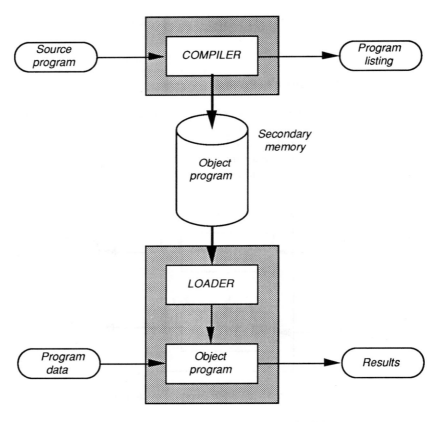

Figure 1.2   *Compile/execute cycle (2)*

With this arrangement the secondary memory copy of the object program can be retained—allowing repeated load and execute cycles to take place without further compilation. On the other hand, the compiler is no longer available in the computer's main memory after any single compile/execute cycle and, in general, has itself to be reloaded (from a secondary memory copy) for each subsequent program compilation.

1.2   What is an object program?

The nature of the object program may also vary from one compile/execute scheme to another. Our discussion so far has implied that the (loaded) object program is a machine code program which is directly executable by the computer hardware. This is normally the case when efficient execution of the object program is required. In some situations, however, it may be preferable to use an *interpretive execution* scheme in which the object program is not directly executable by the machine hardware itself but depends on an *interpreter* program (an item of software) for its execution. In the extreme case an interpreter could be provided which interprets the source program itself—analyzing each individual source statement each time it is to be executed in order to determine its executable action. In almost all practical situations such a pure interpretive scheme is very expensive in terms of the object program's execution time and its size. As we shall see, however, an intermediate scheme in which compilation generates an interpretable object code form, somewhere between source characters and directly executable machine instructions, can have advantages in the provision of error diagnostics and error security.

Thus, in practice, a spectrum of object code forms is possible. As we shall see, the exact nature of the object program will not affect our study of the compilation process for some time. In this book we use the word *compilation* to mean the process of translating a source program into a chosen object program form, whatever that may be.

1.3   The compilation process

The compilation process can be split into two main parts, *analysis* of the source program and *synthesis* of the object program. These parts can, in turn, be further subdivided as follows. Analysis involves the following three phases:

(a) scanning the source program character by character to recognize the basic language *symbols* (i.e. identifiers, reserved words, integer numbers, operators, etc.) which make up the program—this is known as *lexical analysis*;

(b) determining the syntactic structure of the sequence of symbols making up the program and verifying that this structure conforms to the syntax rules of the programming language—this process is known as *syntax analysis*;

(c) recording the meaning given to identifiers by their declarations in the source program and checking that their subsequent usage is compatible with their declarations—known as *semantic analysis*.

Synthesis involves two main phases:

(a) determining how and where the variables declared in the source program will be represented in memory locations within the object program—this is known as *storage allocation*;

(b) determining the object code sequences required to effect in execution the sequence of actions defined by the source program—this is the process of *code generation*.

The overall process of compilation is depicted in Figure 1.3.

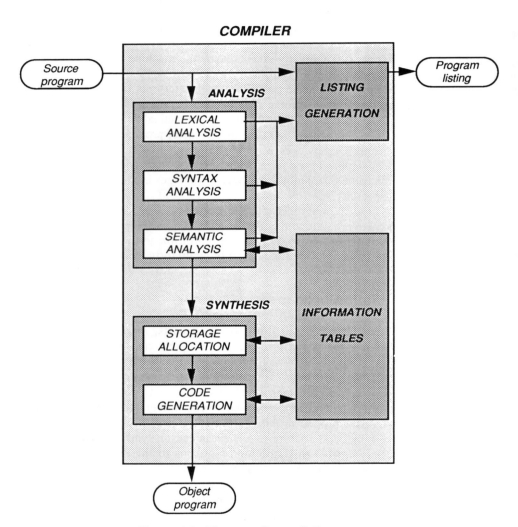

Figure 1.3 *The overall compilation process*

During the analysis process some form of *program listing* is generated, containing the text of the original source program together with indications of the nature and position of any language violations detected by the analysis. The synthesis process makes use of *information tables*, created during the analysis process, which contain information associated with the identifiers and various other source program entities.

A compilation process in which each of these phases of compilation is completed for a given source program before the next phase is begun is known as *multi-pass compilation*. Under certain conditions the phases can, however, be interleaved or carried out in parallel—this is known as *one-pass compilation*.

In general, multi-pass compilation allows a more complex programming language to be translated, as well as the generation of more efficient object code, but is slower and more expensive to use. One-pass compilation imposes particular constraints on the structure of source programs and cannot, in general, produce optimum object code but it does have the advantage of being cheaper to use.

In the remainder of this book we will consider these five phases of compilation, and various subsidiary related topics, in turn.

1.4   Further reading

This book assumes and requires that the reader is familiar with the concepts of high-level programming languages such as Pascal and Modula-2. A detailed treatment of all of the concepts required appears in Ghezzi and Jazayeri (1987).

There is a wide range of introductory texts describing compilers and their construction. For a readable overview of high-level programming languages and an introduction to compilers, see Watson (1989). McKeeman's (1976a) introductory paper at a compiler construction course gives a concise introduction to the various phases of the compilation process.

Chapter 2

The Model compiler

As we saw in the previous chapter, a compiler accepts as input another program expressed in a given *source* language and produces as output an equivalent program in another language (the *object* or *target* language), together with a listing of the source program input. Formally, we might express this translational process as

$$compiler\ (source\ program)\ (object\ program,\ listing)$$

i.e. the *compiler* transforms an input *source program* into an *object program* and a *program listing*. This is shown diagrammatically in Figure 2.1.

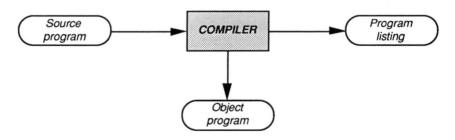

Figure 2.1 *Function of a compiler*

The notation

$$P\ (x_1, x_2, \ldots)\ (y_1, y_2, \ldots)$$

is used to denote that a software component P takes $x_1, x_2, \ldots$ as inputs and produces $y_1, y_2, \ldots$ as outputs.

2.1   Developing a compiler

Any particular compiler is characterized by three aspects:

- The language in which the source program is expressed—the *source language*.
- The *target machine* for which the corresponding object program is generated.
- The language in which the compiler is written—the *implementation language*.

In this book we develop a compiler whose source language is Model, a sequential programming language which is a subset of the language Modula-2. The target machine for this compiler is a hypothetical computer (described later in this chapter) which we choose to name the *Target* computer, and the implementation language is Modula-2 (to be precise, the MetroWerks™ implementation of Modula-2 which runs on the Apple Macintosh™ range of computers). These three characteristics may be summarized diagrammatically in the form of a *T-diagram*. Such a diagram is often used to describe language translator production processes involving different machines and different implementation languages.

In a T-diagram the horizontal arms of the T show the source and target languages of the translation process, and the base of the T indicates the language which is used to implement the translator concerned. The name of the piece of software appears at the top of the T. Figure 2.2 shows the T-diagram for our compiler—the *Target Model compiler* is a Modula-2 program which translates programs written in the Model programming language into Target machine code (*Target M/C*) programs.

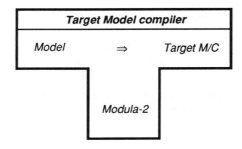

Figure 2.2   *T-diagram for the Model compiler*

Of course, this development process requires the existence of a Modula-2 implementation on which to run our compiler. The MetroWerks implementation of Modula-2 for the Apple Macintosh can thus be used to translate our Model compiler program (written in Modula-2) into an equivalent object program which will run on the Macintosh (which contains a Motorola 68000 series processor). This object program is a Model compiler, but it can only be executed on the Macintosh and not on the Target computer itself—i.e. it is what is known as a *cross-compiler*. The object programs which it produces have to be transported in some way from the *host* Macintosh machine to the Target computer in order for them to be executed. In a composite T-diagram, such as Figure 2.3, the right hand (shaded) T is the program which results when the program denoted by the left hand T is used as input to the program denoted by the middle T, and hence the arms of the middle T match the bases of the Ts to the left and right.

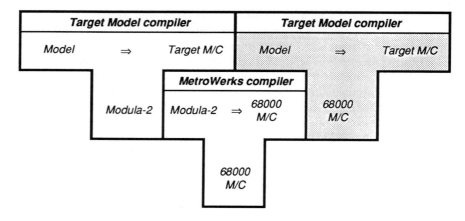

Figure 2.3   *Development process for the Model compiler*

Hence the overall development process consists of

(a)   writing the Target Model compiler in Modula-2;
(b)   compiling this program using the MetroWerks Modula-2 compiler on the Macintosh;
(c)   running the resultant program on the Macintosh to translate Model programs into Target machine code programs.

2.2   The input

At first sight the input which a compiler is required to handle may appear to be perfectly defined, since each source language usually has a defining document which specifies exactly the set of programs for which the compiler may be asked to generate equivalent object code. However, a practical compiler is expected not only to generate object code for the correct programs of the source language, but also to diagnose faults in incorrect ones. In practice therefore all possible inputs must be accepted by a compiler and treated in some appropriate manner.

The source language definition remains the central component of the compiler writer's specification. Definition of the structure or *syntax* of the programs is well understood and a standard notation—the so-called *extended Backus–Naur form* or *EBNF*—is widely used in language definitions. Formal definition of the meaning or semantics given to programs, and the semantic constraints which the language rules impose, is a more difficult problem. No generally accepted method has so far emerged.

Appendix 1 gives a full definition of the principal features of Model in the form of a formal syntax description, using EBNF, accompanied by an informal semantic description expressed in natural language. As we shall see, the formal syntax definition greatly assists the compiler writer in determining the structural framework of the compiler, while the informal description of semantics imposes a much greater burden in the realization of semantic analysis and the generation of object code.

Model has been defined to contain a range of features which make it suitable as a vehicle for illustrating many of the techniques and operations performed within a typical compiler—this range is a balance of facilities for the description of data and performable operations on those data that is useful for the solution of a wide range of programming problems. These features reflect the strong correspondence between the structures of data and the structure of the processing required by those data. Thus Model is also usable as an elementary practical programming language suitable for teaching introductory computer programming.

Model provides three primitive *scalar-types*:

- The type *BOOLEAN* whose two values are denoted by the constant-identifiers *TRUE* and *FALSE*, representing the corresponding logical truth values.
- The type *INTEGER* defines an ordered subset of the whole numbers.
- The values of the type *CHAR* are the ordered set of characters in the ASCII (American Standard Character set for Information Interchange) character set and are denoted by character-literals, e.g. 'A', '&'.

An *array* consists of a number of component data items identical in nature and type, e.g.

    VAR HoursWorkedPerDay: ARRAY[1..7] OF INTEGER

with individual items (*elements*) denoted as e.g.

    HoursWorked[E]

where *E* is an expression whose value must lie in the range *1..7*.

Procedures in Model do not take parameters, but may have local variables declared within them and may be arbitrarily nested—recursive procedure calls are allowed.

Model is a *sequential* programming language. Its executable action is defined by a *statement-sequence*, which consists of a sequence of *statements*, each specifying a corresponding action to be carried out by the program, e.g.

    S1; S2; ... ; Sn

The statements are executed in the order in which they are written.
    In the Model *if-statement*

    IF C THEN SS1 ELSE SS2 END

the expression C must produce a *BOOLEAN* value that determines which of the
alternative sequences of actions *SS1* or *SS2* is executed.   The *ELSE* limb may be
omitted.
    A *case-statement* takes the form

    CASE E OF
    | E1: SS1
    | E2: SS2
        ...
    | En: SSn
    END

    It specifies the selection for execution of one of a set of statement-sequences
SS1,...,SSn depending on which of the distinct values *E1..En* is currently taken by the
so-called *selector* expression E.   E, E1..En must all be of the same scalar-type.
    A *loop-statement*

    LOOP SS END

specifies the repeated execution of the statement-sequence *SS*. This sequence will
normally contain an *exit-statement*, viz.

    EXIT

whose action is to cause the termination of the execution of the immediately enclosing
loop-statement.
    A *for-statement* takes the general form

    FOR v := E1 TO E2 DO SS END

and specifies that each of the ascending subsequence of values *E1..En* is to be
assigned, in turn, to the *control-variable v*.   Following each assignment the
statement-sequence *SS* is to be executed.
    Two input and output statements are provided in Model. The *read-statement*

    READ(v)

allows a value to be input for any variable *v* of type either *INTEGER* or *CHAR*, while
the *write-statement*

WRITE(E)

provides for the output of an expression *E* whose value may be of either of the types *INTEGER* or *CHAR*.

2.3 The outputs

We have already seen that the output from a compiler consists of two parts—the *object program* generated and the *program listing*. Since any compiler will usually have to deal with more incorrect programs than correct ones, the qualities of the program listing and the error messages produced are just as important as those of the object code.

2.3.1 The program listing

The source program listing output by the compiler provides

(a) a confirmation, and permanent visual record, of the text of the source program compiled;
(b) an indication of all the errors detected during the compilation of the source program.

The exact form in which these are provided is usually left for the compiler writer to determine, and is a straightforward, but often neglected, exercise in human–computer engineering. The programmer using the compiler expects it

(a) to enforce all of the language rules and restrictions;
(b) to find all the violations of the language rules within the source program in a single compilation run;
(c) to generate no spurious or misleading error reports due to preceding errors.

Achieving goals (b) and (c) implies that the compiler must resume compilation immediately after detecting each error as if the error had not existed. Clearly this is an impossible task in some situations. However, this need for satisfactory *error recovery* is a dominant influence on the design of a compiler. We shall consider the detailed design and implementation of program listings and the strategy for effective error recovery in subsequent chapters.

2.3.2 The object program

In the case of the object program output by the compiler the ultimate object language will usually be precisely defined, e.g. as the machine language of the object machine, but the compiler writer has the freedom to choose the way in which the various source language features are expressed in the object language. He or she does so subject to specifiable requirements of the object program produced, e.g.

(a) its correctness;
(b) its compactness or storage economy;
(c) its speed of execution;
(d) the security against run-time errors (such as arithmetic overflow or array subscript errors) which it provides;
(e) the run-time diagnostic facilities which it provides.

It is soon apparent, however, that some of these desirable characteristics of the object program are mutually conflicting, and cannot all be realized in a single object program form. For example, providing security against run-time errors will often necessitate the inclusion of additional error checking code in the object program which will obviously increase the size of the program and degrade its execution speed. The code generated by any particular compiler represents some compromise between them, according to the particular priorities adopted in its construction. In some cases there may be different versions of a compiler available, each of which optimizes the object programs it generates in accordance with one or more of the above requirements.

We will consider the alternative forms for object code in some detail later in this book. The exact form chosen has relatively little impact on the early stages of compiler development, but the possibility of adapting the compiler to the generation of different forms of object code is one which the compiler writer should bear in mind when choosing the overall structure of the compiler.

In the Model compiler the generation of compact, reasonably efficient machine code for a realistic machine is illustrated. This machine, the Target computer, is not an actual existing machine, but its features are typical of many available computers and are particularly appropriate for executing programs compiled from Model.

The Target is a *stack* computer, i.e. it provides a stack within its memory for holding intermediate data values. A stack provides a simple method of evaluating expressions—*load* instructions are used to place (*push*) data values on to the top of the stack and various instructions (for performing arithmetic, logical and comparison operations) replace the topmost values on the stack by the result of the application of a particular operation. Other instructions include ones for moving (*popping*) values on top of the stack to specified memory locations.

For example, the evaluation of the arithmetic expression

$$x * (y + w) - z$$

on the Target could be performed by the following sequence of instructions:

```
LOAD        x
LOAD        y
```

```
LOAD        w
ADD
MUL
LOAD        z
SUB
```

Figure 2.4 traces the state of the stack as each instruction in this sequence is executed. We assume that the stack is empty initially, and that it grows downwards.

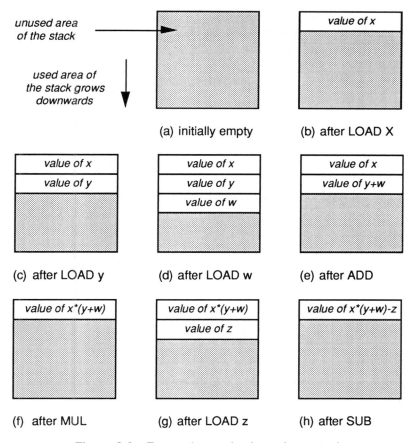

Figure 2.4 *Expression evaluation using a stack*

Each word in the main memory of the Target is 16 bits long, and the total main memory size is 2^{16} words. Within the memory, integer values are represented in twos complement form.

Two *input and output channels* are provided which enable character data (represented using ASCII codes) to be moved to and from the top of the stack.

Four registers on the Target are dedicated to holding the addresses of locations within the main memory:

SP   Stack Pointer register
BP   Base Pointer register
FP   Frame Pointer register
MP   Mark Pointer register

The *SP* register (see Figure 2.5) addresses the location immediately beyond the end of the stack; the *BP* register is used to address the first word of a loaded program; the *FP* and *MP* registers are associated with the execution of procedures and will be considered in detail in Chapter 17.

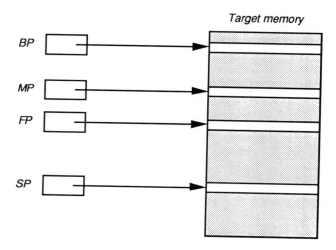

Figure 2.5 *Memory addressing registers*

The *program counter* register *PC* holds the address of the next object program instruction to be executed (the Target's memory is used to hold both data and instructions).

The following conventions are used below to refer to these registers and their contents:

r   denotes   one of the registers *SP, BP, FP, MP, PC*
r^   denotes   the memory location whose address is contained in register *r*
(r)   denotes   the contents of register *r*

Many of the Target's instructions use memory addresses as operands. Such addresses are always expressed as a displacement *n* relative to a base address computed from the contents of a specified register *r*. This base address is expressed by means of a pair *[r, l]* where

*[r, 0] = r^*
[r, 1] = (r^)
[r, 2] = ((r^)) and so on.

Hence, in Figure 2.6,

[FP, 0] denotes the memory address   *3456*
[FP, 1] denotes the memory address   *3171*
[FP, 2] denotes the memory address   *1234*
[FP, 3] denotes the memory address   *791*

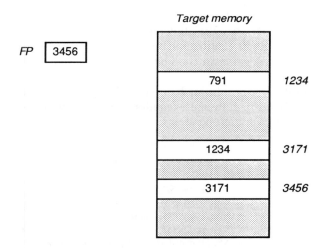

Figure 2.6 *Memory addressing on the Target computer*

Each Target instruction is held as two 16-bit words and consists of four fields (some instructions do not use certain fields). The first word contains

- an 8-bit *operation code* field *f*
- a 2-bit *register* field *r* [where *BP* = 0, *FP* = 1, *MP* = 2, *SP* = 3]
- a 6-bit *address level* field *l*

while the second word consists of a single field

- a 16-bit *operand* field *n*

as shown in Figure 2.7.

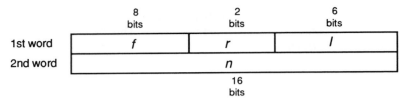

Figure 2.7   *Target instruction structure*

The *processor status word (PSR)* register consists of a sequence of bits as follows:

Bit 0	C	Checks bit
Bit 1	V	Overflow bit
Bit 2	E	Range Error bit
Bit 3	H	Halted bit
Bit 4	M	Memory Violation bit
Bit 5	R	Register Violation bit
Bit 6	I	Illegal Instruction bit

PSR[b] denotes the value of the bit *b* in the PSR register. When a program begins execution *PSR[H]* is set to zero and execution continues until *PSR[H]* is set to 1. The other bits are set by various operations.

NOOP		
LOADL	n	$(SP^\wedge) \leftarrow n; inc(SP, 1)$
LOADR	r	$(SP^\wedge) \leftarrow (r); inc(SP, 1)$
LOAD	n, [r, l]	$transfer(1, m, SP^\wedge); inc(SP, 1)$
LOADA	n, [r, l]	$(SP^\wedge) \leftarrow m; inc(SP, 1)$
LOADI	n	$dec(SP, 1); transfer(n, (SP^\wedge), SP^\wedge); inc(SP, n)$
STORER	r	$dec(SP, 1); (r) \leftarrow (SP^\wedge);$
STORE	n, [r, l]	$dec(SP, 1); transfer(1, SP^\wedge, m)$
STOREI	n	$dec(SP, n+1); transfer(n, SP^\wedge, (SP^\wedge+n))$
INCR	n	$(SP^\wedge{-}1) \leftarrow (SP^\wedge{-}1) + n$
STZ	n, [r, l]	$(m) \leftarrow 0$
INCREG	r, n	$inc(r, n)$
MOVE	n	$transfer(n, (SP^\wedge{-}2), (SP^\wedge{-}1); dec(SP, 2)$
SLL	n	*shift* $(SP^\wedge{-}1)$ *n mod 16 bits to the left*
SRL	n	*shift* $(SP^\wedge{-}1)$ *n mod 16 bits to the right*
ADD		$dec(SP, 1); (SP^\wedge{-}1) \leftarrow (SP^\wedge{-}1) + (SP^\wedge)$
SUB		$dec(SP, 1); (SP^\wedge{-}1) \leftarrow (SP^\wedge{-}1) - (SP^\wedge)$
MUL		$dec(SP, 1); (SP^\wedge{-}1) \leftarrow (SP^\wedge{-}1) * (SP^\wedge)$

DVD		$dec(SP, 1); (SP^\wedge\text{-}1) \leftarrow (SP^\wedge\text{-}1) \; div \; (SP^\wedge)$
DREM		$dec(SP, 1); (SP^\wedge\text{-}1) \leftarrow (SP^\wedge\text{-}1) \; mod \; (SP^\wedge)$
LAND		$dec(SP, 1); (SP^\wedge\text{-}1) \leftarrow (SP^\wedge\text{-}1) \; and \; (SP^\wedge)$
LOR		$dec(SP, 1); (SP^\wedge\text{-}1) \leftarrow (SP^\wedge\text{-}1) \; or \; (SP^\wedge)$
INV		$(SP^\wedge\text{-}1) \leftarrow not \; (SP^\wedge\text{-}1)$
NEG		$(SP^\wedge\text{-}1) \leftarrow - (SP^\wedge\text{-}1)$
CLT		$dec(SP, 1); if (SP^\wedge\text{-}1) < (SP^\wedge) \; then \; (SP^\wedge\text{-}1) \leftarrow 1 \; else \; (SP^\wedge\text{-}1) \leftarrow 0$
CLE		$dec(SP, 1); if (SP^\wedge\text{-}1) \leq (SP^\wedge) \; then \; (SP^\wedge\text{-}1) \leftarrow 1 \; else \; (SP^\wedge\text{-}1) \leftarrow 0$
CEQ		$dec(SP, 1); if (SP^\wedge\text{-}1) = (SP^\wedge) \; then \; (SP^\wedge\text{-}1) \leftarrow 1 \; else \; (SP^\wedge\text{-}1) \leftarrow 0$
CNE		$dec(SP, 1); if (SP^\wedge\text{-}1) \neq (SP^\wedge) \; then \; (SP^\wedge\text{-}1) \leftarrow 1 \; else \; (SP^\wedge\text{-}1) \leftarrow 0$
BRN	n, [r, l]	$(PC) \leftarrow m$
BIDX	n	$dec(SP, 1); (PC) \leftarrow (SP^\wedge)*n + (PC)$
BZE	n, [r, l]	$dec(SP, 1); if (SP^\wedge) = 0 \; then \; (PC) \leftarrow m$
BNZ	n, [r, l]	$dec(SP, 1); if (SP^\wedge) \neq 0 \; then \; (PC) \leftarrow m$
BNG	n, [r, l]	$dec(SP, 1); if (SP^\wedge) < 0 \; then \; (PC) \leftarrow m$
BPZ	n, [r, l]	$dec(SP, 1); if (SP^\wedge) \geq 0 \; then \; (PC) \leftarrow m$
BVS	n, [r, l]	$if PSR[V] \neq 0 \; then \; (PC) \leftarrow m$
BES	n, [r, l]	$if PSR[E] \neq 0 \; then \; (PC) \leftarrow m$
MARK	n	$(MP) \leftarrow (SP); inc(SP, n)$
CALL	n, [r, l]	$(MP^\wedge+1) \leftarrow (FP); (MP^\wedge+2) \leftarrow (PC); (FP) \leftarrow (MP); (PC) \leftarrow m$
EXIT		$(SP) \; \text{"} \; (FP); (FP) \; \text{"} \; (SP^\wedge+1); (PC) \; \text{"} \; (SP^\wedge+2)$
SETSP	n, [r, l]	$(SP) \leftarrow (m)$
SETPSR	n	$PSR \leftarrow n$
HALT		$PSR[H] \leftarrow 1$
CHECK		$dec(SP, 2); if (SP^\wedge) \leq (SP^\wedge\text{-}1) \leq (SP^\wedge+1) \; then \; PSR[E] \leftarrow 0$
		$else \; PSR[E] \leftarrow 1; PSR[H] \leftarrow PSR[E] \wedge PSR[C]$
CHIN		$transfer(1, input \; channel, SP^\wedge); inc(SP, 1)$
CHOUT		$dec(SP, 1); transfer(1, SP^\wedge, output \; channel)$

Table 2.1   *Target instruction set*

The range of Target instructions relevant to our object code generation problem and their effect are shown in Table 2.1, where

m	is the address denoted by *n + [r, l]*
(a)	is the contents of the memory location whose address is *a*
inc(r, n)	means 'increment the value in register *r* by the value *n*'
dec(r, n)	means 'decrement the value in register *r* by the value *n*'
transfer(t, s, n)	means 'transfer a block of *t* words from the source address *s* to the destination address *n*'

If any of the instructions *ADD, SUB, MUL, DVD, REM, INCR, NEG* cause *arithmetic overflow* to occur then

- the values of the operands on the stack are not altered;
- $PSR[V] \leftarrow 1; PSR[H] \leftarrow PSR[C]$

otherwise $PSR[V] \leftarrow 0$.

Execution of a *BVS* instruction always clears *PSR[V]*.

If the *CHECK* instruction determines that a range error has occurred then

- $PSR[E] \leftarrow 1; PSR[H] \leftarrow PSR[C]$

otherwise $PSR[E] \leftarrow 0$.

Execution of a *BES* instruction always clears *PSR[E]*.

Thus, if *PSR[C]* is set to 0, arithmetic overflow and range errors do not cause program execution to terminate. Otherwise they set the *PSR[H]* to 1, thereby causing immediate termination of execution of the program.

The Target machine supports the ASCII character set which thus defines the type *CHAR* for our implementation of Model. Any values moved from and to the input and output channels are ASCII characters and are thus padded out to a 16-bit word, or have their leading 8 bits truncated, by the *CHIN* and *CHOUT* instructions, respectively.

The following Modula-2 definition module *Target* provides a description of the Target's architecture. Appendix 2 contains a complete listing of the module.

```
DEFINITION MODULE Target;

            (* ------- Word Structure ------- *)

CONST   WordLength = 16; (* bits per word *)
CONST   MaxInteger = 77777B - 1; (* i.e. 2**15 - 1 *)
TYPE    Integer =LONGINT [-MaxInteger..MaxInteger-1];

            (* ------- Character Set  ------- *)

TYPE    Ordinal = [0..255]; (* Target uses ASCII *)

            (* ----  Store Dimensions   ---- *)

CONST   MaximumAddress = 177777B;
TYPE    AddressRange = [0..MaximumAddress];

            (* ---- Register Organization --- *)

TYPE    Register = [BP, FP, MP, SP, PC, PSR];
        AddressRegister = [BP..SP];

            (* ------ PSR Organization -------*)

CONST   C = 0;    V = 1;    E = 2;
```

```
        H = 3;    M = 4;    R = 5;    I = 6;

        (* ----    Instruction Set   --- *)

TYPE OrderCode =    (NOOP, LOAD, LOADL, LOADR, LOADA, LOADI,
                     STORE, STORER, STOREI, STZ,
                     INCR,INCREG, MOVE, SLL, SRL,
                     ADD, SUB, MUL, DVD, DREM, LAND, LOR, INV, NEG,
                     CLT, CLE, CEQ, CNE,
                     BRN, BIDX, BZE, BNZ, BNG, BPZ, BVS, BES,
                     MARK, CALL, EXT, SETSP, SETPSR, CHECK, HLT,
                     CHIN, CHOUT);

        (* ----  Instruction Format ---- *)

TYPE Level =    [0..77B];
TYPE Instruction = RECORD
                OpCode: OrderCode; R: AddressRegister; L: Level;
                N: Integer
            END;

        (* -- Object Program Addresses -- *)
    ...

END Target.
```

2.4 Design constraints for the Model compiler

Like any other item of computer software a compiler may be subject to constraints on its design and implementation. These constraints stem from the general objectives of software development such as the following.

Reliability

Compiler reliability is not achieved by techniques peculiar to compiler construction. Since a compiler is an inherently complex piece of software, its reliability results from a simple well-structured design, which gives a logical separation of concerns, and the use of simple well-understood techniques for their realization. The role played by modular development, and modular testing, in achieving reliability is well illustrated by the Model compiler.

Efficiency

Efficiency requirements of object programs were mentioned as part of the compiler's output specification. However, if a compiler is used as frequently as the programs which it produces, then its own efficiency becomes significant. Compiler efficiency involves three factors:

(a) the speed of compilation;
(b) the amount of main memory usage during compilation;
(c) the amount of secondary memory usage during compilation.

All three factors warrant economy in the construction of a compiler. Compilers are often constructed as multi-pass systems for reasons of language design, main memory limitation, or conceptual simplicity. However, the secondary memory transfers involved in multi-pass compilation are a very significant overhead in many environments and the time spent in such transfers may well outweigh the time which is spent in processing the transferred information. As we shall see, the conceptual simplification of the compilation process into several component processes can be achieved without enforcing multi-pass operation on the compiler which carries it out.

We shall examine algorithms for various functions that must be performed as part of the compilation process. Where a choice is available, we shall normally select the one that performs the required task most efficiently.

Flexibility

Flexibility is a vital objective in the construction of any software whose useful lifetime may span many changes in its working environment. An obvious flexibility for a compiler is a capacity to generate object code for a totally different target machine. Much of the effort of writing a compiler for a given language is machine independent, but if this commonality of effort is to be fully exploited in producing compilers for other machines, a compiler structure which separates the machine-dependent and machine-independent aspects must be chosen at an early stage in the design.

A less radical but commonly required flexibility in systems software is device independence. If the environment in which the compiler runs does not support device-independent input and output, then it must be realized within the compiler itself. The ease with which this can be done is again dependent on the degree to which the chosen compiler structure isolates the device dependencies within the overall compilation process.

Another important aspect of the flexibility of a compiler is its *portability*, i.e. we may wish to use a compiler developed for use in a particular environment in a different environment. For instance, we might wish to use the Model compiler developed on the Macintosh to perform compilation on other computers such as an IBM PC or a Sun workstation. Ideally this should involve little or no reprogramming of the compiler. However, the portability of the compiler depends on the avoidance of all unnecessary assumptions about the environment in which it is used. Where it is necessary to make such assumptions, they should be isolated within the compiler in such a way that they may be readily identified and changed for the new environment without requiring consequent changes to those parts of the compiler which depend upon them.

As an illustration of the influence which such considered flexibility may have on a program's development, all the above will be incorporated in the specification of the Model compiler.

In this chapter we have developed an outline specification for the Model compiler, which can be summarized as follows:

(a) it must compile the language Model as defined in Appendix 1;
(b) it must achieve an acceptable level of error recovery;
(c) it must generate reasonably efficient machine code for the Target computer;
(d) it must be reliable;
(e) it should be reasonably efficient in its use of time, main memory and secondary memory;
(f) it should be readily adaptable to
   (i)   the use of a variety of input and output devices on the given machine;
   (ii) use on a different host machine;
   (iii) the generation of object code for different machines.

2.5 Further reading

Much of the early development of T-diagrams was due to Earley and Sturgis (1970). The use of T-diagrams in the description of a range of compiler implementation strategies is well illustrated by Watt (1993).

A somewhat intuitive approach to language definition is taken in this text in order to make its material accessible to readers with a wide range of backgrounds. Although Appendix 1 uses a formalism known as extended Backus–Naur form (see Chapter 6) for defining the syntactic rules of the Model language, we choose to express the semantic rules informally using English. However, there are formal methods available for specifying the semantics of programming languages.

Operational semantics describes the actions of a program in terms of their effect on the state of an abstract machine which is assumed to execute the program. This enables a model implementation to be defined, to which all other implementations must be equivalent.

Other approaches use mathematical logic, e.g. the *axiomatic semantics* approach of Hoare and Wirth (1973) in which axioms define the transformation of predicates that result from the execution of each of the constructs of the language. This approach is particularly relevant to establishing proofs of correctness of programs. *Denotational semantics* involves defining program actions in terms of mappings onto mathematical operations, which allows the semantics of a language to be defined using formal mathematical techniques (which can, however, be quite complex). Watt (1993) makes use of *action semantics*.

Comprehensive reviews of programming language syntax and semantics appear in excellent texts by McGettrick (1980), Tennent (1981) and Watt (1991).

Readers unfamiliar with Modula-2 should refer to Wirth (1982) or one of the many textbooks on programming in Modula-2, such as Welsh and Elder (1987).

Exercises 2

2.1 Draw T-diagrams to represent the following pieces of software:
  (i)   a compiler, written in Modula-2, which translates Pascal into Motorola 68000 series machine code;
  (ii) a translator, written in C, which transforms Pascal programs into Modula-2 programs;
  (iii) a compiler, expressed in Motorola 68000 machine code, which translates Ada programs into Intel 8086 machine code.

2.2 Suppose that you have a Macintosh computer with a Motorola 68000 series processor as well as a program (written in Ada) for translating Modula-2 programs into Ada and an Ada compiler which runs on your Macintosh. Describe, using T-diagrams, how these programs can be used to:
  (i)   compile and execute an Ada program A;
  (ii) compile the Modula-2 to Ada translator into 68000 machine code;
  (iii) translate a program B written in Modula-2 into an equivalent 68000 machine code program.

2.3 A useful property of a compiler which is written in the language which it compiles is that it can be used to compile itself. This process is known as *bootstrapping* and is the basis of a frequently used technique for constructing a compiler incrementally.
  Suppose that we wish to build a compiler for a language L that is to run on a machine M. Initially we could choose a subset of L (say L–0) containing features suitable for compiler writing and proceed as follows:
  (i)   write the compiler for the subset language L–0, using any suitable high-level programming language for which there is a compiler already available on M;
  (ii) compile this using the M compiler for the chosen implementation language, thereby producing an L–0 compiler for M, thus allowing the execution of L–0 programs on the machine M;
  (iii) rewrite the L–0 compiler in the L–0 language itself (this is a fairly straightforward process in most cases) and compile it using the L-0 compiler for M produced at stage (ii)—this removes the dependency on the language and compiler employed at stages (i) and (ii);
  (iv) write a compiler for L using L–0 as its implementation language and compile it using the L–0 compiler produced at stage (iii);
  (v)   rewrite the compiler for L using L itself as the implementation language and compile using the the L compiler produced at stage (iv).
  Draw T-diagrams to show the production of the various compilers developed at each of the stages (i)–(v).

2.4 A Pascal compiler is to be produced for a new model of computer known as the

ORCHARD. The implementors have available a Macintosh computer with a Pascal compiler. Describe, giving appropriate T-diagrams, how the *ORCHARD* Pascal compiler can be produced using a bootstrapping process involving the Macintosh Pascal compiler.

Chapter 3

Communicating with the user

Irrespective of the programmer's working environment, the source program is normally prepared as a text file which is input to the computer's file storage medium via an *editor* program. The compiler is then invoked and produces the error listing, again as a text file which is held within the file store and subsequently may be printed or inspected using the text editor.

In some environments the user indirectly invokes the compiler via an operating system command in which the names of the files corresponding to the source program and error listing are cited. The operating system then runs the compiler and connects the required files to the compiler as its standard input and output streams. In an interactive environment, however, it is preferable for the compiler itself to acquire the identities of the required files from the user by means of a suitable interactive dialogue and then to open and close these files itself. It is the latter approach that we shall adopt in our model compiler.

3.1 The program listing

One of the first tasks to be undertaken by the compiler writer is the design of the format in which the program listing is to be displayed. A program listing usually consists of an identifying *header*, a *line-by-line listing* of the source program, and a *trailing summary* of the compilation performed.

The heading

A compiler should clearly identify itself at the start of each compilation by a heading which incorporates the following minimum information:

- the source language and target machine pair involved;
- the compiler involved—its name, version number, and date of creation;
- the date and time of the particular compilation run;

- the settings of any compilation parameters or options that were selected by the programmer.

Such a heading need not occupy more than two or three lines. While the programmer may totally ignore these headings as irrelevant noise during the process of program development they can play a crucial role in the subsequent documentation and maintenance of the program.

The line-by-line listing

Many compilers generate a line-by-line listing of the source program compiled. This listing provides the programmer with

(a) a visual confirmation that the program text was input correctly;
(b) a frame of reference for subsequent diagnostic messages, and for modification of the source program;
(c) the central component of the program's overall documentation.

To provide a source-related reference framework for the program most compilers output a line or statement number with each source line listed. Where line numbers are used they normally, wherever possible, observe the same conventions as text editors in the program development environment.

Many compiler systems provide source-related diagnostics during object program execution—if, however, subsequent run-time diagnostics are not explicitly related to the text of the source program, the compiler may generate a second frame of reference, based on the data and object code locations within the object program generated, for use in run-time diagnostic messages.

With most programming languages the use of careful source text layout can significantly increase the readability of listed programs. Such layout is usually based on the consistent application of simple rules for indentation, symbol separation, etc. An increasingly popular option is to make this *paragraphing* an automatic feature of the compiler-generated source listing. Alternatively, a separate program paragrapher may be provided as a complementary software item within the overall program development system, leaving the contents of the compile-time listing to reflect precisely the layout of the original input program.

Trailing summaries

It is often useful for the compiler to provide its users with summary information about the source program, either at the end of the program listing or at the end of each major program unit (e.g. each module or procedure). This information might include a table of all the identifiers occurring in the program or unit, the entry for each showing

- its spelling;

- its type or class of usage;
- the source coordinates of its declaration point;
- the number of times it was used in the program, and possibly the source coordinates of each usage (this is known as a *cross-reference table*).

For the convenience of the programmer the identifier entries normally are sorted alphabetically. For large program units the accumulation of cross-references can be extremely expensive in storage, making such a facility impractical within the compiler itself. In such cases the facility may again be provided as a complementary software item within the overall program development system.

3.2 Compile-time error responses

From the user's viewpoint the overriding requirement for error handling in compilation must be that the compiler detects as many as possible, if not all, of the errors in a source program. As we shall see in Chapter 10, adjacent errors in a program may cause a particular error to be missed but the compiler should at least, in principle, enforce every rule of the language. Many compilers do not do so, for reasons of convenience or of economy. Such economy is usually false when measured in terms of user efficiency or the total number of compilation runs needed by the user.

It is also important, however, that the compiler should retain the user's confidence in the significance of the error messages which it generates. A welter of repeated or spurious error messages quickly leads the user to overlook or ignore significant distinct messages in the same section of the listing. Repeated messages arise principally from misused or undeclared identifiers and can, as we shall see, be easily avoided. The avoidance of spurious messages depends critically on the quality of error recovery which the compiler achieves.

Reporting each error

Each error detected by the compiler is in general reported to the user by means of some form of error message incorporated in the program listing. In general an error message should

(a) describe the error as completely as possible, and
(b) define its 'position' in the source program as exactly as possible.

Meeting requirement (a) essentially implies the introduction of as many distinct error messages as there are potential error situations to be described, and thus each message can describe the particular error situation exactly. In practice it is sometimes impractical either to distinguish all distinct error situations within the analysis process or to provide a large enough range of distinct error messages. The practical compromise often employed is to group several error situations under a single message. This solution usually means some loss of detail in the description of any particular error situation. In general the maximum range of error messages which is practical should be used in any compiler and error situations may then be mapped onto these so as to minimize the loss of detail.

Meeting requirement (b) involves relating each error message to a particular point in the source program. This can usually be done by indicating the point in the source text scan at which the compiler discovered the error, e.g. by generating a listing marker such as '^' (as in many compilers for languages like Modula-2) or by a line number and character count within the line. The program error concerned must then involve one of the symbols immediately preceding this marked point. This method can be unsatisfactory or misleading in certain situations, e.g. when an end-of-line control character occurs between the point of the error itself and the point of scan at which the compiler discovers the error. For certain languages it may be justifiable to handle such pathological cases (e.g. in the case of a missing semicolon in a Modula-2 statement-sequence) in a particular way.

Certain errors cannot of course be directly related to any particular point in the source program, e.g. when a goto-statement refers to a statement label which is never sited in the program or if a program has a missing procedure-declaration. Reports for such errors should give as much source relation as possible, e.g. the label or procedure identity should be included in the error message, together with the source coordinates of its occurrence in a goto-statement or procedure-statement, respectively.

The actual error messages themselves may take one of two basic forms:

(a) self-explicit text messages;
(b) numeric or alphanumeric codes referring to a published table of explanations.

The first form has obvious advantages of convenience for users, although the storage of the messages within the compiler can represent a considerable overhead. Also, for large programs with large numbers of errors, if their program listings are printed, they can use a significant amount of paper! A practical compromise is for the compiler to generate code numbers to indicate each individual error, and then at the end of compilation to read from secondary memory a file containing the explicit messages, and print the subset of those corresponding to the code numbers actually generated, as an immediately available error code table for the user.

Two placements of compile-time error messages are commonly used:

(a) on the line(s) immediately following the source line where the error was detected;
(b) at the end of the listing.

The first placement is more convenient for the user in considering individual errors, and is also convenient for a one-pass compiler to generate. For a multi-pass compiler, however, which operates in several passes carrying out some part of the overall compilation process for the entire input program in each pass, the production of an interleaved listing of source lines and corresponding error messages must be postponed until all passes which may generate error messages have been completed. The compiler may then collate the input source text with the messages arising from the various passes to form the listing required. For such multi-pass compilers (which include most COBOL compilers) placement of error messages at the end of the program listing is more convenient if the listing is to be printed.

Many compilers developed for use as part of a program development environment for use on personal computer systems do not include the error messages within the listing of the source program text; indeed they generally do not produce a listing at all. Instead, the error code numbers and positions discovered during a compilation are usually written to an *error file*. The interactive editor in the program development system then provides the user with a facility to step from error to error through the source program text. At each error point the editor will normally highlight the offending text and, often using a special *error window*, display the details of the error concerned. The diagnostic supplied will typically be an explicit message and the window will often include other control facilities to enable the user to obtain a more detailed explanation of the error and, possibly, correct the error and move on to the next one. The exact form in which these facilities is provided varies greatly from one system to another.

3.3 Further reading

Most compiler texts pay scant attention to the problems of user communication and the reporting of errors. However, a paper by Horning (1976a) discusses the design and implementation of program listings and the display of error messages.

Exercises 3

3.1 Examine some listings of long programs produced by some of the compilers that you use. How useful is the information they produce? Do you consider the listing format to be well designed?

3.2 Devise some suitable erroneous test programs in the high-level languages that you use and study the reporting of compile-time errors by the compilers. Is their error detection complete and is the error reporting accurate? Do any of the compilers generate spurious error messages?

Chapter 4

Source handling

Our initial concept of a compiler was that of a program which takes the text of a source program as input and produces both an object program and a listing as its outputs. Our first formal expression of the compiler's structure was defined in Chapter 2 as

compiler (source program) (object program, listing)

where

source program denotes the program to be compiled;
object program denotes the translated program;
listing denotes the program listing produced.

4.1 Isolating device dependencies

All three of the above inputs and outputs involve physical representation on some input, output or storage media. Their format is in general dependent on the devices or media involved. Since device independence has been identified as an important objective for the compiler a logical refinement of this first model is to isolate the device dependencies from the compiler proper, by introducing the following:

- An *input handler* which converts the device-dependent source text into a device-independent stream of characters.
- An *output handler* which composes a device-oriented listing format by collating the source program input with the errors reported by the compiler proper.
- A *code handler* which constructs a device-oriented representation of the object program from the device-independent object code emitted by the compiler proper.

This separation of the device-dependent functions leads to a revised model of our compiler structure which is as follows:

> *input handler (source program) (character stream)*
> *compiler (character stream) (errors, object code)*
> *output handler (source program, errors) (listing)*
> *code handler (object code) (object program)*

and is shown in Figure 4.1.

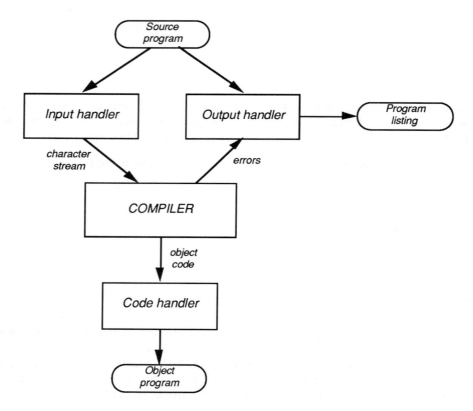

Figure 4.1   *Revised compiler structure*

The notation used is not intended to imply the order in which these activities take place. They might proceed in sequence, in parallel, or by appropriate interleaving of their component actions. That remains to be determined. What the model has achieved is the separation of the device-dependent activities from the process of compilation proper. If this modularity can be carried into the final compiler program a sound basis for device independence will be achieved.

Realising such modular structure involves

(a) defining precisely the communication interfaces between the modules;
(b) choosing program structures to represent them;
(c) proceeding with the refinement of the individual modules.

However, attempting to do so for the compiler model given above quickly reveals a practical flaw in the suggested structure.

Both the *input handler* and the *output handler* process the device-dependent representation of the input source program. Practicalities of course dictate that input from a physical device should take place once only. Likewise simple efficiency considerations suggest that any internal saving and rescanning of the source representation must be avoided whenever possible. The input and output handlers could share a single scan of the source input through a shared line buffer which has associated with it an appropriate access protocol. But the need for such a shared structure calls into question the practical independence of the input and output handlers.

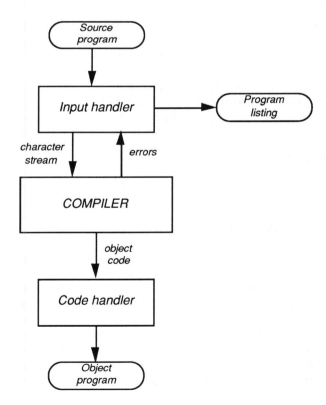

Figure 4.2   *Introduction of a source handler module*

An alternative is to revise our compiler model, merging the input and output handlers into a single *source handler*. It is then a question internal to the source handler as to how the input and listing device pair should cooperate.

Our compiler model now has the form (as illustrated in Figure 4.2)

source handler (source program, errors) (character stream, listing)
compiler (character stream) (errors, object code)
code handler (object code) (object program)

We will find that this model remains a valid basis of all our subsequent Model compiler development. It is not appropriate to consider the interface between the compiler and the code handler further at this stage, but we shall proceed to define the source handler's interface with the compiler and then to develop each module in turn.

4.2 The source handler/compiler interface

The interface between the source handler and the compiler involves the transmission of the source character stream from the source handler to the compiler, and the transmission of error reports from the compiler to the source handler. We consider the source character stream first.

Simple efficiency considerations suggest that the compiler should scan the individual characters in the source character stream once only, presumably in left-to-right order. A sufficient interface therefore is that the source handler should make available to the compiler the 'current' character in the source stream, say as a variable

    VAR CurrentCharacter: CHAR;

together with the ability to replace this character by its successor when the compiler wishes. This could be provided as a procedure

    PROCEDURE GetNextCharacter;

Now consider the error reporting. For each error detected by the compiler it must report to the source handler the *nature* and the *position* of the error.

For denoting the nature of the error we shall adopt a simple numeric code, at the interface level. Whether this code is translated into an explicit text message by the source handler is a listing design decision which affects only the source handler.

It is important to realize that, as was illustrated in Section 3.3, the position of the error is not necessarily related to the current character position in the source character stream. Since we should make no assumptions as to how the compiler actually detects errors in this stream, it may be any position in the stream already scanned by the compiler.

The compiler could keep track of the ordinal position of each character in the source stream scanned and express each error position in terms of these. Equally the source handler could relate an ordinal character position to whatever line or text structure it scanned in the original source program.

A little consideration, however, shows that it is more efficient for the source handler to make available with each character in the source stream a corresponding positional value which the compiler may record. This is more efficient because

- the source handler must maintain some such positional coordinates anyhow;
- the compiler need only copy this position at those points to which a subsequent error report may refer.

The actual details of the representation of the positional coordinates need not be made available to the compiler proper, since it requires only to record positions for possible, subsequent, transmission back to the source handler. So we first extend our source character stream interface by a variable

```
VAR PositionNow: TextPosition;
```

and then the error reporting interface is easily provided as a procedure

```
PROCEDURE Error(Code: CARDINAL; Position: TextPosition);
```

The total interface described can be implemented by defining the source handler as a module with the following interface:

```
DEFINITION MODULE SourceHandler;

    TYPE TextPosition = ...;

    VAR   CurrentCharacter: CHAR;
          PositionNow: TextPosition;

    PROCEDURE GetNextCharacter;
    PROCEDURE Error(Code: CARDINAL; Position: TextPosition);
    PROCEDURE FinalizeIO;

END SourceHandler.
```

Any use of the source handler's facilities by the compiler must be preceded by some initialization, and followed by some finalization, of the source handler's input and output activities. The initialization will be provided by the statement-part of the corresponding implementation module for *SourceHandler*, and the finalization by the interface procedure *FinalizeIO*.

4.3 Programming the source handler

The keynote in programming the facilities provided within the source handler must be efficiency, since the overall efficiency of a compiler is determined largely by the efficiency of its character handling. It is crucial, therefore, that the normal repetitive actions provided by the source handler, primarily the *GetNextCharacter* procedure, be programmed as efficiently as possible. With this in mind, the internal structure of the source handler is now considered.

A first model for the action of *GetNextCharacter* might be

```
IF current character is last in the current line THEN
    list this line;
    read next line
END;
update CurrentCharacter, PositionNow for next character
```

Note that we use italicized text within Modula-2 program fragments to denote abstract actions and operations that are not expressed precisely in Modula-2. This convention is used throughout the book.

We introduce a buffer to hold the characters of the current line under scan. Note that, as anticipated, the position made available to the compiler can also be used within the source handler to control the transmission of characters.

For a line-by-line text format a text position involves a line identity or number, and a character position within the line. Assuming a maximum line length defined by the constant *MaxCharsPerLine* we can define a type

```
TYPE CharPosition = [1..MaxCharsPerLine];
```

and hence

```
TYPE TextPosition =  RECORD
                        LineNumber: CARDINAL;
                        CharNumber: CharPosition
                     END;
```

The line buffer used to hold the source line under scan can now be declared as

```
VAR Line: ARRAY CharPosition OF CHAR;
```

For some input media the actual line in the line buffer at any moment may be preceded by one or more control characters which do not form part of the actual source program. It is convenient to introduce auxiliary variables

```
VAR FirstInLine, LastInLine: CharPosition;
```

to delimit the significant contents of the line buffer at any time. With these decisions our initial model for *GetNextCharacter* is easily translated into

```
PROCEDURE GetNextCharacter;
```

```
BEGIN
   WITH PositionNow DO
      IF CharNumber = LastInLine THEN
         list this line;
         read next line;
          INC(LineNumber);
          CharNumber := FirstInLine
      ELSE INC(CharNumber)
      END;
      CurrentCharacter := Line[CharNumber]
   END
   END GetNextCharacter
```

To complete the programming of *GetNextCharacter* it remains to refine the actions *list this line* and *read next line*. However, since these actions

(a) involve the mechanics of device manipulation, and
(b) are also required in the initialization and finalization of the source handler activities,

it is prudent to abstract them as procedures to be called from *GetNextCharacter*, and elsewhere as required. *read next line* is implemented as a straightforward device-handling procedure which

(a) transfers the next input line to the line buffer;
(b) sets the markers *FirstInLine* and *LastInLine* to denote the positions in the buffer of the first non-blank and last non-blank characters, respectively.

The dynamic setting of the markers *FirstInline* and *LastInLine* enables leading and trailing blanks to be 'stripped' by a fast scan within the procedure *ReadNextLine,* rather than by a slow scan

```
WHILE CurrentCharacter = " " DO GetNextCharacter END
```

within the compiler proper.

ReadNextLine also checks for the input character stream becoming exhausted before the compilation is complete. If this situation occurs it terminates the compilation after first calling *FinalizeIO.*

The form of the procedure *ListThisLine* depends on the particular error and collation mechanisms chosen. We assume that the compiler reports most errors relating to a particular line before moving to the next line, which is a reasonable assumption for a language such as Model. In this case error message lines which are interleaved with the source program text give the most convenient listing format, from the viewpoints of both the compiler and the user. Those messages which refer to a point in the immediately preceding source line can do so by a simple position marker, while those that refer to an earlier line may do so by means of line numbers included in the listing, as the following listing excerpt suggests:

```
... ...
27       A := A+1;
28       B = B*-A
*****       ^ ERROR ...
*****             ^ ERROR ...
*****    ERROR ... ON LINE 24
```

Thus the source handler needs to accept the error reports during the processing of each line, for display only when the last significant character of the line has been transmitted by *GetNextCharacter*. In these circumstances it is reasonable to set a fairly small upper limit on the number of errors reported during any line. If the compiler exceeds this limit it is more likely that the compiler has failed to recover from one of the first errors reported, and thus has generated a welter of spurious messages, than that so many genuine independent errors exist. Of course the compiler must tell the user when such messages have been suppressed. So, given a limit *MaxErrorsPerLine* we introduce an array to hold the error code and position pairs:

```
VAR ErrorList:  ARRAY [1..MaxErrorsPerLine] OF
                RECORD
                  ErrorPosition: TextPosition;
                  ErrorCode: CARDINAL
                END;
```

and a counter to indicate the number of errors collected so far since the last end of line:

```
VAR ErrorsInThisLine: [0..MaxErrorsPerLine];
```

Finally a flag is needed which indicates when error overflow, with the subsequent suppression of further error messages, has occurred during processing of a given line:

```
VAR ErrorOverflow: BOOLEAN;
```

Besides the individual error reports interleaved with the program text, the source handler will provide the user with a count of the total number of errors reported to it, at the end of the compilation listing. For this purpose we introduce an additional variable

```
VAR TotalNumberOfErrors: CARDINAL;
```

With the introduction of these variables the error collecting procedure *Error*, and the listing procedure *ListThisLine*, are both easily programmed. The initialization of the *SourceHandler* module is readily programmed, involving a dialogue with the user to obtain the identities of the files containing the source program text and to receive the error listing text, the printing of listing headers, and suitable initialization of the variables involved. The finalization procedure *FinalizeIO* is responsible for printing the required trailers and closing the various files.

4.4 The host environment interface

It is appropriate at this stage to consider one of our stated design objectives, namely to develop the Model compiler so as to make it as portable as possible. This may be achieved by introducing a module into the compiler which isolates those actions performed by the compiler which depend on the host machine and the Modula-2 system being used, and provides an implementation-independent interface to them.

The source handler requires the use of various input and output operations to open and close text files and to transfer values to and from those files. We shall see during the development of later stages of the compiler that it needs to make use of other facilities provided by the host Modula-2 environment, such as those for dynamic storage management, string manipulation and character set operations.

The following module *Host* defines an interface to these facilities of the compiler's environment. It is incomplete at present but the other facilities will be identified in subsequent chapters.

```
DEFINITION MODULE Host;

   (*  An operation for determining the ASCII ordinal value of
       any character in the the host machine's character set:  *)

   TYPE ASCIIOrdinal = [0..255];

   PROCEDURE ASCIIOrdinalOf(C: CHAR): ASCIIOrdinal;

   CONST EOL = 15C;  (* end-of-line character on host machine *)

   (*  Operations for dynamic allocation and deallocation of  storage  *)
       ...

   (*  Operations for performing text file input and output:  *)

   TYPE FileAccessMode = (Input,Output);
        File;

   PROCEDURE OpenFile(OpenPrompt: ARRAY OF CHAR; Mode: FileAccessMode;
                      VAR F: File; VAR Opened: BOOLEAN);
   PROCEDURE ReadChar(F: File; VAR EndOfInput: BOOLEAN; VAR C: CHAR);
   PROCEDURE WriteChar(F: File; C: CHAR);
   PROCEDURE WriteCardinal(F: File; Number, FieldWidth: CARDINAL);
   PROCEDURE WriteInteger(F: File; Number: INTEGER; FieldWidth: CARDINAL);
   PROCEDURE WriteString(F: File; String: ARRAY OF CHAR);
   PROCEDURE WriteLine(F: File);
   PROCEDURE CloseFile(VAR F: File);
```

(* *Properties of identifiers on the host implementation,*
and spelling comparison operations. *)

...

END Host.

If the Model compiler is moved to a new host machine, then the implementation module for *Host* needs to be rewritten to reflect the implementation of its features on that new environment. The remainder of the compiler will thus not require any modifications. Appendix 3 contains a full listing of the *Host* module interface, together with its implementation for the MetroWerks Modula-2 system on the Macintosh.

Appendix 4 shows the complete source handler module, implemented using the input and output facilities of the *Host* module to realize source input and listing output.

Exercises 4

4.1   Rewrite the implementation module for *Host* given in Appendix 3 to reflect how the various environment-dependent operations it provides are realized in your particular Modula-2 system.

4.2   Write a suitable driver program to test the *SourceHandler* module given in Appendix 4, and then run your test program using a carefully chosen sequence of input lines as test data.

4.3   Amend the *SourceHandler* implementation module given in Appendix 4 so that it outputs explicit error messages at the end of the listing for each distinct error that occurs during compilation of a program. The messages themselves should be stored in a separate text file.

Chapter 5

Compiler structure: analysis and generation

5.1 Structuring the compiler

The isolation of the various device dependencies carried out in Chapter 4 produced a compiler proper of the form

compiler (character stream) (errors, object code)

The two outputs *errors* and *object code* generated by the compiler reflect its underlying twin purposes which are

(a) to determine if the input source program is free of errors, and to diagnose the errors if it is not, and
(b) to generate an equivalent object code program.

In practice action (b) may be conditional on action (a) finding the program to be error free, but in any case it should make use of the program analysis which (a) must involve. This leads immediately to an obvious subdivision of the compiler process, thus

analyzer (character stream) (errors, analyzed program)
generator (analyzed program) (object code)

where *analyzed program* is some representation of the source program produced by the analyzer, enabling the generator to produce the object code required.

This splitting of the compiler into *analyzer* and *generator* processes contributes to the objective of achieving flexibility in the form of object code generated. The analyzer in effect represents those aspects of compilation which are machine dependent or object code independent, and its output, the *analyzed program*, can be thought of as a machine-independent expression of the program's meaning or effect. In contrast, the generator must convert this output from the analyzer into a form which is totally dependent on the object machine code, and thus it embodies those parts of the compiler which must change when the object code is changed. The separation is thus not just a conceptual one but a practical means of achieving the flexibility required within the final compiler program. We adopt therefore a two-part structure for the compiler proper, comprising an analyzer part and a generator part, whose mutual interface, the analyzed program, should permit the generation of a variety of object codes by the generator, without any alteration to the analyzer.

Having made this decision, our next step in principle should be to define the *analyzed program* interface before proceeding with the refinement of either the analyzer or generator part. In practice, however, so much of the analyzer is independent of this interface that it is convenient to postpone its definition to a later stage, proceeding for the moment with the development of an open-ended analyzer of the form

$$analyzer\ (character\ stream)\ (errors, \quad ? \quad)$$

5.2 Structuring the analyzer

The primary task of the analyzer is to apply the rules of the language definition to the input source program, so determining any errors which exist within it, and its meaning. Our definition of the Model language distinguishes in form between the syntax rules formally expressed in EBNF, such as

$$assignment\text{-}statement \ = \ variable \ ``:=" \ expression.$$

and the informally expressed semantic rules, such as

"The variable and the expression must be of identical type "

whose enforcement depends on the contextual information established by previous declarations, etc. Since application of these semantic rules depends on prior application of the syntax rules, a logical and commonly made separation of analyzer activities is as follows:

syntax analyzer (character stream) (syntax errors, program syntax)
semantic analyzer (program syntax) (semantic errors, ?)

In practice a further distinction is usually made within the syntax analyzer between the analysis of those sequences of characters which form the individual symbols of the program, i.e. identifiers, reserved words, constants, etc., and the analysis of the sequence of language symbols itself. This distinction is not particularly reflected in the formal language definition, but follows rather from our intuitive conception of program composition in which we regard the symbols of the programming language as the indivisible atomic building blocks, whose actual representation as character sequences is a mere clerical detail. The symbol recognition process is usually known as *lexical analysis* (or *lexical scanning*), and so our model of the overall analysis process is now

lexical analyzer (character stream) (lexical errors, symbol stream)
syntax analyzer (symbol stream) (syntax errors, program syntax)
semantic analyzer (program syntax) (semantic errors,   ?   )

This separation of the lexical scanning process has some significance in achieving flexibility in transporting the compiler to different host computer systems; while the language as such should not change from one machine to another the character set available for its representation may do so, and may thus enforce variations in the symbol representations, or 'dialects'. This character set dependence is usefully isolated within the lexical scanner.

For this reason, and because of the simplicity of its relationship with the syntax analyzer, we can readily choose to retain the separation of the lexical scanner as a separate module within the final compiler program.

5.3 Further reading

Among the textbooks which consider in some detail the problems of structuring compilers are Aho, Sethi and Ullman (1986), Bornat (1979) and Tremblay and Sorenson (1985). Papers presented by McKeeman (1976a) and Horning (1976b) at an advanced course on compiler construction give overviews of the standard approaches to compiler design.

Chapter 6

Syntax theory

Before we can proceed to consider the lexical analysis and syntax analysis phases of compilation it is necessary to introduce the elementary theory of *context-free languages*. Most high-level programming languages may be considered as simple extensions of such languages and their analysis or compilation is based on the syntax theory of context-free languages. Since our aim in this book is to understand the principles of compilation the theory is developed solely with this aim in mind. We are not concerned in this book with the analysis of languages with arbitrarily complicated syntax, but rather with the conditions under which the efficient analysis of a particular restricted language class can be achieved.

6.1 Terminology and notation

Informally we may think of a natural language as consisting of a set (usually infinite) of allowable sequences of symbols from a given *vocabulary* (which is usually finite in size). These symbols are subdivided into two categories:

(a) the *terminal* symbols T of the vocabulary—these correspond to the words of a natural language (i.e. those entities listed in a dictionary);

(b) the *non-terminal* symbols N of the vocabulary—these correspond to the names of the syntactic categories in a natural language (e.g. *clause*, *predicate*, *phrase* in English).

Hence $\qquad V = T \cup N$

We shall denote terminal symbols by enclosing them in quotes, e.g. "*cat*", and non-terminal symbols by (possibly hyphenated) names, e.g. *expression*.

Sequences of symbols we shall denote by Greek letters α, β, ... The construction of a sequence by juxtaposition of symbols or other sequences we denote simply by juxtaposition of the corresponding denotations, viz. $\alpha\beta$, α"*cat*"... . We shall also be concerned with what is known as an *empty sequence*, which we denote by ε. An empty sequence consists of no symbols at all.

The set of all the sequences that can be derived from a vocabulary V we denote by $V*$.

Axiom 1 $\sigma = \sigma\varepsilon = \varepsilon\sigma$

This states that prefixing a sequence of symbols by the empty sequence, or appending the empty sequence to it, does not change the sequence.

Axiom 2 $\varepsilon \in V*$

The empty sequence is a member of the set of all sequences.

Axiom 3 $\alpha b \in V*$ if and only if $\alpha \in V*$ and $b \in V$

Thus, if an existing sequence of symbols from the vocabulary has another symbol from the vocabulary added to it, then we have a new sequence which is also a member of the set of all sequences.

Given a vocabulary V we wish to be able to define the set of allowable sequences which form the language L. This set is obviously a subset of the set of all sequences which can be derived from the vocabulary (compare this with a natural language, where not all the possible sequences of words are grammatically correct; indeed very few of them are actually correct).

Thus $L \in V*$

Since L is usually infinite it cannot be defined by enumerating the allowable sequences. Instead we use a *grammar* (also known as a *production system or syntax*).

A *context-free grammar* is defined by a vocabulary V and a set P of *productions*, which take the form

$$A = \xi \text{ where } A \in N \text{ and } \xi \in V*$$

The meaning of such a production is that any occurrence of the non-terminal symbol A (i.e. A is the name of a syntactic category) can be replaced by the sequence of symbols ξ.

A context-free language $L(P, V, T, S)$ is defined, by means of a production system P as above, as the set of sequences (called *sentences*) of the terminal symbols T of V which can be obtained by repeated application of the productions P starting from some non-terminal *origin symbol S*.

In a context-free language the only symbols which may appear on the left hand side of a production rule are the symbols in the set N, the *non-terminals* (i.e. syntactic categories). Hence each production rule describes the allowable form of the sequence of symbols derived from a syntactic rule of the language. Since the symbols T of the vocabulary may not appear on the left hand side of any production in P, they cannot lead to any further application of these productions and hence the reason for them being known as *terminal symbols*.

The set of all productions in P whose left element is a given non-terminal A, say

$$A = \xi_1, \ A = \xi_2, \ \dots \ , \ A = \xi_n.$$

is called the *production set* of A, and is denoted by

$$A = \xi_1 \mid A = \xi_2 \mid \dots \mid A = \xi_n.$$

So, given a vocabulary V containing
　　　　a terminal vocabulary $T \ (\in V)$
　　　　a set P of productions $A = \xi$ where $A \in N, \xi \in V^*$
　　　　an origin symbol $S \in N$

we state

(1)　　　　a sequence $\xi = \alpha B \gamma$ *directly generates*
　　　　a sequence $\eta = \alpha \beta \gamma$ (written $\xi \rightarrow \eta$)
　　　　if and only if $B = \beta$ is a production in P

(2)　　　　a sequence ξ *generates* a sequence η (written $\xi \Rightarrow \eta$)
　　　　if and only if there exist sequences $\sigma_1, \dots, \sigma_n$ such that $\xi = \sigma_1, \sigma_n = \eta$
　　　　and $\sigma_i \rightarrow \sigma_{i+1}$ for $i = 1, \dots, n-1$

(3)　　　　the language $L(P, V, T, S)$ is the set of sequences
　　　　$\{ \xi \mid S \Rightarrow \xi \ \text{and} \ \xi \in T^* \}$

6.2 Some simple grammars

Grammar 1: a finite language

$T:$　"x" "y" "z" "w"
$N:$　$A \ B \ S$
$P:$　S　$= AB.$
　　　A　$=$ "x" $\mid$ "y".
　　　B　$=$ "z" $\mid$ "w".

then　　　$L = \{ xz, yz, xw, yw \}$

The sentence *xw* is generated by

$$S \rightarrow AB \rightarrow xB \rightarrow xw$$

or

$$S \rightarrow AB \rightarrow Aw \rightarrow xw$$

The sentences derived by these two generation sequences are not essentially different and they correspond to the same *syntax tree*, as shown in Figure 6.1. Note that, in a syntax tree, the terminal symbols (*"x"* and *"w"*) appear at the edges of the tree, and the non-terminal symbols (*S, A* and *B*) appear at the internal nodes of the tree.

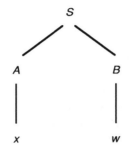

Figure 6.1 *Syntax tree for xw*

A sentence which can be generated via two different syntax trees is said to be *ambiguous*, and a language which contains at least one ambiguous sentence is known as an *ambiguous language*.

Grammar 2: an ambiguous language

T: *"x" "y" "z"*
N: *S A B*
P: *S* = *AB*.
       A = *"x"* | *"x" "y"*.
       B = *"z"* | *"y" "z"*.

and hence $L = \{ xz, xyz, xyyz \}$

The sentence *xyz* is, however, ambiguous since its syntactic structure can be represented by two different trees, as shown in Figure 6.2.

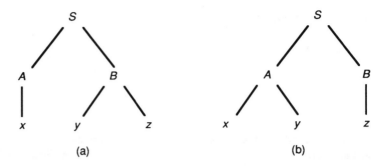

Figure 6.2 *Alternative syntax trees for xyz*

The correspondence to ambiguity in natural language can be seen if we take

x = fruit
y = flies
z = like bananas

which has two quite distinct interpretations, i.e. that a certain type of insect enjoys eating bananas, or that all fruit travels through the air in the same way as bananas do! Since the meaning of a computer program must be precise, the syntactic definitions of programming languages do not allow ambiguous sentences.

Grammar 3: an infinite language

T: "*x*" "*+*" "*–*"
N: *expression tail*
P: *expression* = "*x*" | "*x*" *tail*.
       tail   = "*+*" *expression* | "*–*" *expression*.

Here we have named the syntactic categories *expression* and *tail,* and *expression* is the origin symbol. Some of the sentences of the language defined by this grammar are

   x   x+x   x–x   x+x–x   x–x+x   ...

We extend our formalism for defining languages to include the use of parentheses brackets (and), where necessary, to group syntactic categories together, e.g. the rule for *tail* above may be re-expressed as

   tail   = ("*+*" | "*–*") *expression*.

and defines a *tail* as an *expression* preceded by a "*+*" or "*–*" symbol.

The symbols such as I (and) which form part of the notation for formally defining grammars are known as *meta-symbols*.

The next three example grammars illustrate three commonly used notations for defining arithmetic expressions.

Grammar 4: infix notation

T: "*x*" "+" "*" "(" ")"
N: *expression term factor*
P: *expression* = *term* I *expression* "+" *term*.
    term = *factor* I *term* "*" *factor*.
    factor = "*x*" I "(" *expression* ")".

The origin symbol for this grammar is *expression*. Some sentences with their generation trees are illustrated in Figure 6.3.

Notice that this grammar implies the conventional priority of operators, i.e. that multiplication has higher priority than addition.

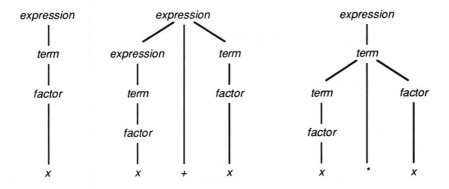

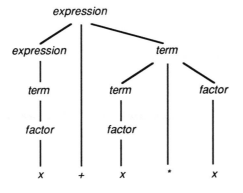

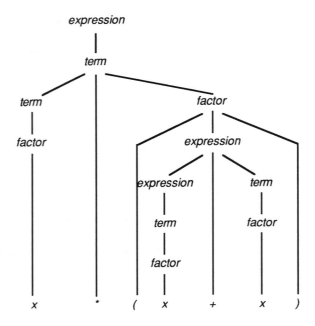

Figure 6.3   *Some sentences and syntax trees for Grammar 4*

Grammar 5: prefix notation

T: "*x*" "+" "*"
N: *expression*
P: *expression*   =   "*x*" | ("+" | "–") *expression expression.*

Again *expression* is the origin non-terminal symbol and some sentences defined by this grammar are

   x   +*xx*   *xx   +*x**xx   *x+*xx*   ...

Grammar 6: postfix notation

T: "*x*" "+" "*"
N: *expression*
P: *expression*   =   "*x*" | *expression expression* "+" | *expression expression* "*" .

Some sentences are

   x   *xx*+   *xx**   *xxx**+   *xxx*+*   ...

Note that neither of these last two grammars requires the use of parentheses to construct sub-expressions. Postfix notation will be of particular importance when we consider the generation of object code for arithmetic expressions in Chapter 18.

6.3 Equivalent grammars

The same language may be generated by two or more distinct grammars or production systems, in which case the grammars are said to be *equivalent*. In general it is an insoluble problem to prove that two grammars are equivalent. However, since in compilation we base our analysis of source programs upon the grammar of the programming language and, as we shall see, the efficiency of this analysis depends on the form of the grammar on which it is based, it is useful to note at this stage certain standard transformations whereby we may translate a given grammar into an equivalent one which has a more suitable form. Some such simple transformations are now presented.

Elimination of non-terminals by substitution

In general a non-recursive non-terminal symbol can be eliminated from a grammar by substituting each of its productions at each point at which it occurs in other productions. Consider the following example grammar:

$$S = \text{``}a\text{''} B.$$
$$B = \text{``}b\text{''} S \mid \varepsilon.$$

Substitution into the rule for S of the two alternatives for B gives an equivalent grammar:

$$S = \text{``}a\text{''} \text{``}b\text{''} S \mid \text{``}a\text{''}.$$

As we shall see, in Chapter 9, it is often convenient to reduce the number of non-terminal symbols in a grammar.

The above example illustrates how the empty sequence ε may be eliminated from a grammar, a task that is frequently required for certain types of syntax analysis. It is in general possible provided $\varepsilon \notin L$, the language being defined.

We can further extend our formal notation for defining grammars to enable all explicit references to the empty sequence ε to be removed from a grammar. Enclosure of a sequence of symbols within the right hand side of a production by the meta-symbols [and] denotes that the enclosed sequence is optional, e.g. the above grammar may be expressed as

$$S = \text{``}a\text{''} B.$$
$$B = [\text{``}b\text{''} S].$$

Factorization

The reverse process is also possible and may be used to take advantage of the occurrence of a common symbol or sequence of symbols in each of the alternatives of a production set. This production set may then be replaced by a single production whose right hand side consists of the common symbols and a new non-terminal symbol whose production set comprises those symbols in which the original alternatives differed. Hence the production set

$$S = \text{“}a\text{”} \text{“}b\text{”} S \mid \text{“}a\text{”}.$$

is returned to its original form by introducing a new auxiliary non-terminal S' thus

$$S = \text{“}a\text{”} S'.$$
$$S' = [\text{“}b\text{”} S].$$

This process is known as *factorization*. Auxiliary non-terminals can also be introduced to reduce the length of the right hand sides of productions. For example, the production

$$S = A_1 .. A_n.$$

could be rewritten as

$$
\begin{array}{lll}
S = A_1 X_1. & \quad\text{or}\quad & S = X_n A_n. \\
X_1 = A_2 X_2. & & X_n = X_{n-1} A_{n-1}. \\
\quad\quad \cdots & & \quad\quad \cdots \\
X_{n-1} = A_n. & & X_2 = A_1.
\end{array}
$$

In Chapter 8 we shall see that it is often necessary to perform such factorizations of some rules of a grammar before efficient analysis of its sentences can be performed.

Inversion of palindromic productions

In natural language, a *palindrome* is a word, such as 'radar', which reads the same both forwards and backwards. If a non-terminal symbol A generates palindromes (i.e. *sentences* which read the same both forwards and backwards, sometimes also referred to as *invertible sentences*) its production rule can be written in two equivalent forms, e.g.

$$A = \text{“}x\text{”} \mid A \text{“}y\text{”} \text{“}x\text{”}. \quad \text{and} \quad A = \text{“}x\text{”} \mid \text{“}x\text{”} \text{“}y\text{”} A.$$

This grammar generates sentences such as

$$x \quad xyx \quad xyxyx \quad xyxyx \quad \cdots$$

The above two forms for *A* are known as *left-recursive* and *right-recursive forms* respectively. Grammar 4 included two such productions and can be written in either of the following forms:

expression = *term* | *expression* "+" *term*.
term   = *factor* | *term* "*" *factor*.
factor   = "x" | "(" *expression* ")".

or

expression = *term* | *term* "+" *expression*.
term   = *factor* | *factor* "*" *term*.
factor   = "x" | "(" *expression* ")".

Removal of recursion

In many practical grammars the use of recursion to describe a repeating sequence of a given form is replaced by an equivalent repetition notation, using the meta-symbols { and } to denote repetition of the enclosed form zero or more times. For example, Grammar 4 could be rewritten as

expression = *term* { "+" *term* }.
term   = *factor* { "*" *factor* }.
factor   = "x" | "(" *expression* ")".

6.4 Parsing

In this chapter we have introduced a notation for defining the grammars of context-free languages and also have looked at how sentences of a language may be generated from its syntax rules. This notation is known as *extended Backus–Naur form* (or simply EBNF). We have also considered how the grammar of a language may be transformed to a more suitable form.

In considering the application of the language theory we have introduced to the compilation of programming languages, the problem of practical interest to us is the following:

> *Given a sequence of symbols, can we determine whether it belongs to the language specified by a given grammar?*

We are interested in developing algorithms to perform this task. The complexity of such algorithms depends on the structural complexity of the language and programming languages are classified by the nature of the algorithms capable of analyzing or *parsing* their sentences.

6.5 Further reading

Most compiler texts deal with the syntax theory introduced in this chapter. Authors such as Hunter (1981) and Terry (1986) use a similar approach to the one adopted here, whereas others such as Tremblay and Sorenson (1985) offer a very much more rigorous treatment.

The area of context-free grammars in particular is well covered by Hopcroft and Ullman (1979), Backhouse (1979) and Watt (1991). Context-free grammars are known as *Type 1 Chomsky grammars*—the original development work on grammars for programming languages was carried out by Chomsky (1959), whose classification grouped grammars according to the form of their production rules.

Extended Backus–Naur form was introduced by Naur (1963) in producing the revised definition of the language Algol 60.

Exercises 6

6.1 Identify the sentences of the language defined by the following grammar:

$$S = xA.$$
$$A = z \mid yA.$$

6.2 Draw syntax trees to show the derivations of
    (i)   the sentences $+x*xx$ and $*x+xx$ derived from Grammar 5;
    (ii)   the sentences $xxx*+$ and $xxx+*$ derived from Grammar 6.

6.3 Draw syntax trees to show the derivations of the sentence *xxxy* derived from the following grammar:

$$A = xB.$$
$$B = xC \mid y.$$
$$C = xC \mid y.$$

Rewrite the grammar to remove the non-terminal symbols B and C.

6.4 Show that the language defined by the following grammar

$$S = [aSbS \mid bSaS].$$

is ambiguous by constructing two syntax trees for the sentence *abab*.

6.5 Show that the language defined by the following grammar

$$E = ``i" \mid ``(" E ``)" \mid EAE.$$

A = "+" | "*".

is ambiguous by constructing two syntax trees for the sentence $i + i * i$.

6.6 Extend the following grammar to include the diadic operators – and / (with their usual precedence), and also the unary operators + and –:

S = $T | S$ "+" T.
T = $F | T$ "*"F.
F = "x" | "(" S ")".

6.7 Rewrite the following production rules in iterative forms so that they are no longer left-recursive:

A = $B | A$ "p" B.
C = "q" | C "t".

Chapter 7

Lexical analysis

7.1 Regular languages

The simplest class of languages is known as *regular languages*. A regular language is one that is generated by either a *left-linear grammar* or a *right-linear grammar*. A production of the form

$$A \ = \ aB \qquad \text{or} \qquad A \ = \ a$$

is said to be *right-linear*, whereas a production of the form

$$A \ = \ Ba \qquad \text{or} \qquad A \ = \ a$$

is said to be *left-linear*. A grammar containing only left-linear productions is known as a *left-linear grammar*, whereas a grammar containing only right-linear productions is said to be a *right-linear grammar*. It is possible that non-linear productions may generate regular languages—in which case an equivalent linear grammar exists.

The following is an example of a right-linear grammar which defines binary integer numbers, i.e. arbitrary-length sequences of zeros and ones:

$$A \ = \ \text{``0''} \ A \ | \ \text{``1''} \ A \ | \ \text{``0''} \ | \ \text{``1''} \ .$$

It has the equivalent left-linear form

$$A \ = \ A \ \text{``0''} \ | \ A \ \text{``1''} \ | \ \text{``0''} \ | \ \text{``1''} \ .$$

7.2 Finite-state acceptors

Regular languages can be parsed or recognized by so-called *finite-state acceptors*. A finite-state acceptor operates in discrete steps called *transitions*. In each transition it changes its *state* and reads (*accepts*) one input *symbol*. The finite-state acceptor for a language L is defined by a set of possible transitions corresponding to the production rules of the grammar for L as follows.

(1) *Right-linear grammars*

$$A = aB$$

A = state before transition
a = symbol accepted
B = state after transition

In other words, if A is the current state of the acceptor and it inputs a symbol a, then its new state is B. Thus acceptance of the symbol a transforms the state of the acceptor from A to B. Rules of the form $A = a$ are rewritten $A = a\varepsilon$ where the empty state ε denotes the *final* state. The origin symbol S denotes the *initial* state.

At any moment the state of the acceptor is a description of the *sequence of symbols it is expecting*. If the acceptor is accepting (i.e. parsing) a sequence of symbols it expects to have been generated from the production A, and the next symbol accepted is a, then it expects the remainder of the sequence to be one generated according to the rule for B.

(2) *Left-linear grammars*

$$A = Ba$$

A = state after transition
B = state before transition
a = symbol accepted

Hence, if B is the current state of the acceptor and a symbol a is accepted, then the acceptor's new state is A. Acceptance of the symbol a in this case changes the state of the acceptor from B to A. Rules of the form $A = a$ are rewritten $A = \varepsilon a$ where ε now denotes the *initial* state, and the origin symbol S denotes the *final* state.

Given an acceptor for a left-linear grammar, at any moment its state is a description of the *sequence of symbols it has accepted so far*. If the acceptor has parsed a sequence of symbols generated from the production B, and the next symbol it accepts is a, then it concludes that it has now parsed a sequence defined by the rule for A.

An acceptor is said to be *deterministic* if and only if its present state and the next symbol to be accepted uniquely determine the next state, i.e. there are no two productions

$$A = aB_1 \quad \text{and} \quad A = aB_2 \qquad B_1 \neq B_2$$

or

$$A_1 = Ba \quad \text{and} \quad A_2 = Ba \qquad A_1 \neq A_2$$

Finite-state acceptors are easily represented as *graphs* or *transition diagrams*. Consider Grammar 3 of Chapter 6, which is a right-linear grammar and hence defines a regular language:

$$expression = \text{"}x\text{"} \mid \text{"}x\text{"} \; tail.$$
$$tail \qquad = \text{"}+\text{"} \; expression \mid \text{"}-\text{"} \; expression.$$

Its acceptor can be depicted as shown in Figure 7.1.

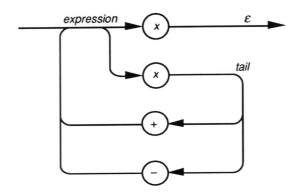

Figure 7.1   *Finite-state acceptor for Grammar 3*

The derivation of this acceptor diagram follows directly from the above production rules. Noting that the rule for *expression* can be rewritten as

$$expression = \text{"}x\text{"} \; \varepsilon \mid \text{"}x\text{"} \; tail.$$

acceptance of an expression involves accepting the symbol "*x*" and then accepting an empty sequence (i.e. no symbols) or accepting an "*x*" followed by a sequence of symbols defined by *tail*. The acceptance of a *tail* involves accepting either a "+" followed by a sequence of symbols forming an *expression*, or accepting a "–" followed by a sequence of symbols forming an *expression*. Therefore, as shown in Figure 7.1, we denote a particular symbol which is to be accepted by labelling a node accordingly, and denote the resultant state following such acceptance by labelling the arc emanating from the node with the name of the sequence then to be accepted. Hence the acceptance of an expression following a "=" or "–" symbol is denoted by connecting the arcs emanating from the nodes concerned to the start of the acceptance process (since acceptance of an expression is effectively a return to the original state of the acceptor and is thus to be performed by repeating the action of the acceptor itself).

The acceptor in Figure 7.1 is not deterministic. However, we can always define an equivalent grammar, e.g. by factorization of the rule for *expression*, to give

$$expression = \text{"}x\text{"} \; tail.$$

tail   = [*"+" expression* | *"–" expression*].

This is still not quite satisfactory since the transition from state *tail* to the empty state ε (as defined by the empty alternative for *tail*) involves the acceptance of no symbol. It is sometimes convenient to introduce a special *stop symbol* ⊥ with which, by convention, all sentences terminate. Now we are able to design a deterministic acceptor, as shown in Figure 7.2.

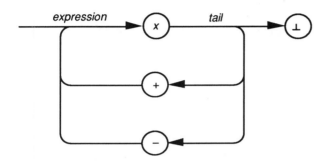

Figure 7.2   *Revised finite-state acceptor for Grammar 3*

A program to carry out the action of the finite-state acceptor can be written with ease—its diagrammatic representation is essentially a flow chart of an equivalent computer program.

Regular languages are examples of Chomsky Type 3 languages and form a restricted subset of the Type 2 context-free languages. While programming languages are not themselves regular languages the preceding theory does underlie the first phase of programming language compilation—*lexical analysis*. We may regard the rules whereby language symbols are constructed from individual characters as a sub-language in which the (language) symbols are the terminal sentences and the individual characters are the terminal symbols of the sub-language. A grammar can be constructed defining this language which can be shown to be a regular grammar and an appropriate finite-state acceptor can then be devised.

7.3   Defining the lexical analyzer interface

The function of the *lexical analyzer* is to transform the character stream transmitted by the *source handler* into a symbol stream suitable for analysis by the *syntax analyzer*. Again we assume that the syntax analyzer will scan the symbols in the symbol stream once only from left to right (a more significant assumption in this case than for the source handler, as we shall see in due course). An adequate interface, analogous to that of the source handler, is that the lexical analyzer makes available to the syntax analyzer the 'current' symbol in the input symbol stream, together with the ability to replace this symbol by its successor whenever the syntax analyzer wishes.

The symbols of Model are the reserved words, identifiers, constants and special-symbols specified in the language definition in Appendix 1. This range of possible symbols may be defined as the values of an enumerated-type

```
TYPE SymbolType =  (Identifier, IntegerNumber, CharConstant,
                    Module, Var, ..., Begin, End, ..., Read, Write,
                    Not, And, Or, ... , Comma, Semicolon, ... , OtherSymbol);
```

where the value *OtherSymbol* denotes an invalid symbol. The suggested interface for the lexical analyzer is then provided by a variable representing a description of the current symbol

```
VAR SymbolDescription: RECORD
                       Symbol: SymbolType;
                       ...
                    END;
```

and a procedure which replaces the description of the current symbol by a description of its successor

```
PROCEDURE GetNextSymbol;
```

The syntax analyzer, upon receiving these symbol descriptions, may subsequently wish to report errors relating to them directly to the source handler, and will require some text position coordinates to do so. The syntax analyzer must not assume that the current position indicated by the source handler is that of the current symbol offered by the lexical analyzer. Instead it is necessary for the lexical analyzer to make available a text position for each symbol, as an additional field of *SymbolDescription*

```
VAR SymbolDescription: RECORD
                       Symbol: SymbolType;
                       Position: TextPosition;
                       ...
                    END;
```

When necessary the syntax analyzer will use this value in reporting errors to the source handler.

The interface defined so far is sufficient for performing the process of syntax analysis itself. However the process of semantic analysis will require additional knowledge of user-defined symbols to be made available, viz. the spelling of each identifier in the source program, and the actual value denoted by each integer or character constant. Whatever interface is defined between the syntax and semantic analyzers must transmit all of this information, and hence the lexical analyzer must enable the syntax analyzer to do so. The interface variable *SymbolDescription* is therefore extended with additional fields

```
VAR SymbolDescription: RECORD
                        CASE Symbol: SymbolType OF
                        | IntegerNumber: IntValue: Target.Integer;
                        | CharConstant: CharValue: Target.Ordinal;
                        | Identifier: Spelling: Host.Word
                        END;
                        Position: TextPosition
                      END;
```

which, respectively, give the relevant identifier spelling when *Symbol* is an *Identifier*, and the equivalent integer value for the target machine when *Symbol* is either an *IntegerNumber* or a *CharConstant*. The type *Word* must provide some means of representing identifier spellings.

The syntax and semantic analyzers will require use of the type *Word* together with various associated operators for performing identifier spelling comparison functions. Since *Word* will be represented most conveniently by a Modula-2 string-type and the host implementation of Modula-2 may provide convenient string-handling operations, it is convenient to extend the *Host* module to export not only a definition of this type but also other aspects of the handling of word spellings which will be required by the various component parts of the compiler. These include definitions of an enumeration of the standard identifiers of Model and the significant length of identifiers:

```
DEFINITION MODULE Host;
    ...
    CONST MaxSignificantIdLength = 12;

    TYPE Word = ARRAY [1..MaxSignificantIdLength] OF CHAR;
    VAR   BlankWord: Word; (* value assumed to be all blanks *)

    TYPE WordRelation = (FirstIsLess, WordsEqual, SecondIsLess);
    PROCEDURE ComparisonOf(W1, W2: Word): WordRelation;

    TYPE StandardIdentifiers = (Integer, Char, Boolean, False, True);
    PROCEDURE GetSpelling(Id: StandardIdentifiers; VAR Spelling: Word);

END Host.
```

Appendix 3 contains a full listing of the *Host* module. The complete interface for the lexical analyzer is specified below as the definition module *LexicalAnalyzer*.

```
DEFINITION MODULE LexicalAnalyzer;

    IMPORT SourceHandler, Host, Target;

    TYPE SymbolType = (Identifier, IntegerNumber, CharConstant, Module, Var,
                        Procedure, Array, Of, Begin, End, If, Then, Else, Case,
```

```
                        Loop, Exit, For, To, Do, Read, Write,
                        Not, And, Or, Div, Times, Plus, Minus, LessThan,
                        LessThanOrEqual, GreaterThanOrEqual, GreaterThan,
                        NotEquals, Equals, RightParenthesis, LeftParenthesis,
                        RightBracket, LeftBracket, Comma, Semicolon,
                        Period, Colon, Becomes, Thru, Separator, OtherSymbol);

  VAR SymbolDescription: RECORD
                        CASE Symbol: SymbolType OF
                        | IntegerNumber: IntValue: Target.Integer;
                        | CharConstant: CharValue: Target.ASCIIOrdinal;
                        | Identifier: Spelling: Host.Word
                        END;
                        Position: SourceHandler.TextPosition
                     END;

     PROCEDURE GetNextSymbol;

  END LexicalAnalyzer.
```

The explicit modularization of the compiler using modules with such interfaces enables the implementation of the facilities defined by individual modules to be hidden from the other modules of the compiler—hence, as in the case of the *LexicalAnalyzer* module above, the permanent tables required by processes associated with distinct parts of the compiler can be provided and protected from the rest of the compiler.

7.4 Programming the lexical analyzer

The lexical analyzer's function, implemented by its principal exported procedure *GetNextSymbol*, is defined by the syntax rules for special-symbols, identifiers and constants given in the language definition in Appendix 1. We will find, however, that this definition is incomplete and must be augmented in order to enable a working lexical analyzer to be programmed.

For a free-format language such as Model, successive calls to the lexical analyzer must deal with not only the characters that actually compose the language symbols but also those characters, such as blanks, that are allowed to occur between them. The usual rule adopted for languages like Modula-2 is that any arbitrary number of blanks may occur between, but not within, the symbols of the program. This might be represented by an additional syntax rule

symbol   = {*separator*} *proper-symbol*.
separator   = *blank*.
proper-symbol   = *identifier* | *integer-number* | *character-constant* |
                    special-symbol.

This modified syntax rule for *symbol* leads us to a finite-state acceptor for *symbol* as shown in Figure 7.3.

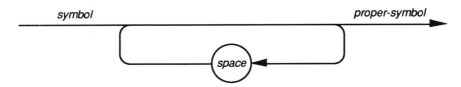

Figure 7.3   *Finite-state acceptor for symbol*

The corresponding coding for the *GetNextSymbol* scan process is as follows:

```
PROCEDURE GetNextSymbol;
   BEGIN
      WHILE SourceHandler.CurrentCharacter = " " DO
         SourceHandler.GetNextCharacter
      END;
      SymbolDescription.Position := SourceHandler.PositionNow;
      scan proper-symbol
   END GetNextSymbol
```

This assumes that each call of *GetNextSymbol* expects the current value of *SourceHandler.CurrentCharacter* to denote the first possible character of the next symbol already and, upon the completion of each call of *GetNextSymbol*, the value of *SourceHandler.CurrentCharacter* denotes the first character which follows that symbol.

The language definition represents the special symbols, DIV, NOT, BEGIN, etc., as sequences of upper-case letters and forbids the use of identifiers of the same spelling. We correspondingly revise our syntax rules as follows:

proper-symbol   = *identifier-or-reserved-word* | *integer-number* |
                                   character-constant | *special-symbol*.
identifier-or-reserved-word = *letter* { *letter* | *digit* }.
special-symbol   = "+" | "–" | ... | ":=" | ":" | ";".

Identifiers and reserved words are thus syntactically indistinguishable and so our analyzer will be able to distinguish them only by a secondary process after their character-by-character scan is complete.

With these changes the definition of *proper-symbol* is readily translatable into an equivalent *scan proper-symbol* process. Rewriting the definition yet again in the form

proper-symbol   = *identifier-or-reserved-word* |
                       integer-number |
                       character-constant |

```
":=" | ":" |
".." | "." |
"<=" | "<>" | "<" |
">=" | ">" |
"+" |
"–" |
"*" |
"=" |
"(" |
")" |
"[" |
"]" |
"|" |
";" .
```

we see that the alternatives on each line are completely distinguished from those on other lines by the first character involved, and that the occurrence of any character other than those shown cannot represent a legal symbol at all. This leads us immediately to a finite-state acceptor for the process *scan proper-symbol* as in Figure 7.4. This acceptor diagram can then be readily translated into the following case-statement:

```
CASE SourceHandler.CurrentCharacter OF
| "A".."Z", "a".."z":   scan identifier or reserved word;
| "0".."9":             scan integer constant;
| "'", "''":            scan character constant;
| ".":                  scan ":=" or ":" symbol;
| ".":                  scan ".." or "." symbol;
| "<":                  scan "<=", "<>", or "<" symbol;
| ">":                  scan ">=" or ">" symbol;
| "+":                  scan "+" symbol;
   ...
| ";":                  scan ";" symbol
ELSE                    scan illegal symbol
END
```

The process *scan identifier or reserved word* must implement the structural rule

identifier-or-reserved-word = *letter* { *letter* | *digit* }.

Since the existence of the initial letter has already been established by the case-statement, this is programmable as

```
SourceHandler.GetNextCharacter;
WHILE SourceHandler.CurrentCharacter is letter or digit DO
   SourceHandler.GetNextCharacter
END
```

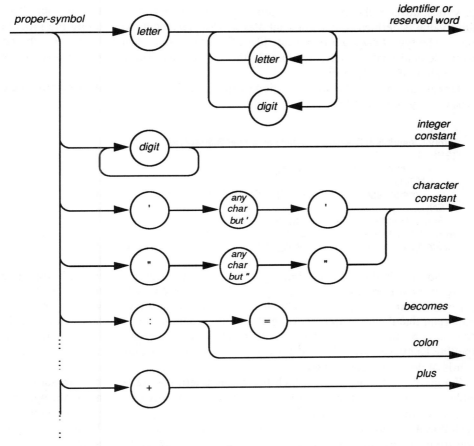

Figure 7.4   *Finite-state acceptor for proper-symbol*

or, more neatly, as

```
REPEAT
    SourceHandler.GetNextCharacter
UNTIL SourceHandler.CurrentCharacter is not a letter or digit
```

However, this scan process must also implement two additional actions, viz.

- the recording of identifier spellings;
- the distinction between identifiers and reserved words.

The language definition imposes a limit on the significant length of identifiers, i.e.

they must differ in the first 12 characters if they are to be considered as distinct. This limit value is defined by the constant *MaxSignificantIdLength* exported by the module *Host*. The type *Host.Word* represents identifier spellings as strings of this length and so the lexical analyzer need retain only the first *MaxSignificantIdLength* characters as the spelling of each identifier.

Having decided on the representation of spellings the *scan identifier or reserved word* process may be elaborated as

```
K := 0;
SymbolDescription.Spelling := SpellingHandler.BlankWord;
REPEAT
   IF K < Host.MaxSignificantIdLength THEN
      INC(K);
      SymbolDescription.Spelling[K] := SourceHandler.CurrentCharacter
   END;
   SourceHandler.GetNextCharacter
UNTIL SourceHandler.CurrentCharacter is not a letter or digit;
decide if SymbolDescription.Spelling denotes an identifier or a reserved word
```

Deciding whether the spelling represents an identifier or a reserved word is a straightforward process of looking up a table of reserved word spellings. However, since up to 50% of symbols in a typical program fall into these two categories it is important that the look-up process be efficiently programmed. The lexical analyzer in Appendix 5 uses a look-up table *WordSymbols* which is sorted and indexed by actual spelling length (Figure 7.5), so that each spelling is compared only with those reserved words of the same actual length.

To give a fast search loop which has a single terminating condition an additional table position is left at the end of each sequence of words of given length, with the preset symbol value *Identifier*. The array *LastOfLength* is initialized to contain, for each possible significant identifier length, the index within the look-up table of this additional position. The spelling scanned is inserted at the particular position associated with its significant length before the search loop is entered. If no preceding entry gives a match the loop will terminate at this entry, and return the symbol value *Identifier* as required:

```
WordSymbols[index of last word symbol of length K].Spelling :=
                                    SymbolDescription.Spelling;
I := index of first word symbol of length K;
WHILE WordSymbols[I].Spelling <> SymbolDescription.Spelling DO
   INC(I)
END;
SymbolDescription.Symbol := WordSymbols[I].Value
```

The process *scan integer constant* implements the structural rule

integer-number = digit { digit }.

	Spelling		Value
1	"	"	Identifier
2	"DO	"	Do
3	"IF	"	If
4	"OF	"	Of
5	"OR	"	Or
6	"TO	"	To
7	"	"	Identifier
8	"AND	"	And
9	"DIV	"	Div
10	"END	"	End
11	"FOR	"	For
12	"NOT	"	Not
13	"VAR	"	Var
14	"	"	Identifier
23	"BEGIN	"	Begin
24	"WRITE	"	Write
25	"	"	Identifier
26	"MODULE	"	Module
27	"	"	Identifier
28	"	"	Identifier
29	"	"	Identifier
30	"PROCEDURE	"	Procedure
31	"	"	Identifier
32	"	"	Identifier
33	"	"	Identifier
34	"	"	Identifier

LastOfLength

0	0
1	1
2	7
3	14
4	21
5	25
6	27
7	28
8	29
9	31
10	32
11	33
12	34

Figure 7.5   *Symbol look-up table*

which again is readily programmed as

```
REPEAT
   SourceHandler.GetNextCharacter
UNTIL SourceHandler.CurrentCharacter is not a digit
```

Computation of the Target machine integer value equivalent to the constant scanned is readily incorporated in this loop, the only complication being that the lexical analyzer must guard against sequences of digits which denote values beyond the Target machine's limit for integers (defined by the constant *Target.MaxInteger*).

The process *scan character constant* implements the structural rule

$$character\text{-}constant \; = \; \text{'''} \; any\text{-}character\text{-}other\text{-}than\text{-}apostrophe \; \text{'''} \; |$$
$$\text{'''} \; any\text{-}character\text{-}other\text{-}than\text{-}quote \; \text{'''}.$$

which can be easily programmed. Computation of the ASCII ordinal value of the character constant concerned on the Target machine is performed using the functions *Host.ASCIIOrdinalOf* and *Target.OrdinalOf*.

The other scanning processes within the case-statement are equally easily programmed. Appendix 5 shows the resultant code for each.

7.5 Further reading

In this chapter we have adopted a pragmatic approach to lexical analysis. More formal approaches to the use of finite scanning techniques are presented in Aho, Sethi and Ullman (1986) and Backhouse (1979). Watson (1989) describes the construction of finite-state automata for performing lexical analysis and examines algorithms used in the construction of such automata. Detailed treatments also appear in Davie and Morrison (1981) and Hunter (1981).

An example of the construction of a complete lexical analyzer for Pascal appears in Welsh and Hay (1986). Watt (1993) constructs a lexical scanner for a model language.

The Model language restricts identifiers to a certain maximum significant length, whereas Pascal allows identifiers of arbitrary length—techniques for the handling of such identifiers are well illustrated in Welsh and Hay (1986).

Software tools have been developed that enable the automatic generation of the source code of lexical analyzers from an input definition of the symbols of the language. A well-known example is the Unix tool *Lex* which generates a C program and is described, together with examples of its use, in Aho, Sethi and Ullman (1986) and Watson (1989).

Exercises 7

7.1 Draw a finite-state acceptor for the language defined by the following regular grammar:

$$A \; = \; \text{"}a\text{"} \; B \; | \; \text{"}c\text{"} \; A \; | \; \text{"}d\text{"}.$$
$$B \; = \; \text{"}b\text{"} \; A.$$

The above grammar is right-linear. Rewrite it in left-linear form.

7.2   The symbols of a certain programming language are defined by the following enumerated-type:

    TYPE SymbolType = (IntegerConstant, RealConstant, CharacterConstant,
                        String, Identifier);

where the lexical structure of these symbols is defined as follows:

integer-number   = *digit-sequence.*
real-constant   = *digit-sequence* "." [*digit-sequence*] [*scale-factor*].
scale-factor   = "E" ["+" | "–"] *digit-sequence*.
digit-sequence   = *digit* { *digit* }.
character-constant = "'" (*letter* | *digit*) "'".
string   = "'" { *letter* | *digit* } "'".
identifier   = *letter* { *letter* | *digit* }.

and a string of length 1 is considered to be a *character-constant*.

(i)   Draw a finite-state acceptor for the symbols so defined.
(ii) Write a procedure with heading

    PROCEDURE NextSymbol(VAR Symbol: SymbolType);

which will determine the next symbol in an input text stream and assign its value to the variable parameter *Symbol*. Assume that the procedure

    PROCEDURE NextCh;

can be invoked to assign successive characters from the input stream to the variable *Ch*, which initially contains the first character of the input stream. Your procedure should report any lexical errors it detects by calling a procedure

    PROCEDURE LexicalError;

7.3   Write a suitable driver program to test the lexical analyzer in Appendix 5. Devise an input program which demonstrates the complete range of Model symbols and use it together with your driver program to test the correctness of the lexical analyzer.

7.4   Modify the Model lexical analyzer in Appendix 5 to allow any sequence of characters enclosed by the double character symbols *(** and *)* to form a *comment*. Comments may appear anywhere that a blank or end of line may occur, but they have no significance as far as the execution of the program is concerned. For example,

(* This is an example of a comment expressed in ordinary English *)

Hint: First rewrite the syntax of *symbol* to allow a preceding *comment*.

Devise a sample Model program and use it as input to the test driver module used in Exercise 7.1 in order to demonstrate that your modifications function correctly.

7.5   Modify the Model lexical analyzer in Appendix 5 to allow identifiers to contain embedded underscore characters "_". For example,

A_long_identifier

Chapter 8

Syntax analysis

In Chapter 6 we were concerned with determining how sentences of unambiguous languages are generated from their grammars. In this chapter we examine how, given such sentences, we can analyze them in order to find their syntactic structure. Thus, given an input sequence of symbols (obtained via a lexical analyzer such as the one developed in Chapter 7), we wish to determine whether it is a valid symbol sequence and, if so, construct the unique syntax tree corresponding to its syntactic structure. We are particularly interested in devising parsing algorithms—such algorithms fall into two categories, *top-down* algorithms and *bottom-up* algorithms, which are characterized by the order in which they construct the parts of the syntax tree.

8.1 Recursive descent analysis

Regular languages exclude one property which is essential to practical programming languages—*nested* or *embedded* structures. Such embedded structures are useful in programming languages as they enable the construction of arbitrarily complex expressions and statements, such as the Modula-2 expression

    (a < 3) OR (b >= ((c + 1) * (d − e) + 10))

which contains a number of nested sub-expressions, or the Modula-2 statement

```
IF a = b THEN
    IF b = c THEN a := a + b; c := c − 1
    ELSE
        REPEAT a := a − b; c := c + 1 UNTIL c = 100
    END;
    IF b > 0 THEN b := 0 END
END
```

which contains a number of nested statements.

Embedded structures are generated by recursively defined grammars. The simplest case of a nested structure is defined by a simplified form of Grammar 4 from Chapter 6, viz.

Grammar 7

T: "*x*" "(" ")"
N: *expression*
P: *expression* = "*x*" | "(" *expression* ")".
L: { (^{n} *x*)^n } $n{\geq}0$

where the (^{n} notation denotes *n* occurrences of the symbol "(".

The sentences of this language consist of the symbol "*x*" embedded in an arbitrary number of matching pairs of left and right parentheses, e.g.

$$x \quad (x) \quad ((x)) \quad (((x))) \quad \ldots$$

Suppose we postulate a finite-state acceptor for this language in which some of the symbols to be read are so far unspecified, as shown in Figure 8.1.

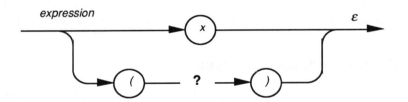

Figure 8.1 *Form of acceptor for Grammar 7*

Clearly the missing action is the acceptance of a sequence of symbols generated by *expression*—the intended action of the acceptor itself, which implies that our unspecified symbol should be the non-terminal *expression*. This leads us to the concept of our acceptor activating itself *recursively* or, more generally, to the concept of sets of acceptors which activate each other (and possibly themselves) recursively.

This concept is in fact the basis of a syntax analysis technique, widely used in compilation, called *recursive descent analysis*, in which the acceptor for each non-terminal is implemented as a procedure which can activate other acceptors, including itself, recursively. These acceptors are often referred to as *recognizers*. For example, a *recognizer* for Grammar 7 could be written as a recursive procedure, thus:

```
PROCEDURE Expression;
   BEGIN
```

```
WITH LexicalAnalyzer.SymbolDescription DO
    IF Symbol = "x" THEN
        LexicalAnalyzer.GetNextSymbol
    ELSIF Symbol = LeftParenthesis THEN
        LexicalAnalyzer.GetNextSymbol; Expression;
        IF Symbol = RightParenthesis THEN LexicalAnalyzer.GetNextSymbol
    ELSE error
    END
ELSE
    error
END
END
END Expression
```

We shall return in due course to a more detailed consideration of recursive descent analysis, after we have looked at the more general aspects and techniques of syntax analysis.

8.2 Top-down analysis

As we have already stated, the objective of syntax analysis is to construct the syntax tree for a given input sequence of symbols. We refer to this syntax tree as a *phrase structure tree*. Recursive descent analysis is a particular form of the more general *top-down analysis*.

In top-down syntax analysis, the syntax tree is constructed starting at the top of the tree (with the origin symbol) and proceeding to its bottom. At each stage of the construction process the analyzer sets itself a goal of building part of the tree—the initial goal is to recognize the origin symbol *S*, and the analysis then proceeding by splitting each goal into a succession of sub-goals according to the production corresponding to that goal. When a sub-goal is achieved (ultimately by matching the next input symbols with those required by the production representing the sub-goal) control passes to the next sub-goal (if any) in the production. When a sub-goal is not achieved the production which generated it is abandoned and the next alternative production is selected.

Analysis is complete when the original goal *S* has been achieved (or abandoned) and the tree has been fully constructed (or it is found that the tree cannot be constructed). Consider the parsing of the sentence

$$x + x$$

of Grammar 4, defined previously as

expression	=	*term* | *term* "+" *expression*.
term	=	*factor* | *factor* "*" *term*.
factor	=	"*x*" | "(" *expression* ")".

Construction of the sentence's phrase structure tree by top-down analysis proceeds as shown in the sequence (1)–(10) below. At each stage the part of the input symbol sequence which has been examined so far is highlighted by shading.

(1)   The initial goal is to match the origin non-terminal *expression* against the input symbol sequence *x+x*.

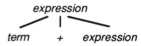

(2)   This goal is replaced by the goals *term +* *expression*, with *term* as the first sub-goal to be attained.

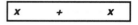

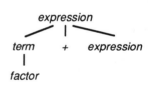

(3)   The sub-goal *term* may be satisfied by achieving the sub-goal *factor*.

(4)   Achieving the sub-goal *factor* may be achieved by satisfying the sub-goal *x*, i.e., by matching the incoming symbol with *x*.

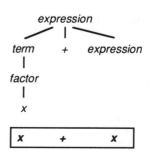

(5)   Compare *x* with the next input symbol.
They match and so the goal *x* is achieved;
and thus the goal *factor* (4) is achieved,
and the goal *term* (3) is also achieved.
The next goal to satisfy is +, i.e., the
incoming symbol must be matched with
+.

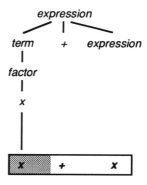

(6)   Compare + with the next input symbol.
They match and hence the goal + has been
achieved.

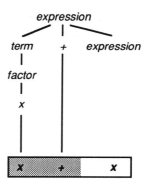

(7)   The next goal to satisfy is *expression*.
This can be satisfied by achieving the
sub-goal *term*.

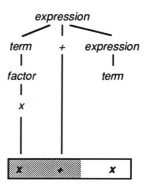

(8)   The next goal to satisfy is *term*.
        This can be satisfied in turn by satisfying
        the sub-goal *factor*.

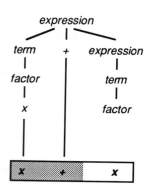

(9)   The next goal to satisfy is *factor*.
        This can be satisfied by satisfying the
        sub-goal *x,* i.e., by matching the
        incoming symbol against *x*.

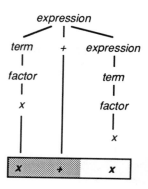

(10)   Compare *x* with the next input symbol. It
        matches and hence goal *x* is achieved;
        and so the goal *factor* (9) is achieved;
        and so the goal *term* (8) is also achieved;
        and so also is the goal *expression* (7),
        and so also is the goal *term + expression* (2);
        and hence the original goal *expression* (1) is
        achieved.
        Therefore, the parse is complete, and the
        syntax tree has been constructed.
        The input is exhausted and so the parse has
        been successful.

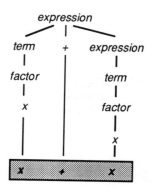

    Some of the decisions that were taken in the construction of the above syntax tree
may be rather mystifying. At various points in the construction process, certain goals
were replaced by particular goals when in fact a number of alternative choices were

available. Why, for instance, at step (2) above, was the goal *expression* replaced with the sub-goals *term "+" expression* rather than the goal *term* (which was the choice made in the same situation at step (7))?

Top-down analysis is a *predictive* technique—each time we try to satisfy a goal which has a number of alternative forms, a prediction is made of which of the alternative forms is the correct one. The problem then arises as to how to make the appropriate prediction. In the next section we examine the conditions under which the correct prediction can be made.

8.3 Conditions for effective top-down analysis

We are interested in determining the conditions under which top-down analysis will work, and work efficiently.

No left-recursion

Top-down analysis cannot work if it is based on any production which is left-recursive, directly, or indirectly, since looping must occur, e.g. analysis of sequences defined by

term = factor | term "" factor.*

will cause a looping situation to occur. If *term* is set as a goal in parsing a symbol sequence, and this goal is replaced by the sub-goals *term "*" factor*, then the first sub-goal to be satisfied is *term* itself, and the parser is back where it started in trying to achieve the goal *term*!

Such left-recursive rules can usually be eliminated by a simple transformation of the grammar. The rule for *term* above defines palindromic sequences of factors separated by "*" operators and can be transformed by inversion into the right-recursive form

term = factor | factor "" term.*

No back-up

The general description of top-down analysis given in Section 8.2 implies that, if an incorrect production is selected as a goal from among a number of alternative possible productions, then at some subsequent point in the analysis it may be necessary to abandon the goal represented by a given production, some of whose sub-goals have already been achieved, and select another goal represented by one of the alternative productions. This 'backing-up' in the analysis process involves a corresponding backing-up in the input symbol stream and, if parallel semantic actions are being taken, a backing-up or undoing of these is also involved. Furthermore the backing-up may extend over an arbitrary number of syntax levels. In consequence an analysis process allowing back-up is potentially an extremely inefficient one, the degree of inefficiency being in general determined by the form of the grammar on which it is based.

The need for back-up can only arise when the analyzer is faced with a choice of two or more alternative productions for a given goal symbol, and has no means of determining which is the correct one to choose. If the wrong choice is made then back-up must eventually occur, possibly after considerable subsidiary analysis. This would have been the case in the construction of the syntax tree in 8.2 if, when faced with a choice of productions for *expression*, *term* or *factor*, we had made a selection other than the one actually chosen.

The obvious question is whether it is possible to restrict or transform a grammar such that the analyzer can always make the correct choice and, if so, how is the choice to be made? A grammar for which an analyzer can always select its next syntactic goal by examining the next k incoming symbols (at most) is called an *LL(k) grammar*. For practical applications the restriction is usually strengthened to $k = 1$, i.e. to *LL(1) grammars*. LL(k) grammars are so called because the correct choice of goal can always be made by an analyzer on the basis of the knowledge of all the symbols occurring to the left (*L*) of the incoming symbol, and the left-most k incoming symbols (*L(k)*).

For languages defined by LL(1) grammars, top-down analysis without back-up is guaranteed simply by examination of the next input symbol at any stage. A necessary and sufficient condition for a grammar to be LL(1) is given in the next section. This condition also fulfils the above requirement for no left-recursion in all practical situations.

An LL(1) condition

An LL(1) grammar must enable the analyzer to choose among the alternative productions for a given goal symbol by examination of the next available input symbol. We may postulate therefore that for each production there exists a set of terminal symbols (which we will call its *director symbols*) such that the occurrence of a director symbol as the next input symbol implies the selection of the corresponding production for the given goal at that moment. Consider the production set for a given non-terminal A:

$$A = \alpha_1 \mid \alpha_2 \mid \ldots \mid \alpha_n.$$

The director symbols for a production α_i obviously include those terminal symbols which can occur at the left hand end of any sequence generated by α_i, i.e. the symbols

$$L_T(\alpha_i) = \{ a \mid \alpha_i \Rightarrow a\beta, a \in T, \beta \in V^* \}$$

These symbols are often referred to as the *starters* of α_i.

We must also consider what happens if α_i is, or can generate, the empty sequence ε (which of course has no starter symbol). In general, when parsing a sequence of symbols generated indirectly from any non-terminal S, we have

$$S \Rightarrow \beta A\delta$$

where A is the current goal symbol, β is the sequence of symbols already accepted, and δ is the sequence of symbols following those generated by A. If the correct production to be selected for A is α_i in its empty generating role then the next input symbol is therefore the first symbol of the sequence δ. Thus, if the production set for A contains a production α_i which can generate the empty sequence, the director symbols for that alternative must include those symbols which can follow sequences generated by A, i.e. the symbols

$$F_T(A) = \{ \; a \mid S \Rightarrow \beta A\delta, \, a \in L_T(\delta), \, b,\delta \in V^* \}$$

These symbols are often referred to as the *followers* of A.

So we define the director symbols for a production α of a non-terminal A as follows:

$$DS(A, \alpha) = \{ \; a \mid a \in L_T(a) \; \textbf{or} \; (\alpha \Rightarrow \varepsilon \; \textbf{and} \; a \in F_T(A)) \; \}$$

The necessary and sufficient condition that a grammar be LL(1) is then that, for each non-terminal in the grammar, *the director symbols of its alternative productions must form mutually disjoint sets*, i.e. for each production set

$$A = \alpha_1 \mid \alpha_2 \mid \dots \mid \alpha_n.$$

$$DS(A, \alpha_i) \cap DS(A, \alpha_j) = \varnothing \; \textit{for } i \neq j$$

It can be verified that this condition implies that all practical left-recursion is excluded. For example, consider the following simple grammar, in which the non-terminal A is defined left-recursively:

$$A = A\text{ ``b'' } \mid \text{ ``c'' } \mid \text{ ``d''}.$$

We can establish the director symbol sets for the three alternatives of A—since there is no empty alternative for A they consist simply of the starter symbols of the sequences generated by the alternatives:

$$
\begin{aligned}
DS(A, A\text{ ``b''}) &= \{ \text{ ``c''}, \text{ ``d''} \} \\
DS(A, \text{ ``c''}) &= \{ \text{ ``c''} \} \\
DS(A, \text{ ``d''}) &= \{ \text{ ``d''} \}
\end{aligned}
$$

which are obviously not disjoint. Hence, if the next input symbol is, say, *"c"*, then the parser cannot tell whether to parse according to the goal A *"b"* or the goal *"c"*. Note that the problem arises because, since sequences generated by the alternative A *"b"* start with the symbols that can start sequences generated by A, the starter symbols for the alternative A *"b"* include all those symbols which can start any alternative of A.

It can be verified that the LL(1) condition implies that at most one production for any non-terminal A may generate the empty sequence. Consider the grammar:

$$X \;=\; \text{"}a\text{"}\, A\, \text{"}y\text{"} \mid A\, \text{"}z\text{"}.$$
$$A \;=\; B \mid C \mid \text{"}d\text{"}.$$
$$B \;=\; [\, \text{"}e\text{"}\,].$$
$$C \;=\; [\, \text{"}f\text{"}\,].$$

The director symbol sets for the three alternatives of A are

$$DS\,(A, B) \;=\; \{\, \text{"}e\text{"},\, \text{"}y\text{"},\, \text{"}z\text{"}\, \}$$
$$DS\,(A, C) \;=\; \{\, \text{"}f\text{"},\, \text{"}y\text{"},\, \text{"}z\text{"}\, \}$$
$$DS\,(A, \text{"}d\text{"}) \;=\; \{\, \text{"}d\text{"}\, \}$$

The director symbol sets for the alternatives $A = B$ and $A = C$ must both contain the followers of A since they can both generate empty sequences and thus cannot be disjoint. The followers of A are determined by examining the contexts in which A appears on the right hand side of any productions, and then working out which symbols can start the sequences which can follow one derived from A. In the above case sequences generated by A are always followed by either *"y"* or *"z"*.

Efficient recursive descent parsing

As we shall see in the next chapter, construction of a recursive descent parser for an LL(1) grammar is a straightforward matter, consisting of a set of recognizers developed as suggested in 8.1. Such a parser, when incorporated in a one-pass compiler for a language like Model, does not construct an actual phrase structure syntax tree but instead builds it implicitly by detecting the beginning and end of each syntactic structure within the input program.

The Model parser will be written in Modula-2 and will provide a syntactic framework in which semantic actions can subsequently be incorporated. It will consist of a set of recognizers, one for each syntactic construct in the grammar. For those syntactic constructs which are defined recursively, such as expressions and statements, the corresponding recognizer will take the form of a recursive procedure.

Recursion, even within a programming system designed to provide it, is not an inexpensive technique and, in many cases where formal notation uses it as a means of syntax description, it is nevertheless unnecessary in the corresponding analysis process.

For example, the production for *term* in Grammar 4 was modified previously to remove the left-recursion and written as

term = factor | *term* *"*" factor.*

However, this still uses (right-)recursion to denote simple repetition, but can be written non-recursively as

    term = factor { "*" factor}.

A corresponding recursive descent recognizer can also be constructed which uses iteration rather than recursion, e.g. as a procedure

```
PROCEDURE Term;
   BEGIN
      Factor;
      WHILE LexicalAnalyzer.SymbolDescription.Symbol = "*" DO
         LexicalAnalyzer.GetNextSymbol; Factor
      END
   END Term
```

which will be more efficient than its recursive equivalent. Moreover, as we shall see later, this iterative form is more natural and convenient for semantic processing.

Note, however, that, since repeated (and possibly empty) sequence $\{\alpha\}$ is equivalent to the occurrence of an auxiliary non-terminal A with two alternatives, one of which is empty

    $A = [\alpha A]$.

the LL(1) condition must be applied. Thus, for every occurrence of a repetition $\{\alpha\}$ in a grammar we must ensure that

$$L_T(\alpha) \cap F_T(\{\alpha\}) = \varnothing$$

Otherwise the decision to terminate the analysis loop for $\{\alpha\}$ cannot be made by inspection of the next input symbol, since it cannot be established whether that symbol is occurring in the context of the starter symbol of another α or as the first symbol following the sequence of αs.

In certain cases recursive analysis is inevitable (e.g. for sub-expressions contained within parentheses) and cannot be avoided. In general the grammar, and the corresponding top-down analyzer, for a given language can be reduced to one recursive procedure for each kind of recursively nested structure in the language. In practice, however, it is not always advantageous to reduce the number of acceptor procedures to this minimal number.

8.4 Bottom-up analysis

Bottom-up syntax analysis is so called because it involves starting the building of a syntax analysis tree from the given sentence (the *bottom* of the tree), performing reductions when appropriate, to approach the top of the tree (the origin symbol of the grammar concerned) on the way *up*. This is in contrast with top-down analysis which, as we have seen, starts at the *top* of the tree and descends *down* by matching parts of the sentence with predicted sub-goals.

In the remainder of this book as we develop the Model compiler we shall be interested only in recursive descent analysis. Nonetheless, it is of interest for comparative purposes to consider the fundamental properties and techniques of bottom-up analysis.

The basic technique of bottom-up analysis is to scan the input sequence symbol by symbol, at each step investigating whether the sequence read so far, or part of it, is reducible, i.e. whether application of a *reduction rule* (which is simply a production rule in reverse) can lead to replacement of (part of) the sequence by a non-terminal symbol. For example, the sentence

$$x + x$$

of Grammar 4, for which we previously performed a top-down parse to construct its syntax tree, can be parsed in a bottom-up fashion as shown in Table 8.1.

Step	Action	Description of symbols scanned so far	Remaining input
1	Initial state		*x + x*
2	input next symbol	*"x"*	*+ x*
3	reduce using *factor* = *"x"*	*factor*	*+ x*
4	reduce using *term* = *factor*	*term*	*+ x*
5	input next symbol	*term* *"+"*	*x*
6	input next symbol	*term* *"+"* *x*	
7	reduce using *factor* = *"x"*	*term* *"+"* *factor*	
8	reduce using *term* = *factor*	*term* *"+"* *term*	
9	reduce using *expression* = *term*	*term* *"+"* *expression*	
10	reduce using *expression* = *term* *"+"* *expression*	*expression*	

Table 8.1   *Bottom-up parse of x + x*

The description of the sequence of symbols seen so far is known as the *handle* of the parse—all additions and reductions of the description take place at the right hand end of the handle, and hence it is effectively a stack of symbols (terminals and non-terminals). After step 10 all of the input sequence has been scanned and it has been reduced to the origin symbol expression, so demonstrating that the original sequence was indeed a sentence generated by *expression*. Figure 8.2 illustrates the order in which the syntax tree is constructed—the annotated numbers refer to the parsing steps listed in Table 8.1.

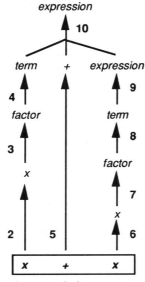

Figure 8.2   *Bottom-up order of construction of syntax tree for x + x*

It should be noted that certain reductions, although possible, were not made as they would have led to an incorrect parse and the need for some back-up within the analysis. Once again, the problem lies in finding some satisfactory criterion for making the correct reduction decisions and thus avoiding any back-up. There exists a variety of methods, each imposing corresponding restrictions on the class of language analyzed.

Parsers based on bottom-up syntax analysis all involve the construction of tables from the original grammar, which are used subsequently to delimit or identify a reducible sequence of symbols, the reduction itself being made by searching the grammar for the appropriate reduction rule. The methods differ in the way in which they identify the reducible sequence and in the amount of information they use in doing so.

All the various bottom-up methods are capable of analyzing more complex languages than those which are amenable to top-down analysis. The underlying reason for this is that, whereas top-down analysis methods must identify the production corresponding to a given sequence of symbols by examining at most one (or in general *k*) of the symbols from the start of the sequence itself, bottom-up analysis methods involve the examination of symbols beyond the end of a sequence before identifying it as reducible—a much more powerful strategy.

Those grammars which enable a reduction to be identified after examining all symbols to the *left* and *k* symbols to the *right* of the reducible sequence are classified as *LR(k)* grammars. A family of analyzers for *LR(0)* and *LR(1)* grammars has been developed—they function in the same bottom-up manner, constructing and using tables to delimit reducible sequences during analysis.

Both top-down analysis and bottom-up analysis methods have advantages and disadvantages in particular situations. As far as pure syntax analysis is concerned top-down methods work well when applied to languages whose grammars meet the LL(1) condition. The bottom-up methods work better for recursive constructs such as arithmetic expressions and allow a wider class of language constructs via an appropriately restructured grammar.

However, in practice we are interested not just in syntax analysis but also in the accompanying process of semantic evaluation. Automatically constructed analyzers, either top down or bottom up, provide facilities whereby calls to semantic actions are plugged into the syntax tables themselves. These facilities must in general impose some constraints on the actions provided. A recursive descent analyzer, on the other hand, is an explicit program written in some programming language and thus permits all the flexibility of the language itself in how the semantic actions are implemented.

8.5 Further reading

For more detailed information on LL grammars and parsing techniques the reader should consult the papers by Lewis and Stearns (1968) and Rosenkrantz and Stearns (1970). Texts such as Davie and Morrison (1981) and Tremblay and Sorenson (1985) provide a thorough coverage of recursive descent analysis. Hunter (1981) includes material on the transformation of non-LL(1) grammars into LL(1) grammars. Detailed coverage of parsing techniques and algorithms appears in Watt (1993).

Bottom-up analysis is not of any further relevance in this text. However, the interested reader will find comprehensive treatments of LR(k) grammars and parsing techniques (and their many variations) in Aho, Sethi and Ullman (1986), Backhouse (1979) and Tremblay and Sorenson (1985).

Much research has been devoted to the investigation of automatic generation of parsers from context-free language definitions. The Unix software tool *Yacc* accepts a suitable-defined context-free grammar for a language, and will generate an LR parser for that language. Details appear in Aho, Sethi and Ullman (1986).

Exercises 8

8.1 Determine the starters and followers terminal symbol sets for the non-terminals of the following grammar:

S = "(" A ")".
A = C B.
B = [";" A].

C = "*x*" | *S*.

8.2 Transform the following set of production rules into a form which ensures that the corresponding top-down analysis is deterministic, without back-up, and complete. Illustrate the need for each condition by a counter-example.

S = $C | T | P | U$.
C = U "=" U.
T = U "+" $T | U$ "+" U.
P = U "*" $P | U$ "*" U.
U = "(" S ")" | "~" $U | L$.
L = "*p*" | "*q*" | "*r*".

8.3 Transform the following grammar into a form which meets the LL(1) conditions and demonstrate in detail that it does so:

E = $A | F |$ "(" L ")".
A = "*i*".
F = "*i*" "(" L ")".
L = $E | L$ "," E.

8.4 Transform the following grammar into a form which meets the LL(1) conditions and demonstrate in detail that it does so:

A = $B | A$ ";" B.
B = $C |$ "[" A "]".
C = $D | C$ "," D.
D = "*x*" | "(" C ")".

8.5 A grammar is defined by the productions

X = $Y | X$ "*p*" Y.
Y = "*q*" Z "*r*" | "*q*" W "*r*".
Z = ["*u*" Z].
W = "*s*" | W "*t*".

Revise this grammar
(i) to eliminate left-recursion;
(ii) to ensure that, for each non-terminal symbol, the director symbols of its alternative productions form mutually disjoint sets;
(iii) to replace all recursion in the productions by simple iteration (denoting zero or more occurrences of *x* by {*x*}).
Write a procedure to parse a correct sentence of the revised grammar. Assume that the sentence is followed by a special stop-symbol, and that the procedure

Next can be invoked to assign successive terminal symbols of the sentence to the variable *Symbol*, which initially contains the first symbol of the sentence. Whenever your procedure parses an occurrence of the non-terminal symbol Y it should output the character 'z' or 'w' depending on which alternative production of Y is parsed.

Chapter 9

A recursive descent analyzer

9.1 Separating syntax and semantics

Now that we have developed the Model lexical analyzer, we move on to consider the remaining components of the analysis process which were previously identified as

syntax analyzer (symbol stream) (syntax errors, program syntax)
semantic analyzer (program syntax, semantic errors, ?)

Before further development can take place some decision must be taken on the structural relationship between these processes. The factors affecting this decision are as follows:

- The language features of Model do not require that semantic analysis of the program as a whole should follow its syntax analysis—they can take place in *parallel*, and efficiency considerations dictate that they should.
- The compiler design constraints specified in Chapter 2 do not, as in the case of the source handler, require the physical separation of the syntax and semantic analysis code. This choice can be made purely on the inherent nature of the two processes and their mutual interaction.
- The conceptual interface *program syntax* is some representation of the program's syntax tree. We have seen that such trees are recursively structured objects—a common property of such recursive tree structures is that the sequence of control involved in their traversal (in our case, by semantic analysis) either mirrors exactly, or is an exact subset of, the sequence of control which creates them (in our case, syntax analysis). Where these creation and traversal processes take place in parallel a common controlling code structure can suffice.

The way forward therefore is not to define any explicit interface at this stage, but to construct the code structure necessary for syntax analysis and then to add to (i.e. enrich) this syntactic 'skeleton' with the 'meat' of semantic analysis. The end product will be a single module which carries out both syntax and semantic analysis.

9.2 Programming the syntax analyzer

In Chapter 8 we introduced the concept of recursive descent acceptors (recognizer procedures)—this concept can be generalized to construct a syntax analyzer directly from the syntax rules of the language. Thus, from the syntax rule for *program*

> *program* = "MODULE" *identifier* ";" *block identifier* ".".

we can immediately formulate a procedure for the analysis of a complete program as

```
PROCEDURE Programme;
   BEGIN
      Accept(Module);
      Accept(Identifier);
      Accept(Semicolon);
      Block;
      Accept(Identifier);
      Accept(Period)
   END Programme
```

where *Accept* is a procedure which checks that the current symbol is that specified and scans to the next input symbol, otherwise it reports a syntax error:

```
PROCEDURE Accept(SymbolExpected: SymbolType);
   BEGIN
      IF LexicalAnalyzer.SymbolDescription.Symbol = SymbolExpected THEN
         LexicalAnalyzer.GetNextSymbol
      ELSE SyntaxError(SymbolExpected)
      END
   END Accept
```

The procedure for the analysis of a *block* is similarly derived from the corresponding syntax rule

> *block* = *declaration-part statement-part.*

leading to a procedure

```
PROCEDURE Block;
   BEGIN
      DeclarationPart;
      StatementPart
   END Block
```

which simply invokes two other recognizer procedures, in turn.

Since these are the only calls on the procedures *DeclarationPart* and *StatementPart* which occur, they could be replaced by the procedure bodies themselves, and these procedures dropped from the analyzer. However, in this case their retention gives a useful structural separation of the very different activities of dealing with declarations and statements.

We could continue developing syntax analysis procedures in this way, one for each syntax rule in the language definition. It may be clear, however, that each procedure developed is a direct translation of the corresponding syntax rule. Before continuing, therefore, it is useful obviously to formulate a set of rules for the translation process.

As we have seen, in a context-free grammar, each syntax rule takes the form

$$non\text{-}terminal\text{-}symbol \quad = \quad allowable\text{-}form.$$

where the *allowable-form* is constructed in terms of

(a) the terminal symbols of the language;
(b) other non-terminal symbols;
(c) the meta-symbols |, [ ] and { } denoting selection, optionality and possible repetition, respectively.

Our objective is to translate the syntax rule for each non-terminal symbol into a recognizer procedure of the same name, whose action is to analyze the incoming sequence of symbols, and verify that it is of the corresponding *allowable-form*, reporting errors if it is not. More precisely, the procedure corresponding to a non-terminal symbol S

(a) assumes initially that *LexicalAnalyzer.SymbolDescription* contains a description of the first symbol of an S;
(b) causes the input of the longest sequence of symbols which are of form S, reporting an error if no such sequence is found;
(c) leaves in *LexicalAnalyzer.SymbolDescription* a description of the first source program symbol which does not belong to S.

The body of the procedure required is clearly some transformation of the *allowable-form* appearing in the syntax rule, so we can depict our translation process as converting a syntax rule

$$S \;=\; \alpha$$

into an equivalent procedure

```
PROCEDURE S;
  BEGIN
    T(α)
  END S
```

The transformation T is defined by a series of rules as follows:

1. If the allowable form α is a single terminal symbol a of the language, the action required is to inspect the current input symbol, and if it is the allowed symbol a then scan to the next symbol, otherwise report an error. Assuming the procedure *Accept* defined above, our first transformation rule is thus

    Rule 1 $T("a") \rightarrow Accept(a)$

2. If the allowable form is itself a single non-terminal symbol, A say, the action required is simply a call to the corresponding recognizer procedure A. Hence:

    Rule 2 $T(A) \rightarrow A$

3. If the allowable form is a sequence of terminal and non-terminal symbols, $\alpha_1 \alpha_2 \ldots \alpha_n$ say, the action required is clearly the corresponding sequence of actions appropriate to each symbol. Hence:

    Rule 3 $T(\alpha_1 \alpha_2 \ldots \alpha_n) \rightarrow T(\alpha_1); T(\alpha_2); \ldots; T(\alpha_n)$

    The *program* and *block* recognizers developed earlier in this section illustrate the application of these first three translation rules.

4. If the allowable form consists of a number of alternative forms

    $$\alpha \mid \beta \mid \ldots \mid \delta$$

    the action required is clearly some selection among the actions appropriate to each alternative

    ```
    CASE ? OF
    | ? : T(α);
    | ? : T(β);
      ...
    | ? : T(δ)
    END
    ```

    On what basis is the selection made? In the lexical analyzer the corresponding decision was made on the first character of the symbol under scan. If the language is assumed to have an LL(1) grammar the choice can be made on the basis of the current symbol. If we denote those symbols $L_T(\alpha)$ which can begin a sequence of symbols of form α as *StartersOf*(α), the necessary transformation is defined by the rule

    Rule 4 $T(\alpha \mid \beta \mid \ldots \mid \delta) \rightarrow$

```
CASE LexicalAnalyzer.SymbolDescription.Symbol OF
| StartersOf(α)   : T(α);
| StartersOf(β)   : T(β);
        ...
| StartersOf(δ)   : T(δ)
ELSE
    error
END
```

The first condition derived in Section 8.3 for an LL(1) grammar requires that no symbol may be a starter of more than one of the alternatives of each allowable form.

The analyzer's action for an empty alternative of an allowable form S is to accept no symbols. This action should be taken when the next input symbol is a follower of the allowable form, i.e.

$T([\alpha | \beta | \dots | \delta]) \rightarrow$

```
CASE LexicalAnalyzer.SymbolDescription.Symbol OF
| StartersOf(α)   : T(α);
| StartersOf(β)   : T(β);
        ...
| StartersOf(δ)   : T(δ)
| FollowersOf(S)    : { do nothing }
ELSE
    error
END
```

Again, for an LL(1) grammar we have already seen in the derivation of the LL(1) conditions that no symbol may be both a possible starter and a possible follower of an allowable form which has an empty alternative.

The case construct used in Rule 4 neatly expresses a choice among any number of alternatives. If only two alternatives exist, and if one of these alternatives is empty, it may of course be re-expressed as an *IF...THEN...ELSE...* statement.

5. If the allowable form involves a possible repetition, $\{\alpha\}$, the action required is clearly a loop of some form. As in the lexical analyzer the criterion for loop termination is again based on the value of the current input symbol. Hence:

Rule 5 $T(\{\alpha\}) \rightarrow$

```
WHILE LexicalAnalyzer.SymbolDescription.Symbol IN StartersOf(α) DO
    T(α)
END
```

Note that, since a repetitive form $\{\alpha\}$ is possibly empty, for an LL(1) grammar no symbol may be both a possible starter of α and a possible follower of $\{\alpha\}$.

Those repetitions that cannot be empty are written in the syntax rules as

$$\alpha\{\alpha\}$$

which transforms to

```
T(α);
WHILE LexicalAnalyzer.SymbolDescription.Symbol IN StartersOf(α) DO
    T(α)
END
```

or, more neatly, as

```
REPEAT
    T(α)
UNTIL NOT (LexicalAnalyzer.SymbolDescription.Symbol IN StartersOf(α))
```

These five rules enable the translation of the set of syntax rules defining a context-free language defined by an LL(1) grammar into an equivalent set of recognizer procedures. The ultimate objective, viz. the analysis of programs of the language, is then achieved by a call to the procedure corresponding to the syntax rule for *program*. This procedure of course calls other procedures, which in turn call others. Such a recursive descent analyzer does not actually construct a syntax tree representing the syntactic structure of the input program at all—instead it produces a gradual tracing of the conceptual syntax tree of the program being analyzed, accompanied by a symbol-by-symbol acceptance of the program each time a 'leaf' of the tree is identified. For those constructs which are nested or recursive in form, such as expressions and statements, the procedures automatically call themselves recursively to deal with nested instances of their allowable forms.

The analyzer operates in a deterministic manner, determining the appropriate analysis path by inspection of the current input symbol, provided each of the underlying syntax rules fulfils the LL(1) conditions.

Constructing the syntax analyzer for Model now involves the systematic application of Rules 1–5 to the syntax rules appearing in its language definition, with a preliminary check that the LL(1) conditions are fulfilled where appropriate. Table 9.1 shows the syntax rules as they appear in Appendix 1 (apart from the omission of certain redundant syntax constructs), but sorted in an order appropriate to recursive descent analysis.

program	=	"MODULE" *identifier* ";" *block identifier* ".".
block	=	*declaration-part statement-part*.
declaration	=	{ *variable-declaration-part* | *procedure-declaration* ";" }.
variable-declaration-part	=	"VAR" { *variable-declaration* ";" }.

variable-declaration	=	*identifier-list* ":" *type.*
identifier-list	=	*identifier* { "," *identifier* }.
type	=	*simple-type* I *array-type.*
simple-type	=	*type-identifier.*
type-identifier	=	*identifier.*
array-type	=	"ARRAY" *index-type* "OF" *component-type.*
index-type	=	"[" *integer-number* ".." *integer-number* "]".
component-type	=	*simple-type.*
procedure-declaration	=	"PROCEDURE" *identifier* ";" *block identifier .*
statement-part	=	"BEGIN" *statement-sequence* "END"
statement-sequence	=	*statement* { ";" *statement* }.
statement	=	*simple-statement* I *structured-statement.*
simple-statement	=	*assignment-statement* I *exit-statement* I *procedure-statement* I *read-statement* I *write-statement.*
assignment-statement	=	*variable* ":=" *expression.*
procedure-statement	=	*procedure-identifier.*
procedure-identifier	=	*identifier.*
exit-statement	=	"EXIT".
read-statement	=	"READ" "(" *input-variable* ")".
input-variable	=	*variable.*
write-statement	=	"WRITE" "(" *output-value* ")".
output-value	=	*expression.*
structured-statement	=	*if-statement* I *case-statement* I *loop-statement* I *for-statement.*
if-statement	=	"IF" *expression* "THEN" *statement-sequence* ["ELSE" *statement-sequence*] "END".
case-statement	=	"CASE" *expression* "OF" *case-limb* { *case-limb* } "END".
case-limb	=	"I" *case-label-list* ":" *statement-sequence.*
case-label-list	=	*constant* { "," *constant* }.
loop-statement	=	"LOOP" *statement-sequence* "END".
for-statement	=	"FOR" *variable-identifier* ":=" *initial-expression* "TO" *final-expression* "DO" *statement-sequence* "END".
initial-expression	=	*expression.*
final-expression	=	*expression.*
expression	=	*simple-expression* [*relational-operator simple-expression*].
simple-expression	=	*sign term* { *addition-operator term* }.
term	=	*factor* { *multiplication-operator factor* }.
factor	=	*variable* I *constant* I "(" *expression* ")" I "NOT" *factor .*
relational-operator	=	"=" I "<>" I "<" I "<=" I ">" I ">=".
sign	=	["+" I "-"].

addition-operator	=	"+"	"-"	"OR".
multiplication-operator	=	"*"	"DIV"	"AND".
constant	=	*integer-number*	*character-constant*	*constant-identifier*.
constant-identifier	=	*identifier*.
variable	=	*entire-variable*	*indexed-variable*.
indexed-variable	=	*array-variable* "[" *expression* "]".
array-variable	=	*entire-variable*.
entire-variable	=	*variable-identifier*.
variable-identifier	=	*identifier*.

Table 9.1   *Model syntax in recursive descent order*

The procedures already devised for program and block analysis followed directly from application of Rules 1–3 to the first two syntax rules. The next syntax rule, viz.

declaration-part = { *variable-declaration-part* | *procedure-declaration* ";" }.

presents a more difficult translation task. Its allowable form involves a possibly empty repetition (a *block* need not contain any declarations). We must check that the LL(1) condition holds in this case. The only symbol which can follow a *declaration-part* is *BEGIN* (we determine this by inspection of the contexts in which a *declaration-part* occurs—it can occur only within a *block* and is always followed by a *statement-part*, which must start with *BEGIN*). The only symbols which can commence either a *variable-declaration-part* or a *procedure-declaration* are the symbols *VAR* and *PROCEDURE*. Hence the LL(1) condition is clearly satisfied and the *declaration-part* recognizer takes the form

```
PROCEDURE DeclarationPart(Followers: SymbolSet);
  BEGIN
    WHILE LexicalAnalyzer.SymbolDescription.Symbol) IN {Var, Procedure} DO
      CASE SymbolDescription.Symbol OF
      | Var:
          VariableDeclarationPart
      | Procedure:
          ProcedureDeclaration;
          Accept(Semicolon)
      END
    END;
  END DeclarationPart;
```

The rule

variable-declaration-part = "VAR" { *variable-declaration* ";" }.

again allows a possibly empty repetition, this time of

variable-declaration ";"

and we must therefore check once more that the LL(1) condition still holds in this case. The only symbol which can begin a *variable-declaration* is an *identifier*, and a legal *variable-declaration-part* is always followed by one of *VAR, PROCEDURE* or *BEGIN* since it is followed by either another *variable-declaration-part* or by a *procedure-declaration* or a *statement-part*. Again these symbols are determined by inspection of the right hand sides of the relevant syntax rules. So we obtain

```
PROCEDURE VariableDeclarationPart;
   BEGIN
      Accept(Var);
      WHILE LexicalAnalyzer.SymbolDescription.Symbol = Identifier DO
         VariableDeclaration;
         Accept(Semicolon)
   END
END VariableDeclarationPart
```

The remaining syntax rules can be checked and transformed in a similar manner. Appendix 6 shows the complete syntax analyzer which results. This analyzer is exactly that dictated by the syntax rules except that

(a) the procedures are nested within each other as tightly as their use permits;
(b) certain redundant procedures are eliminated;
(c) some conflicts with the LL(1) conditions arise which are resolved as shown below.

An obvious conflict with the LL(1) condition arises in the syntax rule for *simple-statement*

simple-statement = *assignment-statement* | ... | *procedure-statement* | ...

Symbol sequences allowed by the alternatives *assignment-statement* and *procedure-statement* both start with an identifier, so the choice between them cannot be made on the basis of the (first) symbol under scan. A similar problem arises in the rule for *factor*

factor = *variable* | *constant*   ...

since both *variable* and *constant* may begin with an identifier (*BOOLEAN* constants in Model are denoted by the identifiers *TRUE* and *FALSE*).

These problems are due to the fact that the syntax constructs *variable-identifier*, *procedure-identifier* and *constant-identifier* are lexically indistinguishable. A purely syntactic solution can be found by eliminating their distinction from the syntax rules, and then factorizing and transforming the revised syntax. However, the distinction can and must be made during semantic analysis. Anticipating that syntax and semantic analyses are to take place in parallel we may assume that a semantic check can be used to resolve the syntactic choice, and so retain the general form of the syntax given by the language definition.

The syntax analyzer requires the construction of starter symbol sets as well as sets of syntactically related symbols such as relational operators and addition operators. These sets have the type *LexicalAnalyzer.SymbolType* as their base-type. Since almost all Modula-2 implementations do not support sets with base-types containing as many values as are in *SymbolType*, we must instead define and implement our own abstraction of such sets. This is specified in the form of a local module *SymbolSets* of the syntax analyzer which exports a data-type *SymbolSet* together with associated set manipulation operators, viz.

```
MODULE SymbolSets;
    IMPORT SymbolType;
    EXPORT SymbolSet, Clear, Include, Remove, Contains, Union;

    TYPE SymbolSet = ...;

    PROCEDURE Clear(VAR S: SymbolSet); ...;
    PROCEDURE Include(I: SymbolType; VAR S: SymbolSet); ...;
    PROCEDURE Remove(I: SymbolType; VAR S: SymbolSet); ...;
    PROCEDURE Contains(VAR S: SymbolSet; I: SymbolType): BOOLEAN; ...;
    PROCEDURE Union(VAR S1, S2, Result: SymbolSet); ...;

    END SymbolSets;
```

The implementation of the type *SymbolSet* uses a Boolean array representation. Unfortunately, use of the *SymbolSets* operators lacks the conciseness and elegance of the corresponding Modula-2 set operations. For example, the abstract set operation

```
WHILE LexicalAnalyzer.SymbolDescription.Symbol) IN {Var, Procedure) DO ...
```

which appeared within the recognizer *DeclarationPart* has to be expressed, rather clumsily, as

```
VAR DeclarationStarters: SymbolSet;
    ...
Clear(DeclarationStarters);
Include(Var, DeclarationStarters); Include(Procedure, DeclarationStarters);
WHILE Contains(DeclarationStarters, SymbolDescription.Symbol) DO ...
```

As Appendix 6 demonstrates, the translation rules presented in this chapter enable a systematic transformation of the syntax rules of a language defined by an LL(1) grammar into a set of recognizer procedures. Indeed, this transformation could itself be performed by a computer program which reads the production rules of the language (presented in some suitable format), stores them, checks that they satisfy the LL(1) conditions, and then generates the source code, in some suitable language, of the recognizer procedures. Such a program is known as a *parser-generator* and is itself a form of compiler which will incorporate a syntax analyzer of its own to parse the input grammar rules.

9.3 Further reading

There are good examples of the construction of recursive descent syntax analyzers available in various books. These include the MiniPascal analyzer in Welsh and McKeag (1980), the PL/0 analyzer in Wirth (1976), the Pascal compiler of Brinch Hansen (1985), and another Pascal subset analyzer in Rees and Robson (1987). The outstanding example, however, is the analyzer which appears in its entirety in Welsh and Hay (1986)—the text of this book is actually the text of a Pascal compiler complete with embedded annotation.

The analyzer developed in this chapter does not construct an explicit syntax tree but instead the sequence of recognizer calls that it makes in analyzing a program implicitly traverses the syntax tree of the program. Watt (1993) develops a recursive descent parser which constructs an *abstract syntax tree* which represents the analyzed program's syntactic structure.

Exercises 9

9.1 Trace the sequence of recognizer calls made by the Model syntax analyzer of Appendix 6 in analyzing the following (meaningless) Model program:

```
MODULE Test;
    VAR I, J: INTEGER; VAR B: BOOLEAN;

    PROCEDURE P;
       BEGIN
          B := (I > 0) AND (J <= 10);
          READ(J);
          IF J = I THEN I :=J; J := 0 END;
       END P;

    BEGIN
       WRITE(I)
    END Test.
```

9.2 Write a recursive descent parser for the transformed grammar of Exercise 8.3.

9.3 Write a recursive descent parser for the transformed grammar of Exercise 8.4.

9.4 A *multiple-assignment-statement* may be defined in EBNF as

multiple-assignment-statement   =   *variable-list* ":=" *expression*.

variable-list   = *variable* { "," *variable* }.

The effect of execution of such a statement is to evaluate the *expression* and assign its value to all the variables of the *variable-list*. Write a recursive descent analysis procedure which will recognize such a *multiple-assignment-statement*.

9.5   Modify the syntax of Model to include a *repeat-statement* of the form

repeat-statement = "REPEAT" *statement-sequence*
                                   "UNTIL" *Boolean-expression*.
Boolean-expression = *expression*.

where a *Boolean-expression* is an expression which denotes a value of type *BOOLEAN*. Modify the Model syntax analyzer of Appendix 6 to recognize such repeat-statements.

9.6   Modify the syntax of Model to include a *while-statement* of the form

while-statement   = "WHILE" *Boolean-expression* "DO"
                                    statement-sequence
                                   "END".
Boolean-expression = *expression*.

where a *Boolean-expression* is an expression which denotes a value of type *BOOLEAN*. Modify the Model syntax analyzer of Appendix 6 to recognize such repeat-statements.

9.7   The Modula-2 *if-statement* is defined in EBNF as

if-statement = "IF" *Boolean-expression* "THEN" *statement-sequence*
                          { "ELSIF" *Boolean-expression* "THEN" *statement-sequence* }
                          ["ELSE" *statement-sequence*]
                          "END".
Boolean-expression = *expression*.

where a *Boolean-expression* is an expression which denotes a value of type *BOOLEAN*. Write a recursive descent syntax analysis procedure which will recognize such an if-statement.

9.8   (*Possible project*) Construct a program which will read in the production rules of a grammar, determine whether it is an LL(1) grammar and, if so, output the text of a Modula-2 program which will recognize programs expressed in the language defined by that grammar.

Chapter 10

Syntax error recovery

At this point it is appropriate to consider the problems of syntax error recovery since they are directly related to the syntax analysis method in use. In Chapter 2 we determined that good error recovery requires that the compiler should

- resume 'normal' compilation as near as possible to the point of error;
- avoid the generation of spurious error messages consequential on some previous error.

In many practical situations these two requirements are conflicting and compromise solutions lead to either some spurious errors being reported or some genuine errors being missed through a recovery that is too slow.

At any point the input program under syntax analysis has the form

$$\beta\, t\, \delta$$

where β is the sequence of symbols that has already been analyzed, t is the next available symbol, and δ is the remainder of the program. A syntax error is detected when t is a symbol that does not enable correct syntax analysis to proceed. This error may be due to

(a) some symbol or symbols which should precede t having been omitted by mistake;
(b) t having been substituted for some other symbol by mistake;
(c) t being an extraneous symbol which has been introduced by mistake.

In order to recover effectively the syntax analyzer must decide which of these situations is actually the case and act accordingly. To help it to make this decision the analyzer has knowledge of the preceding program symbols β and the symbol t itself, but no knowledge of the actual following symbols which make up δ. However, depending on the method of analysis in use, it has some means of predicting some of the symbols which might be expected instead of, or following, t.

10.1 Recovery in top-down analyzers

Consider top-down syntax analysis in which the next available source program symbol t fails to match some terminal symbol a_i in the goal production

$$A = \alpha_1\ a_i\ \alpha_2 \quad \text{(where } \alpha_1, \alpha_2 \in V^*)$$

The analyzer has, or can obtain, knowledge of the following symbols:

(a) the set of terminal symbols $\{a_j \dots a_n\}$ which appear in the production tail α_2 (these are determined simply by examination of α_2);
(b) the set of left-most terminal symbols $L_T(A_j)$ for each non-terminal A_j appearing in α_2 (these are determined by inspection of the production set of A_j);
(c) the set of symbols which can legally follow sequences generated by A, i.e. the set $F_T(A)$—these symbols are found by inspecting the production rules in which A appears on the right hand side.

The analyzer can therefore apply a recovery strategy such as the following:

(i)   if the available input symbol t occurs in those predicted by (a) and (b) above then correct analysis can be restarted at the corresponding point in α_2;
(ii) if the available input symbol t occurs in those given by (c), i.e. $F_T(A)$, then goal A should be abandoned and control within the analyzer returned to the goal production which activated it for possible recovery within that goal;
(iii) otherwise the symbol t should be ignored and the recovery strategy repeated on the next input symbol.

As an illustration of the application of this strategy consider the following grammar:

Block	=	*Header "begin".*
Header	=	*{Declaration}.*
Declaration	=	*Identifier ":" TypeName ";".*
Identifier	=	*"a"	"b"	"c"	... .*
TypeName	=	*"integer"	"real"	"char".*

The following sets of symbols can be determined by inspection of the grammar:

$$
\begin{aligned}
L_T(TypeName) &= \{integer, real, char\} \\
F_T(Declaration) &= \{begin, a, b, c, \dots\}
\end{aligned}
$$

We now examine the analysis of three different input sequences.

Case 1
Analysis of

a : real ; b integer ; begin ...

where analysis has reached the point indicated by ^. The analysis fails when the current symbol under scan t ($=$ *integer*) fails to match the expected terminal symbol ":" within the parsing which is attempting to satisfy the goal *Declaration*. Recovery proceeds as follows:

(1) since ";" is the only terminal symbol appearing to the right of ":" in the production rule for *Declaration*, t is compared with the set $\{;\} \cup L_T(TypeName)$; t is in $L_T(TypeName)$ so the correct recovery point is at the sub-goal *TypeName* within the parsing to satisfy *Declaration*.

Case 2
Analysis of

a : real ; b : integer begin ...

fails when t ($=$ *begin*) fails to match the expected terminal symbol ";" within the parsing to satisfy the goal *Declaration*. Recovery in this case proceeds as follows:

(1) there are no terminal symbols to the right of ";" in the rule for *Declaration* and hence t is compared with $\{\ \}$; there is no match, so
(2) t is compared with $F_T(Declaration)$; t is in $F_T(Declaration)$, so parsing to satisfy goal *Declaration* is immediately terminated and control is returned to the activation point of *Declaration* within the parsing to satisfy *Header*. The normal analysis actions of *Header* will then return control to *Block* where analysis will now progress normally with *begin* as the current input symbol.

Case 3
Analysis of

a : real ; b   . integer begin ...

fails when t ($=$ ".") fails to match the expected terminal symbol ":" within the parsing to satisfy the goal *Declaration*. Recovery proceeds as follows:

(1) t is compared with $\{;\} \cup L_T(TypeName)$; there is no match, so
(2) t is compared with $F_T(Declaration)$; again there is no match, so
(3) the current symbol is skipped (as a result of which we will now have the current symbol $t =$ "integer") and the recovery process continues from step (1). This time $t \in L_T(TypeName)$ so recovery is effected by resuming parsing to satisfy the sub-goal *TypeName*.

This error recovery strategy may be expressed more formally as

```
REPEAT
    IF (t = aj) OR (t ∈ L T(Aj)) for any aj, Aj in α2 THEN
        recover at the corresponding point in α2
    ELSIF t ∈ FT(A) THEN
        abandon the current goal to recover in the goal which activated it
    ELSE
        advance to next source symbol t
    END
UNTIL recovery is achieved
```

The exact form in which such a strategy is implemented is dependent on the exact implementation method used for analysis itself. The following section considers a variation of the above strategy within a recursive descent analyzer.

10.2 Recovery in recursive descent analyzers

The strategy described in the previous section can be readily incorporated in a top-down analyzer which operates by interpreting stored syntax rules. However, for a recursive descent analyzer it implies associating with the acceptance of each symbol some recovery code which may transfer control to various points in the body of the currently active recognizer procedure body, as indicated below:

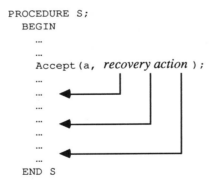

```
PROCEDURE S;
    BEGIN
        ...
        ...
        Accept(a, recovery action );
        ...
        ...
        ...
        ...
        ...
        ...
    END S
```

The incorporation of such coding at every point at which a symbol is accepted would expand and complicate the procedure to an unacceptable degree. Instead we wish to find some means of modifying the strategy which requires less distortion of the syntax procedures but still maintains an acceptable synchronization between the analyzer and the sequence of symbols being parsed.

The syntax analyzer developed in Chapter 9 functions satisfactorily on syntactically correct programs, i.e. it verifies that the programs obey the syntax rules of Model, and in doing so determines their syntactic structures. For an incorrect program, however, the analyzer's behaviour is acceptable only up to the detection of the first syntax error. Thereafter the analysis process is liable to get out of step with the sequence of symbols under scan, and so it will either go into a looping state or produce a welter of irrelevant error messages.

To maintain a reasonable synchronization between the analyzer and the symbol sequence under scan synchronization could be enforced at entry to and exit from each syntax recognizer procedure, thus limiting the effects of desynchronization to the range of symbols that is accepted between any two successive calls or exits. This range is dependent on the particular grammar and the number of procedures used within the analyzer, but for the Model analyzer already constructed it is rarely more than one or two symbols.

It is easy to enforce this synchronization at the start of the recognizer procedure *S* corresponding to a syntax rule *S*. The set of symbols which are legitimate starters for a sequence of form *S* is known from the allowable form of *S* and so a preliminary statement of the form

```
IF NOT (LexicalAnalyzer.SymbolDescription.Symbol IN Starters) THEN
    Error (...);
    SkipTo(Starters)
END
```

can be added to the body of the procedure *S*, where *SkipTo* is an operation which repeatedly accepts symbols from the input stream until one of the specified set of symbols *Starters* is encountered.

The obvious danger in this strategy is that if the intended starter symbol has been omitted from the source program, the *SkipTo* operation may skip over symbols which should have been processed by the procedure(s) which called *S*.

What is meant by synchronization at procedure exit? In practice it implies that the symbol under scan when execution of *S* is complete is one which the procedure which called *S* is prepared to deal with next. The procedure *S* has no intrinsic knowledge of which symbols these are, but it can be passed this information as a parameter at the point at which it is called. A parameter is therefore added to the syntax procedure corresponding to the syntax rule *S*:

```
PROCEDURE S(Followers: SymbolSet);
```

where *Followers* are those symbols which the calling procedure is prepared to deal with immediately after the call to *S* is completed. Now we can readily add to the body of *S* a trailing statement of the form

```
WITH LexicalAnalyzer.SymbolDescription DO
    IF NOT (Symbol IN Followers) THEN
        Error (...); SkipTo(Followers)
    END
END
```

The introduction of the *Followers* parameter also enables the dangers inherent in the statement to enforce synchronization at procedure entry to be avoided, by rewriting it in the rather more complex form

```
WITH LexicalAnalyzer.SymbolDescription DO
    IF NOT (Symbol IN Starters) THEN
        Error (...); SkipTo(Starters+Followers)
    END;
    IF Symbol IN Starters THEN perform normal syntax analysis actions END
END
```

With this prelude, if a follower of S is encountered before a starter symbol of S is found then an immediate exit from the recognizer procedure S will occur without execution of the normal syntax analysis associated with S.

What actual parameter is used in making a call to the procedure S? Clearly it must include the set of symbols which may legitimately occur immediately after the sequence scanned by S. However, since the legitimate immediate follower may itself be missing in an incorrect program the actual set passed to S is strengthened by the addition of

(a) subsequent symbols which the calling procedure expects to deal with after the call to S;
(b) the follower symbols which the calling procedure has itself received as parameter.

The inclusion of (b) guarantees that within any nest of active recognizer procedures a lower-level procedure cannot inadvertently skip over a symbol which some higher-level procedure expects to deal with later.

Our revised picture of the syntax procedure corresponding to a syntax rule S is thus

```
PROCEDURE S(Followers: SymbolSet);
    BEGIN
        WITH LexicalAnalyzer.SymbolDescription DO
            IF NOT (Symbol IN Starters) THEN
                Error (...); SkipTo(Starters+Followers)
            END;
            IF Symbol IN Starters THEN


            [                ]


                IF NOT (Symbol IN Followers) THEN
                    Error (...);  SkipTo(Followers)
                END
            END
        END
    END S
```

where the shaded box represents the normal analyzer body constructed as in Chapter 8, except that each call to any other syntax procedure T within that body now takes the form

T(*{...}+Followers*)

where *{...}* is the set of symbols which *S*, or any procedure which *S* calls, expects to deal with after the call to *T*.

Modification of each syntax procedure of the analyzer in this way would achieve a reasonable level of error recovery, but at a considerable expansion of the size of the analyzer as a whole. However, the same effect can be achieved much more economically by abstracting the entry and exit synchronization actions in the form of two procedures. The additional code structure now bracketing each procedure body differs only in the starters and followers sets which are manipulated, so we may define the procedures

```
PROCEDURE CheckForStarter(Starters, Followers: SymbolSet;
                          VAR Found: BOOLEAN);
   BEGIN
      WITH LexicalAnalyzer.SymbolDescription DO
         IF NOT ( Symbol IN Starters) THEN
            SyntaxError(OtherSymbol);  SkipTo( Starters+Followers)
         END;
         Found := Symbol IN Starters
      END
   END CheckForStarter

PROCEDURE FindFollower(Followers: SymbolSet);
   BEGIN
         WITH LexicalAnalyzer.SymbolDescription DO
         IF NOT ( Symbol IN Followers) THEN
            SyntaxError(OtherSymbol);  SkipTo(Followers)
         END
      END
   END FindFollower
```

and then modify each syntax procedure to take the form

```
PROCEDURE S(Followers: SymbolSet);
   VAR OK: BOOLEAN; StartersOfS: SymbolSet;
   BEGIN
      CheckForStarter( StartersOfS, Followers, OK);
      IF OK THEN
```

```
      FindFollower(Followers)
   END
END S
```

where the shaded box again represents the original procedure body with parameterized recognizer procedure calls as before. The result is an analyzer with the desired error recovery properties at the cost of a very modest increase in the size of the analyzer previously constructed.

Appendix 7 shows a syntax analyzer derived from that in Appendix 6 in this way. It corresponds to a purely mechanical introduction of the follower's parameters and calls of the procedures *CheckForStarter* and *FindFollower* for each syntax procedure, with the following exceptions:

(a) The eight procedures *Assignment*, *ReadStatement*, *WriteStatement*, *IfStatement*, *ExitStatement*, *LoopStatement*, *CaseStatement* and *ForStatement* serve only as alternative paths through the enclosing procedure *Statement* and do not require follower's parameters, or calls of *CheckForStarter* and *FindFollower*, of their own. Also, the recognizers *VariableDeclarationPart* and *ProcedureDeclaration* do not include calls of *CheckForStarter* as they are only called (from within *DeclarationPart*) whenever an appropriate starter symbol for them has already been determined.

(b) The syntax form $S\{aS\}$, consisting of a sequence of one or more sub-forms S separated by terminal symbol separators a, translates to analyzer code of the form

```
S;
WHILE LexicalAnalyzer.SymbolDescription.Symbol = a DO
   Accept(a);
   S
END
```

In adding syntax recovery actions it is logical to guard against a missing separator a by including the starters of S in the actual follower's parameter used for each call of S in this code. However, if this is to be effective, the while-loop repetition condition must also be relaxed to ensure looping continues when a starter of S actually occurs, thus:

```
S({a}+StartersOfS+Followers);
WHILE LexicalAnalyzer.SymbolDescription.Symbol IN {a}+StartersOfS DO
   Accept(a);
   S({a}+StartersOfS+Followers)
END
```

This technique is used in the procedure *StatementSequence* to handle missing semicolons between statements, viz.

```
PROCEDURE StatementSequence(Followers: SymbolSet);
   VAR OK: BOOLEAN;
   BEGIN
      CheckForStarter( StatementStarters, Followers, OK);
      IF OK THEN
         Statement( {SemiColon, End} + StatementStarters − Identifier + Followers);
         WHILE LexicalAnalyzer.SymbolDescription.Symbol
```

```
                    IN {SemiColon} + StatementStarters – Identifier DO
            Accept(SemiColon);
                Statement( {SemiColon, End} + StatementStarters – Identifier + Followers);
            END;
            FindFollower(Followers)
        END
    END StatementSequence;
```

where the set *StatementStarters* contains those symbols which can start a statement. The symbol *Identifier*, which is a valid statement starter symbol, is removed from consideration as it can appear in too many different syntax constructs for it to be useful in this context. The procedure *Term* also uses this technique to handle missing operators in an expression and it is also employed to deal with missing commas in case label lists within case-statements.

The testing of the syntax analyzer in Appendix 7 requires the identification of a carefully chosen sequence of such test programs to verify the analyzer's correct behaviour over the range of possible syntax errors and recovery.

10.3 Further reading

The syntactic error recovery technique described in this chapter is used in many compilers for Pascal and Modula-2. The model implementation of Standard Pascal constructed by Welsh and Hay (1986) is one example of a published compiler which employs it. The MiniPascal compiler of Welsh and McKeag (1980) is written in a superset of Pascal, known as Pascal Plus—the envelope structure of Pascal Plus enables a particularly elegant implementation of the entry and exit synchronizations.

Backhouse (1979) presents the theory of error repair and its application to the design of error recovery mechanisms for recursive descent analyzers. Some compilers attempt to correct errors for the user by trying to repair offending symbol sequences, but most people remain sceptical of the ability of a compiler to make correct repairs.

Exercises 10

10.1 How would the Model syntax analyzer of Appendix 7 react to each of the following input sequences?
   (i)   *IF J+6 THEN J := J+1 END*
   (ii) *IF J<6 THEN THEN J := J+1 END*
   (iii) *IF J<6 J := J+1 END*
   (iv) *IF J<6 THEN J := J 1 END*

10.2 Extend the *multiple-assignment-statement* analyzer developed in Exercise 9.4 to include the syntactic error recovery strategy developed in this chapter.

10.3 Extend the Model syntax analyzer of Appendix 7 to include versions of the *repeat-statement* and *while-statement* recognizers developed in Exercises 9.5 and 9.6 extended with appropriate syntactic error recovery actions.

10.4 Extend the Modula-2 *if-statement* recognizer developed in Exercise 9.7 to include suitable syntactic error recovery actions.

10.5 Consider how the Model compiler developed so far would have to be modified in order to inform the user of those symbols which have been skipped as the result of the analyzer carrying out syntactic error recovery actions.

Chapter 11

Semantic table organization

A source program may contain a range of programmer-defined *symbols*, such as *identifiers* and (in a language such as Pascal which provides goto-statements) *labels*. Semantic analysis involves the recording of the semantics (i.e. the meaning, or *attributes*) associated with such symbols and the verification that each usage of a symbol within a program is consistent with its current attributes. The techniques of semantic analysis depend to some extent on whether the language rules require that the attributes of a given symbol are specified prior to its usage (in an appropriate *declaration*) or are determined by the context in which it is used. In all cases semantic analysis depends on the use of *information tables*, commonly called *semantic tables*, or *symbol tables*. For each symbol currently defined at any point in the compilation of a program there will be an associated *entry* in the table which records its current attributes. In this chapter we consider various methods of overall structure and organization which may be used for such tables.

11.1 Defining the semantic table

A semantic table must provide facilities to

- create a new entry for a symbol with specified attributes;
- update the attributes contained in the entry for a given symbol;
- determine whether an entry for a given symbol exists within it and, if so, make the corresponding attributes available.

Although, as we have already seen, 'symbols' may be any programmer-defined entities allowed by the source language, for simplicity here we consider symbols to be represented by values of an arbitrary type *SymbolRepresentation*. In practice symbols are usually represented as identifiers or (as in the case of labels in the programming language Pascal) as numeric constants. Our presentation in this chapter of the definition and manipulation of semantic tables can trivially be applied to tables containing entries for various symbol representations.

We may thus define the semantic table as an abstract object with the following interface:

```
DEFINITION MODULE Table;
    TYPE SymbolRepresentation = ...;
    TYPE SymbolEntry = ...;
    TYPE AttributeType = ...;
    TYPE SymbolRecord =   RECORD
                            Name: SymbolRepresentation;
                            Attributes: AttributeType;
                            ...
                          END;

    VAR Table: ...;  (* Some data structure containing values of type SymbolRecord *)

    PROCEDURE Initialize;

    PROCEDURE NewSymbol(Identity: SymbolRepresentation;
                        VAR AlreadyInTable, Full: BOOLEAN;
                        VAR WhereEntered: SymbolEntry);

    PROCEDURE SearchSymbol(Identity: SymbolRepresentation;
                           VAR Found: BOOLEAN;
                           VAR WhereFound: SymbolEntry);

    PROCEDURE Finalize;
END Table;
```

The procedure *Initialize* creates a semantic table which does not contain any entries. *Finalize* disposes of all entries currently in the table.

NewSymbol determines whether a symbol with a given representation *Identity* is already entered in the table; if so *AlreadyInTable* is assigned *TRUE* and the values of *Full* and *WhereEntered* are undefined, otherwise

(a)   *AlreadyInTable* is assigned *FALSE*,
(b)   the value of *Full* indicates whether there was room for an insertion in the table—if so,
(c)   a new entry is created for this symbol, and
(d)   the value of *WhereEntered* is set to reference this new entry, thus enabling subsequent updating of the attributes of the entry created.

SearchSymbol locates within the table the entry (if any) for a symbol with given representation *Identity*; if an entry is found then *Found* is assigned *TRUE* and the value of *WhereFound* is set to reference that entry (enabling subsequent access to the entry for inspection and updating of its attributes), otherwise *Found* is assigned *FALSE* and the value of *WhereFound* remains undefined.

The specifications of the various operations in no way indicate the actual structure of the table entries. In the next three sections we consider various commonly used methods of structuring the semantic table and the corresponding implementations of the above four operations. In each case we consider a *contiguous* representation in which a fixed-size array is used to represent the table and the table entries are accessed using subscripting, and a *pointer* representation in which the table entries are created dynamically and accessed via pointers. For convenience, our diagrams will assume that the symbols are identifiers.

11.2 Unsorted tables

The simplest way to organize a semantic table is to hold its entries as an unsorted linear list, adding new entries to one end of the list as they occur, and searching the list in a linear fashion for each symbol. Such a table can be represented with equal efficiency as a one-dimensional array or as a linked list as shown in the following two sub-sections.

11.2.1 Contiguous representation of an unsorted table

Figure 11.1 illustrates the use of an array of size *TableSize* elements to hold an unsorted list of symbol entries where the symbols are identifiers.

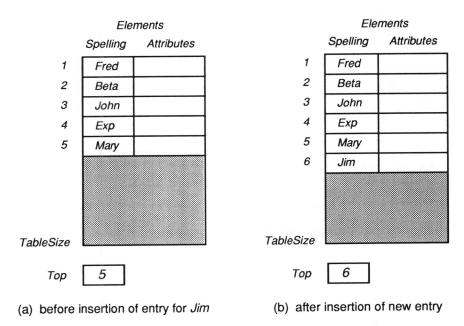

Figure 11.1 *Contiguous representation of an unsorted linear table*

The declarations of the necessary data structures and the implementations of the associated operations are given below:

```
CONST  TableSize = ...;
TYPE   SymbolEntry = [1..TableSize];
VAR    Table :   RECORD
                    Element: ARRAY SymbolEntry OF SymbolRecord;
                    Top: [0..TableSize]
                 END;

PROCEDURE Initialize;
   BEGIN
      Table.Top := 0
   END Initialize;

PROCEDURE NewSymbol(Identity: SymbolRepresentation;
                    VAR AlreadyInTable, Full: BOOLEAN;
                    VAR WhereEntered: SymbolEntry);
   VAR I: SymbolEntry;
   BEGIN
      WITH Table DO
         FOR I := 1 TO Top DO
            IF Element[I].Name = Identity THEN
               AlreadyInTable := TRUE; RETURN
            END
         END;
         AlreadyInTable := FALSE;
         IF Top = TableSize THEN Full := TRUE
         ELSE
            Full := FALSE;
            INC(Top); Element[Top].Name := Identity; WhereEntered := Top
         END
      END
   END NewSymbol;

PROCEDURE SearchSymbol(Identity: SymbolRepresentation;
                       VAR Found: BOOLEAN; VAR WhereFound: SymbolEntry);
   VAR I: SymbolEntry;
   BEGIN
      WITH Table DO
         FOR I := 1 TO Top DO
            IF Element[I].Name = Identity THEN
               Found := TRUE; WhereFound := I; RETURN
            END
         END
      END;
      Found := FALSE
   END SearchSymbol;

PROCEDURE Finalize;
   BEGIN
```

```
    Table.Top := 0
END Finalize;
```

For such a contiguous representation the *WhereEntered* and *WhereFound* parameters returned by *NewSymbol* and *SearchSymbol*, respectively, are the subscripts of the records entered or located in the table and the appropriate table record can then be accessed as an array component, e.g. the updating of the entry for a symbol with representation *SymbolSought* could be performed as follows:

```
Table.SearchSymbol(SymbolSought, Located, Position);
IF Located THEN UpdateAttributes(Table.Element[Position]) END;
    ...
```

11.2.2   Chained representation of an unsorted table

The implementation of an unsorted list of symbol entries represented as a linked list connected by pointers is illustrated in Figure 11.2. In this case it is more convenient to insert new entries at the head of the list.

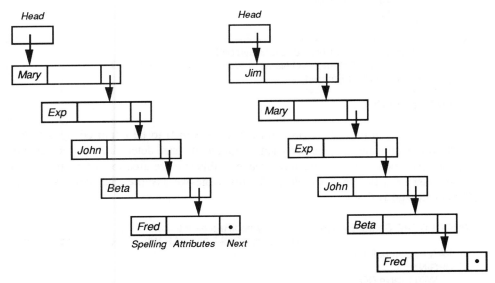

(a) before insertion of entry for *Jim*   (b) after insertion of new entry

Figure 11.2 *Linked list representation of an unsorted linear table*

The overall table is thus represented as a pointer to the head of a linked list of entries and the necessary definitions and declarations are as follows:

```
TYPE SymbolEntry = POINTER TO SymbolRecord;
TYPE SymbolRecord =   RECORD
                          Name: SymbolRepresentation;
                          Attributes: ...;
                          Next: SymbolEntry
                      END;
VAR Table: RECORD Head: SymbolEntry END;


PROCEDURE Initialize;
   BEGIN
      Table.Head := NIL
   END Initialize;


PROCEDURE NewSymbol(Identity: SymbolRepresentation;
                    VAR AlreadyInTable, Full: BOOLEAN;
                    VAR WhereEntered: SymbolEntry);
   VAR P: SymbolEntry;
   BEGIN
      WITH Table DO
         P := Head;
         WHILE P <> NIL DO
            IF P^.Name = Identity THEN AlreadyInTable := TRUE; RETURN
            ELSE P := P^.Next
            END
         END;
         AlreadyInTable := FALSE; Full := FALSE;
         Host.New(WhereEntered, SIZE(SymbolRecord));
         WITH WhereEntered^ DO Name := Identity; Next := Head END;
         Head:= WhereEntered
      END
   END NewSymbol;
```

Here we have introduced a procedure *New*, assumed to be exported by the *Host* module, which allocates an area of dynamic storage of a size determined by the value of its second parameter and assigns a reference to this storage area to its first parameter (which must be a pointer variable). At this stage we assume that there is always sufficient storage available.

```
PROCEDURE SearchSymbol(Identity: SymbolRepresentation;
                       VAR Found: BOOLEAN; VAR WhereFound: SymbolEntry);
   VAR P: SymbolEntry;
   BEGIN
      WITH Table DO
         P := Head;
         WHILE P <> NIL DO
            IF P^.Name = Identity THEN
               Found := TRUE; WhereFound := P; RETURN
            ELSE P := P^.Next
            END
         END
```

```
        END;
        Found := FALSE
      END SearchSymbol;

  PROCEDURE Finalize;
    VAR NextToDisposeOf: SymbolEntry;
    BEGIN
      WITH Table DO
        WHILE Head <> NIL DO
          NextToDisposeOf := Head; Head := Head^.Next;
          Host.Dispose(NextToDisposeOf, SIZE(SymbolEntry))
        END
      END
    END Finalize;
```

The two parameters, i.e. *WhereEntered* and *WhereFound,* returned by *NewSymbol* and *SearchSymbol,* respectively, are references (pointers) to the entries entered or located in the table concerned and the appropriate table record can then be accessed as a referenced-variable, viz.

```
  Table.SearchSymbol(Id, Located, Position);
  IF Located THEN UpdateAttributes (Position^) END;
    ...
```

The extra cost of the *Next* field in each entry of the linked list representation may be more than offset by the fact that the linked list entries may be of variable length (e.g. we shall see in Chapter 12 that variable-identifiers and procedure-identifiers have different numbers and types of attributes associated with them), something which the array representation cannot permit without a wastage of storage. The allocation of variable-length entries in the linked list representation can be supported by including in the parameter list of the *SearchSymbol* operation an additional parameter specifying the class of the symbol, something that we shall illustrate in Chapter 13 in considering the construction of the semantic table for our Model compiler.

The major advantages of linear unsorted tables are their simplicity of manipulation and their storage economy. They are used in some compilers despite their major disadvantage that, for a table containing N entries, on average $N/2$ comparisons must be performed in each search operation. For large values of N this is obviously very inefficient.

11.3   Sorted tables

In this section we consider how the entries in our unsorted representations may be organized in some significant order and the associated insertion and search operations. Obviously, the *key* field in each entry (i.e. the field which uniquely distinguishes each entry) is the representation of the symbol and so the entries must be sorted according to their associated symbol representations.

11.3.1 Contiguous representation of a sorted table

Figure 11.3 shows the entries in the unsorted table of Figure 11.1 organized in sorted order of symbol spelling.

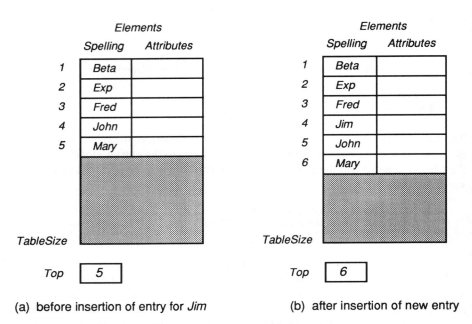

(a) before insertion of entry for *Jim*   (b) after insertion of new entry

Figure 11.3 *Contiguous representation of a sorted linear table*

Such a table which is sorted in alphabetic order of symbol representations may be searched by *binary* or *logarithmic* search techniques. The use of the straightforward binary search which successively splits its search area within an array in half is illustrated by the following search procedure:

```
PROCEDURE Locate(Identity: SymbolRepresentation; VAR Found: BOOLEAN;
                 VAR Position: CARDINAL);
    VAR First, Last, Mid: [1..TableSize+1];
    BEGIN
        WITH Table DO
            First := 1; Last := Top;
            WHILE First <= Last DO
                Mid := (First+Last) DIV 2;
                IF Element[Mid].Name < Identity THEN First := Mid + 1
                ELSE Last := Mid - 1
                END
            END;
```

```
            Position := First;
            IF (First>Top) OR (Element[First].Name<>Identity) THEN Found := FALSE
            ELSE Found := TRUE;
            END
        END
    END Locate;
```

This gives a search time proportional to log_2N for a table of N entries. If an entry for the required *Identity* is found, the value of the parameter *Position* is set by *Locate* to indicate the relevant entry in the table. If no entry is found, then the value of *Position* is set to indicate the appropriate point of insertion for such an entry, if required. This procedure *Locate* may then be used to implement the procedures *NewSymbol* and *SearchSymbol*. The latter operation is expressed trivially using a call of *Locate*, viz.

```
PROCEDURE SearchSymbol(Identity: SymbolRepresentation; VAR Found: BOOLEAN;
                        VAR WhereFound: SymbolEntry);
    VAR Position: CARDINAL;
    BEGIN
        Locate(Identity, Found, Position);
        IF Found THEN WhereFound := Position END;
    END SearchSymbol;
```

The insertion operation, however, becomes more complicated (and slower) as the result of having to insert a new entry at the position appropriate to its representation and the possible repositioning required for existing entries. It is thus expressed as

```
PROCEDURE NewSymbol(Identity: SymbolRepresentation;
                        VAR AlreadyInTable, Full: BOOLEAN;
                        VAR WhereEntered: SymbolEntry);
    VAR Position: CARDINAL;
    BEGIN
        Locate(Identity, AlreadyInTable, Position);
        IF NOT AlreadyInTable THEN
            WITH Table DO
                IF Top = TableSize THEN Full := TRUE
                ELSE
                    Full := FALSE; WhereEntered := Position; INC(Top);
                    FOR I := Top TO Position +1 BY –1 DO Element[I] := Element[I–1] END;
                    Table[Position].Name := Identity
                END
            END
        END
    END Enter;
```

11.3.2   Binary tree representation of a sorted table

We have seen that the major disadvantage of the above method of using a sorted array for representing the table entries is that the insertion of a new entry in the sorted table will almost always involve repositioning of some existing entries and, for tables containing a large number of entries, the repositioning becomes expensive.

This disadvantage can, however, be overcome by representing the ordered table as a *binary sorted tree* (Figure 11.4) in which each entry is a node of a tree which has in turn two sub-trees—all entries in its left sub-tree being less in natural (symbol representation) order than itself, all entries in its right sub-tree being greater in natural order than itself.

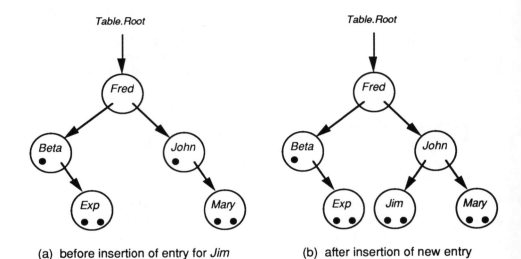

(a) before insertion of entry for *Jim*   (b) after insertion of new entry

Figure 11.4 *Binary tree representation of a sorted table*

A binary tree is thus represented by a pointer to its *root* node and can be defined, together with its associated operators, by the following definitions:

```
TYPE SymbolEntry = POINTER TO SymbolRecord;
TYPE SymbolRecord =   RECORD
                          Name: SymbolRepresentation;
                          Attributes: ...;
                          Left, Right: SymbolEntry
                      END;

VAR  Table: RECORD Root: SymbolEntry END;

PROCEDURE Initialize;
    BEGIN Table.Root := NIL END Initialize;

PROCEDURE NewSymbol(Identity: SymbolRepresentation;
                    VAR AlreadyInTable, Full: BOOLEAN;
                    VAR WhereEntered: SymbolEntry);
    VAR ThisNode, LastNode: SymbolEntry; LeftTaken: BOOLEAN;
```

```
BEGIN
    WITH Table DO
        ThisNode := Root; LastNode := NIL;
        WHILE ThisNode <> NIL DO
            LastNode := ThisNode;
            IF ThisNode^.Name < Identity THEN
                ThisNode := ThisNode^.Right; LeftTaken := FALSE
            ELSIF ThisNode^.Name > Identity THEN
                ThisNode := ThisNode^.Left; LeftTaken := TRUE
            ELSE
                AlreadyInTable := TRUE; RETURN
            END
        END;
        AlreadyInTable := FALSE; Full := FALSE;
        Host.New(WhereEntered, SIZE(SymbolRecord));
        WITH WhereEntered^ DO Name := Identity; Left := NIL; Right := NIL END;
        IF Root = NIL THEN Root := WhereEntered
        ELSIF LeftTaken THEN LastNode^.Left := WhereEntered
        ELSE LastNode^.Right := WhereEntered
        END
    END
END NewSymbol;

PROCEDURE SearchSymbol(Identity: SymbolRepresentation; VAR Found: BOOLEAN;
                        VAR WhereFound: SymbolEntry);
    VAR ThisNode: SymbolEntry;
    BEGIN
        WITH Table DO
            ThisNode := Root;
            WHILE ThisNode <> NIL DO
                IF ThisNode^.Name < Identity THEN ThisNode := ThisNode^.Right
                ELSIF ThisNode^.Name > Identity THEN ThisNode := ThisNode^.Left
                ELSE Found := TRUE; WhereFound := ThisNode; RETURN
                END
            END
        END;
        Found := FALSE
    END SearchSymbol;

PROCEDURE Finalize;

    PROCEDURE DisposeNode(P: SymbolEntry);
        BEGIN
            IF P <> NIL THEN
                DisposeNode(P^.Left); DisposeNode(P^.Right);
                Host.Dispose(P, SIZE(SymbolRecord))
            END
        END DisposeNode;

BEGIN
    DisposeNode(Table.Root)
END Finalize;
```

The binary sorted tree representation retains the improved speed of a binary search and at the same time permits the insertion of new entries without any repositioning of the existing entries in the tree. Its principal disadvantage is that the logarithmic search time is guaranteed only so long as the tree is *balanced* (i.e. the sub-trees of each node contain approximately equal numbers of nodes), and this in turn depends on the presumably random order in which new entries are added to the tree. In the worst case, which is when entries are made in the natural order of their representations, the tree degenerates to a linear list with a linear search time. However, procedures to rebalance out-of-balance trees can be incorporated, although at some expense.

11.4   Hash tables

A substantial increase in the speeds of both insertion and access may be achieved by the use of a fixed-length array of size N to hold the symbol records as a *hash table*. In order to organize the entries in a hash table some arbitrary *hash function* is chosen which maps a symbol representation onto an integer value in the range $1..N$ (since the number of possible symbol representations will, in general, be very much greater than the size N of the table, this is necessarily a many-to-one mapping). When an entry is inserted it is placed (if possible) at the position in the table indicated by *hashing* (i.e. applying the chosen hash function to) the representation of the associated symbol, so that any subsequent access using the same hash function must find it there.

The hash function calculates the position by performing some (usually simple) arithmetic operation on the symbol representation. Hence, to enter a new symbol record within a hash table:

(a) For a given symbol its *preferred position* within the hash table is calculated by hashing the symbol representation in some way.
(b) If the preferred position is found to be occupied by the record for some other symbol a sequence of second, third, etc., preference positions is tried until an empty position is found—which is the required insertion position. The process of selecting second, third, etc., preference positions is known as *rehashing*.

The entry for a particular symbol is subsequently located by retracing the sequence of positions visited during the insertion process:

(a) Its preferred position is determined by again applying the hash function to its representation.
(b) If the preferred position is found to be occupied by the record for some other symbol the second, third, etc., preference positions are tried until either the required entry is found or an empty position is found—meaning that no entry exists for the identifier.

We first consider the detailed representation of hash tables and the associated insertion and searching operations before considering the nature and properties of suitable hash functions.

11.4.1 Representation of a hash table

Figure 11.5 shows a possible hash table representation of the identifier records used to illustrate the various organizations described previously in this chapter.

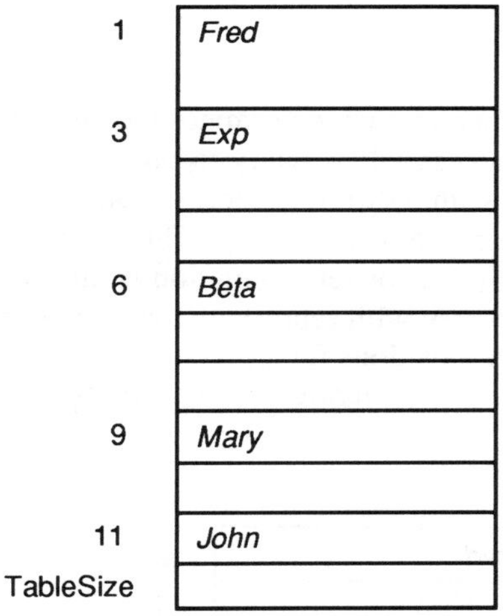

Figure 11.5 *Hash table organization*

Unoccupied table positions are shaded in Figure 11.5 while occupied positions show the spellings of the symbols for which they contain entries. Hence, the table structure may be defined as

```
CONST  TableSize = ...;

TYPE   SymbolEntry = [1..TableSize];

VAR    Table:RECORD
              Occupied: ARRAY SymbolEntry OF BOOLEAN;
              Element: ARRAY SymbolEntry OF SymbolRecord
           END;
```

The Boolean array *Occupied* is used to indicate which elements of the table hold significant entries at any moment (we do not show it explicitly in our diagrams since it is implied by the shading of unoccupied table positions). Alternatively, a Boolean field within each entry of the table might be used to denote whether the field is occupied, if this is convenient. The initialization of the table simply involves setting all the *Occupied* fields to the value *FALSE*, viz.

```
PROCEDURE Initialize;
    VAR I: SymbolEntry;
    BEGIN
        WITH Table DO
            FOR I := 1 TO TableSize DO
                Occupied[I] := FALSE
            END
        END
END Initialize;
```

Because the hash function that determines the preferred position p_1 for an entry with representation w is necessarily a many-to-one mapping, position p_1 may already be occupied by an entry with a different representation. In this case a *collision* is said to occur, and must be resolved in some way. This involves calculating second, third, etc., choice positions $p_2, p_3, \ldots$ for representation w and trying each in turn, until either a vacant position or an entry with representation w is found. This process of generating second, third and so on positions for a given representation is known as *rehashing*, and the sequence of positions generated for any representation w is known as its *probe sequence*.

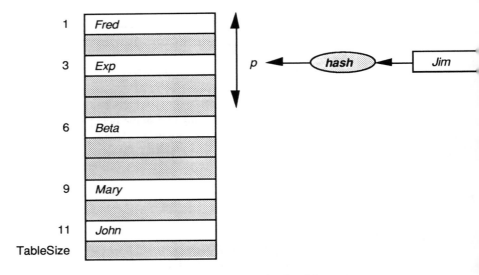

Figure 11.6 *Access to hash table*

We now define the process of locating an entry in a hash table more precisely. The first step in locating an entry with representation w is to calculate its preferred position p by applying the hash function to its representation

p := *Hash*(w)

If entry p in the table is unoccupied, then no entry for the given representation exists in the table and, if necessary, a new entry may be made there. Figure 11.6 illustrates this case—the preferred position p for the identifier *Jim* is unoccupied and a new entry for *Jim* may, if required, be made there. However, if the purpose of the table access is to try to find an entry for *Jim*, then it is concluded that there is no such entry in the table.

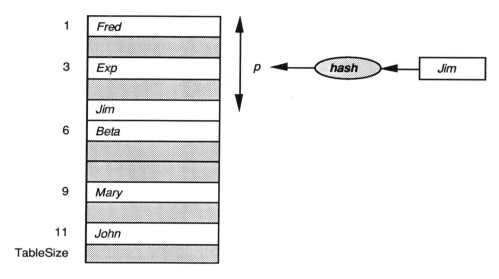

Figure 11.7 *Required entry found at preferred position*

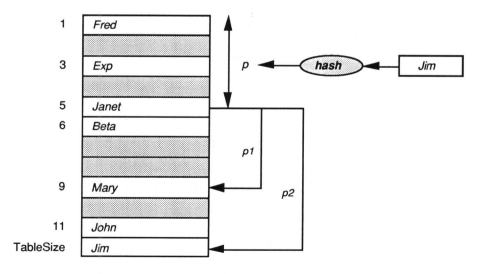

Figure 11.8 *Probe sequence leading to required entry*

If position *p* is already occupied, either it contains the required entry (as in Figure 11.7) or a collision has occurred and further inspection is required. This is performed by applying a *rehash* procedure to compute second and third positions, etc., and applying the same consideration to each, until a conclusion is reached (Figures 11.8 and 11.9).

In Figure 11.8, the first preference position *(p = 5)* is occupied by an entry for another symbol *(Janet)*; the first rehash position *(p+p₁ = 9)* is similarly occupied (by the entry for *Mary*), but success is achieved at the second rehash position *(p+p₂ = TableSize)*.

However, the hash and rehash sequence shown in Figure 11.9 leads to a vacant position without a match being found and thus it can be concluded that the required entry is not in the table.

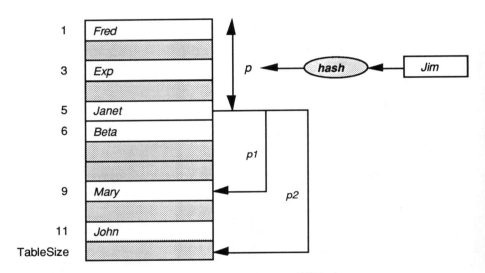

Figure 11.9 *Probe sequence leading to vacant position*

The overall process of locating an entry in the table may thus be expressed as the following procedure:

```
PROCEDURE Locate(Identity: SymbolRepresentation;
                        VAR Found: BOOLEAN; VAR Position: SymbolEntry);
    VAR P: SymbolEntry;
    BEGIN
        WITH Table DO
            Found := FALSE; P := Hash(Identity);
            LOOP
                IF NOT Occupied[P] THEN EXIT
                ELSIF Element[P].Name = Identity THEN Found := TRUE; EXIT
```

```
            ELSE  Rehash P
            END
        END;
            Position := P
    END
END Locate;
```

If an entry for the required symbol representation is found, the value returned for the variable parameter *Position* references this entry in the table. If no entry is found, the value of *Position* references the appropriate point of insertion for such an entry. This procedure could be used to implement the procedures *NewSymbol* and *SearchSymbol*.

The rehash process determines the second, third, etc., choice positions examined if the preferred position is occupied by an entry with another representation. To ensure full utilization of the positions in the table, the sequence of positions generated by rehashing from any initial value should visit each entry position in the table. One simple way of doing so is to use a so-called *linear rehash* which tries successive table positions in turn, cycling back to the first table position after the last position has been tried. This rehash operation is easily expressed as follows:

```
p := p MOD N + 1
```

However, this simple technique makes obvious one new problem. What happens if every table position is occupied, but none contains the entry sought? To prevent looping, this condition must be detected within the *Locate* procedure, but its significance depends on whether or not a subsequent insertion is required. We therefore modify the *Locate* procedure to return a second Boolean result *Full* to indicate when insertion is impossible, thus:

```
PROCEDURE Locate(Identity: SymbolRepresentation;
                        VAR Found, Full: BOOLEAN; VAR Position: SymbolEntry);
    VAR P, P1: SymbolEntry;
    BEGIN
        WITH Table DO
            Found := FALSE; Full := FALSE;
            P1 := Hash(Identity); P := P1;
            LOOP
                IF NOT Occupied[P] THEN EXIT
                ELSIF Element[P].Name = Identity THEN Found := TRUE; EXIT
                ELSE
                    Rehash P;
                    IF P = P1 THEN Full := TRUE; EXIT END
                END
            END;
            IF NOT Full THEN Position := P END
        END
    END Locate;
```

and the *NewSymbol* and *SearchSymbol* procedures can make use of *Locate* as follows:

```
PROCEDURE NewSymbol(Identity: SymbolRepresentation;
                        VAR AlreadyInTable, Full: BOOLEAN;
                        VAR WhereEntered: SymbolEntry);
BEGIN
   Locate(Identity, AlreadyInTable, Full, WhereEntered);
   WITH Table DO
       IF NOT (AlreadyInTable OR Full) THEN
           Occupied[WhereEntered] := TRUE;
           Element[WhereEntered].Name := Identity
       END
   END
END NewSymbol;

PROCEDURE SearchSymbol(Identity: SymbolRepresentation; VAR Found: BOOLEAN;
                        VAR WhereFound: SymbolEntry);
   VAR Full: BOOLEAN;
   BEGIN
       Locate(Identity, Found, Full, WhereFound)
   END SearchSymbol;

PROCEDURE Finalize;
   VAR I: SymbolEntry;
   BEGIN
       WITH Table DO
           FOR I := 1 TO TableSize DO
               Occupied[I] := FALSE
           END
       END
   END Finalize;
```

11.4.2   Alternative representation of a hash table

One possible alternative (non-contiguous) organization for a hash table reduces the overall amount of storage used by representing the table. It does so by representing the table as an array of pointers to the actual entries, which are created dynamically as required. Hence, instead of having a hash table containing a fixed number of entries, the entries are created only when actually required. A pointer having the value *NIL* then denotes an unoccupied table position—otherwise the pointer references the actual entry, as shown in Figure 11.10. This table structure is defined as follows:

```
TYPE    SymbolEntry = POINTER TO SymbolRecord;

CONST TableSize = ...;
TYPE    TableIndex = [1..TableSize];

VAR     Table: ARRAY TableIndex OF SymbolEntry;
```

The various semantic table operations then take the form:

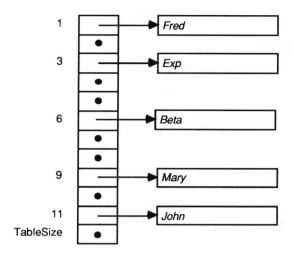

Figure 11.10 *Hash table organized as an array of pointers*

```
PROCEDURE Initialize;
    VAR I: TableIndex;
    BEGIN
        FOR I := 1 TO TableSize DO Table[I] := NIL END
    END Initialize;

PROCEDURE Locate(Identity: SymbolRepresentation;
                        VAR Found, Full: BOOLEAN; VAR Position: SymbolEntry);
    VAR P, P1: TableIndex;
    BEGIN
        Found := FALSE; Full := FALSE; P1 := Hash(Identity); P := P1;
        LOOP
            IF Table[P] = NIL THEN EXIT
            ELSIF Table[P]^.Name = Identity THEN Found := TRUE; EXIT
            ELSE
                Rehash P;
                IF P = P1 THEN Full := TRUE; EXIT END
            END
        END;
        IF NOT Full THEN Position := P END
    END Locate;

PROCEDURE NewSymbol(Identity: SymbolRepresentation;
                        VAR AlreadyInTable, Full: BOOLEAN;
                        VAR WhereEntered: SymbolEntry);
    VAR Position: TableIndex;
    BEGIN
        Locate(Identity, AlreadyInTable, Full, Position);
        IF NOT (AlreadyInTable OR Full) THEN
            Host.New(Table[Position], SIZE(SymbolRecord));
```

```
              Table[Position]^.Name := Identity; WhereEntered := Table[Position]
       END
     END NewSymbol;

  PROCEDURE SearchSymbol(Identity: SymbolRepresentation; VAR Found: BOOLEAN;
                         VAR WhereFound: SymbolEntry);
     VAR Full: BOOLEAN; Position: TableIndex;
     BEGIN
       Locate(Identity, Found, Full, Position);
         IF Found THEN WhereFound := Table[Position]
     END SearchSymbol;

  PROCEDURE Finalize;
     VAR I: TableIndex;
     BEGIN
       FOR I := 1 TO TableSize DO Host.Dispose(Table[I], SIZE(SymbolRecord)) END
     END Finalize;
```

11.4.3   Hash functions

Hashing is usually carried out by performing some simple arithmetic or logical operation on the binary representation of the symbol representation to produce a value suitable for use as an index into the hash table. Ideally this hashing should result in an even distribution of preferred positions throughout the table for the symbols occurring in any program, so avoiding collisions and the need to rehash.

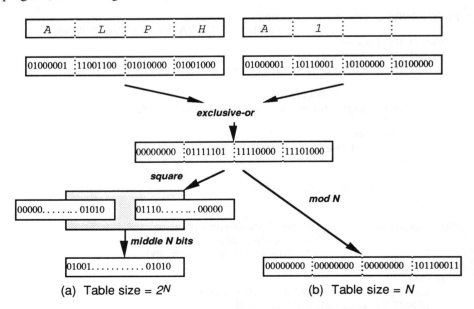

Figure 11.11 *Hashing of identifier ALPHA1*

A typical algorithm for hashing spellings in the case where the symbols concerned are identifiers (Figure 11.11) involves two steps:

(1) If the identifier representation is more than one computer word long it is reduced to one word by adding or exclusive-oring the component words together.
(2) The value of the preferred position (modulo the table size) is produced from the reduced identifier by e.g.
   (a) if the table size is a power of 2, say 2^N, multiplying the reduced identifier by itself and taking the middle N bits (which will be the most random), or
   (b) reducing the identifier modulo the table size (this is not advisable when the table size is a power of 2, since it merely selects the bottom N bits of each identifier, which may always be the same if the programmer chooses short identifiers!).

Another possible hash function for use when symbols are represented as identifier spellings (i.e. values of type *Host.Word*) has the form:

```
PROCEDURE Hash(W: Host.Word): SymbolEntry;
    CONST Factor = ...; K = ...;
    VAR H: SymbolEntry; I: CARDINAL;
    BEGIN
        H := 1;
        FOR I := 1 TO K DO
            H := (H*Factor+ORD(W[I])) MOD N + 1
        END;
        RETURN H
    END Hash;
```

After each iteration of the body of the for-statement *H* has a value in the range *1* to *TableSize* determined by the first *I* characters of the identifier *W*. If *Factor* is co-prime with *TableSize*, then all the characters of *W* have an equal effect on the final hash value. In practice, the number *K* of characters used can be small, so limiting the cost of calculating the hash value.

Any simple transformation is acceptable provided it produces preferred positions which are reasonably randomly distributed for the range of symbol representations which normally occurs. It is usually advisable to check that it works well for the simplest symbol representations (identifiers such as *A, B,* ...) and for the pre-declared symbols of the language.

11.4.4 Rehashing

When a collision occurs, i.e. a given symbol representation is hashed and its preferred position p found to be occupied by some other symbol, rehashing involves in general trying a next position $(p+p_1) \bmod N$ (where N is the table size) and then $(p+p_2) \bmod N$ and so on for some values $p_1, p_2, \ldots$. This continues until, at some position $(p+p_i) \bmod N$, one of the following conditions is satisfied:

(a) the entry for the symbol sought is encountered, or

(b) an empty position is found, meaning no entry exists for the symbol sought, or

(c) $(p+p_i)$ *mod* $N = p$, i.e. the search is back where it started and thus it can be concluded that the table is full. (Note that the table is truly full only if the offsets $p_1, p_2, \ldots$ generate all the values *1..N–1* before generating *0*.)

Some common and simple examples of rehashing methods are now considered.

(1) *Linear rehash*—this is the most simple method in which we choose $p_1 = 1, p_2 = 2, p_3 = 3, \ldots$, i.e. successive entries in the table are compared until a collision is resolved. It can be shown that the average number of symbol comparisons required in seeking a symbol is approximately

$$(1-\alpha/2)/(1-\alpha)$$

where α is the *load factor* or *occupancy*, i.e. the ratio of the number of occupied entries in the table to the total table size. Hence,

    10% occupancy gives an average of 1.06 comparisons per search,
    50% occupancy gives an average of 1.5   comparisons per search,
    90% occupancy gives an average of 5.5   comparisons per search.

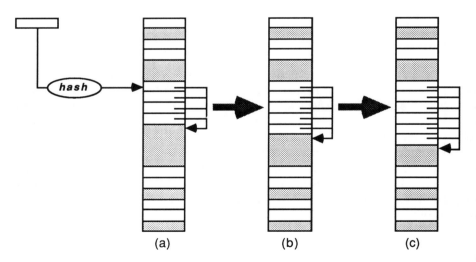

Figure 11.12 *Linear rehashing and clustering*

These example figures demonstrate two significant features of hash tables:

•   The average number of comparisons per search is remarkably low, even at high occupancy levels.

- The speed of the table search varies inversely with the load factor rather than with the absolute number of entries—by using a table of sufficient size, fast insertion and retrieval of entries can be assured, however many entries are involved.

In fact, this linear rehash method that we have used so far is a rather poor rehashing technique, as it suffers from *clustering*—occupied entries tend to cluster together in ever-lengthening sequences, causing a more rapid fall-off in performance. This clustering occurs because the probe sequences leading from each preferred position in the hash table are all cyclic rotations of a single sequence *1, 2, 3, ..., TableSize*. Figure 11.12 illustrates the effect of clustering as successive entries are added to a hash table.

(2) *Random rehash*—the efficiency of table searching may be further improved by adopting an alternative rehash technique which guarantees that, for each distinct starting position *p*, the associated probe sequence is a distinct permutation of the table positions *1..TableSize* (Figure 11.13). *p* is referred to as the *seed* of the probe sequence.

One simple method of doing so is to choose a table size such that *TableSize+1* is a prime number, and then to generate probe sequence values by means of the recurrence relation

$$p_{i+1} = (p_i + p) \bmod (TableSize+1)$$

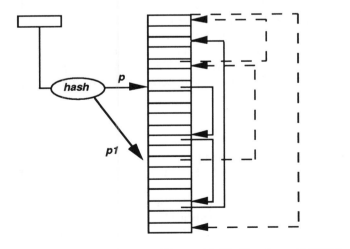

solid lines denote the random sequence generated by p

broken lines denote the random sequence generated by p1

Figure 11.13 *Random rehashing*

Provided *TableSize+1* is prime, this gives a distinct permutation of the values *1..TableSize* for each starting value in the range *1..TableSize*, before generating *0* as the $(TableSize+1)^{th}$ value in every case. With such a rehash function, the average number of symbol comparisons per search is reduced to approximately

$$-(1/\alpha)\ log(1-\alpha)$$

so that   10%   occupancy gives an average of 1.05 comparisons per search,
                50%   occupancy gives an average of 1.39 comparisons per search,
                90%   occupancy gives an average of 2.56 comparisons per search.

Hash tables are undoubtedly the best means of organizing semantic tables when fast searching is required. Their disadvantages are that, for efficient operation, they require more storage than they actually use and that, if they do become full, they cannot be extended easily. They also require each entry to be the same size although this can be overcome, as shown in Section 11.4.2, by holding the hash table as an array of pointers to a corresponding set of variable-length symbol entries. This also minimizes the storage wastage required for efficient operation. Many improved variations on these basic methods of hash table representation using pointers can be devised easily.

11.5   Tables for block-structured languages

In considering possible table organizations so far we have assumed that all the entries in the table were associated with unique symbols of equal significance in any search. This is not so when block-structured languages are considered. In this case the same symbol may be declared and used in different blocks and thus distinct entries must coexist in the semantic table corresponding to each declaration. The basic scope rules associated with most block-structured languages imply that, to find the correct entry for a given symbol requires that all entries arising from declarations in the current block are inspected first, then those from the surrounding block, and so on, i.e. a *hierarchical* table search is required. How this search is provided depends upon the underlying table organization.

11.5.1   Blocked unsorted tables

The blocks of the example Modula-2 program of Figure 11.14 have been enclosed in boxes and each block allocated a block number which is shown at the top right of the corresponding box.

Within the statement-part of each block the numbers of the blocks whose local identifiers are accessible at that point have also been indicated.

A block structure is easily superimposed on a linear table by

(a) numbering the blocks of the source program, say in the order in which they are opened;
(b) keeping a *scope table* in which the entry for each block delimits the linear sequence of semantic table entries created for that block.

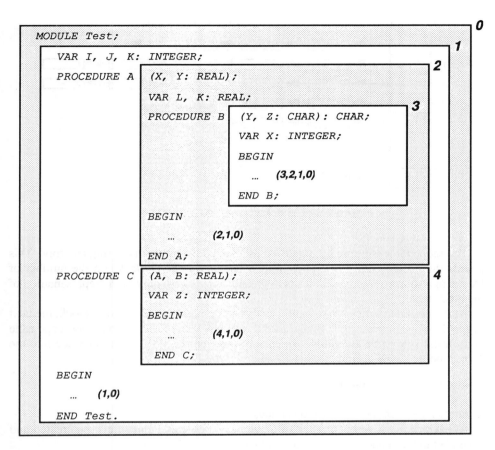

Figure 11.14 *Block structure of an example Modula-2 program*

For languages with pre-declared symbols it is customary to create a *pseudo-block* which surrounds the whole source program and which is initialized before compilation begins with entries for all these standard symbols. These are then locatable by the same mechanism as program-defined symbols. Figure 11.15 illustrates the structure of a linked list semantic table for the Modula-2 program of Figure 11.14.

Such a structure may be defined as follows:

```
TYPE    SymbolEntry = POINTER TO SymbolRecord;
CONST   MaximumNumberOfScopes = ...;
VAR     ScopeTable:  RECORD
                        NumberOfScopes: [0.. MaximumNumberOfScopes];
                        Table: ARRAY [1.. MaximumNumberOfScopes] OF
                                RECORD Head: SymbolEntry END;
                     END;
```

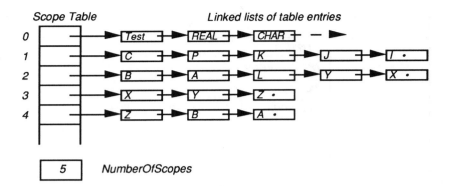

Figure 11.15 *Blocked unsorted table structure*

The scope table is normally organized as a linked list rather than using an array. This avoids the need to place an upper limit *MaximumNumberOfBlocks* on the number of blocks in a source program and leads to greater storage economy in the representation of the block table.

At the commencement of semantic analysis of a new source program block, the next available scope number must be assigned to this block and the corresponding scope table entry initialized to be an empty sequence of table entries. Thus we introduce into the *Table* module a new operator

PROCEDURE OpenScope;

to perform these scope initialization actions.

At each declarative occurrence of a symbol a new table entry must be created and appended to the sequence for the current block.

To search the semantic table for a particular entry involves a hierarchical search of the individual collections of entries for each block accessible at that point in the source program—starting with the current block, and then the enclosing block, and then its enclosing block, and so on. Hence, in Figure 11.14, a search performed during compilation of the statement-part of the procedure *C* must search the entries for blocks (*4, 1, 0*), in that order. Searching the entries for any given block involves extracting the block table entry for that block and then searching the sequence of table entries delimited by it.

Note that in one-pass compilation the symbol entries for a given block are no longer needed as soon as the analysis of that block is completed. These entries can thus be discarded at that point and the scope table structure therefore collapses to a stack in which the topmost entry is always that for the current block. We therefore introduce a further *Table* module operation, complementary to *OpenScope*, which is responsible for performing the necessary scope finalization actions, viz.

PROCEDURE CloseScope;

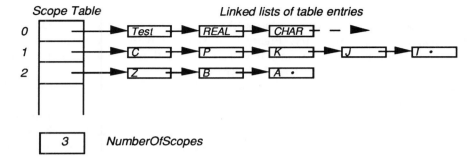

Figure 11.16 *Blocked unsorted table structure for one-pass compilation*

The table search operation thus is modified to search the semantic tables for all the currently defined scopes, beginning at the topmost one in the stack. Figure 11.16 illustrates the state of the semantic table during the analysis of the procedure *C* in the program of Figure 11.14.

11.5.2 Blocked sorted tables

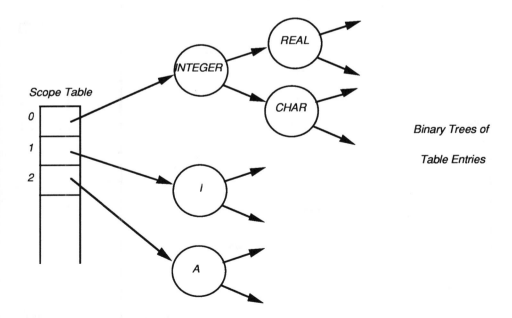

Figure 11.17 *Blocked binary tree table structure*

Binary tree tables for a block-structured language can be organized in the same way as linear tables—with a tree for each block, the root of each tree being pointed to by a corresponding scope table entry. Figure 11.17 shows a tree-structured table for one-pass compilation in which the only trees retained are those of currently accessible blocks, i.e. the table structure is that of a *stack* of trees.

This representation is considered in further detail when we construct the semantic analyzer for Model in Chapter 13.

The use of an array representation for an ordered table in contiguous storage is convenient only in one-pass compilation where the ordered sub-table to which an entry is to be added is always the topmost one and so adjacent to the unused elements of the array.

11.5.3 Blocked hash tables

It is not practical to adopt a scheme which uses a separate hash table for each program block as this implies setting a bound on the maximum number of entries in each block rather than in the program as a whole. This, together with the need to have each table lightly loaded so as to achieve fast search times, must lead to an unacceptable waste of storage.

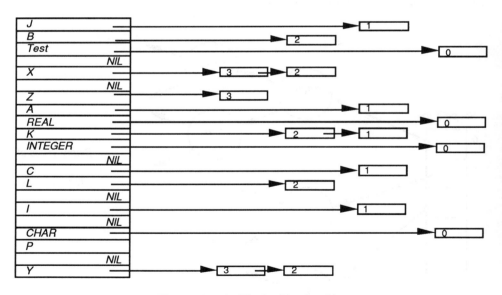

Figure 11.18 *Blocked hash table*

However, we can devise some alternative representations which use a single hash table for the entire program.

(1) The block number may be combined with the symbol representation to produce a composite search key which is unique for each entry. Thus, finding an entry corresponding to a given symbol involves searching the table for this symbol combined with the current block number, then combined with the enclosing block number, and so on.

(2) All of the entries for a given symbol may be held as a linked list to which the hash table entry for the symbol points (Figure 11.18 illustrates the state of such a table during the analysis of the body of procedure *C* in Figure 11.14). When searching for the entry for a given symbol, once the relevant hash table entry for the symbol representation is found, the linked list which it references must then be searched for the entry with the correct block number.

Once again, in the case of one-pass compilation, only the entries for symbols declared in the currently accessible blocks need be retained and entries for a given block may be discarded once analysis of that block is complete. Thus the required entry in a search for a given symbol is always that at the head of the linked list concerned, provided that new entries are always inserted at the head of each list.

11.6 Further reading

McKeeman (1976b) gives a detailed treatment of symbol table organization and access, and gives comparative figures for table access speeds derived from experimental results. Symbol tables and searching algorithms are also examined in depth in Knuth (1973), Aho, Hopcroft and Ullman (1983) and Aho, Sethi and Ullman (1986). Tremblay and Sorenson (1985) consider the searching of sub-tables in detail.

A discussion of hashing algorithms appears in Morris (1968) and Wirth (1976). Various alternatives to hash tables for representing semantic tables are described in the chapter on sparse data structures in Welsh, Elder and Bustard (1984).

Exercises 11

11.1 Assuming
  (i)   an unsorted table organization (as in Figure 11.16),
  (ii)   a binary tree organization (as in Figure 11.17),
  (iii) a hash table organization (as in Figure 11.18 and using the hash function suggested in 11.4.3),
  trace, by means of diagrams, the state of the semantic table as the identifiers declared in the following outline Model program are entered into the tables by a one-pass compiler:

```
MODULE Main;
    VAR X, C, Y, H: INTEGER;

    PROCEDURE P;
```

```
VAR A, M, H: CHAR;
BEGIN ... END P;

VAR B1, B: BOOLEAN;

PROCEDURE A; BEGIN ... END A;

BEGIN ... END Main.
```

11.2 Use the hash function suggested in 11.4.3 to convert identifiers of up to 16 letters to a hash index in the range 1..100. Use this in a test program which computes
   (i)   the distribution of hash indices for the names of the states of the USA;
   (ii)   the average number of comparisons required to locate a valid state name in a hash table of size 100 which uses this function, together with linear rehashing to resolve collisions (assume any convenient order of insertion for the state names, and that no other entries other than state names are present);
   (iii)   the average number of comparisons required to determine that a state name is invalid.

11.3 Implement the binary tree representation of the semantic table described in Section 11.3.2, using an array rather than a pointer representation for the binary tree (i.e. each node link is represented as an array subscript value rather than as a pointer value).

11.4 Implement a block-structured semantic table in which identifier spellings are recorded, using a linked list representation for each sub-table.

11.5 Implement a block-structured semantic table in which identifier spellings are recorded, using a binary tree representation for each sub-table.

11.6 Design a hash table representation consisting of a table in which each position *p* contains a pointer to the head of a linked list containing the entries for those symbols with preferred position *p*.

11.7 Implement the semantic table as a single hash table in which all entries for a given identifier are held as a chain to which the hash table entry for the identifier points (as described in Section 11.5.3 and illustrated in Figure 11.18). The hash table should be large enough to accommodate at least 500 different identifier spellings at any time.

11.8 Write a driver program which can be used to compare the search speeds (i.e. by measuring the number of symbol comparisons) for the various table organizations described in this chapter and developed for Exercises 11.2–11.6.

Chapter 12

Semantic table contents and usage

In this chapter we consider what information concerning symbol attributes requires to be stored within the entries of the semantic table and how this information is placed in the table and subsequently used for semantic analysis purposes. Much of the material of the chapter is illustrated by its application within the Model compiler in Chapter 13.

12.1 Semantic table contents

As we noted in the previous chapter, programmer-defined symbols within a program are usually denoted by identifiers or by numeric values (as in the case of statement labels in many languages). Ignoring this possible distinction in representation we first consider the attributes held within the table entry for an identifier occurring in a program. This information depends in general on the nature of the objects that can be defined in the programming language concerned and, in particular, on the range of data structuring methods which it provides. For a programming language such as Pascal or Modula-2, the following attributes (in addition to the spelling of the identifier) are typical:

- In general an identifier may denote a *constant-*, *type-*, *field-*, *variable-*, *procedure-*, *function-* or *label*. This is known as the *class* of the identifier.

  If it is a *constant-identifier* what is
  - the *type* of the constant value so denoted?
  - the *value* of the constant?

  If it is a *variable-identifier* then
  - is it an *actual-variable* or a *formal-variable* (i.e. a formal parameter of a procedure)?
  - if it is a formal-variable what is its *parameter-mode* (in Modula-2, for instance, a parameter may be passed as a *value* or *variable* parameter)?

- what is the *type* of the variable?

If it is a *field-identifier* (i.e. denotes a field within a record-type) then
- what is the *type* of the field?

If it is a *procedure-identifier* then
- is it an *actual-* or *formal-procedure* (some languages allow a procedure to be passed as a parameter to another procedure)?
- how many *parameters* has the procedure?
- what is the declared *type* of each parameter?
- what *mode* is used for passing each parameter?

If it is a *function-identifier* then its attributes are as for a *procedure-identifier* plus
- the *result-type* produced by a call of the function.

If the identifier is a *type-identifier* then
- what are the details of the structural *form* of the type, i.e. is it a *scalar-type* (such as an enumeration or a subrange-type) or is it a *structured-type* (e.g. an *array-type*, a *record-type* or a *set-type*)?
  If it is a *subrange-type* then
  - what is the *host-type* (i.e. the ordinal-type of which its values form a subrange)?
  - what are the bounds of the subrange?
  If it is an *array-type* then
  - how many *dimensions* are there?
  - what is the *type* of each dimension?
  - what is the *element-type*?
  If it is a *record-type* then
  - what are the *fields* of the record-type?
  If it is a *set-type*
  - what is the *base-type* of the set-type?
  For a language with more complex types available the information needed is correspondingly more complex.

If the identifier is a *label-identifier* then
- the *status* of the label, i.e. whether the statement it labels has already *occurred*, is still *expected*, or lies within a part of the program which is now *inaccessible*;
- other attributes which depend upon the rules governing the range of definition of a label (Pascal, for instance, only allows a labelled-statement to be referenced by a goto-statement within the same, or an enclosing, compound-statement as the labelled-statement).

How should type attributes be represented? Each type in a program is shared by, and must be associated with, a number of data objects. For storage economy each association with a given type should be represented by some reference to a single descriptor of the attribute's type, rather than by duplication of the attribute descriptor at each point of association. Thus we introduce into the *Table* definition an exported type

```
TYPE TypeEntry = ...;
```

The lifetime of a type descriptor is that of the table entries that are associated with it. To enable these to be dealt with in the same way a further extension is made to the *Table* interface—to put the creation of type descriptor records, and hence their collection and disposal, under its control. This is done by a further interface procedure

```
PROCEDURE NewType(VAR Entry: TypeEntry; FormNeeded: TypeClass);
```

where

```
TYPE TypeClass = (Scalars, Arrays, Records, ...);
```

A suitable form for the type descriptors is thus defined by

```
TYPE TypeRecord =  RECORD
                       CASE Form: TypeClass OF
                       | Scalars:    ...
                       | Arrays:     ...
                       | Records:    ...
                   ...
                       END;
                   ...
                   END
```

Note that no explicit discrimination between the individual scalar types is necessary within the descriptors. The descriptor for the type *INTEGER* is that pointed to by the entry for the identifier *INTEGER* and by all entries whose associated type is *INTEGER*. Any type represented by the same pointer value must be *INTEGER*.

Figure 12.1 illustrates the semantic table identifier and type descriptors associated with the Model variable-declaration

```
VAR B: BOOLEAN;
```

and Figure 12.2 illustrates the various semantic table entries associated with the array variable-declaration

```
VAR A: ARRAY [1..10] OF INTEGER;
```

In some languages labels are denoted by numbers rather than identifiers, in which case it will be necessary to hold details of labels in a separate, but similarly organized, table.

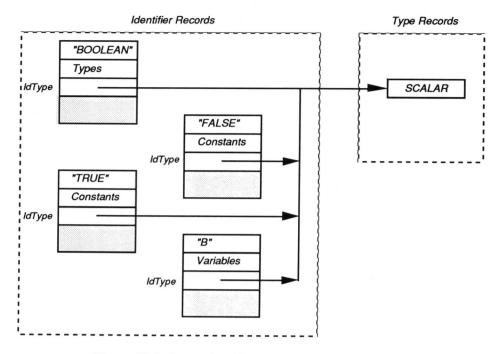

Figure 12.1 *Semantic table entries for VAR B: BOOLEAN*

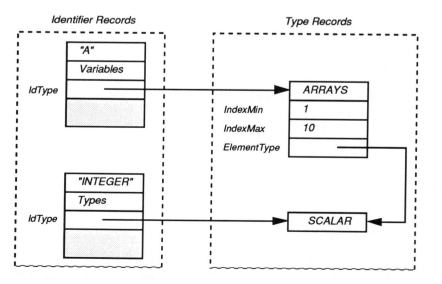

Figure 12.2 *Semantic table entries for VAR A: ARRAY [1..10] OF INTEGER*

The attributes defined in this section are sufficient for the implementation of semantic analysis. However, when we consider the run-time representation of programs and the generation of object code we shall define additional attributes which will require to be stored in the existing entries for identifiers and types within the semantic table.

12.2   Recording and using attributes

The information outlined in the previous section must be recorded at the (explicit or implicit) declarative occurrence of each symbol, and used at each subsequent occurrence to check that the symbol is being used correctly. More precisely, the semantic analysis which must be carried out using the semantic table is as follows:

- At the *declarative occurrence* of a symbol
  (a) check that it is not already declared (in the current scope);
  (b) record its attributes as defined in Section 12.1.

- At *each subsequent* occurrence of a symbol, check that
  (a) it has already been declared;
  (b) its usage at that occurrence is consistent with its declaration.

In particular, checking the consistency of declaration and usage involves the following actions:

(1) Within expressions, extracting the attributes of those *variable-, field-, constant-* and *function-identifiers* appearing as factors, for use in the expression analysis outlined in the next section.

(2) Within subscripted identifiers, checking that
  (a) the identifier is a variable-identifier whose associated type is an array-type;
  (b) the correct number of index-expressions occur;
  (c) each such expression produces a value of the correct type.

(3) Within procedure and function calls, checking that
  (a) the identifier is a procedure-identifier or function-identifier;
  (b) the correct number of actual parameters is supplied;
  (c) each actual parameter is of the correct type;
  (d) each actual parameter is compatible with the declared parameter mode of the corresponding formal parameter.

(4) When a statement is labelled or used as the destination of a goto-statement, various actions must be performed which check the consistency and correctness of use of the label and may also update the attribute information associated with the label. Section 12.5 considers label checking in greater detail.

(5) A variable used as a control-variable in a for-statement must be checked to ensure it is of an acceptable ordinal type. However, some languages place constraints on the range of operations that may be performed on a control-variable (e.g. it must not be explicitly assigned a value within the body of the for-statement). This requires analysis of the use of control-variables throughout the scope of their declarations.

12.3   Semantic analysis of expressions

In the analysis of expressions it is necessary to analyze not only the attributes of each identifier appearing within the expression but also the attributes of every operand, i.e. variable, constant, function call or sub-expression which is involved in the evaluation of the expression. To do so the semantic analysis process requires some means of representing the attributes of such operands outside of the semantic table itself. Since the attribute required is the type of the operand, a convenient representation is simply as a reference to the type descriptor for the type of the operand. Given this representation the analysis involves the following:

(a) Constructing the attributes for each primary operand involved. For variables and function calls this will involve extraction of these attributes from the semantic table; for explicit constants such as *integer-constants* they may be made available by, for instance, the lexical analyzer; for (parenthesized) sub-expressions the attributes are generated by preliminary analysis of the sub-expressions themselves.
(b) Checking that the attributes of the operands for each operator in the expression are compatible with the operator involved.
(c) Deducing the attributes of the result of applying the operator to its operands.

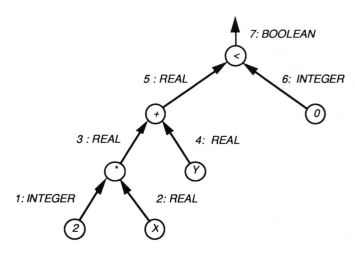

Figure 12.3 *Semantic processing of Pascal expression 2*X+Y<0*

Consider the Pascal expression

$$2\,{}^*X + Y < 0$$

where the identifiers *X* and *Y* denote variables of type *REAL*. Figure 12.3 shows the significant nodes of the syntax tree associated with the primary operands and operators of this expression and the order in which type attributes are associated with these nodes. This form of syntax tree is known as an *abstract syntax tree*—it is a reduced form of the *phrase structure tree* introduced in Chapter 6 with redundant (non-terminal) information extracted. The reduction can be expressed using a *transformational grammar*. Note that Pascal allows *INTEGER* and *REAL* values to be used as operands to an arithmetic operator—if either operand is of type *REAL* then the result of the operation is also of type *REAL*.

With reference to the numbering of the arcs in Figure 12.3, the following are the actions associated with establishing the various sub-expression attributes:

(1) The lexical analyzer gives the type of the constant *factor 2* as *INTEGER*.
(2) The variable-identifier entry for the *factor X* in the semantic table gives its type as *REAL*.
(3) For the operator * the operands are of type *INTEGER* and *REAL*, respectively—these are acceptable types for the operands and the resultant *term* is of type *REAL*.
(4) The semantic table entry for *Y* gives its declared type as *REAL*.
(5) For the operator + the operands are both of type *REAL* —this is acceptable and the resultant *simple-expression* is of type *REAL*.
(6) The lexical analyzer gives the type of the constant *0* as *INTEGER*.
(7) For the operator < the operands are of type *REAL* and *INTEGER*, respectively—these are acceptable and the resultant *expression* type is *BOOLEAN*.

12.4 Semantic analysis of statements

Once the types of expressions have been established, it is a simple matter to perform the semantic analysis associated with statements according to the semantic rules stated in the language definition. For example, given an assignment-statement

    v := e

the types of the variable *v* and the expression *e* must be checked to ensure that they are assignment-compatible with each other.

For a procedure call the actual parameters must be checked to ensure that they are compatible in mode and type with the declared formal parameters of the procedure.

In the case of conditional and repetition statement forms, for example. a while-statement

    WHILE c DO ... END

the type of the controlling expression *c* must be of type *BOOLEAN*.

In a for-statement

```
FOR v := e1 TO e2 DO ... END
```

the control-variable *v* and the *initial-* and *final-expressions e1* and *e2* must all be of the same ordinal type (i.e. in Modula-2 this will be a scalar-type other than *REAL*).

Selector-expressions in *case-statements* must be of an ordinal-type and all *case-labels* must be of the same type (and must appear in at most one case-limb).

The semantic analysis associated with *loop-statements* and *exit-statements* involves checking that an exit-statement occurs within a textually enclosing loop-statement.

The application of these semantic checks within statements will be well illustrated by the implementation of the Model semantic analyzer in Chapter 13.

12.5   Semantic analysis of labels

As an illustration of a language feature in which symbols are not necessarily defined before they are used, consider the semantic analysis required for label checking in a language providing *statement-labels* and *goto-statements*. In a structured language restrictions are usually imposed on the relative positions of goto-statements and the labels that they may reference. In languages such as Pascal, for instance, a *goto-statement* must not attempt to transfer control to a label other than one which occurs within the same statement-sequence or in an enclosing statement-sequence. Labels themselves must be unique within the block in which they occur. Such rules can be enforced by maintaining the following information within each block:

(a)   the current level of *nesting* of compound-statements;
(b)   a *label table* in which the entry for each label records the following information:
    (i)   the label *identity*;
    (ii) whether the label itself has *occurred*, is *expected*, or is *inaccessible* (i.e. has occurred in a compound-statement whose analysis is already completed);
    (iii) the *defined depth* of nesting of a label which has already occurred or the *maximum depth* of nesting at which an expected label may occur.

Each such entry may be described by the following type definitions:

```
TYPE LabelDepth = CARDINAL;
      LabelRange = ...;
      LabelStatus = (Expected, Occurred, Inaccessible);

      LabelRecord = RECORD
                       Identity: LabelRange;
                       CASE Status: LabelStatus OF
                       | Occurred:  DefinedDepth: LabelDepth;
                       | Expected: MaximumDepth: LabelDepth;
```

```
        | Inaccessible: ;
        END
END
```

The label tables for the accessible blocks at any point during analysis may be organized using any of the organizations described in Chapter 11.

The analyzer must now process these label table entries, not only at each occurrence of a label or a goto-statement, but also at the closure of each compound-statement— updating the entries for those labels, expected or occurred, which are currently associated with this level. A label which has occurred within a completed compound-statement becomes inaccessible, while the expected level of occurrence of an expected label must be decremented.

For example, on the right below are indicated the label analysis actions associated with the semantic checking of the sample program fragment shown on the left which uses numeric label values.

Example procedure	*Label analysis*
procedure P;	Create a label table for this procedure;
	Initialize *NestingLevel* to *0*;
begin	*INC(NestingLevel);*
...	
goto 1;	Create an entry for label *1* with attributes:
	Status := Expected; MaximumDepth := 1;
...	
loop	*INC(NestingLevel);*
...	
2: ...	Create an entry for label *2* with attributes:
	Status := Occurred; DefinedDepth := 2;
loop	*INC(NestingLevel);*
...	
goto 2;	OK since for label *2*: *DefinedDepth ≤ NestingLevel*
...	
goto 3;	For label *3*: *MaximumDepth := 3*
...	
end;	For label *3*: *MaximumDepth := 2*;
	DEC(NestingLevel);
1: ...	Invalid, since *NestingLevel > MaximumDepth* for label *1*,
	but now, for label *1*:
	Status := Occurred; DefinedDepth := 2;
goto 4;	For label *4*: *MaximumDepth := 2*
...	
end;	For labels *1* and *2*: *Status := Inaccessible*;
	For labels *3* and *4*: *MaximumDepth := 1*;
	DEC(NestingLevel);

3: ...	Valid, since for label *3*: *NestingLevel = MaximumDepth*;
	For label *3*: *Status := Occurred; DefinedDepth := 1*;
goto 2;	ERROR since, for label *2*, *Status = Inaccessible*;
...	
end {P};	*DEC(NestingLevel)*;
	For label *3*: *Status := Inaccessible*
	Invalid, since for label *4*, *Status <> Occurred*

12.6   Recovery from semantic errors

The requirements of good error recovery, given earlier for syntactic error recovery, apply equally to recovery from semantic errors. However, it turns out that recovery from semantic errors—those arising from misuse of labels, identifiers, or expressions— is considerably easier than recovery from syntactic errors.

When an incorrectly used identifier or operand is detected consequential error reports can be avoided by adopting for the identifier or operand an attribute description which indicates that an associated error has been detected and that the attributes are therefore in doubt. Subsequent semantic checks are then suppressed in any situation in which a 'doubtful' operand is involved and in this way spurious error messages are avoided. To ensure the fastest possible recovery this doubtful status should be removed from the analysis process as soon as possible.

For example, consider the analysis of the comparison $A < B$ where A is an identifier that has not been declared:

(a) on finding A to be undeclared the analyzer should report this error and adopt an attribute description for A indicating that its type is unknown;
(b) in analyzing the $<$ comparison the analyzer should suppress the type compatibility check for operands once it has found that the attributes of the first operand are in doubt;
(c) The analyzer should then generate an attribute description for the comparison which is not 'doubtful' since it is entitled to conclude that the comparison will produce a *BOOLEAN* result whatever its operands should have been.

In the case of incorrect expression operands in general, the transient attribute descriptors for them automatically disappear. In the case of misused identifiers it can be profitable to retain a knowledge of such misuses within the semantic table (by constructing additional entries for the misuses of each identifier) so that the reporting of subsequent similar misuses can be suppressed but further distinct misuses reported.

When an undeclared symbol is detected, semantic error recovery demands that a new entry be created at that point. This will prevent repeated flagging of the same undeclared identifier at its every occurrence in the program being compiled. Creation of this new entry can be incorporated within the specification of *SearchSymbol*.

Duplicate declaration errors may be handled in a similar manner. When a second declaration of some symbol occurs in a given scope, whose attributes differ from the first declaration, effective semantic error recovery suggests that entries should be created for both declarations and the more appropriate one chosen at any subsequent occurrence of the symbol. Provided *NewSymbol* makes the duplicate entries, *SearchSymbol* will sometimes be able to choose among them—on the basis of appropriate symbol class.

12.7   Implementing semantic analysis

Given a suitable representation of semantic attributes the corresponding semantic actions outlined above are relatively straightforward to define and to program. The ease with which they are incorporated into the overall compilation process depends on whether it is a multi-pass or one-pass process, and if it is one-pass, on the method of syntax analysis chosen. For top-down analysis by recursive descent, semantic analysis actions can be coded directly at appropriate points in the recursive syntax procedures, with the full flexibility which the implementation language provides. This is illustrated for the Model compiler in the next chapter.

12.8   Further reading

Most compiler texts such as Bornat (1979), Tremblay and Sorenson (1985), Davie and Morrison (1981) and Hunter (1981) provide extensive coverage of type checking and its implementation. Watt (1993) presents an algorithm for performing the type checking of an abstract syntax tree and illustrates its application to his model language. However, the most comprehensive treatment of type checking within expressions and statements is provided by Aho, Sethi and Ullman (1986). They examine in detail additional concerns such as *coercion* (implicit conversions between types) and *overloading* (procedures and functions with different actions but the same name).

Language definitions are often ambiguous in their definition of type compatibility, i.e. whether the type equivalence of two constructs depends upon them having the same structural properties or requires them to be of the same named type. A paper by Welsh, Sneeringer and Hoare (1977) drew attention to these type equivalence problems in the definition of Pascal as well as to other problems relating to the notion of scope in the language.

Various methods that have been used to represent the type attributes of Pascal expressions are illustrated in Welsh and Hay (1986) and Pemberton and Daniels (1982).

Exercises 12

12.1   Define a possible form for the semantic table records in a one-pass compiler for a language similar to Modula-2 in which the only programmer-defined symbols are identifiers which may denote scalar variables, one-dimensional arrays of scalars over *INTEGER* index-ranges, procedures or functions producing scalar results (with parameters which may be only scalar- or array-variables).

12.2 Define a possible form for the semantic table records in a one-pass compiler for a programming language in which identifiers may denote *INTEGER* or *CHAR* constant values, types, variables, or functions (with variable parameters only).

12.3 Define a possible form for the identifier and type descriptors in a one-pass compiler for a language which supports the standard types *INTEGER* and *BOOLEAN*, as well as allowing users to define enumerated-types and (non-variant) record-types. Identifiers may denote types, constants, variables, and record-fields. Assuming a sorted binary tree organization of the identifier descriptors and a chained list representation of the type descriptors, draw a detailed diagram of the descriptors (and information included within them) associated with the following declaration-part:

```
TYPE Colours = (Red, Blue,Yellow, Silver, White, Black);
TYPE Car = RECORD
                    YearOfManufacture: INTEGER;
                    Imported: BOOLEAN;
                    Colour: Colours
                END;
VAR   MyCar: Car;
```

12.4 Assuming the following variable-declarations

```
VAR B: BOOLEAN; C: CHAR, K, J: INTEGER;
```

construct abstract syntax trees for the following Model expressions and label the nodes of the trees with their associated type attributes:

```
(K DIV J + 3) < J * 4
NOT B OR (J = 2)
(C = '?') AND ((K + J) > 3)
```

12.5 Model is to be extended to include *statement-labels* (denoted by non-negative integer values) which are not declared in advance of their use, and *goto-statements* which transfer control to a labelled-statement which must occur within the same, or an enclosing, statement-sequence in the *same* block as the goto-statement.

statement	=	[*label* ":"] (*simple-statement* | *structured-statement*).
simple-statement	=	*assignment-statement* | ... | *goto-statement*.
label	=	*integer-constant*.
goto-statement	=	"GOTO" *label*.

Define a suitable data structure, in the form of a chained list of records of type

LabelRecord linked by pointers of type *LabelEntry*, which may be used to record the semantic attributes of labels during compilation of a program. Construct a procedure

PROCEDURE SearchLabel(L: Label; VAR Entry: LabelEntry);

which searches the data structure to find an entry for the label with integer value *L*—if such an entry exists a reference to the entry is returned via the parameter *Entry*, otherwise *Entry* is assigned the value *NIL*; and a procedure

PROCEDURE NewLabel(L: Label; VAR Entry: LabelEntry);

which creates a record for the label with integer value *L* in the data structure and returns a reference to the entry so created in *Entry*.

Use these procedures to perform the semantic analysis of labels and goto-statements at the following points within the text of a program:
* the start of a *block*;
* the start of a *statement-sequence*;
* the end of a *statement-sequence*;
* a *label* prefixing a *statement*;
* a *goto-statement*;
* the end of a *block*.

Chapter 13

Semantic analysis for Model

In this chapter we consider the informally defined semantic rules which accompany the formal syntax definition of Model. Their application involves the collection and examination of the attributes associated with the identifiers, constants and (sub-) expressions which appear in Model programs. For the time being we confine our attention to those attributes necessary for semantic checking. The construction of attributes which reflect the object program to be produced are considered with the generator interface in Chapter 14.

13.1 Attributes and their representation

For identifiers appearing in Model programs the attributes necessary to facilitate semantic checking are

(a) the declared *class of usage* of the identifier—in Model identifiers may denote types, constants, variables and procedures, and so their possible classes of usage may be represented by an enumerated-type

    TYPE IdentifierClass = (Types, Constants, Variables, Procedures);

(b) for type-, constant- and variable-identifiers, the associated *type* itself (Model's parameterless procedures require no further attributes for semantic checking).

As we saw in Chapter 12, the association of each identifier with its attributes must involve the maintenance of some record of the form

    TYPE IdRecord = RECORD
                        Name: Host.Word;
                        Class: IdentifierClass;
                        IdType: ?
                     END;

The number of such records required is determined by the program being compiled, and varies greatly from one program to another. In the interests of compile-time storage economy, therefore, the representation of the records in dynamically allocated storage is preferable to any statically allocated structure, hence

```
TYPE IdentifierEntry = POINTER TO IdRecord;
```

The creation and access of all *IdRecords* required will be made through pointers of type *IdentifierEntry*.

We established in the previous chapter that, in order to achieve storage economy, each association with a given type should be represented by some reference to a single descriptor of the type. Where the number of types to be represented is not predetermined, the pointer is again the natural means of denoting such references in Modula-2, so we define

```
TYPE TypeEntry = POINTER TO TypeRecord;
```

In Model a type is either one of the built-in types (*INTEGER*, *CHAR*, *BOOLEAN*) or an array-type whose index-range and element-type are determined by the type definition within a variable-declaration. A suitable form for the type descriptors is thus defined by

```
TYPE TypeClass  =  (Scalars, Arrays);
     TypeRecord =  RECORD
                       CASE Form: TypeClass OF
                       | Arrays:  IndexMin,
                                  IndexMax: Target.Integer;
                                  ElementType: TypeEntry
                       | Scalars:
                       END
                   END
```

13.2   The semantic table

In this section the functions of the semantic table access procedures are examined in greater detail so as to facilitate further their use in performing semantic analysis.

13.2.1   The table interface

The semantic analysis of Model identifiers involves

(a) creation of a new identifier record for each identifier on encountering its declaration, and recording of its attributes therein;
(b) location of the entry for a particular identifier on each of its subsequent occurrences, and inspection of the attributes recorded therein.

For a block-structured language such as Model, these processes are complicated by the fact that more than one entry for an identifier may exist and the appropriate entry, as determined by the scope rules of the language, must always be selected.

The organization of the table is independent of the actual analysis applied to the attributes stored there and hence it is logical to isolate this organization from the semantic analyzer proper. This separation can be achieved by the use of a module whose interface is based on that of the *Table* module specified in Chapter 12. The following module's interface is derived from that developed in Chapter 12, with a systematic re-naming of its exported procedures and their parameters to reflect the fact that the symbols whose attributes are to be recorded are identifiers:

```
DEFINITION MODULE Table;
   IMPORT Host, Target;

   TYPE TypeEntry = POINTER TO TypeRecord;
        TypeClass = (Scalars, Arrays);
        TypeRecord =  RECORD
                        CASE Form: TypeClass OF
                        | Arrays:
                            IndexMin, IndexMax: Target.Integer;
                            ElementType: TypeEntry
                        | Scalars:
                        END;
                        …
                      END;

   TYPE IdentifierEntry = POINTER TO IdRecord;
        IdentifierClass = (Types, Constants, Variables, Procedures);
        IdRecord =  RECORD
                      Name: Host.Word;
                      IdType: TypeEntry;
                      Class: IdentifierClass;
                      …
                    END;

   PROCEDURE OpenScope;
   PROCEDURE CloseScope;

   PROCEDURE NewId(Spelling: Host.Word; VAR Entry: IdentifierEntry; …);
   PROCEDURE SearchId(Spelling: Host.Word; VAR Entry: IdentifierEntry; …);
   PROCEDURE NewType(VAR Entry: TypeEntry; FormNeeded: TypeClass);

END Table.
```

The semantic analyzer signals the beginning and end of each scope range, as determined by the syntactic block structure of the program, by means of calls of *OpenScope* and *CloseScope*. Between these calls the analyzer may create a new identifier entry in the current scope by a call to *NewId*, or locate an appropriate entry for an identifier, in the current or any enclosing scope, by a call to *SearchId*.

13.2.2   Context-error detection and recovery

The above *Table* interface reflects the basic functions of the semantic table in the semantic analysis process. However, its precise behaviour may be further refined in relation to the errors of identifier context which semantic analysis must detect and recover from. Consider, for example, the handling of an identifier encountered as the first symbol of a statement. The analyzer actions must take the general form

```
locate identifier in table;
IF none exists THEN
    report error – undeclared identifier
ELSIF NOT identifier class IN {Variables, Procedures} THEN
    report error – identifier is of wrong class
ELSE ...
END
```

It turns out that the screening tests for detecting

(a) undeclared identifiers, and
(b) identifiers of inappropriate class,

are common to every context in which *SearchId* is required. It is logical therefore to incorporate them within *SearchId*. To do so, however, requires a further parameter in the parameter list—to specify the acceptable classes of identifier at that point—thus

```
PROCEDURE SearchId(Spelling: Word; VAR Entry: IdentifierEntry;
                   AllowableClasses: IdClassSet);
```

where

```
TYPE IdClassSet = SET OF IdentifierClass;
```

When an undeclared identifier is detected, semantic error recovery demands that a new entry be created at that point so as to prevent repeated flagging of this undeclared identifier at its every occurrence in the program. This can be readily incorporated within *SearchId*.

With these refinements the procedure *SearchId* is guaranteed to return a pointer to an identifier entry of appropriate class at every call. This guarantee considerably simplifies the semantic analysis code around the point of call. For example, the statement analysis outlined above becomes

```
Table.SearchId(LexicalAnalyzer.SymbolDescription.Spelling, FirstIdentifier,
               IdClassSet {Variables, Procedures});
CASE FirstIdentifier^.Class OF
| Variables: Assignment;
| Procedures: ...
END
```

When *NewId* discovers that a duplicate declaration of some identifier occurs in a given scope, with attributes different from the first, it facilitates semantic error recovery by creating and retaining entries for both declarations. Once *NewId* has made the duplicate entries, *SearchId* will sometimes be able to choose the more appropriate one at any subsequent occurrence of the identifier.

13.2.3   Storage control and recovery

NewId is responsible for the creation of the dynamically allocated records used to hold the attributes of identifiers. While our concept of these attributes so far is simple, in general they, and the storage required for their representation, may vary considerably from one class of identifier to another. To achieve storage economy *NewId* must therefore be aware of the required class of identifier and hence of its storage requirement. We therefore extend the parameter list of *NewId* to accommodate this information, thus

```
PROCEDURE NewId(Spelling: Word; VAR Entry: IdentifierEntry;
                ClassNeeded: IdentifierClass);
```

This additional parameter enables *NewId* to fill each new identifier record with a set of default attributes, thus further simplifying the programming of the analyzer proper.

In a one-pass compiler all usage of the identifier entries takes place between the opening and closing of the scope in which they are created. It is possible therefore to reclaim the storage occupied by the local identifier entries and associated type descriptors when closing any scope, and storage economy dictates that this should be done. This storage recovery can be programmed into the procedure *CloseScope*, according to the organization chosen for identifier records within the *Table* module.

13.3   Programming the table module

With these refinements of its interface settled, the required internal organization of the *Table* module can now be considered. To reflect the block structure and corresponding identifier scopes in the program being compiled the table must clearly be held as a stack of sub-tables, one for each scope currently in existence, with the topmost sub-table holding the identifier and type descriptors for the current local scope. This organization can be represented in Modula-2 by introducing types

```
TYPE Scope = POINTER TO ScopeRecord;
     ScopeRecord =    RECORD
                          Local Identifiers: ...;
                          Local Types: ...;
                          EnclosingScope: Scope
                      END
```

and a pointer-variable which always references the *ScopeRecord* representing the current local scope:

    VAR LocalScope: Scope;

Figure 13.1 illustrates the structure of these scope records during the analysis process.

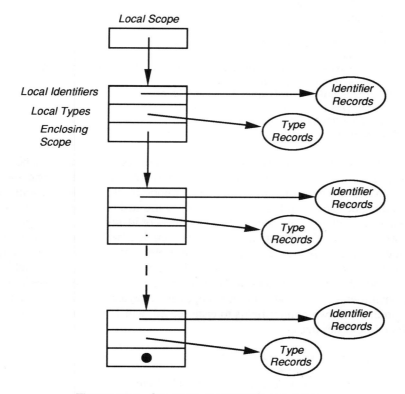

Figure 13.1 *Structure of semantic sub-tables*

The action required on entering a new scope is to create a new scope record with (initially) no identifier and type descriptors, and this is readily expressed as

```
PROCEDURE OpenScope;
   VAR NewScope: Scope;
   BEGIN
      Host.New(NewScope, SIZE(ScopeRecord));
      WITH NewScope^ DO
         Local Identifiers := none; Local Types := none;
         EnclosingScope := LocalScope
```

```
        END;
        LocalScope := NewScope
    END OpenScope
```

The hierarchical search which block structure demands of *SearchId* will have the form

```
PROCEDURE SearchId(...);
    VAR ThisScope: Scope;
    BEGIN
        ThisScope := LocalScope;
        REPEAT
            search for identifier required in the sub-table ThisScope^.Local Identifiers
                and return if found;
            ThisScope := ThisScope^.EnclosingScope
        UNTIL ThisScope = NIL;
        Identifier not found
    END SearchId
```

How best may the sub-tables holding the identifiers local to each scope be organized and searched? After character handling, table searching is the second most time-consuming activity in most compilers, so it is important that an organization allowing fast searching be chosen. It has already been demonstrated that simple linear lists are too slow when compiling programs with large numbers of identifiers. Although hash tables undoubtedly provide the fastest organization for simple table look-up, we have also seen that their advantage is blunted when used in a block-structured environment. As a simpler compromise a binary tree organization is adopted for each sub-table, which gives a reasonably fast search time without incurring excessive storage overheads.

The identifier records created in each scope can be organized as nodes in a binary tree by the addition of two pointer fields to each record, which reference the root nodes of the left and right sub-trees, thus

```
TYPE IdRecord =   RECORD
                    Name: Word;
                    LeftLink, RightLink: IdentifierEntry;
                    IdType: TypeEntry;
                    Class: IdentifierClass
                END
```

Trees are organized according to the alphabetic ordering of identifier spellings. Each sub-table within a scope record is now representable by a pointer to the root node of the corresponding binary tree, hence

```
TYPE ScopeRecord =   RECORD
                       FirstLocal: IdentifierEntry;
                       Local Types: ...;
                       EnclosingScope: Scope
                     END
```

and the process of searching a sub-table within *SearchId* is now expressible as follows:

```
ThisEntry := ThisScope^.FirstLocal;
WHILE ThisEntry <> NIL DO
    IF Spelling < ThisEntry^.Name THEN ThisEntry := ThisEntry^.LeftLink
    ELSIF Spelling > ThisEntry^.Name THEN ThisEntry := ThisEntry^.RightLink
    ELSE entry found; RETURN
    END
END;
entry not found
```

The process of inserting a new entry in the local scope's sub-table performed within *NewId* is similar except that the occurrence of a *NIL* pointer denotes the appropriate point for insertion. Appendix 8 shows the detailed realization of this logic for both *NewId* and *SearchId*.

Since there is no searching of the collections of type records, the type records for each scope may be organized simply as a linear list by the addition of a chaining pointer field to each type descriptor record, thus

```
TYPE TypeRecord =  RECORD
                        Next: TypeEntry;
                        CASE Form: TypeClass OF
                        | Arrays:
                            IndexMin, IndexMax: Target.Integer;
                            ElementType: TypeEntry
                        | Scalars:
                        END
                   END
```

and each scope record then contains a pointer to the first type descriptor at the head of the local chain, thus

```
TYPE ScopeRecord =   RECORD
                        FirstLocal: IdentifierEntry;
                        TypeChain: TypeEntry;
                        EnclosingScope: Scope
                     END
```

NewType then creates a new type descriptor, fills it with a set of default attributes for the required type form, and places the new descriptor at the head of the local type descriptor chain.

Upon completion of compilation of a block, as indicated by a call of *CloseScope*, the storage used by the local binary tree of identifier records and the type descriptor chain entries must be released. This is readily expressed as

```
PROCEDURE CloseScope;
    VAR OldScope: Scope;
    BEGIN
```

```
    OldScope := LocalScope;
    LocalScope := LocalScope^.EnclosingScope;
    WITH OldScope^ DO
        Dispose of local IdRecords(FirstLocal);
        Dispose of local TypeRecords(TypeChain)
    END;
    Host.Dispose(OldScope)
END CloseScope
```

A simple recursive procedure may be programmed to dispose of the nodes of the binary
tree.

13.4   Programming the semantic analyzer

Having chosen a representation for identifiers and their attributes, as well as type
descriptors, and then defined a table module to maintain them, we may easily add to the
existing syntax analyzer framework the additional coding necessary to carry out semantic
analysis.

Scope housekeeping is achieved simply by calling *OpenScope* and *CloseScope* as
the first and last actions, respectively, within the block analysis procedure *Block*. The
built-in types and identifiers which are provided for every Model program are
implemented by further calls of *OpenScope* and *CloseScope* within the program
analysis procedure *Programme*, and creating appropriate entries for the standard types
and identifiers before program analysis begins, thus

```
PROCEDURE Programme;

    PROCEDURE Block( ... );
        BEGIN
            OpenScope;
            ...
            CloseScope
        END Block;

    VAR Entry: IdentifierEntry;

    BEGIN (* Programme *)
        OpenScope;
        NewType(IntegerType, Scalars);
        NewId("INTEGER ", Entry, Types);
        Entry^.IdType := IntegerType;
        NewType(BooleanType, Scalars);
        NewId("BOOLEAN", Entry, Types);
        ...
        NewId("FALSE   ", Entry, Constants);
        Entry^.IdType := BooleanType;
        ...
        Accept(Program);
```

```
        ...
        Block(...);
        ...
        CloseScope
    END Programme
```

where

```
    VAR IntegerType, BooleanType, CharType: TypeEntry;
```

The identifier and type descriptors resulting from this initialization are shown in Figure 13.2.

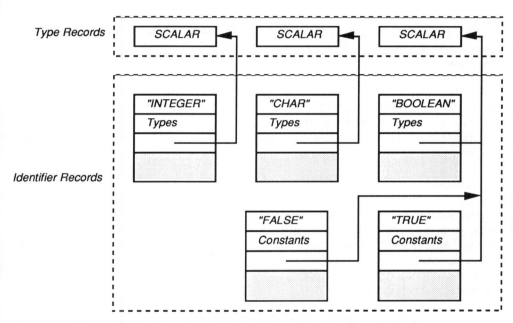

Figure 13.2 *Descriptors for Model standard types and identifiers*

The pointer-variables *IntegerType, BooleanType* and *CharType* are used throughout the semantic analyzer for type checking purposes.

Within the procedure *StatementPart* the attributes of identifiers denoting variables, constants or procedures are obtained by calls to *SearchId*. Thereafter semantic analysis involves a copying and comparison of *TypeEntry* values which represent the types of the variables, operands and expressions occurring within statements. By extending each syntax procedure which recognizes a typed construct (*Variable, Expression*, etc.) with an additional parameter through which it returns the type descriptor reference for the construct scanned, the transmission of type information between procedures is neatly and securely programmed.

For example, the syntax recognizer procedure *Assignment*, extended with semantic checks, becomes

```
PROCEDURE Assignment;
    VAR VariableType, ExpressionType: TypeEntry;
    BEGIN
        Variable(..., VariableType);
        Accept(Becomes);
        Expression(..., ExpressionType);
        IF NOT Table.Compatible(VariableType, ExpressionType) THEN
            SemanticError(...)
        END
    END Assignment
```

The *Table* predicate (i.e. Boolean function) *Compatible* is one needed throughout the semantic analysis code. How should it be defined? Clearly the Model types denoted by two *TypeEntry* values are compatible:

(a) if they reference the same type descriptor (i.e. the pointers are equal), or
(b) if they reference distinct type descriptors which describe array-types with the same bounds and element-types (this is known as *structural equivalence*—some languages, including Modula-2, do not consider structurally equivalent types to be compatible).

Situations may arise, however, due to some preceding error in the program, in which the type of some data item is in doubt or is unknown. As we saw in Chapter 12, error recovery requires that an unknown type should be regarded as compatible with any other type, to avoid unnecessary semantic error messages. By including this tolerance of unknown types within the function *Compatible*, repeated screening against the effects of previous errors can be avoided in this case.

In the Model compiler unknown types are denoted by a further extension to the *Table* interface, an exported function

```
PROCEDURE Undefined(Type: TypeEntry): BOOLEAN;
```

which determines whether a type descriptor pointer *Type* denotes an unknown type (a type descriptor pointer-variable may be made to denote an unknown type by means of a call of another *Table* function *SetUndefined*). Internally, *Table* defines a reference to an unknown type to have the value *NIL* and so the appropriate definition for the function *Compatible* has the following recursive form:

```
PROCEDURE Compatible(Type1, Type2: TypeEntry): BOOLEAN;
    BEGIN
        IF Type1 = Type2 THEN RETURN TRUE
        ELSIF (Type1 = NIL) OR (Type2 = NIL) THEN RETURN TRUE
        ELSIF (Type1^.Form = Arrays) AND (Type2^.Form = Arrays) THEN
            RETURN (Type1^.IndexMin = Type2^.IndexMin) AND
```

```
                    (Type1^.IndexMax = Type2^.IndexMax) AND
                    Compatible(Type1^.ElementType, Type2^.ElementType)
        ELSE RETURN FALSE
        END
    END Compatible;
```

With this function the semantic analysis required in the remainder of the analyzer is easily added to the existing syntax analyzer. For example, the *Factor* recognizer, with the addition of semantic analysis actions, becomes

```
PROCEDURE Factor(Followers: SymbolSet; VAR FactorType: TypeEntry);
    VAR   OK: BOOLEAN; FirstIdentifier: IdentifierEntry;
    BEGIN
        CheckForStarter(FactorStarters, Followers, OK);
        IF OK THEN
            WITH SymbolDescription DO
                CASE Symbol OF
                | Identifier:
                    SearchId(Spelling, FirstIdentifier,  IdClassSet{Variables, Constants});
                    CASE FirstIdentifier^.Class OF
                    | Constants:
                        FactorType := FirstIdentifier^.IdType; Accept(Identifier)
                    | Variables:
                        Variable(Followers, FactorType);
                    END
                | IntegerNumber:
                    FactorType := IntegerType; Accept(IntegerNumber)
                | CharConstant:
                    FactorType := CharType; Accept(CharConstant)
                | LeftParenthesis:
                    Accept(LeftParenthesis);
                    Expression(Followers + {RightParenthesis}, FactorType);
                    Accept(RightParenthesis)
                | Not:
                    Accept(Not); Factor(Followers, FactorType);
                    IF NOT Compatible(FactorType, BooleanType) THEN
                        SemanticError(63)
                    END;
                    FactorType := BooleanType
                END
            END;
            FindFollower(Followers)
        ELSE
            SetUndefined(FactorType)
        END
    END Factor;
```

The semantic analysis checks associated with loop- and exit-statements require the use of a variable

```
VAR CurrentLoopCount: CARDINAL;
```

declared local to the *StatementPart* recognizer, which is used to record the number of loop-statements enclosing the current analysis point in the source program. Each entry to (and exit from) a loop-statement must cause *CurrentLoopCount* to be incremented (and decremented), thus

```
PROCEDURE LoopStatement;
   BEGIN
      INC(CurrentLoopCount);
      Accept(Loop); StatementSequence(Followers + {End}); Accept(End);
      DEC(CurrentLoopCount)
END LoopStatement;
```

Upon encountering an exit-statement, it is necessary to check the value of *CurrentLoopCount*:

```
PROCEDURE ExitStatement;
   BEGIN
      Accept(Exit);
      IF CurrentLoopCount = 0 THEN SemanticError(...) END
   END ExitStatement;
```

For case-statements it is necessary to check that any given case label occurs in at most one case label list within the case-statement. This necessitates the construction, by the case-statement analyzer, of a list of all those case labels which occur in the case-statement under analysis. A case label may be an explicit integer constant or character constant (in which case its value is obtained from the lexical analyzer) or it may be a constant-identifier (in which case its value must be extracted from its entry in the semantic table). The case-statement recognizer makes use of the following procedure which ascertains the type and value of the current symbol whenever it is known to be a case label:

```
PROCEDURE CaseLabel(VAR CaseLabelType: TypeEntry;
                    VAR CaseLabelValue: Target.Integer);
   VAR ConstantIdentifier: IdentifierEntry;
   BEGIN
      WITH SymbolDescription DO
         IF Symbol = IntegerNumber THEN
            CaseLabelType := IntegerType; CaseLabelValue := IntValue
         ELSIF Symbol = CharConstant THEN
            CaseLabelType := CharType; CaseLabelValue := CharValue
         ELSIF Symbol = Identifier THEN
            SearchId(Spelling, ConstantIdentifier, IdClassSet{Constants});
            WITH ConstantIdentifier^ DO
               CaseLabelType := IdType; CaseLabelValue := ConstantValue
            END
         ELSE SetUndefined(CaseLabelType)
         END
      END
   END CaseLabel;
```

The case-statement and for-statement recognizers are required to check that the values of their selector-expressions and control-variables, respectively, are of ordinal-types. Thus we augment the *Table* interface with an additional function:

PROCEDURE IsOrdinalType(Type: TypeEntry): BOOLEAN;

which is used to perform these checks.

Appendix 9 gives a complete listing of the syntax analyzer which has been augmented with semantic analysis actions. The testing of this analyzer again requires the use of a carefully chosen sequence of test programs to verify the analyser's correct behaviour over the range of possible semantic errors and recovery.

13.5   Further reading

For further examples of the implementation of semantic error analysis in complete recursive descent compilers, the reader should consult Brinch Hansen (1985), Wirth (1981), Tremblay and Sorenson (1982) and Pemberton and Daniels (1982).

The semantic error recovery techniques used in the Model compiler for handling re-declarations and misuses of identifiers were introduced in Welsh and McKeag (1980). Their application to a language with a wider range of identifier classes can be seen in the Pascal compiler of Welsh and Hay (1986).

Exercises 13

13.1 Amend the semantic table module of the Model compiler so that it exports a procedure which, when called, will output (in a suitable format) the average number of identifier entries inspected per search (the *search ratio*) so far during analysis of a program. Devise a suitable test driver module and a suitable Model test program, and then establish the search ratio for analysis of your Model program.

13.2 Replace the existing binary tree organization of the semantic table identifier entries in the Model compiler by an unsorted linear list organization. Using the procedure developed in Exercise 13.1, remeasure the search ratio for your Model test program.

13.3 Replace the existing binary tree organization of the semantic table identifier entries in the Model compiler by a suitable hash table organization. Remeasure the search ratio for your Model test program.

13.4 Extend the *multiple-assignment-statement* analyzer developed in Exercise 10.2 to include appropriate semantic analysis and semantic error recovery actions.

13.5 Extend the Model semantic analyzer to include versions of the *repeat-statement* and *while-statement* recognizers developed in Exercise 10.3 which are extended with suitable semantic analysis and semantic error recovery actions.

13.6 Extend the Modula-2 *if-statement* recognizer developed in Exercise 10.4 to include suitable semantic analysis and semantic error recovery actions.

Chapter 14

The code generation interface

In this chapter an interface is developed which enables object code generation actions to be embedded within the analyzer as a set of procedure calls. These calls denote operations on a hypothetical machine and, together with the types which underlie their parameters, provide a generation interface which is independent of the precise object code to be generated by the Model compiler. The code generator itself performs the task of transforming these interface operations into equivalent object code sequences for the chosen target machine. This process is described for the Target computer in Chapters 16 to 18.

14.1 A hypothetical machine

The compilation process was previously split between analyzer and generator modules thus:

analyzer (character stream) (errors, analyzed program)
generator (analyzed program) (object code)

where *analyzed program* is some representation of the program being compiled which enables the generator to produce equivalent object code. The motive in rigidly enforcing this split was to isolate the machine-dependent and object-code-dependent aspects of the compilation process, thereby facilitating adaptation of the compiler to a variety of object codes and/or machines. It follows that the interface, the analyzed program, must be such that

- no features peculiar to any particular object code or machine are implied, and
- generation of any particular object code can be achieved without additional knowledge of, or access to, the internal functioning and data of the analyzer.

A commonly used technique in such situations is to define a *hypothetical machine* whose features are those convenient for execution of programs of the source language, but which can be readily realized in whatever object code and hardware environment is actually selected. The action of the analyzer is then to translate the source program into an equivalent sequence of operations, or program, for the hypothetical machine. The generator's task is to translate this sequence of operations into whatever object code form is required for the chosen target machine.

In principle the analysis and generation actions may take place either in sequence or in parallel. In sequential mode the analyzer must create and 'output' the entire sequence of hypothetical operations for subsequent input to the generator. In parallel mode the analyzer need only signal each hypothetical operation; the generator then acts immediately to translate this operation into an equivalent object code sequence. In practice, however, the analyzer need not be aware of which mode is in use, since it may in either case transfer the hypothetical operation by a *procedure call*, whose effect may either be to file the operation for subsequent translation, or to translate it immediately.

The general interface is thus a group of procedures, calls of each of which correspond to a hypothetical machine operation and are independent of the nature of the precise object code to be generated ultimately. The analyzed program consists of a sequence of such procedure calls. Our next task is to determine the range of hypothetical operations, and hence procedure calls, required. We note, however, that the term 'operation' must be interpreted loosely, since the interface must cover all aspects of program generation—such static operations as determining data representations and data storage as well as the dynamic operations required in program execution.

14.2   Data representation and storage

On any machine which is to execute a program, a means of representing the data items which the program manipulates must first be determined. For a simple typed language such as Model, all items of a given type share a common form of representation. The generator must determine, therefore, a representation within the object program for each type in the source program. To denote these representations a type

```
TYPE TypeRepresentation = ...;
```

is introduced within the generator, whose form will depend on the particular object machine involved. A value of this type must be created by the generator for each Model type encountered in the program being compiled. This value describes how items of the type are to be represented on the object machine. Although the analyzer should not have any understanding of type representations as such, it can be used to maintain the association between types and their representations—by requesting from the generator some indication of the representation for a type when the type is created, and supplying this representation each time an item of the type is to be manipulated. If the analyzer and the generator run in parallel, the representation details themselves may be passed to and fro in this way. If they run in sequence, then the 'representation' given to the analyzer may just be an index to the actual details to be created at generation time.

The generator makes representations available in two ways. For the built-in types *INTEGER, CHAR, BOOLEAN* corresponding built-in representations in the generator are assumed, and thus the generation interface includes the following variables:

```
VAR  BooleanRepresentation,
       CharRepresentation, IntegerRepresentation: TypeRepresentation;
```

For array-types the generator will construct a representation on request, given the array-type's index range and the representation of its elements, through a call to the procedure

```
PROCEDURE ArrayRepresentation(BoundMin, BoundMax: Target.Integer;
                    ElementRepresentation: TypeRepresentation;
                    VAR Representation: TypeRepresentation);
```

Thus, the array-type definition

```
VAR ...: ARRAY [1..10] OF CHAR;
```

gives rise to the call

```
ArrayRepresentation(1, 10, CharRepresentation, representation of the type)
```

Individual data items within a source program require storage locations in the object program which will hold their associated values during execution of the program. Hence, the generator must also determine these storage locations. It is assumed that these locations are specified within the generator as values of a type

```
TYPE RunTimeAddress = ...;
```

whose details again depend on the storage structure and organization of the particular object machine.

The analyzer must maintain the association between variables and their run-time addresses. Thus, when processing variable-declarations the analyzer must request a run-time address for each variable through a call to the procedure

```
PROCEDURE AddressFor(Representation: TypeRepresentation;
                    VAR Address: RunTimeAddress);
```

The variable-declaration-part

```
VAR B: BOOLEAN; C: INTEGER;
```

gives rise to the following pair of generator calls:

```
AddressFor(BooleanRepresentation, address for B )
```

AddressFor(IntegerRepresentation, *address for C*)

Block-structured languages permit the sharing of storage used by variables since the lifetime of variables declared within a block is that of the block itself, i.e. the variables of a procedure exist only for the duration of a call of that procedure. Recursive execution of a block requires that one set of variables for that block exists for each instance of the block that is in existence at any time. Hence, to enable the generator to exploit this store sharing which block structure allows, and to implement recursion correctly, the analyzer must also signal this block structure to the generator. Thus we may consider the overall storage organization for a program to consist of a collection of storage areas, or *frames*, one frame for each variable space currently in existence, The signalling of the block structure is carried out by calls to procedures

```
PROCEDURE OpenFrame;
PROCEDURE CloseFrame;
```

which are made on commencing the analysis of a block, and completing that analysis, respectively. These calls occur at the same analysis points as the calls of *OpenScope* and *CloseScope*, since the storage frames are simply the run-time structures which correspond to the collections of variables declared in a particular scope. Within each matching pair of calls of *OpenFrame* and *CloseFrame* all storage addresses will be allocated in the storage frame associated with the bracketed block.

14.3   Variables, expressions and assignments

For variable access, expression evaluation and assignment the hypothetical machine is assumed to use an *evaluation stack*, the operands in which are either *references* (to storage locations) or *values*. The stack manipulation operations are transmitted by the analyzer as sequences in *postfix form* (see Chapter 6) in which operations to stack operands are followed by the operation to be performed on these operands. Variable access is represented by calls to the following procedures:

```
PROCEDURE StackReference(Location: RunTimeAddress);
```

StackReference is the basic operation for generating a reference to a variable (i.e. an operand address) and pushes the reference onto the evaluation stack.

```
PROCEDURE IndexedReference(BoundMin, BoundMax: Target.Integer;
                          ElementRepresentation: TypeRepresentation);
```

IndexedReference combines an array-variable reference (next to top of the stack) with the value of an index-expression (on top of the stack), to produce a reference to the indexed array element (which is pushed back onto the stack). For example, given the declaration

```
VAR A: ARRAY [2..20] OF CHAR
```

a variable access of the form

```
A[i]
```

would generate the following sequence of interface calls:

```
StackReference(address of A )
...stack value of i...
IndexedReference(2, 20, CharRepresentation,
                 representation of ARRAY [2..20] OF CHAR )
```

A call of the following procedure pops a reference from the evaluation stack and pushes the value of the variable so referenced:

```
PROCEDURE Dereference(Representation: TypeRepresentation);
```

Explicit constants are stacked by means of calls of

```
PROCEDURE StackConstant(ConstantValue: Target.Integer;
                        ConstantRepresentation: TypeRepresentation);
```

which pushes the given constant value with representation *ConstantRepresentation* onto the evaluation stack.

Operand values on the evaluation stack may be removed from the top of the stack and modified or combined by a variety of operations which produce new operands on the stack. The range of possible arithmetic operations is representable as the corresponding subrange of the language symbols defined by the type *LexicalAnalyzer.SymbolType*, thus

```
TYPE OperatorType = [Not..Equals];
```

and the corresponding integer arithmetic postfix operations on the hypothetical machine are then representable as calls to the procedures:

```
PROCEDURE NegateInteger;
```

which negates the topmost (integer value) on the stack, and

```
PROCEDURE BinaryIntegerOperation(Operator: OperatorType);
```

which pops the topmost two values from the stack, applies the required operator (which denotes one of +, −, * or *DIV*) and pushes the result back onto the stack. Thus, the integer-expression

```
−I+J*4
```

would involve the following sequence of calls:

```
StackReference(address of I )
Dereference(IntegerRepresentation)
NegateInteger
StackReference(address of J )
Dereference(IntegerRepresentation)
StackConstant(4, IntegerRepresentation)
BinaryIntegerOperation(Times)
BinaryIntegerOperation(Plus)
```

Boolean arithmetic is performed by means of calls of the following procedures:

```
PROCEDURE NegateBoolean;
```

which inverts the (Boolean) value on top of the stack, and

```
PROCEDURE BinaryBooleanOperation(Operator: OperatorType);
```

which pops two Boolean values from the stack, applies the required operation (*AND* or *OR*) to the values, and pushes back the result. The expression

```
A AND NOT B OR C
```

generates the corresponding interface sequence

```
StackReference(address of A)
Dereference(BooleanRepresentation)
StackReference(address of B)
Dereference(BooleanRepresentation)
NegateBoolean
BinaryBooleanOperation(And)
StackReference(address of C)
Dereference(BooleanRepresentation)
BinaryBooleanOperation(Or)
```

```
PROCEDURE Comparison(Operator: OperatorType);
```

applies the given relational operator $<$, $<=$, $=$, $<>$, $>$, or $>=$ to the two values on top of the stack and replaces them with the Boolean result of applying the operator to them.

An assignment operation is expressed as a postfix operation which assumes that the reference to the variable being assigned and the value of the expression being assigned have already been stacked. It is representable as a call of the procedure

```
PROCEDURE Assign;
```

Thus, the sequence of hypothetical operations, or procedure calls, resulting from the

Model assignment-statement

    A := B + 4

would be as follows:

    StackReference(*address of A*);
    StackReference(*address of B*);
    Dereference(IntegerRepresentation);
    StackConstant(4, IntegerRepresentation);
    BinaryIntegerOperation(Plus);
    Assign

14.4 Input and output operations

For input and output operations the hypothetical machine is assumed to have an input channel and an output channel, both of which may be operated in either character or integer mode:

    TYPE IOMode = (CharMode, IntegerMode);

Input and output operations to and from the evaluation stack are then represented by calls to the procedures

    PROCEDURE ReadOperation(ReadMode: IOMode);
    PROCEDURE WriteOperation(WriteMode: IOMode);

The effect of a call of *ReadOperation* is to read from the input channel a value according to the chosen mode of operation of the channel and push it on top of the evaluation stack. *WriteOperation* pops a value from the stack and outputs it to the output channel in the form appropriate to the stated mode of operation of the channel.

   Thus the sequence of hypothetical machine operations resulting from the Model read-statement

    READ(A)

is equivalent to that of an assignment operation in which the input value is pushed onto the evaluation stack by means of a *ReadOperation*, and is as follows:

    StackReference(*address of A*);
    ReadOperation(IntegerMode);
    Assign

and the sequence of hypothetical operations resulting from the Model write-statement

    WRITE (A*3)

would be:

```
StackReference(address of A);
Dereference(IntegerRepresentation);
StackConstant(3, IntegerRepresentation)
BinaryIntegerOperation(Times)
WriteOperation(IntegerMode)
```

14.5   Sequence control operations

The object code generated, whatever its form, is assumed to be executed in the order of its generation except where explicit control operations intervene. The code generated for the hypothetical machine can therefore be modelled as a series of code sequences, each of which can be entered either sequentially from its predecessor, or by an explicit transfer of control to a label at its head.

To represent each label the generator provides a type

```
TYPE CodeLabel = ...;
```

Variables of this type can be used by the analyzer to identify labelled points in the code sequence under generation. Binding of these variables to the appropriate points in the actual sequence under generation is enabled by three generator procedures:

```
PROCEDURE NewCodeLabel(VAR Sequence: CodeLabel);
PROCEDURE FutureCodeLabel(VAR Sequence: CodeLabel);
PROCEDURE ExpectedCodeLabel(VAR Sequence: CodeLabel);
```

The first is used for labels that are bound before they are referenced by any control operations (i.e. *backward* jumps). *FutureCodeLabel* is used to announce a code label which is referenced (by some control operation) before the code which it labels has been generated, and *ExpectedCodeLabel* is used to bind such a label when this code is eventually generated (i.e. they enable *forward* jumps).

With this code labelling facility the control operations necessary to support Model's if-statements and loop-statements can be expressed as calls of procedures:

```
PROCEDURE Jump(VAR Destination: CodeLabel);
PROCEDURE JumpOnFalse(VAR Destination: CodeLabel);
```

The first operation represents an unconditional jump, while the second represents a jump conditional on the (Boolean) value on the top of the evaluation stack (which is popped from the stack). Thus, the sequence of interface calls arising from a loop-statement of the form

```
LOOP S END
```

involves the introduction of an analyzer-defined code label variable ($L1$, say) as follows:

```
NewCodeLabel(L1)
...code for statement-sequence S...
Jump(L1)
```

An if-statement

```
IF e THEN S END
```

generates the following sequence using an analyzer-defined code label *L2*, say:

```
...code to evaluate expression e...
FutureCodeLabel(L2)
JumpOnFalse(L2)
...code for statement-sequence S...
ExpectedCodeLabel(L2)
```

An exit-statement must occur within a textually enclosing loop-statement, e.g.

```
LOOP ... EXIT ... END
```

in which case the required hypothetical machine operations involve two code labels (*L3* and *L4*, say) and take the form

```
NewCodeLabel(L3)
FutureCodeLabel(L4)
...
Jump(L4)                        code for the exit-statement
...
Jump(L3)
ExpectedCodeLabel(L4)
```

The hypothetical machine provides some additional operations to support the more complex control actions associated with case-statements and for-statements. The interface operation

```
PROCEDURE OpenCase;
```

is called immediately following evaluation of the case selector expression. The analyzer must signal each label in a case-limb by a call of

```
PROCEDURE NextIsCase(CaseLabel: Target.Integer);
```

and, following the analysis of the final case-limb, a call must be made of

```
PROCEDURE CloseCase;
```

Also, a future code label is required to label the code of the statement immediately following the case-statement—each case-limb must be followed by a jump to this code label. Thus, a case-statement of the form

```
CASE K OF
| 1: S1
| 3, 2, 4: S2
...
END
```

generates an interface call sequence as follows:

```
...stack value of K...
FutureCodeLabel(AfterCase)
OpenCase

NextIsCase(1)

...code for statement-sequence S1...
Jump(AfterCase)

NextIsCase(3)
NextIsCase(2)
NextIsCase(4)
...code for statement-sequence S2...
Jump(AfterCase)

...
CloseCase
ExpectedCodeLabel(AfterCase)
```

The following special operations are provided for handling for-statements and are used to bracket the interface calls of the statement-sequence controlled by a for-statement:

```
PROCEDURE OpenFor;
PROCEDURE CloseFor;
```

The for-statement

```
FOR K := 1 TO 10 DO S END
```

involves the following interface calls:

```
StackReference(address of K )
...stack value of expression e1...
...stack value of expression e2...
OpenFor
...code for statement-sequence S...
CloseFor
```

14.6   Procedures

Besides a simple transfer of control, procedure calls in a block-structured language involve housekeeping activity to maintain variable access. To represent the information necessary to support a procedure call, the generator provides a type

```
TYPE ProcedureLinkage = ...;
```

a value of which must be associated with each procedure in the program. The analyzer must request this *linkage* at the point of declaration of a procedure, by a call of

```
PROCEDURE NewLinkage(VAR Linkage: ProcedureLinkage);
```

and must supply this linkage in translating each call of the procedure into the hypothetical operation

```
PROCEDURE CallProcedure(VAR Linkage: ProcedureLinkage);
```

Besides the calling sequence, procedure activation also requires some entry and exit code to be located at the beginning and end of the procedure's code body. This can be represented as additional hypothetical operations

```
PROCEDURE EnterBody(VAR Linkage: ProcedureLinkage);
PROCEDURE LeaveBody(VAR Linkage: ProcedureLinkage);
```

The corresponding entry and exit code required for the execution of the main program body itself can be similarly represented as calls of

```
PROCEDURE EnterProgram;
PROCEDURE LeaveProgram;
```

For the Model program structure below, the code generation actions associated with procedure call, entry and exit are shown on the right. *p* and *q* denote references to the identifier-table entries associated with the procedure identifiers *P* and *Q*, respectively.

PROCEDURE P;	Generator.NewLinkage(*linkage for P*)
PROCEDURE Q;	Generator.NewLinkage(*linkage for Q*)
BEGIN (* Q *)	Generator.EnterBody(*linkage for Q*)
...	
Q;	Generator.CallProcedure(*linkage for Q*)
...	
END Q;	Generator.LeaveBody(*linkage for Q*)
BEGIN (*P *)	Generator.EnterBody(*linkage for P*)
...	
Q;	Generator.CallProcedure(*linkage for Q*)
...	

END P;	Generator.LeaveBody(*linkage for P*)
BEGIN (* main program *)	Generator.EnterProgram
...	
END.	Generator.LeaveProgram

These operations complete the range of hypothetical operations necessary for the execution of Model programs. A summary of the complete generation interface which they define is given in Appendix 10.

14.7   Using the interface

After definition of the code generation interface, the incorporation of its use within the existing analyzer is easily accomplished.

Storage of the various additional code generation attributes (i.e. type representations, run-time addresses, procedure linkages and constant values) which the analyzer must associate with types, procedures, variables and constant-identifiers is readily achieved by the extension of the type and identifier records within the semantic table as follows:

```
TYPE TypeRecord = RECORD
                    Next: TypeEntry;
                    Representation: Generator.TypeRepresentation;
                    CASE Form: TypeClass OF
                    | Arrays:  IndexMin, IndexMax: Target.Integer;
                               ElementType: TypeEntry
                    | Scalars:
                    END
                  END;

     IdRecord = RECORD
                    Name: Word;
                    LeftLink, RightLink: IdentifierEntry;
                    IdType: TypeEntry;
                    CASE Class: IdentifierClass OF
                    | Constants:   ConstantValue: Target.Integer;
                    | Variables:   VariableAddress: Generator.RunTimeAddress;
                    | Procedures:  Linkage: Generator.ProcedureLinkage
                    END
                  END
```

The revised form of the semantic table is given in Appendix 11.

The generation and assignment of values to these additional attributes are then coded as generator calls within the analyser's variable-declaration and procedure-declaration recognizers which create the type and identifier records themselves. Generation of hypothetical machine operations for the various statement forms of the language is easily achieved, simply by inserting appropriate code generation interface calls at points in the existing analyzer recognizer procedures—these points are illustrated by the sample sequences given in the previous sub-sections.

Thereafter, generation of object code for the statement-parts of the program being analyzed is easily added at appropriate points in the analyzer code.

For example, the assignment-statement analyzer is trivially extended to become

```
PROCEDURE Assignment;
    VAR VariableType, ExpressionType: TypeEntry;
    BEGIN
        Variable(..., VariableType);
        Accept(Becomes);
        Expression(..., ExpressionType);
        IF NOT Compatible(VariableType, ExpressionType) THEN
            SemanticError(...)
        ELSE Generator.Assign
        END;
    END Assignment
```

The use of code labels to generate the necessary control structure in the object code is well illustrated by the if-statement analyzer, which in its final form is as follows:

```
PROCEDURE IfStatement;
    VAR  ExpressionType: TypeEntry;
             AfterTrueAction, AfterFalseAction: Generator.CodeLabel;
    BEGIN
        Accept(If);
        Expression(Followers+{Then, Else, End}, ExpressionType);
        IF NOT Compatible(ExpressionType, BooleanType) THEN
            SemanticError(69)
        END;
        Generator.FutureCodeLabel(AfterTrueAction);
        Generator.JumpOnFalse(AfterTrueAction);
        Accept(Then);
        StatementSequence(Followers+{Else, End});
        IF SymbolDescription.Symbol = Else THEN
            Generator.FutureCodeLabel(AfterFalseAction);
            Generator.Jump(AfterFalseAction);
            Generator.ExpectedCodeLabel(AfterTrueAction);
            Accept(Else);
            StatementSequence(Followers+{End});
            Generator.ExpectedCodeLabel(AfterFalseAction)
        ELSE
            Generator.ExpectedCodeLabel(AfterTrueAction)
        END;
        Accept(End)
    END IfStatement;
```

This coding illustrates one remaining problem with the interface. Can an error during the call to *Expression* sabotage the subsequent generator call *JumpOnFalse* by failing to generate a code sequence whose execution will leave a Boolean result on top of the evaluation stack? More generally, can analysis of an erroneous program produce a malformed sequence of hypothetical operations with which the generator cannot cope? Obviously it can, and possible solutions to the problem are

- to guard against the generation of malformed sequences within the analyzer, or
- to detect and ignore malformed sequences within the generator.

Various complicated ways of implementing either of these strategies can be conceived, but a simpler expedient adopted in many compilers is to suppress code generation permanently at the occurrence of the first error. With the form of interface chosen it is easier to make this suppression test within the generator, and so we extend the interface with one further procedure:

```
PROCEDURE NoFurtherCode;
```

which the analyzer will call on detecting any syntax or semantic error.

When executed, an exit-statement must cause termination of execution of the immediately enclosing loop-statement with the program. We saw previously the form of the generator calls required to effect such an exit. However, since loop-statements may be arbitrarily nested, for generation of the correct exit-statement *Jump* operation it is necessary, during the analysis of the statement-part of a block, to maintain details of the code label for the end of each enclosing loop-statement. This information is held in a loop descriptor of the form

```
TYPE LoopEntry = POINTER TO LoopRecord;
     LoopRecord = RECORD
                    EndOfLoop: Generator.CodeLabel;
                    EnclosingLoop: LoopEntry
                  END;

VAR  CurrentLoop: LoopEntry;
```

where these descriptors must be organized as a stack within the analyzer (and it is no longer necessary to retain the analyser's depth of nesting counter *CurrentLoopCount*). Hence, on commencing analysis of a loop-statement a new descriptor must be pushed onto this stack and its code label field *EndOfLoop* bound by means of a *FutureCodeLabel* operation. On completion of the loop-statement analysis this label is bound by an *ExpectedCodeLabel* operation and the associated loop descriptor is then popped from the loop descriptor stack.

```
PROCEDURE LoopStatement;
   VAR StartOfThisLoop: Generator.CodeLabel;
   BEGIN
      create a new loop descriptor;
      Generator.NewCodeLabel(StartOfThisLoop);
      Generator.FutureCodeLabel(CurrentLoop^.EndOfLoop);
      Accept(Loop);
      StatementSequence(Followers+{End});
```

```
        Accept(End);
        Generator.Jump(StartOfThisLoop);
        Generator.ExpectedCodeLabel(CurrentLoop^.EndOfLoop);
        destroy the topmost loop descriptor
    END LoopStatement;
```

An exit-statement thus obtains the appropriate destination code label from the topmost entry in the loop descriptor stack, viz.

```
    PROCEDURE ExitStatement;
        BEGIN
            Accept(Exit);
            IF CurrentLoop <> NIL THEN Generator.Jump(CurrentLoop^.EndOfLoop)
            ELSE SemanticError(72)
            END
        END ExitStatement;
```

A complete listing of the final augmented analyzer with all its generator calls is given in Appendix 12.

14.8 Further reading

The hypothetical machine developed in this chapter is based upon the interface used in the MiniPascal compiler of Welsh and McKeag (1980). A more comprehensive interface which supports a wider range of data-types, parameters, file handling and dynamic storage allocation is used in the Pascal compiler of Welsh and Hay (1986). A further extension of the interface to support concurrent process execution was developed for the Pascal Plus language of Welsh and Bustard (1979), an extension of Pascal which provides concurrent programming features.

Probably the best known code generation interface is that provided by the P-machine (Nori et al., 1981), a hypothetical stack-based machine with a much lower-level instruction set than that of the machine described in this chapter. Its operations are designed to support Pascal programs and many compilers, including Welsh and Hay (1986), generate P-code. P-code programs can be executed using a standard interpreter written in Pascal. Welsh and Hay include a complete model P-code system.

Another commonly used approach to defining the analyser's interface with the code generator is the use of abstract syntax trees 'decorated' with information relevant to code generation. The construction of such trees is described in different levels of detail in McKeeman (1976a), Watt (1993), Aho, Sethi and Ullman (1986) and Watson (1989).

Exercises 14

14.1 Determine the hypothetical machine code sequences corresponding to the following Model program fragments:

```
VAR   B: BOOLEAN; I: INTEGER;
      A: ARRAY [10..99] OF INTEGER;

B := (I > 10) OR (I <= A[I*3])

FOR I := 2 TO 8 DO READ(I) END

CASE I OF
| 1, 2, 4, 9: B := TRUE
| 3, 5, 7: B := FALSE
END
```

14.2 Modify the definition of the hypothetical machine developed in this chapter to allow generation of object code for *multiple-assignment-statements* as defined in Exercise 9.4. Extend the multiple-assignment-statement analyzer developed in Exercise 13.4 to generate the required hypothetical object code.

14.3 Extend the Model analyzer of Appendix 12 to include a version of the *repeat-statement* recognizer developed in Exercise 13.5 which is extended with suitable code generation actions.

14.4 Extend the Model analyzer of Appendix 12 to include the *repeat-statement* and *while-statement* recognizers developed in Exercise 13.5 and extended with suitable code generation actions.

14.5 Extend the Modula-2 *if-statement* recognizer developed in Exercise 13.6 to include suitable actions for the generation of object code for the hypothetical machine described in this chapter.

14.6 Indicate the structure of the hypothetical machine code that would be generated for the following Pascal program:

```
PROGRAM LabelExample2;
    LABEL 1, 2, 3;
    BEGIN
        ...
        GOTO 3;
        ...
        GOTO 1;
    2: ...
    3: ...
        GOTO 1;
        ...
        GOTO 3;
    1: ...
        GOTO 2;
        ...
    END.
```

14.7 Extend the data structure developed in Exercise 12.5 for recording the semantic attributes of labels during compilation of a program to include also the attributes necessary for generation of hypothetical machine code.

Make the necessary modifications to the label processing routines developed for Exercise 12.5 to generate correct hypothetical machine code for *goto-statements*.

Chapter 15

Forms of object code

In Chapters 16, 17 and 18 we shall consider the organization of, and access to, the storage areas associated with object programs and the generation of object code for the target machine. Although the general problems considered are independent of the exact form of the associated object code, it is nonetheless useful to distinguish among the several classes of object code generated by compilers before examining how such code itself is generated.

15.1 Absolute machine code

Figure 15.1 illustrates the structure of an *absolute machine code* program. It consists of machine code instructions whose absolute location in the final object program is completely determined by the compiler.

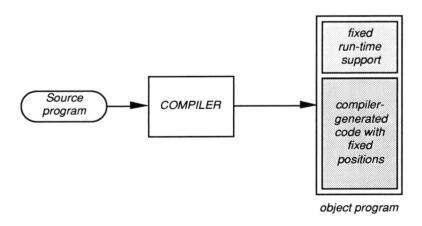

Figure 15.1 *Generation of absolute machine code programs*

The code may actually be generated in these locations by the compiler and so is immediately executable (*in-memory compilation*) or more often it is output to secondary memory, requiring only to be copied back *en bloc* into the correct memory locations to produce an immediately executable machine code program.

The object program normally contains calls to standard routines, such as input and output operations and pre-defined arithmetic functions, which are contained in a fixed *run-time support package* containing the object code of the complete set of standard routines provided by the language, whether the particular program requires them all or not.

Figure 15.2 shows the detailed structure of such an object program. The routines at addresses *RINT* and *WINT* are assumed to be integer input and output routines, respectively, which are called from within the object program (the compiler will implement calls of the language's standard input and output procedures as calls to these routines). The other routines included in the run-time support code are not shown in the diagram. The storage required by the variables of the program begins at address *VARS* and is followed by the machine code instructions for the compiled program.

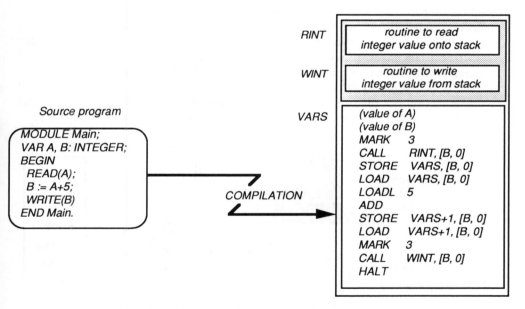

Figure 15.2 *Detail of absolute machine code program*

The principal advantage of generating absolute machine code is that it minimizes the overall time taken in the conversion of a source program to loaded executable form. Its principal disadvantage is that the entire source program must be compiled from scratch each time any part of it is altered. In addition, the object program is obviously not portable, in that it cannot be executed on a machine with a different architecture.

15.2   Relocatable object code

Most Modula-2 compilers, as well as many commercial compilers for languages such as COBOL, generate object code in the form of *relocatable object modules*. Within each such module all its static storage and instruction addresses are undetermined but are expressed as addresses relative to start addresses also as yet undetermined.

One or more relocatable object code modules are converted to an absolute object program by processes known as *linking* and *loading*. Linking is performed by a program (usually referred to as a *linker* or *link editor*) which determines the total storage required for data and instructions in the overall set of modules making up the program, as well as the start addresses of data and instruction storage for each module. The loading process (performed by a *loader* program) uses this information to 'de-relativize' all addresses within the object code as it is loaded into memory to form an absolute object program ready for execution.

The advantages of generating relocatable code modules and subsequently linking them are that individual source program modules can be pre-compiled or recompiled independently and later combined to form a complete object program by linking and loading. In particular, library routines for standard operations such as input and output transfers can be held permanently in relocatable object form and need never be compiled for incorporation in any particular object program. Source modules may also be written in different languages, provided that all the compilers for the languages concerned generate relocatable object code modules in the same format as required by the linker.

The principal disadvantage of generating relocatable code is that the linking and loading process is a time-consuming one and hence the combined compile–link–load sequence is considerably slower than the direct generation of absolute machine code.

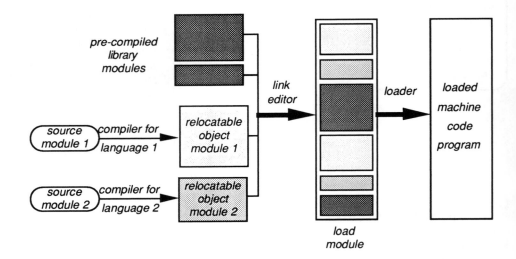

Figure 15.3 *Generation of relocatable object code programs*

Figure 15.3 shows two source modules, assumed to have been written in different programming languages, which have been converted by their respective compilers into relocatable object code modules in the same format. The input and output routines they require already exist, in relocatable format, in a library and have therefore not been included within their respective relocatable modules. The link editor then processes the four modules shown to produce a single object module (the *load module*) in secondary memory which is then ready for processing by the loader prior to its execution.

Figure 15.4 shows the detailed structure of a typical relocatable object code scheme (it is in no way definitive but is presented purely for illustrative purposes). Each module is translated by the appropriate compiler into a text file which will subsequently be read by the link editor.

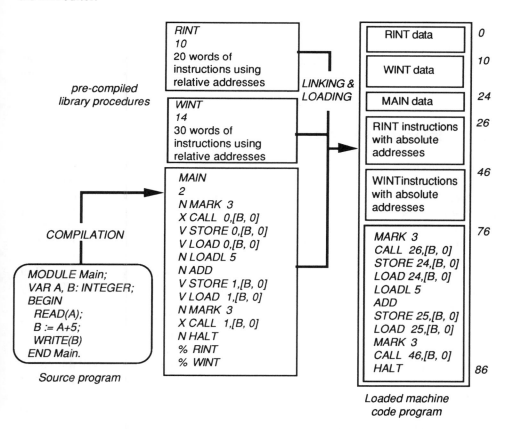

Figure 15.4 *Detail of relocatable object modules and link-editing*

Here the first line of each file contains the name of the module. The second line defines the amount of data storage required for the module. Subsequent lines contain the instructions of the object program with relative addresses used instead of absolute addresses. Each instruction is preceded by a letter indicating the required de-relativization. *N* indicates that no adjustment is required, *V* indicates that the address given is relative to the starting address of the data storage allocated to the module, and *X* means that the instruction refers to an external procedure defined in another module. The file ends with a list of lines (in this case each begins with %) naming the external procedures referenced by the module—the earlier instructions refer to these procedures according to their position in this list. Hence, in the instruction

    CALL 0, [SB, 0]

the procedure being called is *RINT*, whereas

    CALL 1, [SB, 0]

is a call of *WINT*.

Given a set of such files, the linker can determine their overall storage requirements and enable the loader to produce a final loaded program of the form suggested in Figure 15.4.

15.3   Interpretive object code

In an *interpretive object code* program the sequence of actions to be carried out by the object program is represented not by directly executable machine instructions but by *abstract interpretive operations* in some encoded form. The compiler in this case translates the source program into an object program which is expressed in terms of these abstract operations. This object program is then 'executed' by an *interpreter* program which sequences through its operations, decodes each one, and calls a corresponding routine to carry out the required executable action.

The abstract operations define an abstract machine which is usually designed to reflect the nature of the high-level language being processed. The interpreter is thus effectively a simulator for this abstract machine.

The interpreter program is usually written in a high-level language and, as shown in Figure 15.5, contains a set of routines, one for each abstract operation. In addition it contains data structures which provide a model of the architecture of the abstract machine. The semantic table generated by the compiler may also be available to the interpreter (possibly for use in generating source-related diagnostics, as discussed later in this section).

Figure 15.6 gives greater detail of the typical form of such an abstract machine code and the internal structure of the interpreter program. It is possible, for instance, to base the design of the abstract machine on that of the hypothetical machine and executable operations used as the interface between the Model analyzer and code generator in Chapter 14.

The use of an interpretive object code scheme offers significant advantages in certain circumstances and environments:

- *Ease of implementation* of the compiler—most interpretive object codes are designed to reflect the nature of the high-level language concerned and hence object programs are, in general, easy to generate.
- *Compactness* of the object program—an operation requiring several machine instructions for its execution may be encoded as a single abstract operation within a single machine word or less.
- Extensive *run-time diagnostic* facilities can be incorporated in the interpreter, but without any expansion of the object program itself—only of the interpretive routines which execute it. In particular, if the compile-time semantic table is retained through execution time, all references to variables within the object code can be indirect, via their semantic table entries, so that not only their run-time values but also their source program identifiers and type attributes are available for executable and diagnostic actions.

  Hence, if we wish to base an interpreter on the hypothetical machine developed in Chapter 14, it might be more appropriate for operations such as *StackReference* to take the corresponding variable's semantic table entry as parameter, rather than, as at present, the run-time address stored in that entry.

  Likewise, for procedure calls the procedure's semantic table entry might be passed by *CallProcedure* rather than just the linkage information stored therein. However, it would then be necessary for the compiler to retain all the semantic table entries it creates rather than disposing of entries once analysis of the block in which they are created has been completed.
- *Portability* of the language implementation—if the interpretive routines are written in a high-level language, then the object program may be executed on any computer which has an implementation of that particular language.

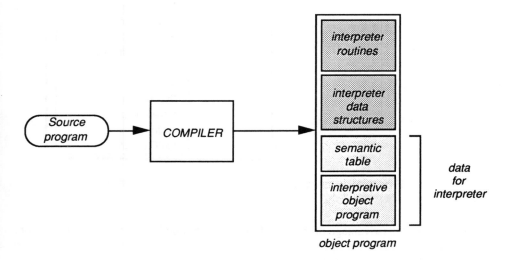

Figure 15.5 *Generation of interpretive object code*

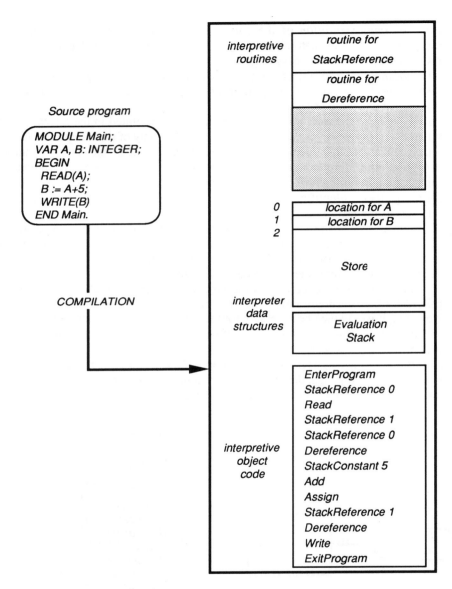

Figure 15.6 *Detail of interpretive object code programs*

The principal disadvantage of the use of interpretive code is its slowness in execution. However few diagnostic options are incorporated in the interpretive routines, the intrinsic overhead of the decode and interpret cycle itself might make it anything from 5 to 100 times slower than the equivalent absolute machine code.

Interpretive object code is used in those situations where its disadvantage in execution speed is outweighed by the range of diagnostic aids it permits. Many programming systems designed for use in teaching environments (such as the MacPascal system and Wirth's Pascal-S system) fall into this category. Many compilers for languages in the Pascal and Modula-2 family have been implemented to generate an interpretive code known as *P-code*—their object programs can then be executed by a portable P-code interpreter written in, say, Pascal. This allows an existing compiler to be made available on a new machine (for which there is already a compiler for its implementation language) and also enables the rapid development of compilers for new languages (the compiler can generate P-code object programs which can then be interpreted immediately and, if faster execution is required, a translator may be written at some later stage to translate the P-code to the required machine code or the compiler's code generator may be rewritten to generate the machine code directly).

15.4 Object code form for the Model compiler

We shall implement the code generator of the Model compiler so that it generates absolute machine code. The input and output operations, together with certain other standard operations, will be provided as part of the run-time support package which will be included in every object program generated by the Model compiler. The detailed structure of its object programs is described in Chapters 17 and 18.

Although the Target machine does not actually exist it would, of course, be possible to build it in hardware. However, we could also write an interpreter program for it so that we can actually execute the programs generated by our Model compiler in the absence of such hardware. Thus it is possible to have both a hardware processor and a software processor (an interpreter program) available for the execution of a given machine code. Although hardware processing is obviously very much faster, it can often be helpful to have a software processor available for experimentation with the design of the computer before it is actually constructed, or for incorporating diagnostic routines to assist in the development of machine code programs.

Appendix 16 contains the listing of an interpreter for the Target machine code, written in Modula-2. Those readers wishing to learn more about the construction of interpreters will find it useful to study the interpreter, while those wishing to gain experience of machine code programming might find it profitable to use the interpreter to execute their programs!

15.5 Further reading

Most books on assembly language programming contain details of absolute machine code and relocatable object program structures. Complete descriptions of P-code and the P-machine can be found in Pemberton and Daniels (1982) and Welsh and Hay (1986). An implementation of the language Concurrent Pascal is described in Hartmann (1977).

Details of interpretive codes and implementations of interpreters appear in books by Wirth (1981), Ben-Ari (1982), Brinch Hansen (1985) and Watt (1993). Although some implementations of the list processing language LISP (such as the InterLISP and MacLISP compilers) generate machine code, many other implementations generate interpretive code, as described in MacLennan (1983).

Exercises 15

15.1 Amend the Target interpreter given in Appendix 16 so that it displays a summary of the machine state following the execution of each instruction. The display should include the address registers' contents, the instruction just executed and relevant areas of the memory (e.g. the topmost stack locations).

15.2 Extend the Target interpreter given in Appendix 16 so that it supports the interactive debugging of Target programs. The user should be able to set breakpoints at given instructions and the interpreter should operate in one of two modes—either executing one instruction at a time or until the next breakpoint is reached (at which stage the machine state should be displayed as in Exercise 15.1).

Chapter 16

Data representation

In the next three chapters we consider the generation of the Target machine code program which corresponds to a given Model source program. Before we can do so, however, we must consider the problems of representing on the Target machine the data items which appear in the source program. Having done so, we must then examine how storage on the Target machine can be allocated to the variables and other data items of the source program. Since the object program produced by the code generator must reference this storage its organization must be determined before code generation can begin.

The problems of organizing the storage which is to be occupied by the object program produced by a compiler are considered in these next two chapters. Storage organization, like most aspects of compilation, is determined by the nature of the source language being compiled. It is neither possible to generalize over all languages nor, given the aims of this book, to look at the particular problems of every language. Instead we look at the problems of languages such as Ada and Modula-2.

Storage occupied by an object program is basically divided between storage for *data* and storage for the *object code instructions*. We consider first the organization of data storage. Various aspects of the organization of code storage are considered in Chapter 18.

Data storage is occupied by the run-time representations of source program variables and constants (and any housekeeping information necessary to its organization). The compiler must decide how the data-types of the source language are to be represented on the machine available. In some cases the hardware offers an obvious solution, in others the compiler must superimpose its representation on the hardware's facilities.

16.1 Unstructured data-types

For the most common unstructured data-types (usually referred to as *scalar-types*) provided in most programming languages—*Real* and *Integer*—the target computer usually offers a built-in representation and a corresponding repertoire of machine operations. Integer values are normally represented in a single computer word using either ones complement or twos complement representations to provide integer arithmetic over an implementation-defined range of negative and positive values. Real values are generally represented in a floating-point format using one or two words, again with the available hardware usually providing signed arithmetic operations over the resultant range of values.

Boolean or logical values may be represented in a single bit (*0* for *false*, *1* for *true*) although most compilers opt for the conventional representation which uses a single computer word or byte, the representations of *true* and *false* being chosen to make best use of the machine's *AND*, *OR* and *NOT* logical instructions to carry out the truth operations of conjunction, disjunction and negation. Usually *0* is used to denote *false* and a non-zero value (normally *1*) for *true*. Since most languages define the ordering of Boolean values to be such that *false* is less than *true*, the choice of *0* and *1* allows operations such as *succ* and *pred* to be implemented trivially using integer addition and subtraction.

For *character* values the hardware again offers an automatic, single byte, representation (usually in terms of the ASCII character set). On most machines it is best to use a full word for each simple character variable although packing of character sequences (*strings*) may be considered.

For *enumerated-types* the standard representation chosen by most compiler writers is to map the values, in their order of enumeration, onto the machine integers $0... N-1$, where N is the number of values, or *cardinality*, of the type. For example, given

TYPE Suit = (Club, Diamond, Heart, Spade)

the individual values will be represented by *0* for *Club*, *1* for *Diamond*, *2* for *Heart*, and *3* for *Spade*. It is in fact possible to represent any of these values in just 2 bits, i.e. $log_2(cardinality(Suit))$.

Hence, once again the *succ* and *pred* operations can be implemented by simple integer increment and decrement operations (many machines provide such operations within their instruction set), and the *ord* function again requires no physical machine operation. This similarity between the implementation of *succ*, *pred* and *ord* for the Boolean type and for enumerated-types is because, in most languages, the type *Boolean* is effectively a standard enumerated-type, viz.

TYPE Boolean = (false, true)

Conventionally, values of *subrange-types* are simply represented by giving each value the same representation as it has in the original type (known as the *host-type*). Hence transfers between subrange-types and host-types involves no physical operation. Once again, however, it is possible to represent a value whose type has an upper bound of N in M bits, where M is the smallest integer such that $M \geq 2^N$ bits.

Pointer values are merely the addresses of the storage locations occupied by the data values which they reference, or some representation of the *NIL* pointer. How they are represented thus depends on the complexity of the target machine's memory architecture and addressing scheme, although on most machines they are usually represented in one computer word. Some value which cannot possibly be a memory address (e.g. -1) is normally chosen for the *NIL* pointer value. In certain situations, however, it is necessary that a pointer also carries with it a descriptor indicating the size, in memory units, of the value which it references.

16.2 Arrays

Arrays are normally represented using blocks of contiguous memory locations, each array element occupying the number of words (*size*, say) appropriate to its type, such that the address of the location(s) corresponding to any subscript value or values is easily calculated.

16.2.1   One-dimensional arrays

The simplest case is that of a *vector* or *one-dimensional array*, e.g.

VAR A: ARRAY[M..N] OF *ElementType*

as illustrated in Figure 16.1, where it is assumed that a value of the type *ElementType* occupies *size* words.

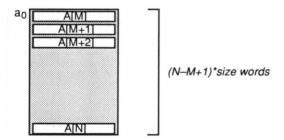

Figure 16.1 *Representation of a one-dimensional array*

Hence, the array *A* will occupy a total of *(N–M+1)*size* contiguous locations which are allocated to corresponding elements in ascending (or descending) order of subscript value. Thus, if the address of the first location of the entire array storage is a_0, then the address of the first location of *A[e]*, where *e* is an expression whose value lies in the range *[M..N]*, is given by

$$a_0 + (e-M)*size$$

which reduces to

$$b_0 + b_1 * e$$

where b_0 and b_1 are constants, such that

$$b_0 = a_0 - size * M$$
$$b_1 = size$$

Note that b_0 is effectively the address of the array element *a[0]*, even though such an element may not actually exist. However, this address is nonetheless useful to us in determining the addresses of actual array elements.

The values b_0 and b_1 are calculable at compile-time and so the compiler can generate efficient code for accessing *A[e]*, e.g. on the Target machine the instruction sequences (assuming $size \neq 1$)

```
LOADA    b0
evaluate expression e
LOADL    b1
MUL
ADD
```

or (assuming $size=1$)

```
LOADA    b0
evaluate expression e
ADD
```

leave the address of *A[e]* addressable on top of the Target machine's stack.

Notice that, if *size* is a power of *2* (and is not equal to *1*), it is more efficient to use a logical left shift instruction

```
LOADA    b0
evaluate expression e
SLL      log2 size
ADD
```

since small shift operations are usually much faster than multiplication operations on most machines.

16.2.2   Multi-dimensional arrays

For the representation of *two-dimensional arrays* there are a number of possibilities. The usual scheme is to store the elements in a contiguous storage block either row by row, or column by column.

In row-by-row storage of an array (as illustrated in Figure 16.2)

```
VAR A: ARRAY [M1..N1, M2..N2] OF ElementType
```

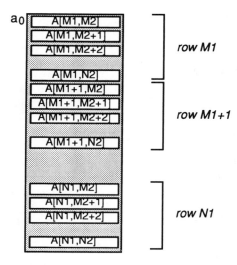

Figure 16.2 *Representation of a two-dimensional array*

the elements are held in the order

```
[M1, M2],    [M1, M2+1],   ...,[M1, N2],
[M1+1, M2], [M1+1, M2+1], ...,[M1+1, N2],
   ...
[N1, M2],    [N1, M2+1],    ...,[M2, N2]
```

and the address of *A[e₁, e₂]* (where *e₁* is a value of type *[M1..N1]* and *e₂* is a value of type *[M2..N2]*) is thus

$$a_0 + ((e_1{-}M1)*(N2{-}M2{+}1) + e_2{-}M2)*size$$

which collapses to

$$b_0 + b_1*e_1 + b_2*e_2$$

where the values b_0, b_1, b_2 can all be calculated at compile-time, i.e.

$$b_0 = a_0 - (M1*(N2{-}M2{+}1) + M2)*size$$
$$b_1 = (N2{-}M2{+}1)*size$$
$$b_2 = size$$

and so the code for loading the address of *A [e₁, e₂]* on top of the Target machine's stack takes the form

    LOADA b_0

```
        evaluate expression e1
        LOADL    b1
        MUL
        ADD
        evaluate expression e2
        LOADL    b2
        MUL
        ADD
```

or, if *size=1*, i.e. $b_2 = 1$,

```
        LOADA    b0
        evaluate expression e1
        LOADL    b1
        MUL
        evaluate expression e2
        ADD
        ADD
```

A similar address function and code format can easily be devised for column-by-column storage.

An alternative method representation of a two-dimensional array uses a separate storage block for each row and an array of pointers (an *access vector*) to these blocks. Elements of each row are held in ascending subscript order within the corresponding block, as shown in Figure 16.3.

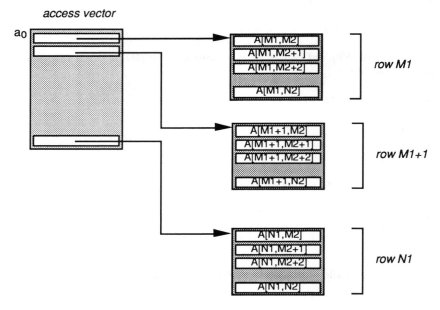

Figure 16.3 *Representation of a two-dimensional array using an access vector*

If a_0 is the address of the first location of the access vector, then the address of the element $A[e_1, e_2]$ is now given by the formula

$$contents[a_0 + e_1 - M1] + (e_2 - M2)*size$$

and the code for loading this address onto the Target stack is

```
LOADA      address (a₀–M1)
evaluate expression e₁
ADD
LOADI      1              [replace address on top of stack by contents of the address
evaluate expression e₂
LOADL      M2
SUB
LOADL      size
MUL
ADD
```

In the case where *size* = *1*, the multiplication becomes redundant and the code sequence becomes two instructions shorter.

Although it requires the additional storage associated with the access vector, there are two principal advantages of this *tree representation*:

- it reduces or eliminates the need for multiplication operations within the addressing code;
- it allows a more flexible allocation of element storage—the individual row blocks need not be contiguous with each other, or even all be in main memory at any given time.

Both of the above methods can be generalized to represent *n*-dimensional arrays—for example, the row-by-row storage of an array

VAR A: ARRAY [M1..N1, M2..N2, ..., Mn..Nn] OF *ElementType*

gives an addressing formula for $A[e_1, e_2, e_3,..., e_n]$ which reduces to

$$b_0 + b_1*e_1 + b_2*e_2 + ... + b_n*e_n$$

where, again, $b_0, b_1,..., b_n$ are calculable at compile-time so that access code of the form

```
LOADA      b₀
evaluate expression e₁
LOADL      b₁
MUL
ADD
...
```

evaluate expression e_n
LOADL b_n
MUL
ADD

can be generated.

16.2.3   Dynamic arrays

Compile-time calculation of the coefficients $b_0,..., b_n$ requires that the bounds *M1*, *N1,..., Mn, Nn* are fixed at compile-time. This is not so in languages like Ada which allow *dynamic arrays* whose bounds are not determined until run-time, e.g. in the following Ada declarations

```
type List is array(Integer range <>) of ItemType;
    L1: List (1..N)
    L2: List(M+1..N-1)
```

the bounds of the arrays *L1* and *L2* are expressed as arbitrary *expressions* involving the values of variables *M* and *N* declared in the surrounding scope(s).

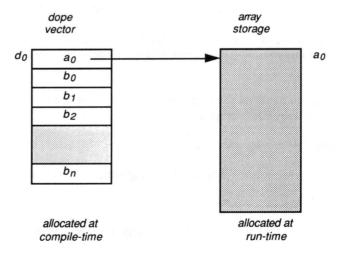

Figure 16.4 *Representation of a dynamic array*

For such arrays, storage cannot be allocated until these bounds are known, neither can the coefficients $b_0,..., b_n$ be calculated. In such languages the compiler allocates only a *dope vector* with origin address d_0, whose size is determined by the number of dimensions of the array (an *n*-dimensional array requires a dope vector of length *n+1*). At run-time, when the actual bounds are known, an *array allocation routine* is called, with the dope vector address and actual bound values as parameters, which

- calculates the amount of element storage needed;
- allocates this storage;
- calculates a corresponding set of values $b_0, \ldots, b_n$;
- stores these in the dope vector.

This routine forms part of the run-time support package in the object program (see Chapter 15). It is convenient to hold the origin address a_0 of the element storage in the dope vector as well as b_0 if the language allows operations on arrays as a whole. The representation of an *n*-dimensional dynamic array *A* is then as shown in Figure 16.4 and the corresponding access code for an array element $A[e_1, e_2, e_3, \ldots, e_n]$ is

```
LOAD        d₀+1
evaluate expression e₁
LOAD        d₀+2
MUL
ADD
...
evaluate expression eₙ
LOAD        d₀+n
MUL
ADD
```

16.2.4 Subscript checking

In describing the various possible representations for arrays and the corresponding access code we have not allowed for the possible need for *array subscript checking*, i.e. to check that the value of a given indexing expression lies within the stated bounds of the dimension concerned. To provide this the compiler must generate code which checks the validity of subscript values before accessing the locations to which they lead, e.g. given

VAR A: ARRAY [M1..N1, M2..N2] OF *ElementType*

and a reference to the element $A[e_1, e_2]$, the compiler must generate additional object program instructions to check that each subscript value lies within its lower and upper bounds before using it in the access calculation

$M1 <= e1 >= N1$
$M2 <= e2 >= N2$

For arrays whose bounds are known at compile-time it is a simple matter to generate this checking code. However, for dynamic arrays it requires that each pair of bounds *Mi, Ni* must be held in the dope vector as well as the coefficient b_i (Figure 16.5).

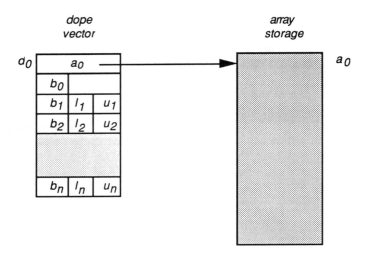

Figure 16.5 *Dynamic array representation with subscript-checking information*

The detailed nature of such checking code is described in Chapter 19 along with details of other run-time checking which may be required within an object program.

16.3   Records

Many languages, including COBOL, Modula-2 and Ada, provide some form of *record structure* within which *fields* of various types can be defined. The basic operation associated with a record-variable is that of *field selection*, in which a particular field is referenced by means of its identifier, or *field-name*. In most cases these record structures are simple from a compilation point of view—since the attributes of all the fields are known to the compiler, the total storage requirement and the address (*offset*) of each field relative to the origin address of the record is easily calculated at compile-time. Figure 16.6 illustrates the representation of a record-variable:

```
VAR R:  RECORD
             Field-1: T1;
             Field-2: T2;
             ...
             Field-n: Tn
        END
```

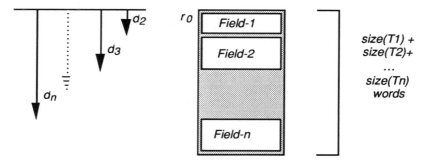

Figure 16.6 *Representation of a record-variable*

size(T1) denotes the number of words occupied by a value of type *T1*. Thus the object code for a field access simply involves an additional offset on the origin address r_0 for the record as a whole, however this is obtained. The semantic table entry for each record-field *Field-i* must maintain its associated offset value d_i and hence the address of

R.Field-i

is simply

$r_0 + d_i$

where (see Figure 16.6)

$d_1 = 0$
$d_2 = d_1 + size(T1)$
...
$d_n = d_{n-1} + size(Tn-1)$

and thus, given the origin address of a record, there is no additional cost (in terms of object program instructions generated) in selecting a particular field of the record.

Ada record structures are more complex in that a field may be a dynamic array—in which case the field simply is represented within the record storage by a dope vector which at run-time enables addressing of the dynamically allocated array storage itself.

For languages such as Ada and Modula-2 which provide records with so-called *variant-parts*, the representation of the variant-part is the same as for a simple record, except that the fields of the alternative *variants* share the same storage (i.e. are *overlayed*), since only one variant can exist at any moment. However, values of the alternative variants may occupy different amounts of storage. It is then necessary to pad out shorter representations so that all the variant representations use the same amount of storage. Figure 16.7 illustrates the representations of two values of a type *PokerCard* defined as follows:

```
TYPE CardType  = (Normal, Wild);
     Rank      = (Two, Three, Four, Five, Six, Seven, Eight, Nine, Ten, Jack,
                  Queen, King, Ace);
     Suit      = (Clubs, Diamonds, Hearts, Spades);
     Joker     = (RedJoker, BlackJoker);
     PokerCard = RECORD
                    CASE Which: CardType OF
                    | Normal: S: Suit; R: Rank
                    | Wild: J: Joker
                    END
                 END;
```

(a) Three of Diamonds   (b) Black Joker

Figure 16.7 *Representation of variant records*

The field *Which* is known as the *tag field* and its value determines the variant in existence at any given time. The representation of a variant record of type *PokerCard* consists of the representation of the tag field *Which* followed by the representation of the variant-part. The variant-part is represented by overlaying the storage for its two variants. Here the variant corresponding to the tag field value *Which* = *Normal* occupies two words (one for the *S* field and one for the *R* field) while the variant *Which* = *Joker* requires only one word (for the *J* field) and hence is padded out with an additional, unused, word.

16.4 Packed structures

In languages like Modula-2 each component of a data structure normally occupies an integral number of words. However, *packed* representations may be employed in which components occupy natural or convenient subdivisions of a word (such as a byte) as determined by the hardware, or each component may occupy only enough bits for its representation and components are directly juxtaposed. Figure 16.8 shows possible packed and unpacked representations on a machine with 4 bytes per word for a record-type *Date* defined as follows:

```
TYPE DayOfMonth = [1..31];
     Month      = (Jan, Feb, Mar, Apr, May, Jun, Jul, Aug, Sep, Oct, Nov, Dec);
     Year       = [1900..1999];
```

```
Date       = RECORD
              y: Year;  m: Month;  d: DayOfMonth
           END;
```

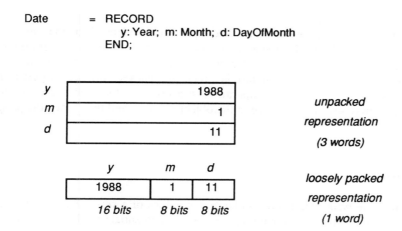

Figure 16.8 shows the following representations:

y | 1988
m | 1
d | 11

unpacked representation (3 words)

y   m   d
1988 | 1 | 11
16 bits 8 bits 8 bits

loosely packed representation (1 word)

Figure 16.8 *Packed and unpacked representations for a record-type*

In the unpacked representation each component uses an integral number of words appropriate to its type. However, loosely packed components occupy 'natural' or convenient subdivisions of a word as determined by the hardware, e.g. the *y* field can occupy 2 bytes since its value cannot be greater than *1999*, and the *m* and *d* fields can be represented in 1 byte each as their representations cannot be greater than *11* and *31* respectively. The packed representation shown in Figure 16.8 is often referred to as a *loosely packed* representation, since it is possible to use less storage than 1 byte for the three individual fields—the *y* field actually needs just 11 bits, the *m* field needs only 4 bits and the *d* field could be represented in 5 bits.

Packed array representations may be employed in circumstances where copying and comparison operations predominate (such as for character strings) and involve storage of more than one element within a computer word—with consequently more complex addressing code to unpack component values and to pack them when they are being updated. Pascal allows the programmer to declare explicitly that a record or array structure is to be represented in a packed form, e.g.

TYPE Name = PACKED ARRAY [1..NameLength] OF CHAR

Since selection and selective updating operations on a data structure such as a record or array depend only on each component occupying a fixed position within the overall representation of a record, it is permissible to rearrange the order of components when designing a packed representation so that they fit conveniently within word or part-word boundaries.

However, when a packed representation is employed it is usually not desirable (if access to components is to be efficient) to allow components to overlap word or byte boundaries—it is normal practice to leave some unused space (padding) at the end of words to avoid such overlaps.

The choice between packed and unpacked representation depends on the nature of the manipulation involved. If selection and selective updating operations are permitted then the unpacked representation is usually chosen, since the field-access code usually becomes more complex if the structure is stored in a packed form. If copying of the value as a whole is the dominant operation in a program then the use of a packed representation may save both storage in the object program and time when the program is executed.

16.5 Sets

Provided that the *base-type* is not too large, the values of a *set-type* are conveniently represented by bit-sequences containing 1 bit for each potential member of the set. This bit takes the value *1* if the corresponding base value is a member, value *0* otherwise. For example, given the type definitions

```
TYPE PrimaryColour  = (Red, Yellow, Blue);
     Colour         = SET OF PrimaryColor;
```

then, since the base-type *PrimaryColour* is an enumeration of three values, a value of the set-type *Colour* may be represented as a sequence of 3 bits, e.g.

101	represents	*Colour{Red, Blue}*
010	represents	*Colour{Yellow}*
000	represents	*Colour{}*

These representations are usually padded out to full-word representations—this leads to efficient target machine implementation of most of the basic set manipulation operations provided by languages such as Modula-2. For example, the Modula-2 set operators * (set *intersection*), + (set *union*) and – (*relative complement*) may be implemented directly by most machines' logical instructions for *and*-ing, *or*-ing, and *exclusive-or*-ing of pairs of machine words, respectively. For example, given set variables declared as

```
VAR S1, S2: Colour;
```

the operation *S1* + *S2* (the union of *S1* and *S2*) may be implemented on the Target machine by the instruction sequence

```
LOAD    address of S1
LOAD    address of S2
LOR
```

which leaves the resultant union set on top of the stack.

Likewise, the *IN* operation (which tests if a given value is included in a particular given set) can be implemented by shifting the relevant bit into the sign bit of a word and testing it.

Many languages place an upper bound on the cardinality of acceptable base-types, and thus on the size of sets. This upper bound is often determined by the word length of the computer on which the language is to be implemented, so as to ensure that sets are always representable within a single machine word.

16.6 Files

Many programming languages provide facilities enabling the input and output of information from objects existing on external media generally referred to as *files*. In some languages the input and output objects are explicitly declared as data structures (e.g. *sequential files* in Pascal), in others they exist by the mapping of input and output operations to them. In all cases some storage representation of these objects must be provided within the object program.

In general, transfers of information to and from such files are specified by the program in *program-determined units* (typically record values, although they can usually be values of any particular type supported by the language), while the physical characteristics of the storage media demand that transfers take place in standard *system-* (or *compiler-)determined units* (typically the operating system will define a standard size of information blocks on an external file). To match these requirements with one another the compiler must generate within the object program a *buffer area* which can hold the total information involved in one physical transfer and a *pointer* which indicates the position within this buffer which the next conceptual program unit of information is to be read from or written to. Figure 16.9 illustrates the storage associated with a Pascal sequential file *F*, declared as

```
TYPE    FileElementType = ...type of elements in the file...;
VAR     F: FILE OF FileElementType;
```

Declaration of such a file *F* in Pascal automatically introduces a *file buffer variable*, denoted as *F^*, which effectively addresses the next accessible position within the element buffer. The element buffer size is usually chosen to be the same size as (or a multiple of) the system block size and hence the number of elements which can be stored in the element buffer depends on the relative sizes of that buffer and the size *FileElementType* of the items in the file. The file buffer variable *F^* thus references the next available element position in the buffer (if the file is being used as an output file) or the next available element (if the file is being read).

The conceptual Pascal sequential file transfer operations *get* and *put* involve advancing the buffer pointer to the next element position within the buffer, and the calling of a support routine to clear or fill this buffer when the pointer reaches the end of it.

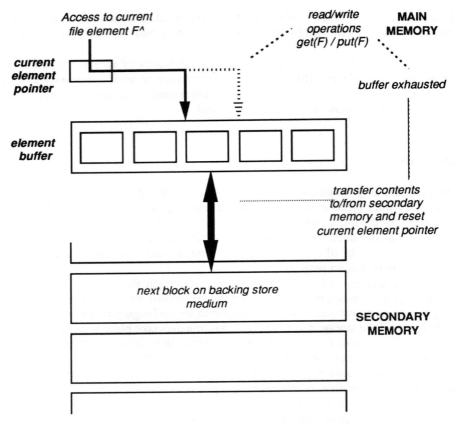

Figure 16.9 *Representation of a Pascal file*

16.7   Data representation in the Model compiler

The generator interface developed in Chapter 14 introduced the type *TypeRepresentation* to describe how values of each type in a Model program are represented. The Target is a strictly word-oriented machine with a word length of 16 bits. For the range of types which Model permits, the obvious representation is one Target word for each of the built-in scalar-types *INTEGER*, *CHAR* and *BOOLEAN*, and *n* contiguous words for each array of *n* elements. The only information required on the representation of each type is its size in words, which may in principle be any size within the available address space of the Target computer. We therefore define *TypeRepresentation* as follows:

    TYPE TypeRepresentation = Target.AddressRange;

and the built-in representations thus have the following values:

```
IntegerRepresentation := 1;
BooleanRepresentation := 1;
CharRepresentation := 1;
```

The array representation procedure *ArrayRepresentation* then becomes simply

```
PROCEDURE ArrayRepresentation(BoundMin, BoundMax: Target.Integer;
                                ElementRepresentation: TypeRepresentation;
                                VAR Representation: TypeRepresentation);
    BEGIN
        Representation := (BoundMax-BoundMin+1)*ElementRepresentation
    END ArrayRepresentation
```

16.8   Further reading

Most books on data structures deal with the machine-level representation of the range of data-types considered in this chapter. Hoare (1972, 1975) made influential contributions to the field, as did Wirth (1976), and current programming language design and implementation owes much to their work. Ghezzi and Jazayeri (1987) provide a thorough treatment of a wide range of data representations, including data-types not found in languages such as Modula-2 and Ada. Welsh, Elder and Bustard (1984) suggest representations for higher-level abstract data-types than those dealt with in this chapter, including stacks, queues, lists, trees, graphs and sparse data structures. They deal also with secondary memory representations for these data-types.

Dynamic arrays are found in Algol 60, Algol 68 and Ada, although Pascal and Modula-2 do not support them. Ada was developed by the United States Department of Defense and provides an interesting range of data structuring and data manipulation features. Its official definition was drawn up by the American National Standards Institute (1983).

Exercises 16

16.1 What storage would be allocated on an 8-bit machine for variables of the following types?

```
TYPE Range1 = [0..255];
     NewChar = CHAR;
     Range2 = [100..999];
     ArrayType = ARRAY [Range1] OF BOOLEAN;
```

16.2 Define a suitable data representation for values of the following types:

```
TYPE Name = PACKED ARRAY[1..16] OF CHAR;
     Age= [0..99];
     Sex = (Male, Female);
```

```
Features = SET OF (Glasses, Beard, Moustache, ScarFaced);
MarriageDetails =   RECORD
                        CASE Status: (Married, Single, Widowed, Divorced) OF
                        | Single, Divorced, Widowed: ();
                        | Married: (NumberOfChildren: CARDINAL)
                    END;
```

Assume that the target machine is a 32-bit machine using the ASCII character set, and single-word representations are to be used for *INTEGER* data items.

16.3 Define suitable unpacked and loosely packed data representations for values of the following type:

```
TYPE  Person =    RECORD
                    Name: PACKED ARRAY[1..16] OF CHAR;
                    Age: [0..99];
                    Sex: (Male, Female);
                    National: BOOLEAN;
                    Features: SET OF (Glasses, Beard, Moustache, ScarFaced);
                    CASE Status: (Married, Single, Widowed, Divorced) OF
                    | Single, Divorced, Widowed: ();
                    | Married: (NumberOfChildren: CARDINAL)
                    END
                  END;
```

Assume that the target machine is a 32-bit machine using the ASCII character set, and single-word representations are to be used for *INTEGER* data items.

16.4 Assuming the following declarations

```
CONST  N = 50;
TYPE   IntRange = 0..N;
VAR    I, J: IntRange;
       IntArray: ARRAY [1..N] OF IntRange;
```

and that the array *IntArray* is located at address 300 onwards in memory, translate the following statement into Target machine code:

```
I := IntArray [J+I*3]
```

16.5 Write a Target machine code fragment to perform the assignment-statement

```
Page [i, j] := Ch
```

where

```
TYPE Line = [1..40];  Column = [1..60];
VAR   Page: ARRAY Line, Column OF CHAR;
      i: Line; j: Column; Ch: CHAR;
```

using
(i)   an unpacked representation of the array *Page*;
(ii)   a tree representation of the array *Page*.

16.6 Given

```
TYPE Date =    RECORD
                     D: DayOfMonth;
                     M: Month;
                     Y: Year
               END
```

write Target machine code sequences to update the variable

```
VAR Day: Date;
```

to denote the date of the day following its present value, using
(i)   a standard representation for *Day*;
(ii)   a loosely packed representation for *Day*.

16.7 Assuming representation of the sets *A, B, C* each within a single word, translate
the following set operations into Target machine code sequences:
(i)   *A := (A * B) + C*
(ii)   *B := B – A*
(iii)   *IF min(A) IN B THEN C := A END*
where the function *min(A)* determines the smallest value in the parameter set *A*.

Chapter 17

Allocating and accessing data storage

Using the range of representations for data of various types described in the previous chapter, the variables associated with any program unit can be represented within an associated data storage area, sufficient for all these variables. We now consider how the data areas associated with different program units are interrelated and how storage is allocated within these areas.

17.1   The run-time stack

Modula-2 is typical of a range of languages which provide a nested block structure with recursive execution and which require some form of run-time administration of data areas. Each execution of a Modula-2 block must have associated with it a data area within which storage for variables local to the block is provided. For a procedure under recursive execution a separate data area must exist for each execution currently in progress. These requirements can be met by dynamic allocation and deallocation of such data areas within a large available storage area on a *stack* basis. This is illustrated in Figure 17.1 for execution of the program skeleton shown below.

```
MODULE A;

    PROCEDURE B;
        BEGIN ... END B;

    PROCEDURE C;
        BEGIN ... C; ...  END C;

    PROCEDURE D;
        PROCEDURE E;
            BEGIN ... C; ... END E;
        BEGIN ... E; ... END D;

    BEGIN ... B; ... D; ... END A;
```

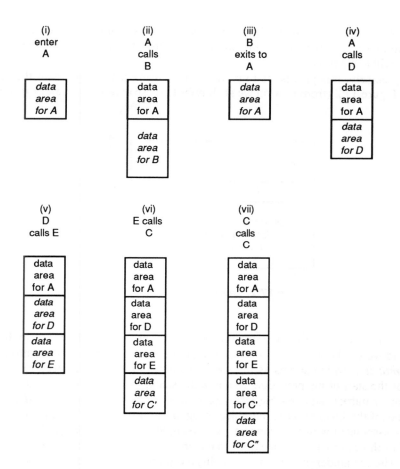

Figure 17.1 *Run-time stack during program execution*

At program entry the stack is initially empty. At each entry to a block a data area of appropriate size is allocated on the top of the stack which is used to hold the values of all variables local to that block for this execution; at exit from the block this data area is popped off the stack, freeing the storage locations used by it.

Thus, on entry to the statement-part of the module *A* a data area is created to hold the variables of *A* (i). *A* subsequently calls *B* and a new data area, of a size sufficient to hold the variables of *B*, is pushed onto the stack (ii). *B* then completes its execution and its data area is popped off the stack (iii). *A* then continues execution and calls *D* which results in a data area for *D* being created on the stack (iv) and when *D* calls *E* another data area, this time for the local variables of *E*, is allocated on the stack (v). At (vi) *E* has called *C* and a data area for *C* (shown as *C'*) has been created on top of the stack. *C* then makes a recursive call of itself and so another data area, of the same size (but shown as *C''*), is allocated (vii). This process of allocating and deallocating data areas continues until execution of the program is complete, at which time the stack of data areas will again be empty.

More precisely, this process is implemented by using a data area with the format shown in Figure 17.2 (from now on we shall refer to these data areas as *stack frames*).

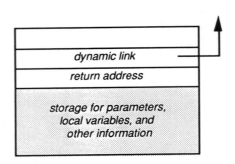

Figure 17.2 *Layout of stack frame (1)*

The first location in the stack frame is used for a purpose that is described in the next section and we shall consider it, in the interim, to be empty. The second location holds the *dynamic link* which serves as the stack chaining pointer and is used to hold the address of the start of the preceding frame in the stack. An additional location in each stack frame is introduced to enable recursion to work correctly. The *return address* (i.e. the address of the instruction in the object program to be executed once the call of the procedure associated with the frame has been completed) is stored in the third location. Retrieval of this return address at exit from the procedure thus ensures the correct control transfer. The remainder of the frame contains the storage associated with a procedure's local variables, parameters, and other information required during execution of the procedure.

During program execution it is necessary to hold the address of the current (topmost) data area on the stack. It is usual practice to dedicate a hardware addressing register (e.g. the *FP* register in the Target computer) to this purpose, and to ensure that no object program instructions other than those which allocate and deallocate the stack frames ever change the value of this register.

Entry to a procedure then involves the creation of a new frame immediately beyond the current one, and recording the values of the *FP* register and the target machine's program sequence register in the dynamic link and return address locations, respectively, of the new frame (see Figure 17.3); and exit from a procedure involves resetting the *FP* register to the value of the dynamic link in the current frame and then returning control to the calling environment at the instruction whose address is in the return address location.

These operations associated with procedure entry and exit can be efficiently implemented using the available instructions of all machines. However, the instruction set of the Target computer contains some instructions which implement many of these operations directly.

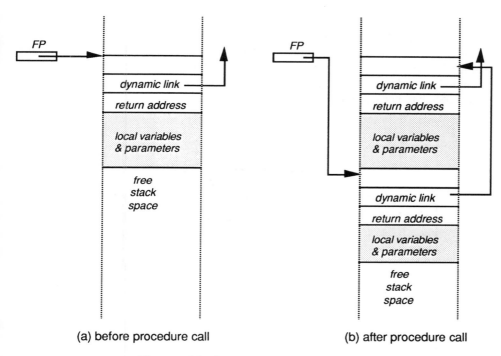

(a) before procedure call   (b) after procedure call

Figure 17.3 *Creation of new stack frame*

The *MARK* instruction records the previous value of the Target's *stack pointer* register *SP* in the *mark register MP* and then extends the stack by a specified number of words. The *CALL* instruction places the current value of the *frame register FP* and the *program counter register* (*PC*) in the second and third words of the frame addressed by the mark register. Moreover, the value in the mark register is then copied into the *FP* register and execution is switched to the address of the procedure specified in the *CALL* instruction. The combined effects of the *MARK* and *CALL* instructions enable the creation of the new stack frame and the recording of the dynamic link and return address values.

The Target's *EXIT* instruction copies the current *FP* register value into the stack register *SP*, and resets the *FP* register and the program sequence register *PC* to the contents of the dynamic link and return address locations, respectively, in the topmost frame. In other words, it performs exactly the necessary procedure exit actions that we identified above.

Thus, the object code corresponding to a call of a procedure *P* takes the following form:

    MARK   3
    CALL   *address of code body for P*

i.e. we use the *MARK* instruction to allocate and mark the three words that are required for the 'header' of the new stack frame (i.e. for the blank word and the dynamic link and return address) as shown in Figure 17.4(b). The *CALL* instruction then stores the dynamic link and return address, adjusts the *FP* register contents and switches control to the procedure body (Figure 17.4(c)).

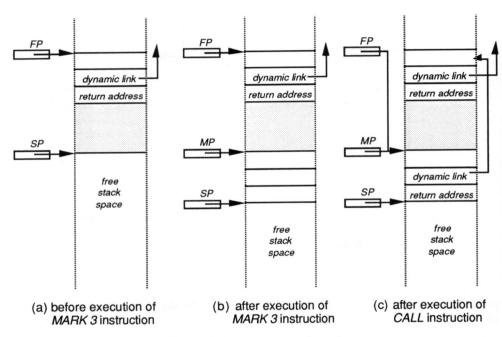

(a) before execution of
   MARK 3 instruction

(b) after execution of
   MARK 3 instruction

(c) after execution of
   CALL instruction

Figure 17.4 *Stages in calling a procedure*

Note, however, that the stack frame is not completely allocated at this stage since the storage area for the local variables and parameters has not been allocated as yet. Although the size of this area is known at compile-time, it is not a property of the calling procedure but rather of the procedure being called.

The object code for the statement-part of each procedure must be preceded by a *prelude*, which is a sequence of instructions that completes the construction of the associated stack frame (including the allocation of the area for the local variables, parameters, etc.), and followed by a *postlude*, which is another sequence of instructions that ensures correct exit is made from the procedure.

For example, the necessary storage administration for procedure entry on our Target machine can be provided, for the present, by a simple prelude as follows:

INCREG   SP, *amount needed for local variables, etc*

and for procedure exit all that is required is the following postlude:

EXIT

These preludes and postludes take an identical form for all procedures except that the value in the operand field of the prelude's *INCREG* instruction depends upon the requirements of the procedure concerned.

The implementation of functions takes a similar form to that of procedures with one major difference. It is necessary to allocate storage to hold the result of the function. This can be done by reserving one or more locations (depending upon the representation of the function's result-type) immediately before the start of the stack frame for the procedure (Figure 17.5).

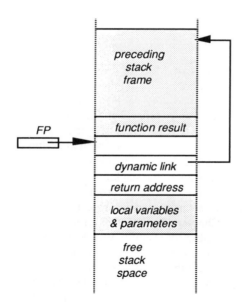

Figure 17.5 *Stack frame for execution of a function*

When it is required to assign a result value to a function (e.g. by means of a *RETURN* statement in Modula-2) then the value is assigned to the location(s) whose starting address is $-n$ relative to the function's stack frame, where n is the number of words required by the result. Thus, upon exit from the function, its result is on top of the stack (and thus, as we shall show in the next chapter, is immediately usable in the evaluation of the expression in which it occurs).

17.2   Access to local and non-local variables

During execution of a procedure the values of its local variables are, as we have seen, held in the topmost frame of the stack of such frames. At compile-time the compiler can determine the relative address of each variable within this stack frame and at run-time its actual address can be obtained by combining this relative address with the address in the register which references the topmost frame. For local variables then the compilation actions required are to record in the semantic table entry for each variable-identifier at the time of its declaration its relative address (*ra*) within the stack frame for the block in which it is declared, and at each subsequent reference to the variable within the block to generate access code of the form

$$X \qquad ra, [FP, 0]$$

where X is an arbitrary machine operation on the variable concerned and we are assuming that the Target's FP register always addresses the topmost of the frames on the stack.

However, the scope rules of Modula-2 (and indeed all other block-structured languages) permit access not only to local but also to non-local variables, i.e. variables declared in any block which textually encloses the current block. At run-time these variables are stored in stack frames other than the topmost frame and are therefore not immediately accessible via the register addressing the topmost frame. This is illustrated in Figure 17.6 where the local variable A is stored at address *ra* relative to the start of its (topmost) stack frame, while the non-local variable X is stored at relative address *rx* within another frame further back in the stack.

How can the object program locate the appropriate frame for access to each non-local variable? At compile-time the semantic table for a block-structured language is organized, as we saw in Chapter 11, as a stack of sub-tables, one for each block level currently in existence. Variable accessibility was determined by searching the sub-tables at successive levels until the appropriate entry is found. Since stack frames are the run-time equivalent of these sub-tables this leads to an analogous approach to run-time access of non-locals—given the difference in textual nesting levels between the block in which a variable is declared and the block in which it is accessed, code can be generated to step back through the run-time stack of stack frames the correct number of levels and so access the correct stack frame. This concept is complicated by two facts:

(i)   procedures and functions may be called, and hence their stack frames created, at levels other than their level of declaration;

(ii) recursive re-entry into blocks creates a series of frames on the run-time storage stack all at the same (compile-time) level.

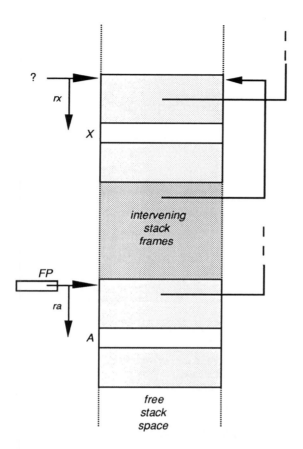

Figure 17.6 *Run-time access to local and non-local variables*

As an illustration of these points, consider the following program fragment

```
PROCEDURE A;

    PROCEDURE B;
        BEGIN ... END B;

    PROCEDURE C;
        BEGIN ... ; B; ...; C; ... END C;

    BEGIN ... ; B; ... END A
```

in which the procedure *B* is called both at its level of declaration (i.e. from within the statement-part of *A*) and at an enclosed level of declaration (from within the statement-part of *C*); and also the procedure *C* calls itself recursively.

It follows that the stack chaining pointer introduced so far, the dynamic link, is inadequate for non-local variable access, since stepping *n* levels down this chain will not necessarily lead to the stack frame for the enclosing program block at *n* levels of enclosure. Instead some run-time equivalent of the compile-time block table is required—this run-time *display* will automatically lead to the current frame within the stack for each textual level of block enclosure in the original source program.

The simplest way of representing the run-time display is to introduce into each frame a second stack chaining pointer, the *textual link*, which in each frame always points to the frame in the stack most recently created for the block which textually encloses its own block in the source program. Access to non-locals is then achieved by stepping the appropriate number of levels down the chain of textual links. To provide for this the concept of each stack frame is revised as shown in Figure 17.7. The first word in each frame, which we previously left empty, is now used to hold the frame's textual link.

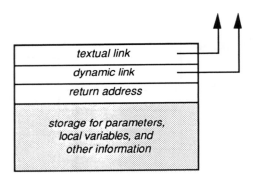

Figure 17.7 *Layout of stack frame (2)*

Suppose now that a procedure *A* encloses procedures *B* and *C*, and that *A* calls *C* which calls *B*, as shown:

```
PROCEDURE A;

    PROCEDURE B;
       BEGIN ... END B;

    PROCEDURE C;
       BEGIN ... ; B; ... END C;

    BEGIN ... ; C; ... END A
```

During the resultant execution of *B* the state of the run-time storage stack would be as shown in Figure 17.8 where, for the sake of clarity, only the textual links have been shown in each stack frame. The frame for the procedure which textually encloses *A* in the source program is assumed to lie further up the stack (Figure 17.8(a)). When *A* calls the procedure *C*, the address of the stack frame for *A* becomes the textual link to be stored in the frame for *C* since *A* textually encloses *C* (Figure 17.8(b)). Subsequently *C* calls *B*. In this case, it is not *C* but *A* which is the textually enclosing procedure for *B*, so it is the address of the stack frame for *A* which is the correct textual link for this execution of *B* rather than the address of the frame of the calling procedure *C*.

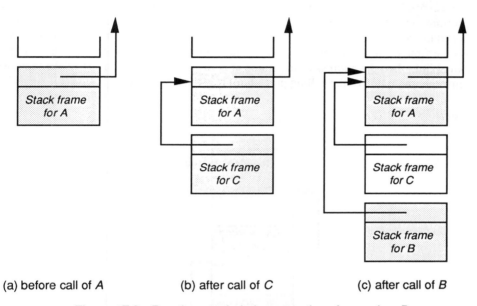

(a) before call of *A*   (b) after call of *C*   (c) after call of *B*

Figure 17.8 *Run-time stack during execution of procedure B*

Note that, within this stack of frames, at any moment there is exactly one frame accessible for each level of textual nesting in the corresponding source program—the accessible frames being those on the chain of textual links emanating from the topmost frame (these frames are shown shaded in Figure 17.8). Hence, to address any variable, the information needed is the textual level of its declaration, which identifies the stack frame's position on the textual link chain, and its relative address within that frame.

How do we determine the correct textual link for each frame? As the example in Figure 17.8 suggests, the appropriate textual link for a newly created stack frame cannot be determined by the procedure being called but instead must be determined at the point of call. For example, if *B* is called by *A* it is the calling procedure *A* which is the textually enclosing procedure. However, if *B* is called by *C*, then it is not the calling procedure *C* which is the textually enclosing procedure but in fact *C*'s textually enclosing procedure, i.e. *A*.

The required textual link is determined according to the difference in textual levels between the declarations of the calling procedure and the called procedure. If a procedure declared at *n* levels of textual nesting in a program calls a procedure declared at *m* levels of textual nesting, then the textually enclosing procedure of the called procedure is at *n–m+1* levels of enclosure of the calling procedure.

On a conventional machine this link could be determined by the calling procedure by means of a sequence of object code instructions which progressively climbs back *n–m+1* levels through the chain of textual pointers linking frames until the required frame is reached. However, the addressing mechanism of the Target machine makes the determination of the address of the frame for the called procedure's textually enclosing procedure very simple. Since the *FP* register addresses the topmost frame on the stack and the first word of the topmost frame (and every other frame) contains that frame's textual link, then the address of the frame at *n–m+1* levels of enclosure of the topmost frame (i.e. the frame of the calling procedure) is given simply by

0, [FP, n–m+1]

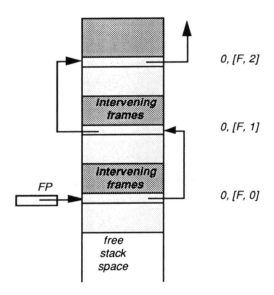

Figure 17.9 *Addressing stack frames on the Target machine*

For example, as Figure 17.9 shows, *0, [FP, 0]* gives the address of the topmost stack frame since it is the frame addressed by *FP* itself. *0, [FP, 1]* gives the address of the frame for the most recent activation of the procedure which textually encloses the currently executing procedure since its address is in the first word (word *0*) of the topmost frame. *0, [FP, 2]* gives the address of that frame's textual enclosure since it is in the first word of that frame, and so on.

We now amend the object code sequence for a call of a procedure *P* so that it determines the required textual link and leaves it on top of the stack immediately prior to execution of the *CALL* instruction (as shown in Figure 17.10(a)), viz.

```
MARK    3
LOADA   0, [FP, n–m+1]
CALL    address of code body for P
```

where *n* is the level of textual nesting of the declaration of the calling procedure, and *m* is the level of nesting of the declaration of *P*.

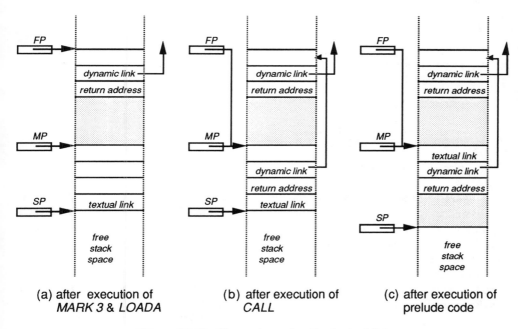

(a) after execution of
    MARK 3 & LOADA

(b) after execution of
    CALL

(c) after execution of
    prelude code

Figure 17.10 *Stages in saving the textual link*

The prelude within the object code for the procedure *P* must be amended to pop this textual link off the top of the stack (Figure 17.10(c)) and store it in the first word of the called procedure's stack frame (which is addressed by the *FP* register at that point), viz.

```
PRELUDE    STORE    0, [FP, 0]
           INCREG   SP, amount needed for local variables, etc
```

As we have seen, access by a procedure to a non-local variable, declared at *n* levels of textual enclosure, involves climbing back *n* levels through the chain of textual pointers emanating from the topmost stack frame. On a conventional machine this would typically involve execution of a sequence of *n* instructions in which each instruction climbs back one level of the chain. However, the Target's addressing mechanism again simplifies this operation by making the variable accessible in a single instruction, since its address is given by

   ra, [FP, n]

where *ra* is the relative address of the variable within its stack frame.

As an illustration of the calling code sequences and access code required to implement the determination of the textual links for procedure calls and subsequent access to non-local variables, consider the following program skeleton:

```
MODULE A;
  VAR X:...;

  PROCEDURE C;
    BEGIN ... ; X := 0; ... C; ... END C;

  PROCEDURE D;
    PROCEDURE E;
      BEGIN ...; C; ... END E;
    BEGIN ...; E; ... END D;

  BEGIN ...; D; ... END A;
```

Figure 17.11 shows the state of the run-time stack during execution of the procedure calls and assignment-statement included in the program. The accessible frames at each point are shown shaded. For the sake of clarity only textual links have been shown within stack frames and dynamic links have been omitted since they are implicit in the stack structure.

In Figure 17.11(a) the main program is currently executing—the main program has no textual enclosure and hence the textual link is not defined. The variable *X* is assumed to be located at a relative address *rx* within the frame for *A*.

When *A* calls its local procedure *D* (Figure 17.11(b)) the difference in textual levels between *A* and *D* is *1* (i.e. *n*−*m*+*1* = *0*) and hence the textual link required for the call is the address of the stack frame for *A* itself, i.e. the required calling sequence is

```
        MARK    3
        LOADA   0, [FP, 0]
        CALL    address of code body for D
```

D then calls its own local procedure *E* (Figure 17.11(c)) and again the difference in textual levels of declaration of the two procedures is *1*. Thus the address of the frame for *D* is the required textual link for the called procedure *E* and the calling sequence is similar to the one above, viz.

```
        MARK    3
```

```
LOADA    0, [FP, 0]
CALL     address of code body for E
```

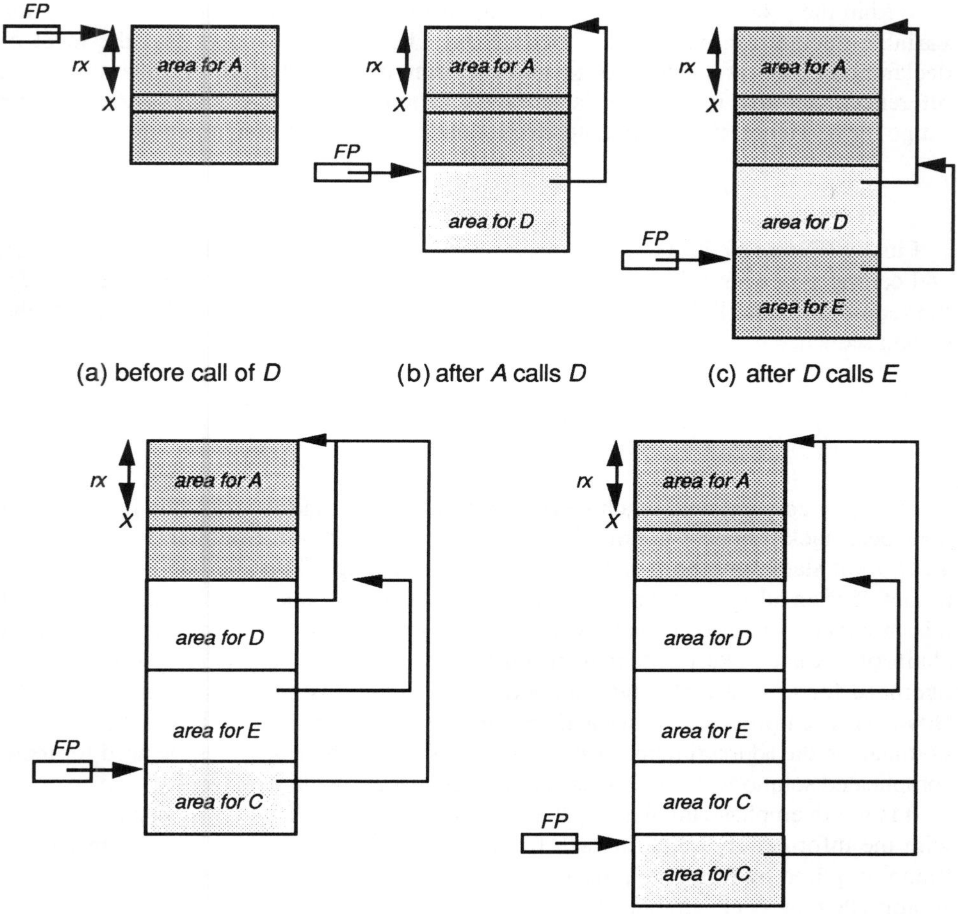

(a) before call of *D* (b) after *A* calls *D* (c) after *D* calls *E*

(d) after *E* calls *C* (e) after *C* calls *C*

Figure 17.11 *Code for procedure calls and non-local data access*

E calls procedure *C* which is declared at the textual level which immediately encloses that of *E*. Hence $n-m+1$ equals 2 in this case (i.e. the required stack frame for the textually enclosing procedure is two levels up the textual chain from the stack frame for *E*, as shown in Figure 17.11(d)) and so the calling sequence required in this case is

```
MARK    3
LOADA   0, [FP, 2]
CALL    address of code body for C
```

Within the procedure *C* there is an assignment of *0* to the variable *X* declared in the variable-declaration-part of the module *A*. The compiler knows that the level of declaration of *X* is at one level of textual enclosure of the procedure in which it is being referenced, and that it occupies the storage location with relative address *rx* within the frame for *A*. Hence, the appropriate instruction to perform the assignment is

```
STZ     rx, [FP, 1]
```

Finally (Figure 17.11(e)) *C* calls itself recursively. In this case, since both the called and calling procedures are obviously at the same textual level (i.e. $n-m+1$ equals 1), the required textual link is the same as that of the calling instance of *C* and hence the calling sequence is

```
MARK    3
LOADA   0, [FP, 1]
CALL    address of code body for C
```

On many conventional machine architectures an alternative technique for access to non-local stack frames is to hold the display of accessible frame pointers at any time as an explicit stack, one pointer for each level of nesting. This method is particularly attractive if an adequate set of addressing registers is available to hold this display—in this case there is no need to execute a series of instructions which climb back through the chain of textual links in order to reach the required stack frame—non-local access overhead for any variable and the maximum overhead is one instruction per access. However, each procedure entry and exit requires a saving and resetting of the display. Fortunately, the addressing mechanism of the Target machine removes the need for more complicated solutions to the problems of addressing non-local variables!

It is worth emphasizing that the stack organization described in this chapter, together with the information stored in each frame, automatically provides the multiple stack frames required by recursive procedure or function execution and enables access to the appropriate non-local variables from any level of recursion.

17.3   Parameters

In the previous sections we developed a model of the run-time storage structure required for the implementation of block-structured languages and also showed how the additional code required for stack control is easily incorporated in prelude and postlude sequences within an object code subroutine which represents the procedure body. However, the transmission and access of parameters to procedures pose some additional problems.

Parameter passing is implemented in general by (see Figure 17.12)

(a) allocating storage within the stack frame of the receiving procedure for each formal parameter specified (how this storage is used depends on the mode of parameter passing, as we shall see);
(b) planting actual parameters in this storage from the calling procedure immediately prior to procedure entry;
(c) generating code within the body of the receiving procedure to access parameters via the contents of these storage locations, according to the mode of passing.

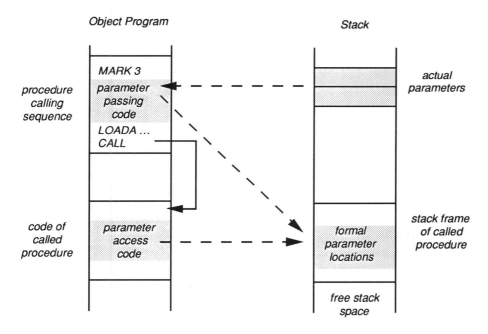

Figure 17.12 *Parameter passing: general case*

In Figure 17.12, the *MARK 3* instruction allocates the first three words of the new stack frame required for the called procedure. The parameter passing code then pushes the actual parameters onto successive locations on top of the stack (i.e. within the new stack frame about to be created for the called procedure), after which the *LOADA* instruction will push the textual link on top of the parameters. As we have seen, the procedure's prelude code will then pop the textual link into the first word of the new stack frame and complete the extension of the frame according to its total storage requirements for parameters and local variables. Hence, within each stack frame the parameters will be stored before the local variables.

A number of different modes of passing parameters are used in various programming languages. We will consider two major modes—*call by reference* and *call by value*—which are two of the most common modes provided in programming languages. Other languages have variations on these particular mechanisms, e.g. *call by result* (in some languages derived from Algol 60) and *dummy arguments* (in the language PL/1). The above two modes, however, adequately illustrate the major options in designing and generating code for parameter mechanisms.

17.3.1 Call by reference

The simplest parameter passing mechanism is known as *call by reference*. In the calling procedure (see Figure 17.13) the actual parameter is evaluated and, if it is not a variable or stored constant, a temporary location is created and the value stored therein.

The *address* of this variable, constant or temporary location is then planted in a corresponding formal parameter location in the stack frame of the receiving procedure. Within the latter procedure all accesses within the object code to the parameter take place indirectly via the address stored in the formal parameter location.

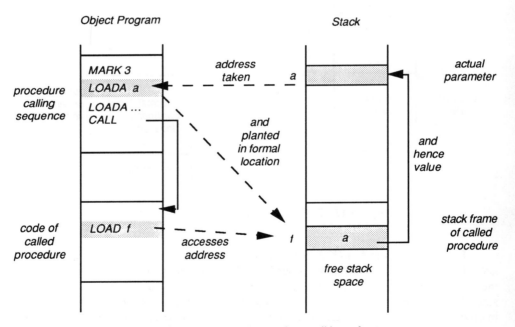

Figure 17.13 *Parameter passing: call by reference*

Assuming that we wish to pass a variable declared at *n* levels of enclosure of the calling procedure and that this variable is stored at some relative address *ra* within its stack frame, the parameter passing code takes the form

>   LOADA   *ra*, [FP, *n*]

Assuming that, within the called procedure's stack frame, the formal parameter occupies location *rf* relative to the start of the frame, then the address of the actual variable passed as the corresponding parameter can be loaded onto the top of the stack by the single instruction

>   LOAD   *rf*, [FP, 0]

and the value of the actual parameter can then be placed on top of the stack in place of its address by means of an additional instruction

>   LOADI   1

This call by reference mechanism is used in Modula-2 for the passing of actual parameters when the corresponding formal parameters have been declared as *variable parameters* only, and in Ada for passing *input–output parameters* only. In both these cases the actual parameters can be variables only, and hence temporary locations are never required.

17.3.2 Call by value

In the case of parameters passed using the *call by value* mechanism, the receiving procedure (Figure 17.14) has sufficient storage allocated within its stack frame to hold the *value* of the actual parameter. The actual parameter is evaluated in the calling procedure and its value then planted in these formal storage locations. Within the receiving procedure this value is then accessible in the same way as that of a local variable and there is no way in which the receiving procedure can change the value of the actual parameter in the calling procedure.

If we wish to pass the value of a variable declared at *n* levels of enclosure of the calling procedure and this variable is stored at some relative address *ra* within its stack frame, the parameter passing code in this case takes the form

>   LOAD   *ra*, [FP, *n*]

(Often the actual parameter value is that of an expression, in which case the actual parameter location does not exist and evaluation of the expression will itself leave the required value on top of the stack.)

Assuming again that the formal parameter occupies location *rf* relative to the start of the called procedure's stack frame, then the value passed as the corresponding parameter can be loaded onto the top of the stack by the single instruction

>   LOAD   *rf*, [FP, 0]

Object Program   Stack

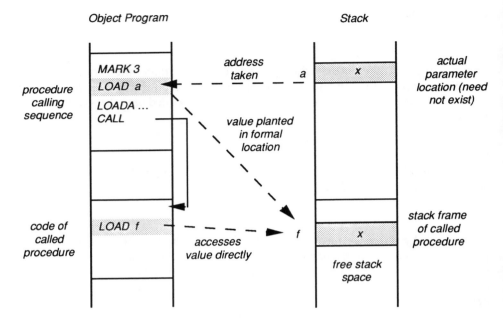

Figure 17.14 *Parameter passing: call by value*

The call by value mechanism is used in Modula-2 for passing actual parameters corresponding to formal parameters declared as *value parameters* and in Ada for passing *input parameters*.

The following example program fragment is introduced to illustrate the difference in effect between the passing of actual parameters by call by reference and by call by value, and subsequent reference to the formal parameters:

```
PROCEDURE Main;
    VAR X, Y: INTEGER;

        PROCEDURE Copy(A: INTEGER; VAR B: INTEGER);
        BEGIN B := A END Copy;

    BEGIN
    ...
    Copy(X, Y);
    ...
    END Main
```

The Target object code for the call *Copy(X, Y)* is

```
                MARK     3          [ allocate space on stack for header of new stack frame
                LOAD     rx, [FP, 0] [ push value of X into word 3 of new stack frame
```

```
LOADA    ry, [FP, 0]   [ push address of Y into word 4 of new stack frame
LOADA    0, [FP, 0]    [ push value of textual link
CALL     address of code for Copy
```

where *rx* and *ry* are assumed to be the relative addresses of the storage locations for the variables *X* and *Y* within the stack frame for *Main*. The value of *X* is loaded into the first word of the new stack frame beyond the three-word header area allocated by the *MARK* instruction, i.e. word *3* of the frame. The address of *Y* is thus loaded into word *4* of the new frame.

Figure 17.15 shows the state of the run-time stack immediately before and after execution of the above instruction sequence implementing the call of *Copy(X, Y)*.

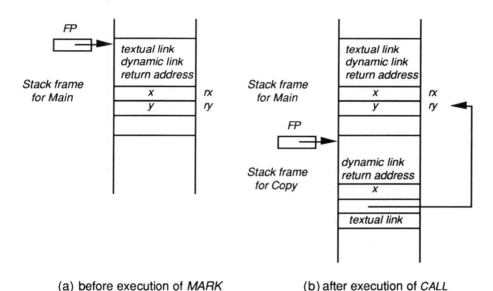

(a) before execution of *MARK*   (b) after execution of *CALL*

Figure 17.15 *Run-time stack for procedure call with mixed parameter modes*

Within the body of the procedure *Copy* the code for the assignment-statement *B:= A* is thus

```
LOAD     3, [FP, 0]    [ load value of A from word 3 of topmost stack frame
LOAD     4, [FP, 0]    [ load address of B from word 4 of topmost stack frame
STOREI   1             [ assign value of A to address of B
```

17.3.3   Procedure and functions as parameters

One further parameter passing problem which is worthy of consideration is that of passing procedures and functions as actual parameters. To enable the code body of an actual procedure (or function) to be entered on execution of a corresponding formal procedure (or function) call, the address of this code body must be passed to the procedure within which the formal procedure (or function) is declared.

For block-structured languages, however, this is not enough. We have seen that the textual link for a procedure or function block must be determined within its calling sequence. The calling sequence for a formal procedure or function, however, has no automatic means of determining the appropriate textual link for the actual procedure or function which has been passed to it. Instead this textual link can and must be determined at the point of first passing the actual procedure (or function) name as a parameter, and carried, together with the code address, into the storage locations allocated to the receiving formal procedure (or function). Subsequent calls to this formal procedure or function then simply pick up this stored textual link prior to activating the corresponding code body.

17.4 Other dynamic storage

The use of the run-time stack organization described in the previous sections of this chapter is possible because the lifetime of data objects represented within each stack frame is determined by the lifetime of the program block in which they are declared and, since the lifetime of a stack frame is that of the block to which it corresponds, their lifetime is the same as that of the stack frame itself. Some languages, however, support features whereby the lifetime of data objects is not related to the program structure creating them. Records created dynamically in Modula-2 using pointer-variables, and list structures in the language LISP, are examples of such data objects. Some other means of storage allocation and recovery must be used for the run-time representation of such objects. How this is done depends on whether the particular language concerned enables the discarding of such storage to be explicitly identified by the compiler or the run-time system.

When the language supports explicit discarding of storage (e.g. the standard procedures *new* and *dispose* in Pascal) then the implementation of these operations will allocate and free storage using a list of available storage which at any moment holds details of all storage not currently in use (as shown in Figure 17.16). Because of the random order of storage allocation and recovery made possible by these language facilities the storage involved, and its controlling mechanisms, are often referred to as a *heap*.

When the discarding of storage cannot be explicitly identified by means of language-defined operations (as in Ada and LISP), then an alternative strategy known as *garbage collection* must be adopted. As illustrated in Figure 17.17, the heap at any time will consist of various storage areas which are currently in use, other areas which are on the list of available space, and some storage which is no longer in use by the program (shown as *debris* in Figure 17.17). In this scheme no storage recovery takes place until the list of available space is exhausted, at which point all storage currently in use is identified and marked by a systematic scanning of the data structures which are currently known to the program, and the remaining unmarked storage is collected to form a new list of available space.

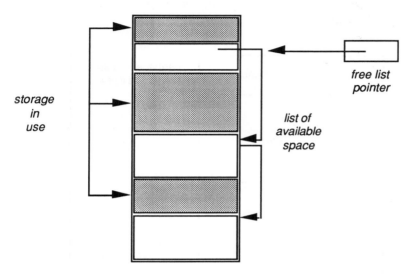

Figure 17.16 *The run-time heap*

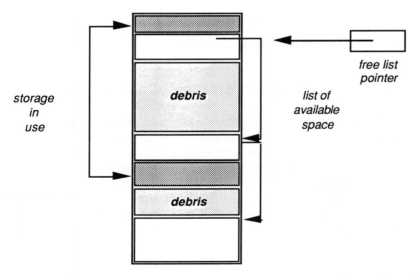

Figure 17.17 *Snapshot of the state of a heap*

The run-time stack and the heap usually compete for space from opposite ends of the total available storage space. This avoids setting an upper bound on the size of either storage structure and allows each to grow to the limit of the available storage. If overlap between the two occurs then the object program is too large to run in the available space and must be abandoned. Figure 17.18 illustrates the typical layout of an object program which uses a stack and a heap.

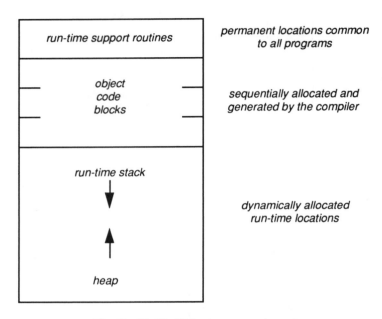

Figure 17.18 *Object program layout*

17.5 The Model compiler: storage allocation and control

Following the run-time storage model developed in the previous sections, the storage organization used for Model object programs will be a dynamically allocated stack of storage frames, one for each procedure currently under execution. The topmost frame holds the variables local to the procedure being executed, the one below holds those of the procedure which called it, and so on.

In order to address any variable the information needed is the textual level of its declaration, which identifies the stack frame's position on the textual link chain, and its relative address within this frame. Hence the type *RunTimeAddress* exported by the code generator is defined as

```
TYPE RunTimeAddress =    RECORD
                         TextualLevel: CARDINAL;
```

```
        RelativeAddress: Target.AddressRange
END
```

In a one-pass compiler for Model it is possible to allocate the global variables to fixed object program locations. On some machines this may have the advantage of locating as many as possible, perhaps all, of the global variables within low-address locations which are more efficiently accessible than those beyond. However, because of the nature of the Target machine's memory addressing mechanism, it is convenient to allocate the global variables locations within a main program stack frame which will be allocated at the beginning of execution of the object program. This has the advantage also of enabling us to develop a consistent approach to storage allocation and data access. The overall picture of the object program to be generated is thus as shown in Figure 17.19, with the generator sequentially allocating the locations from *FirstAvailable* to *FirstStack*.

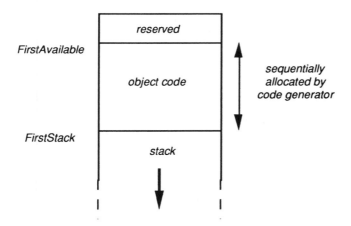

Figure 17.19 *Storage allocation by the Model compiler*

To represent the progress of the allocation of the object program locations we introduce a module *Code* which is also responsible for the assembly of a Target instruction from its component fields, appending it to the current object code sequence and transferring sequences of instructions to the code handler module:

```
MODULE Code;
    IMPORT CodeHandler, AddressRange, CodeRange, CodeMax, OrderCode,
            AddressRegister, Integer, Level, FirstAvailable, SystemRoutines, ...;
    EXPORT QUALIFIED NewCodeSpace, EndOfCodeSpace, Ins0, InsD, Ins, JumpIns,
                FixUp, ReserveInstruction, EnterHere, SystemCall, CodeMax,
                GenerationComplete, ...;

    VAR  CurrentAddress: AddressRange;  NextInstruction: [1..CodeMax+1];
```

```
PROCEDURE NewCodeSpace; ...;
   (* Performs actions associated with start of code generation for a new block. *)

PROCEDURE EndOfCodeSpace; ...;
   (* Outputs code generated for a block to the object code handler. *)

PROCEDURE ReserveInstruction(VAR CodeAddress: CodeRange); ...;
   (* Reserves an instruction and assigns its address to CodeAddress. *)

PROCEDURE Ins(Op: OrderCode; D: Integer; R: AddressRegister; L: Level); ...;
   (* Generates Target instruction Op D, [R, L] *)

PROCEDURE Ins0(Op: OrderCode); ...;
   (* Generates Target instruction Op *)

PROCEDURE InsD(Op: OrderCode; D: Integer); ...;
   (* Generates Target instruction Op D *)

PROCEDURE JumpIns(JumpType: OrderCode; VAR Sequence: CodeLabel); ...;
   (* Generates Target jump instruction to the CodeLabel described by Sequence. *)

PROCEDURE FixUp(FixUpAddress: CodeRange;
                Op: OrderCode; D: Integer; Reg: AddressRegister; Lev: Level);
      ...;
   (* Places instruction Op D, [R, l] in object code location FixUpAddress. *)

PROCEDURE SystemCall(RoutineNeeded: SystemRoutines); ...;
   (* Generates call to specified system routine *)

PROCEDURE EnterHere; ...;
   (* Causes execution of the object program to commence at the next instruction. *)

PROCEDURE GenerationComplete; ...;
   (* Performs actions associated with end of object code generation. *)


   ...


BEGIN
   CurrentAddress := FirstAvailable; NextInstruction := 1;
END Code;
```

The precise range of facilities which this module provides will emerge as we consider the various aspects of code generation which the generator interface procedures imply.

To allocate variable addresses correctly the generator must maintain a record of the level of nesting of the stack frames and the number of locations allocated within each. This it can do by the introduction of a variable

```
VAR FrameLevel: CARDINAL;
```

and a stack of frame description records of the form

```
TYPE FrameEntry    =  POINTER TO FrameRecord;
     FrameRecord   =  RECORD
                            NextLocal: AddressRange;
                            NextFrame: FrameEntry
                      END;
```

The top of this stack can be located by means of a variable

```
VAR LocalFrame: FrameEntry;
```

The appropriate initialization for the frame stack is thus

```
LocalFrame := NIL;
FrameLevel := PseudoLevel;
```

where

```
CONST PseudoLevel = 0;
```

The generator interface operations *OpenFrame* and *CloseFrame* are then readily programmed as straightforward pushing and popping operations on this stack, viz.

```
PROCEDURE OpenFrame;
   VAR NewFrame: FrameEntry;
   BEGIN
      INC(FrameLevel);
      Host.New(NewFrame, SIZE(FrameRecord));
      WITH NewFrame^ DO
         NextLocal := FirstLocal; NextFrame := LocalFrame
      END;
      LocalFrame := NewFrame;
   END OpenFrame;
```

where

```
CONST FirstLocal = 3;
```

defines the first three words of each frame as being reserved for the header information to be stored therein.

```
PROCEDURE CloseFrame;
   VAR OldFrame: FrameEntry;
   BEGIN
      OldFrame := LocalFrame; LocalFrame := LocalFrame^.NextFrame;
      Host.Dispose(OldFrame, SIZE(FrameRecord));  DEC(FrameLevel)
   END CloseFrame;
```

The address allocation procedure *AddressFor* is programmable as follows:

```
PROCEDURE AddressFor(Representation: TypeRepresentation;
                            VAR Address: RunTimeAddress);
   BEGIN
      Address.TextualLevel := FrameLevel;
      WITH LocalFrame^ DO
         Address.RelativeAddress := NextLocal;
         INC(NextLocal, Representation)
      END
   END AddressFor;
```

17.6 Implementing procedure calls

The problems of generating code for procedure calls in Model is made simpler by the
absence of parameters from the language. A *procedure linkage* for our target machine
consists of the address of the object code body for the procedure concerned and the
recording of the textual level of declaration of the procedure-identifier—the latter is
necessary in order to generate the appropriate code for establishing the textual frame
pointer at run-time. Thus

```
TYPE ProcedureLinkage =  RECORD
                            TextualLevel: CARDINAL;
                            CodeBody: CodeLabel;
                            EntryPoint: CodeRange
                         END
```

The third field, *EntryPoint*, is used to record the address of the *INCREG* instruction
which appears in the prelude code of every procedure. This instruction (see Section
17.1) is used to extend the procedure's stack frame to its required size at run-time.
However, the operand field of the instruction (the amount by which the frame is to be
extended) is not known until all of the statement-part of the procedure has been
compiled—at which stage it is necessary to go back and *fix up* the *INCREG*
instruction with the required operand value.

The action of the generator procedure

```
PROCEDURE NewLinkage(VAR Linkage: ProcedureLinkage);
```

in creating a new linkage *P* is thus to

(a) set *P.TextualLevel* to the current level of textual nesting within the source program
    (i.e. the current value of *FrameLevel*);
(b) define *P.CodeBody* as a future code label by means of a call of *FutureCodeLabel*
    (P.CodeBody);

and the action of

```
PROCEDURE CallProcedure(VAR Linkage: ProcedureLinkage);
```

in calling a procedure with linkage *P* is to generate the procedure calling sequence described in Section 17.2, viz.

(a) generate a *MARK* instruction to allocate space on the stack for the three words of the frame header via a call of *Code.InsD(Mark, 3)*;
(b) use the value of *P.TextualLevel* in an instruction which loads the required textual link for the called procedure onto the top of the stack, i.e. by a call of *Code.Ins (LOADA, 0, FP, FrameLevel–P.TextualLevel)*;
(c) generate a procedure call instruction via *Code.JumpIns(CALL, P.CodeBody)*.

Note that the addressing registers *BP, FP, MP, SP* are defined by the *Target* module as the subrange-type

    TYPE AddressRegister = Register [BP..SP]

where

    TYPE Register = (BP, FP, MP, SP, PC, PSR);

The actions associated with

    PROCEDURE EnterBody(VAR Linkage: ProcedureLinkage);

are to generate the procedure prelude for a procedure with linkage *P* as described in 17.1 and 17.2, viz.

(a) call *Code.NewCodeSpace* to indicate that code generation for a new block is about to commence;
(b) call *ExpectedLabel(P.CodeBody)* as the code body of the procedure concerned is about to be generated;
(c) generate an instruction to store away the textual link currently on top of the stack by means of a call of *Code.Ins(STORE, 0, FP, 0)*;
(d) reserve a word in the object code of the procedure for the *INCREG* instruction which will extend the procedure's run-time stack frame—by means of a call of *Code.ReserveInstruction(P.EntryPoint)*.

The action of

    PROCEDURE LeaveBody(VAR Linkage: ProcedureLinkage);

is to generate the procedure postlude for a procedure with linkage *P* as described in 17.1, viz.

(a) fix up the instruction reserved in the prelude as an *INCREG* instruction whose operand field defines the required extension to the stack frame, by means of a call of

Code.FixUp(P.EntryPoint, INCREG, LocalFrame^.NextLocal–FirstLocal, SP, 0);
(b) generate the procedure exit instruction, i.e. *Code.Ins0(EXT);*
(c) call *Code.EndOfCodeSpace* to indicate that code generation for this block is now complete.

The interface operations *EnterProgram* and *LeaveProgram* implement the prelude and postlude operations, respectively, associated with entry to, and exit from, the main program itself. Entry to the main program as defined by *EnterProgram* is rather more complex than entry to a procedure in that

(a) the start of a new code space must again be signalled to the *Code* module by a call of *Code.NewCodeSpace;*
(b) the *Code* module must be informed that code generation for the main program is about to commence so that it can record the starting address of the main program (so that the *Code* module can arrange for program execution to begin at the appropriate instruction) — this is done by means of a call of the procedure *Code.EnterHere;*
(c) space for the header for the main program's stack frame must be allocated (as there is no procedure call to allocate it)—this is done via a call of *Code.InsD(MARK, 3);*
(d) a word must again be reserved in the object code of the main program prelude for the *INCREG* instruction which will extend the main program's stack frame—by means of a call of *Code.ReserveInstruction(MainProgramFixUp)* where *MainProgramFixUp* is a variable declared within the code generator;
(e) the input and output devices required by the program must be initialized by an instruction that calls a routine in the run-time support package to perform this task— this instruction is generated via a call of *Code.SystemCall(InitializeIO)* where the *Target* module defines the run-time support operations required for Model as the enumeration

TYPE SystemRoutines = (InitializeIO, FinalizeIO, ReadInteger, WriteInteger);

Implementation of the *LeaveProgram* operation involves the following sequence of actions:

(a) the stack frame extension instruction reserved in the prelude by *EnterProgram* must be fixed up by means of a call of *Code.FixUp(MainProgramFixUp, INCREG, LocalFrame^.NextLocal–FirstLocal, SP, 0);*
(b) the program's input and output devices are disconnected from the program by a call of the appropriate run-time support routine—this instruction is generated by a call of *Code.SystemCall(FinalizeIO);*
(c) an *HLT* instruction, whose execution will cause termination of the object program at run-time, is generated by a call of *Code.Ins0(HLT);*
(d) *Code.EndOfCodeSpace* is called to indicate that code generation for the main program block is now complete;
(e) *Code.GenerationComplete* is called to indicate that the code generation process has been completed.

17.7 Further reading

Further descriptions of stack-based run-time execution models for block-structured programming languages which support parameter passing appear in Ghezzi and Jazayeri (1987), Watt (1993) and most compiler texts. Most of the original work on stack allocation of run-time storage, and the use of an explicit display (i.e. stack of registers) to enable non-local data access, was done by Dijkstra (1960).

The Algol 60 and Algol 68 languages both supported *call by name* parameter passing—the use of a *name parameter* is equivalent to a textual substitution of the formal parameter by the actual parameter in the procedure body. Textual substitution is not a practical means of implementing name parameters, and Algol compilers instead generated parameterless routines (known as *thunks*) which, at run-time, returned the address of the actual parameter itself. Further details are given in Ghezzi and Jazayeri (1987). For a treatment of various parameter passing modes and implementation techniques, see also Kowaltowski (1981).

In contrast with Modula-2 and Pascal, which provide explicit heap deallocation operations, SNOBOL, a string processing language, and LISP, a list processing language, both depend on the use of heap allocation and associated garbage collection, as does Ada. Algorithms for storage allocation and deallocation using a heap are presented in Knuth (1973) while garbage collection algorithms are covered in Aho, Hopcroft and Ullman (1983).

Exercises 17

17.1 Draw diagrams to show the state of the run-time stack and the contents of each stack frame at every procedure entry and exit during the execution of the following Modula-2 program, assuming the input data to be the integer *13579*:

```
MODULE Test;
    FROM InOut IMPORT ReadCard, WriteCard;

PROCEDURE Reverse(N: CARDINAL);
    BEGIN
        WriteCard(N MOD 10, 1);
        IF N DIV 10 <> 0 THEN Reverse(N DIV 10) END
    END Reverse;

VAR TestValue: CARDINAL;

BEGIN
    ReadCard(TestValue)
    Reverse(TestValue)
END Test.
```

17.2 A Pascal program contains the following global data definitions:

```
TYPE Courses = (SoftwareEngineering, Compilers, FormalMethods,
                   TheoryOfProgramming, DataBase, ComputerArchitecture);
     StudentNumber = 0..9999;
     Student = RECORD
                   Number: StudentNumber;
                   Name: PACKED ARRAY[1..20] OF CHAR;
                   Sex: (Male, Female);
                   Year: 1..4;
                   Attends: SET OF Courses
               END;
VAR DepartmentFile = FILE OF Student;
```

A procedure of this program has the form

```
PROCEDURE ExtendFile(VAR Department: DepartmentFile;
                       VAR S: StudentNumber);
     VAR NewStudent: Student; TemporaryFile: DepartmentFile;
     BEGIN
         (*  obtains details of NewStudent from user at keyboard;
             extends the file Department to contain this new student record;
             returns in S the student number of this new student *)
     END {ExtendFile}
```

Describe how a compiler might allocate storage for the housekeeping information, parameters and local variables within the run-time stack frame for the procedure *ExtendFile*. Assume that the target machine is a 16-bit machine using the ASCII character set, the standard operating system block size is 256 words and single-word representations are to be used for integer data items.

17.3 Consider the following Modula-2 program fragment:

```
MODULE M;

PROCEDURE A;
     VAR X: INTEGER;

     PROCEDURE B (V: INTEGER);

         PROCEDURE C;
             BEGIN ...; C; ...; A; ... END C;

         BEGIN ...; A;  V := X; ... END B;

     PROCEDURE D (VAR I: INTEGER);
         BEGIN ...; B(5);  ...; I:= 0; ... END D;

     BEGIN ...;  D(X); ... END A;

BEGIN ...; A; ... END M;
```

Outline the form of the object code sequences which would be generated by a compiler generating absolute machine code for the Target machine for each of the following statements in the program fragment:

(i)   the procedure call *C* within the statement-part of *C*;

(ii)   the procedure call *A* within the statement-part of *C*;

(iii)   the procedure call *A* within the statement-part of *B*;

(iv)   the procedure call *B(5)* within the statement-part of *D*;

(v)   the procedure call *D(X)* within the statement-part of *A*;

(vi)   the assignment-statement *V := X* within the statement-part of *B*;

(vii)   the assignment-statement *I := 0* within the statement-part of *D*.

Chapter 18

Object code generation

Beyond the code generation interface all design decisions reflect the particular object code form to be generated. Our aim here is to generate directly executable machine code for the Target computer described in Chapter 2. In this chapter we consider how the Target machine and object code characteristics influence the generation process and how they can be handled in the Model compiler's *Generator* module.

Within the overall form of object code chosen there remains a considerable flexibility in the design of the actual code generated for particular language features. Since this code design involves the realization of programming language features in terms of actual computer hardware features it is highly dependent on the characteristics required of the code. For example, speed in execution, economy of code size, security against error, are all characteristics which depend upon the exact code designs chosen as well as their overall format. In many situations these objectives are themselves conflicting and the object code chosen is some compromise within the available features of the hardware involved.

The ease with which the generation of object code is incorporated within the overall compilation process depends on whether a multi-pass or one-pass compilation scheme is in use and in the latter case on the method of analysis in use. It also depends on the degree of optimization required in the final object code—highly optimized code can only be generated by using several passes for code generation alone. However, as many compilers for languages such as Modula-2 demonstrate, acceptably efficient code can be generated within a simple one-pass scheme.

In examining the code generation process for our Model compiler we shall look at a number of typical aspects of code design and generation and the problems that arise.

18.1 An overview of code generation

Much of the intricacy of the code generation process, and most of the correspondingly elaborate techniques associated with it, are concerned with the generation of effective code for arithmetic expressions.

In principle, the generation of sequential code for arithmetic expressions is equivalent to their translation to postfix notation since access code for each operand must be executed before the corresponding operation can be carried out. This translation from infix to postfix notation is easily carried out using a *compile-time operator stack*. in recursive descent analysis this stack is provided by the recursion mechanism itself and the infix to postfix translation process has been illustrated in the generation of the postfix hypothetical machine code generated by the Model analyzer. At run-time evaluation of this postfix form can then be carried out equally easily using a *run-time evaluation stack* to hold the operand values. For a machine which has an adequate set of computation registers these can be employed as the evaluation stack and code generation is relatively simple. For machines with only one computation register a memory-based stack must be used and much of the effort of code generation for expressions is then devoted to avoiding the generation of unnecessary store and load operations to and from this stack.

Consider as an example the expression

$$A + B * C - F * (D - E)$$

Translation of this expression to postfix form gives

$$A B C * + F D E - * -$$

For a machine with an adequate set of computation registers $X1$, $X2$, ... and which provides interregister arithmetic operations, the evaluation code exactly mirrors this postfix form, viz.

LOAD	X1	*address of A*	[X1 := A
LOAD	X2	*address of B*	[X2 := B
LOAD	X3	*address of C*	[X3 := C
MULT	X2	X3 X2	[X2 := X2 * X3
ADD	X1	X2 X1	[X1 := X1 + X2
LOAD	X2	*address of F*	[X2 := F
LOAD	X3	*address of D*	[X3 := D
LOAD	X4	*address of E*	[X4 := E
SUB	X3	X4 X3	[X3 := X3 – X4
MULT	X2	X3 X2	[X2 := X2 * X3
SUB	X1	X2 X1	[X1 := X1 – X2

For a one-address instruction machine which has a single computation register X and uses register-store arithmetic (this is typical of the floating-point arithmetic facilities provided on many machines) the object code involving minimum use of memory locations for stacking intermediate results no longer exactly mirrors the postfix code, viz.

LOAD	B	[X := B
MULT	C	[X := X * C
ADD	A	[X := X + A
STORE	S1	[save result in stack location S1

```
LOAD    D       [ X := D
SUB     E       [ X := X – E
MULT    F       [ X := X * F
STORE   S2      [ save result in stack location S2
LOAD    S1      [ X := S1
SUB     S2      [ X := S1 – S2
```

Such code can be generated by *simulating the run-time evaluation stack* at compile-time. When an operand is scanned its *description* rather than its *value* is stacked. Likewise, when a postfix operation arises, object code is generated to carry out that operation, using the operands whose descriptions are on top of the stack, and these operand descriptions are then replaced by a description of the result. This description will in general indicate that the run-time result is in the run-time computation register. Code to transfer this result to a temporary memory location need only be generated if a subsequent operand has to be loaded into the register before this first one has been disposed of.

Figure 18.1 illustrates the steps in the simulation of the run-time evaluation of the postfix expression $A\ B\ C\ * + F\ D\ E\ - * -$ and the generation sequence for the actual object code shown above. A stack entry containing X denotes that the run-time result is actually in the computation register at that point in the simulation and $S1$, $S2$, ... are consecutive locations within an area of the target machine's memory reserved for use as a stack.

At step (i) the pushing of the operand A onto the run-time evaluation stack is simulated by pushing a description of A onto the simulated stack. The pushing of the operands B and C are likewise simulated at steps (ii) and (iii) by pushing descriptions of B and C, respectively. The effect of the operator * on the run-time evaluation stack (step (iv)) would be to pop the top two values and push their sum back onto the stack. This is simulated by popping the top two descriptions of C and B (which are presumed to contain information about the locations of the operands concerned) from the stack, generating code to perform the multiplication operation and pushing a description of the result back onto the stack of operand descriptions. The register X will be unused at this point so instructions are generated to load the content's of B's location into X and then to perform a multiplication involving the contents of C's location, viz.

```
LOAD    B
MULT    C
```

The result of the *MULT* operation is simulated by pushing a new description on top of the stack indicating that the value will now be in the register X. The simulation of the + operation (step (v)) is similar in that it involves popping two descriptors from the top of the stack—these indicate that one operand will be in the register and the other will be in the memory location allocated to A. Hence code is generated to multiply them and, since one operand will already be in the register, the required instruction sequence is simply

```
ADD     A
```

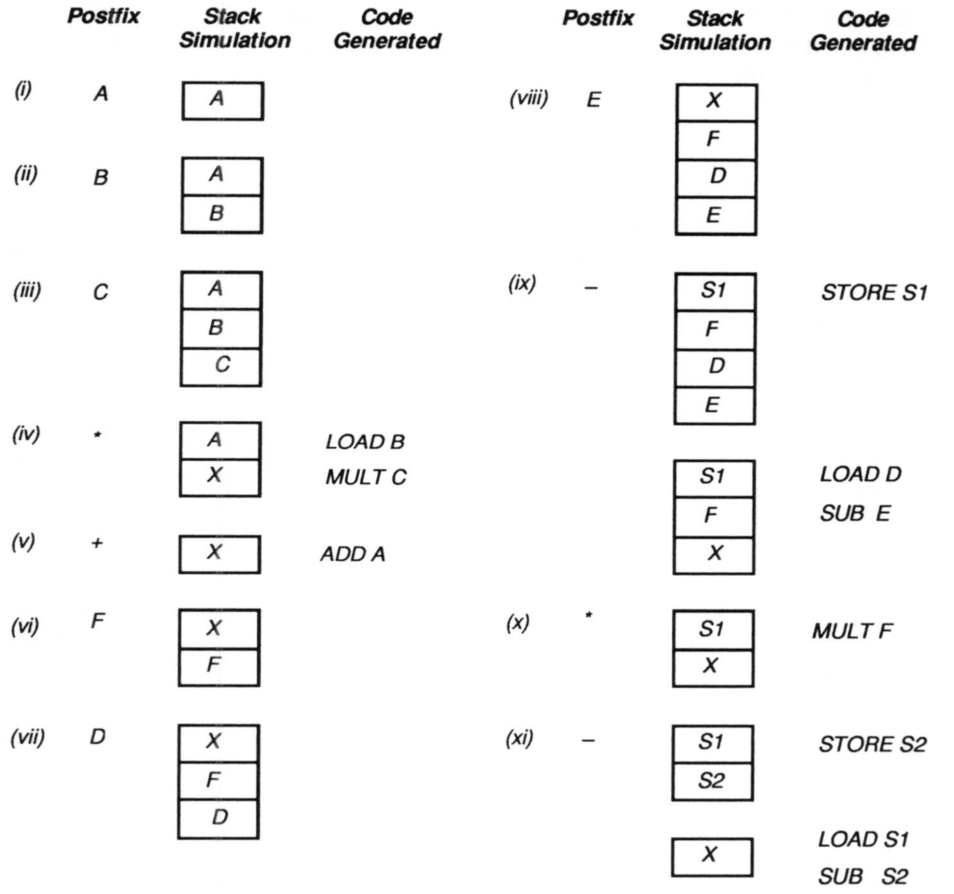

Postfix	Stack Simulation	Code Generated		Postfix	Stack Simulation	Code Generated
(i) A	A			(viii) E	X / F / D / E	
(ii) B	A / B					
(iii) C	A / B / C			(ix) –	S1 / F / D / E	STORE S1
(iv) *	A / X	LOAD B MULT C			S1 / F / X	LOAD D SUB E
(v) +	X	ADD A				
(vi) F	X / F			(x) *	S1 / X	MULT F
(vii) D	X / F / D			(xi) –	S1 / S2	STORE S2
					X	LOAD S1 SUB S2

Figure 18.1 *Generation of expression code by simulation of the run-time evaluation stack*

A description of the result, i.e. that it will be in the register, is then pushed onto the stack.

The simulation of the pushing of the values of the operands F, D and E onto the run-time evaluation stack (steps (vi)–(viii)) once more involves pushing descriptions of the operands onto the stack. However, at step (ix), it is necessary to simulate a subtraction of the value of E from that of D. Since neither value will be in the register at this point at run-time, but the register will contain a value, it is necessary to generate code to store the register contents in a memory stack location, i.e. $S1$. Hence a register-to-memory instruction must be generated, viz.

STORE S1

and the operand description concerned (the one at the bottom of the stack) updated to indicate that the operand concerned will actually be in location *S1*. Instructions to load the register and perform the subtraction are now generated:

$$
\begin{array}{ll}
\text{LOAD} & \text{D} \\
\text{SUB} & \text{E}
\end{array}
$$

To complete the simulation of the − operation a descriptor must be pushed onto the stack to indicate that the result is in the register. Step (x) involves a simulation of the multiplication of the value of the register contents (the value of *D–E*) by the value of the operand *F*. Thus these top two descriptions are popped, the instruction

$$
\begin{array}{ll}
\text{MULT} & \text{F}
\end{array}
$$

is generated, and a descriptor pushed onto the stack indicating that the result will be in *X*. At this stage the simulation of the run-time evaluation stack indicates that there are two operands on the stack which are the values of two intermediate computations (i.e. of *A+B*C* and *(D–E)*F*) and at run-time these values are actually in the memory location *S1* and the register *X* respectively.

Simulation of the subtraction operation required at step (xi) involves subtracting the register contents from those of *S1*. However, the Target *SUB* instruction subtracts from the register contents. Hence, it is necessary to generate code, firstly, to store the register contents in the next available memory stack location (*S2*), then load the contents of *S1* into the register and, finally, subtract the contents of *S2*, viz.

$$
\begin{array}{ll}
\text{STORE} & \text{S2} \\
\text{LOAD} & \text{S1} \\
\text{SUB} & \text{S2}
\end{array}
$$

The simulation of this operation is completed by pushing a description of the result, i.e. that it will be in the register. The simulation of the evaluation of the complete expression and the generation of the actual evaluation code for the single register machine are now complete with the stack simulation indicating that the result of the execution of the instruction sequence generated will leave the expression value in the register.

Note that the correctness of the above object code sequence depends only on the *commutativity* of the operators + and *, a property common to all machine arithmetics. For example, it actually computes *B*C + A* rather than *A + B*C*. However, it does not make any assumptions about the *associativity* of operators, a property which is not guaranteed by machine arithmetics. In general care must be taken that the code sequences generated for arithmetic expressions are consistent with the exact rules for expression evaluation (as stipulated or implied by the programming language) when executed on the particular machine involved.

For machines which have more than one computation register, but still insufficient to accommodate a strict evaluation stack, the above technique can be generalized to make use of these additional registers by

(a) simulating at compile-time the run-time binding of the contents of registers to stack values,
(b) selecting free registers for loading whenever possible, and
(c) generating instructions to store register contents in a memory-held stack only when all of the available registers are in use.

Hopefully it is becoming clear by now that the generation of efficient expression evaluation code for a machine which has a limited number of computation registers is a tricky process. However, generation of the object code for our Target machine is a comparatively simple process since the Target's architecture provides an evaluation stack and associated stack manipulation operations.

Since the code generation interface that we defined in Chapter 14 is that of a hypothetical machine which is assumed to have a run-time evaluation stack, the analyzer signals the required hypothetical machine actions as a sequence of postfix operations using this stack. Hence, with an actual target machine such as our Target computer which also has a run-time evaluation stack, it is a simple matter to generate a corresponding sequence of Target stack manipulation operations.

However, for the purposes of generating efficient object code (and, as we shall see in Chapter 19, for the implementation of run-time error checks) it is still desirable nonetheless for the code generator to simulate all the interface operations defined on the hypothetical machine on a compile-time evaluation stack. Code generation may then be *delayed* until all the information relating to the operands and operations of an expression are known. The use of such a simulation also simplifies the task of adapting the code generator to different target machine architectures.

Thus the interface calls made by the analyzer will cause our code generator to construct a *tree representation* of each variable reference and expression evaluation that is required. Code generation for the Target machine is then delayed until the complete context of a variable reference or expression evaluation has been established. Thus, for the range of language constructs supported by the Model language, generation of variable access code and expression evaluation code takes place only when one of the following situations occurs:

(a) an assignment-statement makes an assignment to a variable (i.e. a hypothetical machine *Assign* operation);
(b) the value of a Boolean expression is tested by a conditional jump instruction (*JumpOnFalse*);
(c) the start or end of a case-statement or for-statement.

To carry out this simulation the generator must keep track of the operands held by the hypothetical stack machine at any moment. A local module of the generator

    MODULE Stack;

provides the operations necessary to look after the simulation of the stack. The precise range of facilities which this module must provide will emerge in due course. However, the records in the stack are assumed to be of a type

    TYPE StackNode = ...;

each instance of which contains a description of an operand value or a variable reference.

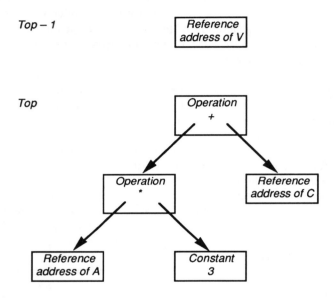

Figure 18.2 *Stack records during simulation of assignment-statement* V := A*3+C

For an operand value, this record is actually the root of an expression tree of such records which define the computation required to generate the operand value. Each node in such a tree is a *StackNode* record of variant *Operation* and denotes an operation whose operands are denoted by the left and right sub-trees attached to the node. The leaf nodes of the tree represent the primary operands of the expression and are of a variant *Reference* (denoting a variable access) or of a variant *Constant* (denoting an explicit constant value). There are two further variants, *Address* and *Result*, which are used to describe references and operands after the generation of evaluation code.

Figure 18.2 shows the stack record structure associated with the simulation of the hypothetical machine's execution of the assignment-statement

    V := A*3+C

immediately prior to execution of the *Assign* operation.

The primary strategy in achieving the generation of efficient object code is therefore delay. Thus the code generator, when it ultimately generates object code instructions, is able to examine the complete details of an expression or variable reference and generate the best code possible. Hence, instead of simply translating an expression such as

    2+A

directly into Target stack manipulation code such as

                LOADL   2
                LOAD   *address of A*
                ADD

by delaying the code generation until the complete expression tree is constructed the code generator can produce improved code such as

                LOAD   *address of A*
                INCR   2

There is a wide range of similar optimizations and some of these will be described later in this chapter.

The *Code* module introduced in the previous chapter looks after the management of the Target object code instructions as they are generated. The details of the architecture of the Target computer, such as its memory characteristics, registers, instruction format, and instruction order codes, are specified in the module *Target*, which was introduced in Chapter 2. The reader may find it useful at this stage to examine once again the description of the Target machine, as well as the Target definition module, before proceeding to consider the more intricate details of code generation.

18.2 Programming the basic stack operations

Simulation of the hypothetical stack contents involves maintaining within the generator operand descriptions of the type *StackNode* introduced in the previous section:

```
TYPE NodeKind  =  (Reference, ...);
     StackEntry =  POINTER TO StackNode;
     StackNode  =  RECORD
                     NextNode: StackEntry;
                     CASE Kind: NodeKind OF
                     | Reference: ...;
                     | ...
                     END
                   END;
```

When a new reference has to be added to the stack by the procedure *StackReference*, no addressing code is generated at that stage. The address coordinates are simply copied across into a new operand description, for which a suitable form is thus

```
TYPE StackNode =    RECORD
                        NextNode: StackEntry;
                        CASE Kind: NodeKind OF
                        | Reference:
                            RefAddress: RunTimeAddress;
                            Indexed: BOOLEAN;
                            ...;
                        |...
                        END
                    END;
```

The field *Indexed* anticipates that indexed references will in some way form an extension of this simple case. The procedure *StackReference* is then expressible as

```
PROCEDURE StackReference(Location: RunTimeAddress);
    VAR NewEntry: StackEntry;
    BEGIN
        Stack.NewNode(NewEntry);
        WITH NewEntry ^ DO
            Kind := Reference; RefAddress := Location; Indexed := FALSE
        END;
        Stack.Push(NewEntry)
    END StackReference;
```

where the *Stack* module operation *NewNode* creates a new stack record and the operator *Push* adds a given record to the top of the stack.

The *IndexedReference* operation also avoids the generation of any code. It uses the *Stack* module's *Pop* operation to remove the array reference and index value descriptions from the stack and adjusts the starting address of the array reference to correspond to the address of the array element with index value 0, even though no such element exists. This adjustment effectively computes the compile-time constant b_0 introduced in the discussion of array element accessing code in Section 16.2. Computation of this value simplifies the later generation of the required access code.

If the index value is a constant, *IndexedReference* makes a direct adjustment of the array reference to address the element required, otherwise it appends the description of the index value to the array reference, together with sufficient information to enable the subscripting code to be generated when it becomes necessary to do so. The suitably adjusted array reference record is then pushed back onto the stack.

A suitable extension of the stack record variant concerned is thus

```
Reference:
    RefAddress: RunTimeAddress;
    CASE Indexed: BOOLEAN OF
    | TRUE:
        Index: StackEntry;
        IndexMin, IndexMax: Target.Integer;
    | FALSE:
    END;
```

and the procedure *IndexedReference* takes the form

```
PROCEDURE IndexedReference(BoundMin, BoundMax: Target.Integer;
                              ElementRepresentation: TypeRepresentation);
   VAR ArrayVariableEntry, IndexEntry: StackEntry;
   BEGIN
      Stack.Pop(IndexEntry); Stack.Pop(VariableEntry);
      WITH ArrayVariableEntry ^ DO
         (* first adjust starting address of array as if lower bound = 0 *)
         DEC(RefAddress.RelativeAddress, BoundMin * ElementRepresentation);
         IF IndexEntry^.Kind = Constant THEN
            INC(RefAddress.RelativeAddress,
               IndexEntry^.Value * ElementRepresentation);
            Stack.FreeNode(IndexEntry)
         ELSE
            Indexed := TRUE; Index := IndexEntry;
            IndexMin := BoundMin; IndexMax := BoundMax
         END;
      Stack.Push(ArrayVariableEntry)
   END IndexedReference;
```

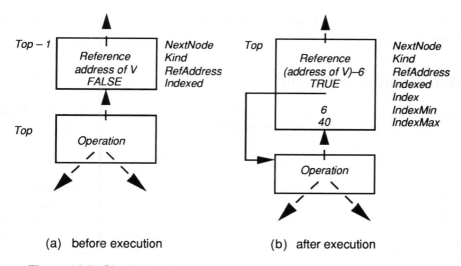

(a) before execution   (b) after execution

Figure 18.3 *Simulation of* IndexedReference(6, 40, IntegerRepresentation) *(i)*

Figures 18.3 and 18.4 illustrate the state of the hypothetical machine's stack before and after execution of *IndexedReference* operations. In Figure 18.3 the stack contains records corresponding to those generated for an array reference *V[e]* where *V* is an array assumed to have been declared as

VAR V: ARRAY [6..40] OF INTEGER;

and *e* is an arbitrary (non-constant) expression. In Figure 18.4 the stack records correspond to those generated for a reference to *V[10]*.

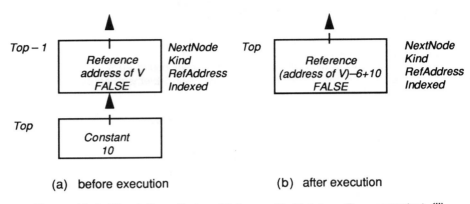

(a) before execution   (b) after execution

Figure 18.4 *Simulation of* IndexedReference(6, 40, IntegerRepresentation) *(ii)*

The generation of stack records for explicit constant and expression values is considered in the following section.

18.3 Expression evaluation

In this section we consider the construction of the tree of stack nodes that represents the evaluation of an expression. The primary operands in an expression tree are

- variable values obtained from accesses to variables;
- explicit constant values which appear in the source program.

The hypothetical machine operation *Dereference* represents the conversion of a variable reference to the corresponding value. In practice no code need be generated at that stage and the only action required is to add to the reference the representation details necessary when object code to access the value does have to be generated. Since this representation information is common to other forms of operand we add it thus:

```
TYPE StackNode =   RECORD
                       NextNode: StackEntry;
                       Rep: TypeRepresentation;
                       CASE Kind: NodeKind OF
                       ...
                       END
                   END;
```

and the operation *Dereference* requires only the following actions:

```
PROCEDURE Dereference(Representation: TypeRepresentation);
   VAR TopEntry: StackEntry;
   BEGIN
      Stack.Pop(TopEntry);
      TopEntry ^.Rep := Representation;
      Stack.Push(TopEntry)
   END Dereference;
```

Figure 18.5 illustrates the effect of a *Dereference(IntegerRepresentation)* operation on a variable reference (to a variable *V* of type *INTEGER*) on top of the stack.

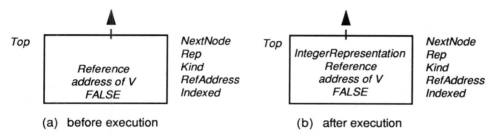

(a) before execution   (b) after execution

Figure 18.5 *Effect of a* Dereference(IntegerRepresentation) *operation*

Constant operands are also processed without any immediate generation of code. To accommodate them a second form of operand record is defined thus:

```
TYPE NodeKind = (Reference, Constant, ...);
      StackNode =    RECORD
                        NextNode: StackEntry;
                        Rep: TypeRepresentation;
                        CASE Kind: NodeKind OF
                        | Reference: ...;
                        | Constant: Value: Target.Integer;
                        | ...
                        END
                     END;
```

The procedure *StackConstant* then creates a stack node of variant *Constant* which holds the constant's value together with the representation appropriate to the value concerned.

```
PROCEDURE StackConstant(ConstantValue: Target.Integer;
                            ConstantRepresentation: TypeRepresentation);
   VAR ConstantEntry: StackEntry;
   BEGIN
      Stack.NewNode(ConstantEntry);
      WITH ConstantEntry^ DO
         Rep := ConstantRepresentation;
```

```
        Kind := Constant; Value := ConstantValue
    END;
    Stack.Push(ConstantEntry)
END StackConstant;
```

The leaves of expression trees are thus constructed by means of *Dereference* and *StackConstant* operations. The nodes of the trees, which represent binary and unary operators on these primary operands, are created by means of the hypothetical machine's integer and Boolean negation, arithmetic and comparison operations:

NegateInteger
NegateBoolean
BinaryIntegerOperation
BinaryBooleanOperation
Comparison

All of these generator operations examine their operand(s) (whose descriptions are on top of the stack) and, if the operands are constant values, the operation is *folded*, i.e. the necessary operation is performed by the code generator at compile-time and the (constant) result determined, thereby avoiding the generation of unnecessary object code to compute the result at run-time.

If folding is not possible, a new stack node of variant *Operation* is created and the operand descriptor(s) popped off the stack. Depending on whether the operator is a binary or unary operator the operand descriptor(s) are appended to the new stack node as either left and right sub-trees (in the case of a binary operator) or as a single sub-tree (in the case of a unary operator). The new stack node is then pushed onto the stack. To cater for this additional information required in stack nodes of variant *Operation*, the *StackNode* definition is expanded to

```
TYPE NodeKind     = (Reference, Constant, Operation, ...);
     OperatorKind = (Unary, Binary, ...);
     StackNode    = RECORD
                        NextNode: StackEntry;
                        Rep: TypeRepresentation;
                        CASE Kind: NodeKind OF
                        | Reference: ...;
                        | Constant: ...;
                        | Operation:
                            CASE OpKind: OperatorKind OF
                            | Unary:
                                UnaryOp: OperatorType;  UnaryEntry: StackEntry;
                            | Binary:
                                BinaryOp: OperatorType;
                                LeftEntry, RightEntry: StackEntry;
                            | ...
                        | ...
                        END
                    END;
```

The *NegateInteger* and *NegateBoolean* operators behave in a similar manner. The descriptor of the value to be negated is popped from the stack. If it is a constant value then the negation or inversion operation may be folded, i.e. the constant value is negated or inverted and the descriptor is pushed back onto the stack. Hence no object code will subsequently be generated for the folded operation. Otherwise a new stack record of variant *Operation* is created, the required operator is recorded (as a *Unary* operator) and the descriptor for the operand is appended to this new stack record, via its *UnaryEntry* field. Hence, *NegateInteger* takes the form

```
PROCEDURE NegateInteger;
   VAR IntegerEntry, ResultEntry: StackEntry;
   BEGIN
      Stack.Pop(IntegerEntry);
      IF IntegerEntry^.Kind = Constant THEN
         WITH IntegerEntry^ DO Value := –Value END;
         Stack.Push(IntegerEntry)
      ELSE
         Stack.NewNode(ResultEntry);
         WITH ResultEntry^ DO
            Rep := IntegerRepresentation;
            Kind := Operation; OpKind := Unary; UnaryOp := Minus;
            UnaryEntry := IntegerEntry
         END;
         Stack.Push(ResultEntry)
      END
   END NegateInteger;
```

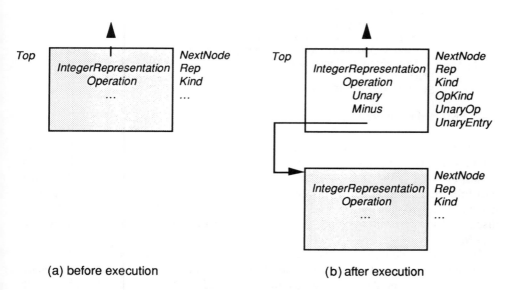

(a) before execution   (b) after execution

Figure 18.6 *Effect of a* NegateInteger *operation (i)*

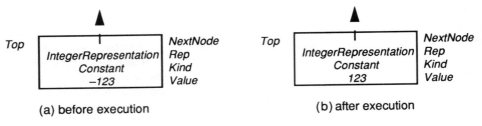

(a) before execution   (b) after execution

Figure 18.7 *Effect of a* NegateInteger *operation (ii)*

Figures 18.6 and 18.7 illustrate the effect of a *NegateInteger* operation on different operands—in Figure 18.6 the operand is an arbitrary non-constant integer expression, while in Figure 18.7 it is an integer constant with value *–123*.

The operation *NegateBoolean* takes a similar form to that of *NegateInteger*. Remember that the Boolean constant values *FALSE* and *TRUE* are represented on the hypothetical machine by the integer values *0* and *1*, respectively.

```
PROCEDURE NegateBoolean;
    VAR BooleanEntry, ResultEntry: StackEntry;
    BEGIN
        Stack.Pop(BooleanEntry);
        IF BooleanEntry^.Kind = Constant THEN
            WITH BooleanEntry^ DO Value := ABS(Value-1) END;
            Stack.Push(BooleanEntry)
        ELSE
            Stack.NewNode(ResultEntry);
            WITH ResultEntry^ DO
                Rep := BooleanRepresentation;
                Kind := Operation; OpKind := Unary;  UnaryOp := Not;
                UnaryEntry := BooleanEntry
            END;
            Stack.Push(ResultEntry)
        END
    END NegateBoolean;
```

BinaryIntegerOperation, when called, will have both of its operands on top of the stack, with its right hand operand descriptor uppermost. It first pops these two descriptors and, if they are both constant values, calls a procedure *DoArithmetic* which will fold the operation by performing the required integer arithmetic within the code generator. It will then push the description of the constant result back onto the stack and dispose of the constant operand stack records by calling the *Stack* module procedure *FreeNode*.

However, if folding is not possible (i.e. at least one operand is not a constant) it must create a new stack node of variant *Operation*, record the required operator as a *Binary* operator, and append the stack records for the operands as the left and right sub-trees of the node, via its *LeftEntry* and *RightEntry* fields.

```
PROCEDURE BinaryIntegerOperation(Operator: OperatorType);
    VAR LeftOperand, RightOperand, ResultEntry: StackEntry; ResultValue: Integer;
    BEGIN
        Stack.Pop(RightOperand); Stack.Pop(LeftOperand);
        IF (LeftOperand^.Kind = Constant) AND (RightOperand^.Kind = Constant) THEN
            DoArithmetic(Operator, LeftOperand^.Value,
                            RightOperand^.Value, ResultValue);
            StackConstant(ResultValue, IntegerRepresentation);
            Stack.FreeNode(LeftOperand); Stack.FreeNode(RightOperand)
        ELSE
            Stack.NewNode(ResultEntry);
            WITH ResultEntry^ DO
                Rep := IntegerRepresentation;
                Kind := Operation;
                OpKind := Binary; BinaryOp := Operator;
                LeftEntry := LeftOperand; RightEntry := RightOperand
            END;
            Stack.Push(ResultEntry)
        END
    END BinaryIntegerOperation;
```

Figures 18.8 and 18.9 illustrate the effect of a *BinaryIntegerOperation(Plus)* operation when folding is possible (in Figure 18.8 the operands are the values *15* and *–7*) and when folding is not possible (Figure 18.9).

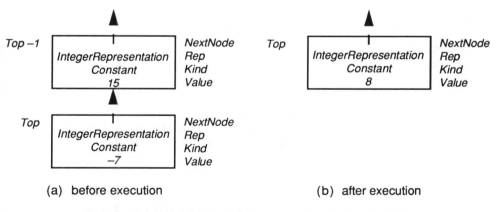

(a) before execution   (b) after execution

Figure 18.8 *Effect of* BinaryIntegerOperation(Plus) *with folding*

The *DoArithmetic* procedure checks for possible target machine overflow when performing arithmetic operations. It must be able to perform safe target machine arithmetic at compile-time without risk of overflow on the host machine. It does so as follows, assuming the *Integer* range of the target machine is no greater than that of the host machine.

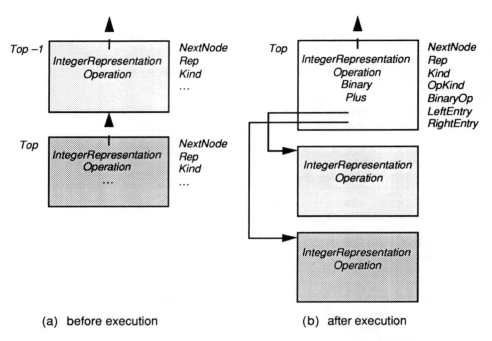

(a) before execution   (b) after execution

Figure 18.9 *Effect of* BinaryBooleanOperation(Plus) *without folding*

```
PROCEDURE DoArithmetic(Operator: OperatorType; Left, Right: Integer;
                       VAR Result: Integer);
    VAR Overflow: BOOLEAN;
    BEGIN
        Overflow := FALSE;
        CASE Operator OF
        | Plus, Minus:
            IF Operator = Minus THEN Right := –Right END;
            IF (Left > 0) AND (Right > 0) THEN Overflow := (Left > MAX(INTEGER) – Right)
            ELSIF (Left < 0) AND (Right < 0) THEN Overflow := (Left < MIN(INTEGER) – Right)
            END;
            IF NOT Overflow THEN Result := Left + Right END
        | Times:
            IF Right = 0 THEN Result := 0
            ELSIF ABS(Left) > MAX(INTEGER) DIV ABS(Right) THEN Overflow := TRUE
            ELSE Result := Left * Right
            END
        | Div:
            IF Right = 0 THEN GeneratorError(94); Result := MAX(INTEGER)
            ELSE Result := Left DIV Right
            END
        END;
        IF Overflow THEN GeneratorError(...); Result := MAX(INTEGER) END
    END DoArithmetic;
```

The action of the *BinaryBooleanOperation* is similar, in that it folds *AND* and *OR* operations which have constant operands, viz.

```
PROCEDURE BinaryBooleanOperation(Operator: OperatorType);
    VAR LeftOperand, RightOperand, ResultEntry: StackEntry; ResultValue: Integer;
    BEGIN
        Stack.Pop(RightOperand); Stack.Pop(LeftOperand);
        IF (LeftOperand^.Kind = Constant) AND (RightOperand^.Kind = Constant) THEN
            CASE Operator OF
            | And: ResultValue := LeftOperand^.Value * RightOperand^.Value
            | Or:  ResultValue := ORD(LeftOperand^.Value + RightOperand^.Value > 0)
            END;
            StackConstant(ResultValue, BooleanRepresentation);
            Stack.FreeNode(LeftOperand); Stack.FreeNode(RightOperand)
        ELSE
            Stack.NewNode(ResultEntry);
            WITH ResultEntry^ DO
                Rep := BooleanRepresentation; Kind := Operation;
                OpKind := Binary; BinaryOp := Operator;
                LeftEntry := LeftOperand; RightEntry := RightOperand
            END;
            Stack.Push(ResultEntry)
        END
    END BinaryBooleanOperation;
```

The hypothetical machine's *Comparison* operation pops the descriptor records for its operands off the stack and again, if possible, it folds the operation concerned by determining the result of the specified comparison for constant operands. If folding is possible it pushes the appropriate Boolean value back onto the stack as part of a stack record of type *Constant*. Otherwise a stack node of variant *Operation* is created, the required comparison operation is recorded as a *Binary* operation, and the operands are appended as the left and right sub-trees of this new node. It is then pushed onto the stack. Note that the number of distinct comparison operators is reduced by interchanging the operands for > and >= operations, thus equivalencing them to < and <=, respectively. Hence *e1* < *e2* is implemented as *e2* > *e1*.

```
PROCEDURE Comparison(Operator: OperatorType);
    VAR LeftOperand, RightOperand, ResultEntry: StackEntry; ResultValue: BOOLEAN;
    BEGIN
        Stack.Pop(RightOperand); Stack.Pop(LeftOperand);
        IF (LeftOperand^.Kind = Constant) AND (RightOperand^.Kind = Constant) THEN
            WITH LeftOperand^ DO
                CASE Operator OF
                | LessThan:              ResultValue := Value < RightOperand^.Value
                | LessThanOrEqual:       ResultValue := Value <= RightOperand^.Value
                | GreaterThanOrEqual:    ResultValue := Value >= RightOperand^.Value
                | GreaterThan:           ResultValue := Value > RightOperand^.Value
                | NotEquals:             ResultValue := Value <> RightOperand^.Value
                | Equals:                ResultValue := Value = RightOperand^.Value
```

```
                    END
              END;
              StackConstant(ORD(ResultValue), BooleanRepresentation);
              Stack.FreeNode(LeftOperand); Stack.FreeNode(RightOperand)
          ELSE
              Stack.NewNode(ResultEntry);
              WITH ResultEntry^ DO
                  Rep := BooleanRepresentation; Kind := Operation;  OpKind := Binary;
                    IF (Operator = GreaterThan) OR (Operator = GreaterThanOrEqual) THEN
                        IF Operator = GreaterThan THEN BinaryOp := LessThan
                        ELSE BinaryOp := LessThanOrEqual
                        END;
                        LeftEntry := RightOperand; RightEntry := LeftOperand
                    ELSE
                        BinaryOp := Operator;
                        LeftEntry := LeftOperand; RightEntry := RightOperand;
                    END
              END;
              Stack.Push(ResultEntry)
          END
      END Comparison;
```

Figure 18.10 illustrates the effect of a *Comparison(LessThan)* operation when folding is possible and Figure 18.11 shows the effect of the same operation when folding is not possible. In Figure 18.10 the two Boolean constants being compared are *FALSE (0)* and *TRUE (1)* giving a folded result value *TRUE*, while in Figure 18.11 the comparison is of two arbitrary Boolean expressions.

We have now completed our examination of the simulation of the range of hypothetical machine operations which construct expression trees and their leaves. As yet we have not actually generated any evaluation code—this is the subject of the following sections.

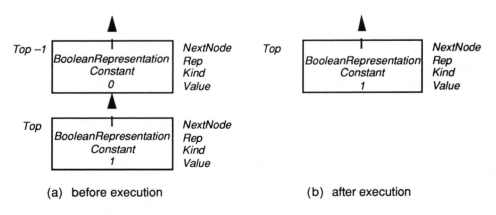

(a) before execution   (b) after execution

Figure 18.10 *Effect of a* Comparison(LessThan) *operation with folding*

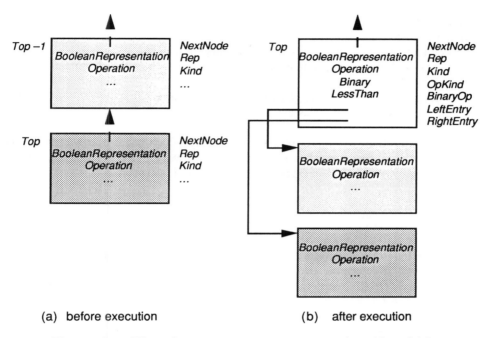

(a)   before execution   (b)   after execution

Figure 18.11 *Effect of a* Comparison(LessThan) *operation without folding*

18.4   Generating code for assignment-statements

The previous section described how all primary operands are handled by the generator without any immediate code generation. How the code is ultimately generated is well illustrated by the assignment operation, which we consider next.

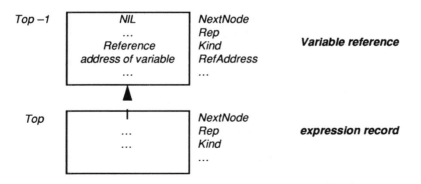

Figure 18.12 *The hypothetical machine's state prior to an* Assign *operation*

When the interface operation *Assign* is called by the analyzer, the state of the simulation of the hypothetical machine's stack is as shown in Figure 18.12, i.e. an expression tree, variable reference or constant entry for the value to be assigned is on top of the stack, with the variable reference for the variable to which the assignment is to be made lying below it.

The form of the code that is generated for an assignment-statement on the Target machine falls into one of four classes:

(a) if the value being assigned is that of an array which requires *n* words for its representation, then a multi-word assignment is involved and the Target's *MOVE* instruction will be used and the code will take the following form:

> LOADA   *address of array being assigned*
> LOADA   *address of array to which assignment is being made*
> MOVE   *n*

(b) if the variable being assigned is an array element then a computation needs to be performed to determine its address and the assignment code makes use of the Target's *STOREI* instruction to assign the one-word expression value to the addressed memory location, viz.

> *load value to be assigned onto the stack*
> *load address of array element onto the stack*
> STOREI   1

(c) if the value *0* is being assigned to a variable that it is not an array element, then the simplest object code uses an *STZ (store zero)* instruction, viz.

> STZ   *address of variable*

(d) otherwise an assignment is being made to a simple variable and the object code form required for the Target is

> *load value to be assigned onto the stack*
> STORE   *address of variable*

A general strategy for Model assignment-statements on the Target computer is thus

```
IF more than one word is being assigned THEN
    generate code to use store-to-store MOVE instruction
ELSIF assigning to an array element THEN
    generate code to store the value in  the array element
ELSIF assigning zero THEN
    generate code using STZ instruction
ELSE
    generate code to load and store value
END
```

Using the stack refinements developed so far, and introducing some basic procedures for code generation, we can program this strategy as follows:

```
PROCEDURE Assign;
   VAR ExpressionEntry, VariableEntry: StackEntry; Size: CARDINAL;
   BEGIN
      Stack.Pop(ExpressionEntry); Stack.Pop(VariableEntry);
      Size := ExpressionEntry^.Rep;
      IF Size > 1 THEN
         LoadAddress(ExpressionEntry);
         LoadAddress(VariableEntry);
         Code.InsD(MOVE, Size)
      ELSIF VariableEntry^.Indexed THEN
         Load(ExpressionEntry);
         LoadAddress(VariableEntry);
         Code.InsD(STOREI, 1)
      ELSIF (ExpressionEntry^.Kind = Constant) AND (ExpressionEntry^.Value = 0) THEN
         AccessWord(VariableEntry^.RefAddress, STZ)
      ELSE
         Load(ExpressionEntry);
         AccessWord(VariableEntry^.RefAddress, STORE)
      END;
      Stack.FreeNode(ExpressionEntry); Stack.FreeNode(VariableEntry)
   END Assign;
```

Here we have introduced

- A procedure *LoadAddress* which generates code to load the *address* of the operand specified onto the top of the Target's run-time stack.

  ```
  PROCEDURE LoadAddress(Entry: StackEntry);
  ```

- A procedure *Load* which generates code to load the *value* of the operand specified onto the top of the Target's stack.

  ```
  PROCEDURE Load(Entry: StackEntry);
  ```

- A procedure *AccessWord* which generates code to perform the memory access operation specified by its *AccessOpCode* parameter using the memory location whose address is indicated by the parameter *WordAddress*.

  ```
  PROCEDURE AccessWord(WordAddress: RunTimeAddress;
                       AccessOpCode: OrderCode);
  ```

These three procedures are the basic work-horses for all the code generation logic associated with the manipulation of hypothetical stack operands, e.g. integer arithmetic. We carry their development further in the following sub-sections.

18.4.1 Loading operands

The procedure *Load* generates the object code required to load onto the Target's evaluation stack the result of the evaluation of an expression tree constructed as described in 18.3. Its action is based directly upon the form of expression trees, the operations that they represent, and the Target machine instructions available for their implementation.

Expression evaluation code is generated by simple traversal of an expression tree in which the left and right sub-trees are evaluated as operands, followed by an appropriate Target machine instruction corresponding to the required operation. The evaluation of a reference (which will be a leaf of the tree) is equivalent to traversal of a degenerate tree and results in the generation of appropriate memory access code. Likewise the evaluation of a constant (again at the edge of a tree) results in the generation of code to load the appropriate value onto the Target's evaluation stack. Hence the basic form of the procedure *Load* is

```
PROCEDURE Load(Entry: StackEntry);

    PROCEDURE DoUnaryOperation;
      VAR OpCode: OrderCode;
      BEGIN
        WITH Entry^ DO
          Load(UnaryEntry);
          IF UnaryOp = Minus THEN OpCode := NEG ELSE OpCode := INV END;
          Code.Ins0(OpCode);
          Stack.FreeNode(UnaryEntry)
        END
      END DoUnaryOperation;

    PROCEDURE DoBinaryOperation;
      VAR Folded: BOOLEAN;
      BEGIN
        WITH Entry^ DO
          Folded := FALSE;
          attempt to fold the binary operation;
          IF NOT Folded THEN
            Load(LeftEntry); Load(RightEntry); Code.Ins0(BinaryOpCode[BinaryOp])
          END;
          Stack.FreeNode(LeftEntry); Stack.FreeNode(RightEntry)
        END
      END DoBinaryOperation;

    BEGIN
      WITH Entry^ DO
        CASE Kind OF
        | Reference:
          IF Indexed THEN LoadAddress(Entry); Code.InsD(LOADI, 1)
          ELSE AccessWord(RefAddress, LOAD)
          END
```

```
| Constant: Code.InsD(LOADL, Value)
| Operation:
    CASE OpKind OF
    | Unary: DoUnaryOperation
    | Binary: DoBinaryOperation
    ...
    END
  END
END;
Entry^.Kind := Result
END Load;
```

The reference evaluation code makes use of *LoadAddress* and *AccessWord* for addressing array elements and simple variables, respectively. In the case of a simple variable its value is loaded onto the stack by means of a *STORE* instruction, whereas the value of an array element is loaded onto the stack by first loading the address of the element's memory location and then performing a *LOADI* operation to replace the address of the location by its contents.

The array *BinaryOpCode* used within the procedure *DoBinaryOperation* is assumed to contain the Target instruction codes corresponding to the binary operator symbols of Model, i.e. it is declared as

```
VAR BinaryOpCode: ARRAY OperatorType OF Target.OrderCode;
```

x + 0	*x*
0 + x	*x*
*x * 0*	*0*
*0 * x*	*0*
*x * 1*	*x*
*1 * x*	*x*
x DIV 1	*x*
0 DIV x	*0*
x AND FALSE	*FALSE*
FALSE AND x	*FALSE*
x AND TRUE	*x*
TRUE AND x	*x*
x OR FALSE	*x*
FALSE OR x	*x*
x OR TRUE	*TRUE*
TRUE OR x	*TRUE*

Table 18.1 *Range of operations folded by* DoBinaryOperation

DoBinaryOperation attempts to perform further folding of operations by examining their operands to determine whether it is possible to carry out the specified operation at compile-time (and thereby avoid generating any evaluation code whatsoever but instead generate code which simply loads the result determined by the code generator onto the Target's stack) or whether it is possible to perform some optimization of the generated code for the Target machine.

DoBinaryOperation examines the left and right operands of an operation looking for the special cases shown on the left in Table 18.1 and generates code to load the result value shown on the right.

For an addition operation such as $x+y$, the normal Target evaluation code takes the form

```
LOAD      address of x
LOAD      address of y
ADD
```

If either of x or y is a constant value (say y) then this code could take the form

```
LOAD      address of x
LOADL     value of y
ADD
```

However, improved code would make use of the *INCR* instruction, viz.

```
LOAD      address of x
INCR      value of y
```

Likewise, *DoBinaryOperation* checks for a possible subtraction involving constant values and again generates improved code using the *INCR* instruction. The analysis carried out within *DoBinaryOperation* to attempt folding is as follows:

```
IF RightEntry^.Kind = Constant THEN
    CASE BinaryOp OF
    | Plus, Minus:
        Load(LeftEntry);
        IF RightEntry^.Value <> 0 THEN
            IF BinaryOp = Plus THEN Code.InsD(INCR, RightEntry^.Value)
            ELSE Code.InsD(INCR, –RightEntry^.Value)
            END
        END;
        Folded := TRUE
    | Times, And:
        IF RightEntry^.Value = 0 THEN Code.InsD(LOADL, 0); Folded := TRUE
        ELSIF RightEntry^.Value = 1 THEN Load(LeftEntry); Folded := TRUE
        END
    | Div:
        IF RightEntry^.Value = 1 THEN Load(LeftEntry); Folded := TRUE END
    | Or:
        IF RightEntry^.Value = 0 THEN Load(LeftEntry); Folded := TRUE
        ELSIF RightEntry^.Value = 1 THEN Code.InsD(LOADL, 1); Folded := TRUE
        END
    ELSE (* cannot fold relational operations *)
```

```
      END
   END;
   IF LeftEntry^.Kind = Constant THEN
      CASE BinaryOp OF
      | Plus:
         Load(RightEntry);
         IF LeftEntry^.Value <> 0 THEN Code.InsD(INCR, LeftEntry^.Value) END;
         Folded := TRUE
      | Times, And:
         IF LeftEntry^.Value = 0 THEN Code.InsD(LOADL, 0); Folded := TRUE
         ELSIF LeftEntry^.Value = 1 THEN Load(RightEntry); Folded := TRUE
         END
      | Div:
          IF LeftEntry^.Value = 0 THEN Code.InsD(LOADL, 0); Folded := TRUE END
      | Or:
         IF LeftEntry^.Value = 0 THEN Load(RightEntry); Folded := TRUE
         ELSIF LeftEntry^.Value = 1 THEN Code.InsD(LOADL, 1); Folded := TRUE
         END
      ELSE (* cannot fold relational operations or minus *)
      END
   END;
```

As the expression tree is traversed, the stack records for traversed nodes and leaves are deallocated, and the tree itself is ultimately replaced on the hypothetical machine's stack by a record of variant *Result*. Hence the definition of *StackNode* is extended to

```
TYPE NodeKind  =  (Reference, Constant, Operation, Result, ...);
     StackNode  =  RECORD
                      NextNode: StackEntry;
                      Rep: TypeRepresentation;
                      CASE Kind: NodeKind OF
                      | Reference: ...
                      | Constant: ...
                      | Operation: ...
                      | Result:
                      | ...
                      END
                   END;
```

18.4.2 Addressing operands

The role of the procedure *LoadAddress* is to generate the Target object code necessary to load the address of a referenced variable onto the top of the Target's evaluation stack. Its form follows directly from the form of a variable reference description in a stack record, i.e. whether or not it is an indexed-variable, and also the Target instruction codes available for memory access.

For a non-indexed-variable, its run-time addressing coordinates are given by the *RefAddress* field of the associated stack record and its address can be loaded using a

LOADA instruction. In 16.2 we saw that the address of an element (with index value *e*) of a one-dimensional array with starting address a_0 and elements requiring *size* words each for their representation, is given by the formula

$$b_0 + b_1*e$$

where b_0 and b_1 are compile-time constants such that

$$b_0 = a_0 - size*M$$
$$b_1 = size$$

Note that the value b_0 (which is effectively the address of the array element *a[0]*) is the value of the *RefAddress* field for an indexed reference (this address adjustment having been performed previously by the *IndexedReference* operation).

The instruction sequences derived in 16.2 for loading the address of an array element were (assuming *size* $\neq 1$)

```
LOADA    b0
evaluate index e
LOADL    b1
MUL
ADD
```

or (assuming *size* = *1*)

```
LOADA    b0
evaluate index e
ADD
```

Hence the form of the procedure *LoadAddress* is

```
PROCEDURE LoadAddress(Entry: StackEntry);
   BEGIN
      WITH Entry^ DO
         AccessWord(RefAddress, LOADA);
         IF Indexed THEN
            Load(Index);
            IF Rep > 1 THEN Code.InsD(LOADL, Rep); Code.Ins0(MUL) END;
            Code.Ins0(ADD);
            Stack.FreeNode(Index, SIZE(StackEntry))
         END
      END;
      Entry^.Kind := Address
   END LoadAddress;
```

LoadAddress disposes of the stack record for the index and adjusts the operand description referenced by *Entry* to indicate that it now describes a loaded *address*, i.e. the stack record type *StackNode* is extended to include a final variant, *Address*, viz.

```
TYPE NodeKind  = (Reference, Constant, Operation, Result, Address);
     StackNode = RECORD
                    NextNode: StackEntry;
                    Rep: TypeRepresentation;
                    CASE Kind: NodeKind OF
                    | Reference: ...
                    | Constant: ...
                    | Operation: ...
                    | Result:
                    | Address:
                    END
                 END;
```

18.4.3 Accessing stored data

The procedure *AccessWord* generates code to perform a specified Target machine code instruction on a specified location within the memory of the Target computer.

```
PROCEDURE AccessWord(WordAddress: RunTimeAddress;
                     AccessOpCode: OrderCode);
```

From the discussion of the nature of Target data access code in 17.2, it follows that the Target instruction required to perform the specified access operation is easily generated using the compile-time relative address and textual frame level information contained in the given *WordAddress*, thus

```
WITH WordAddress DO
   Code.Ins(AccessOpCode, RelativeAddress,
            FP, FrameLevel–TextualLevel)
END
```

The generation of object code to load constant values onto the stack of the Target is trivial since the operand field of a *LOADL* instruction is a full-word value—such an operand which is embedded within an instruction is known as an *immediate* operand. The use of immediate operands wherever possible usually provides the most compact and efficient code for constant manipulation.

However, in the instruction sets of some machines immediate operands are not full-word values but may occupy only part of a word within an instruction. For such machines, when the value of a constant data item is too large to be represented as an immediate operand, the compiler must create a stored copy of the constant somewhere in the object program and then generate instructions which address this stored copy to perform the constant manipulation required. Thus, on a 16 bit per word machine whose instruction set allows only 8-bit operands, say, the object code generated for the assignment-statement

A := 5000

would take the form

$$
\begin{array}{lll}
& \text{LOAD} & \textit{address of C} \\
& \text{STORE} & \textit{address of A} \\
& : & \\
\text{C} & 5000 &
\end{array}
$$

where *C* is a preset location in the object program containing the value *5000*.

The locations holding such stored constants are allocated in a different way from those for variables for several reasons:

(a) their contents must be determined at compile-time;
(b) since their contents do not change, a single copy suffices even for recursive procedure code;
(c) a single stored copy may be shared by several constants with the same internal representation.

In general these preset constant locations are regarded as part of the object code storage rather than the program's variable data storage. The compiler should accumulate a single *constant table* throughout program generation and locate this table in the final object program immediately beyond the object code. Constants within this table are then addressed in the object code relative to a fixed base location which holds the table address. Relocatable object code systems often provide a means of creating and addressing such preset locations.

18.5 Generating code for input and output operations

The code generator interface operation *ReadOperation* is called as part of the sequence of interface calls

```
StackReference(address of v)
ReadOperation(CharMode)
Assign
```

made by the analyzer when processing a read-statement

```
READ(v)
```

where *v* is a variable declared to be of type *CHAR*. Read-statements in Model programs also permit input values to be assigned to *INTEGER* variables.

The *Assign* operation following the *ReadOperation* will, as we have seen in the previous section, ultimately generate the necessary object code—provided that *ReadOperation* builds an expression tree to define the required input operation and the procedure *Load* is extended to generate object code for such an input operation. An input operation is therefore treated as a postfix operator with no operands and, as shown in Figure 18.13, the action of *ReadOperation* is to create a stack record of variant *Operation* in which the *OpKind* field is defined to be a *ReadOp* and the transfer *Mode* and *Rep* fields reflect the type of the variable concerned (which is the type *CHAR* in this case).

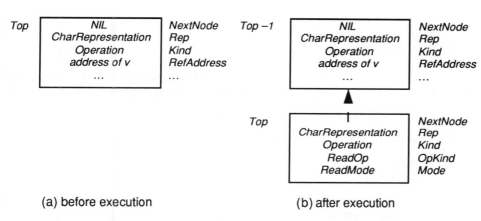

(a) before execution   (b) after execution

Figure 18.13 *Effect of a* ReadOperation *on the hypothetical machine stack*

The definition of *StackNode* is thus extended as follows:

```
TYPE NodeKind      = (Reference, Constant, Operation, Result, Address);
     OperatorKind  = (Unary, Binary, ReadOp);
     StackNode     = RECORD
                        NextNode: StackEntry;
                        Rep: TypeRepresentation;
                        CASE Kind: NodeKind OF
                        ...
                        | Operation:
                            CASE OpKind: OperatorKind OF
                            | Unary: ...
                            | Binary:...
                            | ReadOp:  Mode: IOMode
                            END;
                        ...
                        END
                     END;
```

and the action of *ReadOperation* is defined as

```
PROCEDURE ReadOperation (ReadMode: IOMode);
   VAR ValueRead: StackEntry;
```

```
BEGIN
   Stack.NewNode(ValueRead);
   WITH ValueRead^ DO
      Kind := Operation; OpKind := ReadOp; Mode := ReadMode;
      CASE ReadMode OF
      | IntegerMode: Rep := IntegerRepresentation
      | CharMode:    Rep := CharRepresentation
      END
   END;
   Stack.Push(ValueRead)
END ReadOperation;
```

The procedure *Load* must be amended so that, when it encounters a node of variant *Operation* which defines a *ReadOp* operation, it generates the necessary object code to perform the input transfer.

```
PROCEDURE Load(Entry: StackEntry);
   BEGIN
      WITH Entry^ DO
         CASE Kind OF
            ...
         | Operation:
             CASE OpKind OF
             | Unary:  DoUnaryOperation
             | Binary: DoBinaryOperation
             | ReadOp: DoReadOperation
             END
         END
      END;
      Entry^.Kind := Result
   END Load;
```

The local procedure *DoReadOperation* uses the Target machine's *CHIN* instruction (which loads the next available character from the input channel onto the top of the Target's stack at run-time) to perform the input of a character value. However, for input of an integer value, it must instead generate a call of a routine within the run-time support package of the object program which will read sufficient characters to form an integer value and then push this value onto the top of the Target's stack, thus

```
PROCEDURE DoReadOperation;
   VAR OpCode: OrderCode;
   BEGIN
      WITH Entry^ DO
         CASE Mode OF
         | IntegerMode:  Code.SystemCall(ReadInteger)
         | CharMode:     Code.Ins0(CHIN)
         END
      END
   END DoReadOperation;
```

The output of character and integer values is somewhat simpler. The interface operation *WriteOperation* uses the procedure *Load* to traverse the expression tree on top of the hypothetical machine's stack and generate the object code necessary to load the value that is to be output onto the top of the Target's stack at run-time. If the value is a *CHAR* value then it can be transferred from the top of the run-time stack to the output device by means of the Target's *CHOUT* instruction. In the case of an *INTEGER* value, the object program must again call a run-time support routine which will generate, and output, the corresponding sequence of characters. Hence

```
PROCEDURE WriteOperation(WriteMode: IOMode);
    VAR ExpressionValue: StackEntry;
    BEGIN
        Stack.Pop(ExpressionValue);
        Load(ExpressionValue);
        CASE WriteMode OF
        | IntegerMode:  Code.SystemCall(WriteInteger)
        | CharMode:     Code.Ins0(CHOUT)
        END;
        Stack.FreeNode(ExpressionValue)
    END WriteOperation;
```

18.6 Code labels and jumps

In Chapter 14 we saw that the hypothetical machine program generated by the analyzer contains *code labels* to which control may be transferred from elsewhere. In practice the code generator distinguishes two kinds of label:

(a) *New labels* which are not referenced by any jump instruction before the generation of the instruction which they label.
(b) *Future labels* which are referenced by jump instructions which precede the instruction labelled in the object program—in which case the address of the instruction to which a jump is to be made will not yet be known. Such instructions can only be partially generated and must subsequently be *fixed up* when the information required becomes available. For these the generator must create a record of all jump instructions which reference each future label, and when the label position is determined, the destination of the jump instructions must be fixed up.

Since a compiler in general cannot hold all the object code it generates in main memory, how fix-ups are effected depends on the range over which the fix-ups are required. In Modula-2, for example, fix-ups arising from control statements such as if-, while- and for-statements, etc., are only required within the code for any one procedure or program block, and in-memory fix-ups can be provided by holding the code for each block until the end of that block is reached. To do so the compiler must put an implementation limit on the length of code generated by any block, but such a limit need not be a problem to users. A corresponding limit on total program size would be intolerable.

Since the *Code* module is responsible for the assembly and organization of the instructions of the object program, it is logical to place the handling and fix-up of the various forms of jump instructions under its control also. Hence we add three procedures to those already exported by the *Code* module, namely

```
PROCEDURE NewLabel(VAR Sequence: CodeLabel);
PROCEDURE FutureLabel(VAR Sequence: CodeLabel);
PROCEDURE ExpectedLabel(VAR Sequence: CodeLabel);
```

NewLabel, *FutureLabel* and *ExpectedLabel* correspond directly to the code generator interface procedures *NewCodeLabel*, *FutureCodeLabel* and *ExpectedCodeLabel* whose action is thus merely to call the equivalent *Code* module procedure.

Within the *Code* module the instructions generated for the block currently being compiled are held in a code buffer of size *CodeMax* instructions, declared as

```
VAR Code: ARRAY [1..CodeMax] OF Target.Instruction;
```

A variable

```
VAR NextInstruction: [1..CodeMax + 1];
```

gives the index of the next unoccupied position in the code buffer while the value of

```
VAR CurrentAddress: Target.AddressRange
```

denotes the address of the next available memory location in the overall object program being generated.

The *Code* module procedures *NewCodeSpace* and *EndOfCodeSpace*, introduced in 17.5, are respectively responsible for initializing the code buffer and transferring its contents to a code handler module (described in more detail in 18.9) whose function is to organize the storage of the generated object code.

The interface type *CodeLabel* has two variants:

(a) For *expected* code labels, i.e. those whose labelled object code sequence (its *site*) has not yet been determined, the field *LastCodeReference* addresses the most recently generated instruction in the code buffer which references that label. This instruction is the head of a chain of those instructions awaiting fix-up, i.e. which all reference the particular expected label—the chain is formed by holding the code buffer index of each instruction in the chain in the full-word *N* field of its predecessor, as shown in Figure 18.14. The final instruction in the chain contains *0* (which is not a legal code buffer index) in its *N* field.

(b) For a code label whose site has already been established, the field *Address* gives the object program address of the site of the labelled object code instruction within the current block.

```
TYPE CodeLabel =    RECORD
                    CASE Expected: BOOLEAN OF
                    | FALSE: StartAddress: Target.AddressRange;
                    | TRUE:  LastCodeReference: CodeRange;
                    END
                END;
```

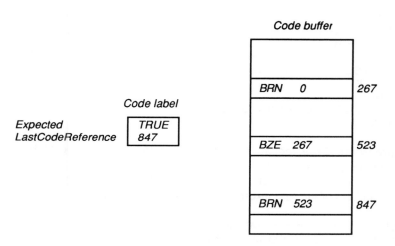

Code buffer

Code label

Expected	*TRUE*
LastCodeReference	*847*

Figure 18.14 *Instructions awaiting fix-up in the code buffer*

The action of *NewLabel* is thus to record the code label as not expected since the instruction being addressed is the next one to be generated in the object program, viz.

```
PROCEDURE NewLabel(VAR Sequence: CodeLabel);
   BEGIN
      WITH Sequence DO Expected := FALSE; StartAddress := CurrentAddress END
   END NewLabel;
```

FutureLabel records the code label concerned as expected and assigns *0* to the *LastCodeReference* field—thus initializing the chain of jump instructions to be fixed up subsequently as empty. Hence

```
PROCEDURE FutureLabel(VAR Sequence: CodeLabel);
   BEGIN
      WITH Sequence DO Expected := TRUE; LastCodeReference := 0 END
   END FutureLabel;
```

JumpIns is responsible for generating the given jump instruction to the label concerned— a backward jump instruction (i.e. one whose label is no longer expected) can be generated directly, otherwise it must enable a later fix-up to be performed.

Hence, for forward jumps, the jump instruction is partially generated by setting its operation code field and the instruction is then entered at the head of the chain of instructions awaiting a fix-up for this code label by chaining it via its *N* field. Thus, *JumpIns* takes the form

```
PROCEDURE JumpIns(JumpType: OrderCode; VAR Sequence: CodeLabel);
    VAR Destination: Integer;
    BEGIN
        WITH Sequence DO
            IF Expected THEN
                Destination := LastCodeReference; LastCodeReference := NextInstruction;
            ELSE Destination := StartAddress
            END
        END;
        Ins(JumpType, Destination, BP, 0)
    END JumpIns;
```

The procedure *ExpectedLabel*, which is used to site an expected label, is thus responsible for performing the fix-ups required. It traverses the chain of jump instructions to be fixed up (such as in Figure 18.14), adjusting the *N* field in each to contain the address of the next instruction in the object program, viz.

```
PROCEDURE ExpectedLabel(VAR Sequence: CodeLabel);
    VAR ThisFixUp, NextFixUp: [0..CodeMax];
    BEGIN
        WITH Sequence DO
            NextFixUp := LastCodeReference;
            WHILE NextFixUp <> 0 DO
                ThisFixUp := NextFixUp; NextFixUp := Code[ThisFixUp].N;
                Code[ThisFixUp].N := CurrentAddress
            END;
            Expected := FALSE; StartAddress := CurrentAddress
        END
    END ExpectedLabel;
```

The interface procedure *Jump* requires an unconditional jump to the instruction denoted by its code label parameter and hence is implemented as a call of

```
PROCEDURE Jump(VAR Destination: CodeLabel);
    BEGIN
        Code.JumpIns(BRN, Destination)
    END Jump;
```

where *BRN* is the Target's unconditional jump instruction.

When the interface operation *JumpOnFalse* is invoked by the analyzer, the compile-time evaluation stack contains a stack record (of variant either *Reference*, *Constant* or *Operation*) which is an expression tree for the Boolean expression upon whose run-time value the transfer of control to the specified code label is conditional. Hence, the object code generated must load the expression value onto the Target's evaluation stack followed by a *BZE* (branch on zero) instruction. The latter will pop the topmost value off the run-time stack and, if its value is zero (i.e. the Boolean value *FALSE*), cause the required transfer of control. Thus, the basic form of *JumpOnFalse* is

```
PROCEDURE JumpOnFalse(VAR Destination: CodeLabel);
  VAR BooleanEntry: StackEntry;
  BEGIN
    Stack.Pop(BooleanEntry);
    Load(BooleanEntry); Code.JumpIns(BZE, Destination);
    Stack.FreeNode(BooleanEntry)
  END JumpOnFalse;
```

However, if the Boolean expression is simply a constant, then folding of the evaluation code can take place—if the value is the constant *FALSE* then only an unconditional jump instruction need be generated, but if the value is *TRUE* then no code need be generated at all! Hence we can re-express *JumpOnFalse* as follows:

```
PROCEDURE JumpOnFalse(VAR Destination: CodeLabel);
  VAR BooleanEntry: StackEntry;
  BEGIN
    Stack.Pop(BooleanEntry);
    WITH BooleanEntry^ DO
      IF Kind = Constant THEN
          IF Value = 0 THEN Code.JumpIns(BRN, Destination) END;
      ELSE
          Load(BooleanEntry); Code.JumpIns(BZE, Destination)
      END
    END;
    Stack.FreeNode(BooleanEntry)
  END JumpOnFalse;
```

In general, for language features generating a need for code fix-ups over a range which exceeds the compiler's code buffer capacity (such as calls in Modula-2 to procedures declared as *forward* procedures or Pascal goto-statements which reference a label declared in a textually enclosing block), a two-pass technique must be adopted—the first pass generating code without fix-ups on backing store, the second pass reading and rewriting this code while carrying out any fix-ups necessary. This second pass can, however, often be incorporated in the loading process which gets the final code into main memory prior to its execution—most link-loaders incorporate such a fix-up capability. Such compilation is sometimes referred to as *one-and-a-half-pass compilation*.

18.7 Generating case-statement code

In Chapter 14 we saw that the following example of a case-statement

```
CASE K OF
| 1: S1
| 3, 2, 4: S2
...
END
```

produced the interface call sequence shown below:

```
...stack value of K...
FutureCodeLabel(AfterCase)
OpenCase

NextIsCase(1)

...code for statement-sequence S1...
Jump(AfterCase)

NextIsCase(3)
NextIsCase(2)
NextIsCase(4)
...code for statement-sequence S2...
Jump(AfterCase)


...
CloseCase
ExpectedCodeLabel(AfterCase)
```

Since the number of case limbs in a case-statement is not known until after all of the limbs have been compiled, the object code generated for a case-statement takes the form shown in Figure 18.15. The initial object code generated by the interface operation *OpenCase* jumps over the code for the case limbs to an object code sequence which evaluates the selector expression and then makes the appropriate statement limb selection. The selection, the object code for which is generated by the interface procedure *CloseCase*, is achieved by means of an indexed jump, using the Target's indexed branch instruction *BIDX*, into a table of jump instructions known as a *jump table*.

A jump table has one entry for each case label value in the range of label values that appears in the case-statement, each entry containing either a jump to the corresponding statement labelled by the case value concerned, or else (in the case of an unspecified label value) a jump to an error routine.

When *OpenCase* is called, the expression tree for the selector expression will be on top of the compile-time evaluation stack. Thus *OpenCase* generates an unconditional jump to a future code label (the point labelled *SELECT* in Figure 18.15) which is pushed, together with the expression tree, onto a stack of case-statement records for later inspection by the corresponding *CloseCase* operation. The use of a stack to store these records is necessary since case-statements may be arbitrarily nested within other case-statements. Hence we have

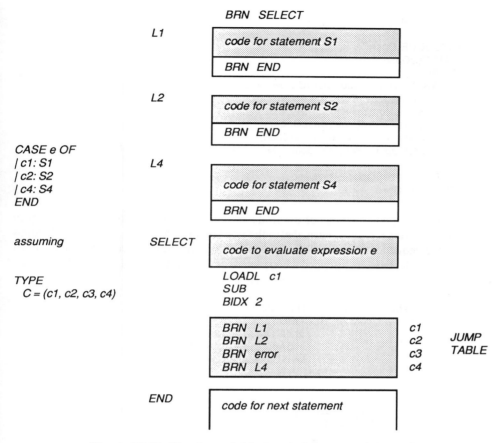

Figure 18.15 *Structure of object code for a case-statement*

```
TYPE CaseEntry   =  POINTER TO CaseRecord;
     CaseRecord =  RECORD
                      Selector: StackEntry;
                      CaseCode: CodeLabel;
                      MinLabel, MaxLabel: Target.Integer;
                      FirstLabel: CaseLabelEntry;
                      Next: CaseEntry
                   END;
```

The top of this stack is referenced by a variable

```
VAR  TopOfCaseStack: CaseEntry;
```

which is initialized by the code generator procedure *InitializeCaseStack*. The action of

OpenCase is thus

```
PROCEDURE OpenCase;
  VAR ThisCase: CaseEntry;
  BEGIN
    Host.New(ThisCase, SIZE(CaseRecord));
    WITH ThisCase^ DO
      Stack.Pop(Selector);
      Code.FutureLabel(CaseCode);
      Code.JumpIns(BRN, CaseCode);
      FirstLabel := NIL; MinLabel := MAX(Integer); MaxLabel := MIN(Integer)
    END;
    TopOfCaseStack := ThisCase
  END OpenCase;
```

During subsequent analysis of the limbs of the case-statement the topmost entry in this stack contains a pointer *FirstLabel* to the head of an ordered list of case label values built by the sequence of calls of the interface operation *NextIsCase*. These case label entries record the label identity and a code label for the statement so labelled. The entries are organized in order of case label value. Hence

```
TYPE CaseLabelEntry = POINTER TO CaseLabelRecord;
     CaseLabelRecord =  RECORD
                          LabelValue: Integer;
                          LimbAddress: CodeLabel;
                          Next: CaseLabelEntry
                        END;
```

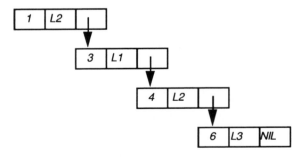

Figure 18.16 *A list of case label entries*

Figure 18.16 shows the case label list corresponding to the following case-statement:

```
CASE e OF
| 3: S1
| 4, 1: S2
```

```
| 6: S3
END
```

where *L1, L2, L3* are assumed to be the code labels for the statements *S1, S2, S3*, respectively.

Thus *NextIsCase* takes the form

```
PROCEDURE NextIsCase(CaseLabel: Integer);
    VAR ThisLabel: CaseLabelEntry;
    BEGIN
       Host.New(ThisLabel, SIZE(CaseLabelRecord));
       WITH ThisLabel^ DO
          LabelValue := CaseLabel; Code.NewLabel(LimbAddress); Next := NIL
       END;
       WITH TopOfCaseStack^ DO
          insert entry ThisLabel^ into case label list at appropriate ordered
             position and, if necessary, adjust MinLabel and/or MaxLabel.
       END
    END NextIsCase;
```

Using the information in the topmost record of the stack of case-statement records, *CloseCase* first announces the siting of the expected code label introduced by *OpenCase* and calls *Load* to generate the object code to evaluate the selector expression. It then calls a procedure *GenerateJumpTable* to generate the case selection code, viz.

```
PROCEDURE CloseCase;
    VAR ThisCase: CaseEntry;
    BEGIN
       WITH TopOfCaseStack^ DO
          Code.ExpectedLabel(CaseCode);
          Load(Selector);
          GenerateJumpTable;
          Stack.FreeNode(Selector)
       END;
       pop and deallocate top record on case record stack
    END CloseCase;
```

GenerateJumpTable generates code to subtract the smallest code label value from the selector expression. Next a

```
BIDX      2
```

instruction is generated which will multiply the result of the subtraction by 2 (since each Target instruction is two words long and hence each jump table entry occupies two words) and add this new result to the current program counter value (which is the first word of the jump table). The generation of the jump table itself then involves a traversal of the case label list, outputting either a *BRN* instruction which transfers control to the appropriate statement code (whose code label is held in the corresponding case label entry), or else a *NOOP* instruction for case label values which do not appear in the case-statement. Strictly speaking the selection of an unspecified case label should cause a jump to an error routine at run-time—the handling of run-time errors within case-statements is discussed in the next chapter. Thus *GenerateJumpTable* takes the form

```
PROCEDURE GenerateJumpTable;
    VAR ThisLabel, PreviousLabel: CaseLabelEntry; L: Integer;
    BEGIN
        WITH TopOfCaseStack^ DO
            Code.InsD(LOADL, MinLabel); Code.Ins0(SUB); Code.InsD(BIDX, 2);
            ThisLabel := FirstLabel;
            FOR L := MinLabel TO MaxLabel DO
                IF L = ThisLabel^.LabelValue THEN
                    Code.JumpIns(BRN, ThisLabel^.LimbAddress);
                    PreviousLabel := ThisLabel; ThisLabel := ThisLabel^.Next;
                    deallocate case label entry PreviousLabel^
                ELSE
                    Code.Ins0(NOOP)
                END
            END
        END
    END GenerateJumpTable;
```

The use of a single jump table to implement case-statement selection can cause problems in certain circumstances, e.g. the jump table generated for

```
CASE e OF
| 1: S1;
| 10: S2;
| 1000: S3
END
```

would contain 1000 entries, of which 997 would be for unspecified case label values. An alternative technique is for *CloseCase* to partition the ordered list of case label entries into a sequence of sub-lists, with each sub-list having its own sub-table associated with it. The maximum gap allowed between successive entries in a sub-table is then chosen to minimize the overall length of the object code sequence that results. These sub-tables are then built into a *binary decision tree* which enables the appropriate sub-table to be selected by a number of comparison tests involving the selector value. Thus the object code generated uses a combination of such comparison operators and smaller jump tables to implement the selection operation.

18.8   Generating for-statement code

We saw in Chapter 14 that the sequence of interface calls that takes place during the analysis of the for-statement

FOR V := e1 TO e2 DO S END

is as follows:

```
StackReference(address of V)
...stack value of expression e1...
...stack value of expression e2...
OpenFor
...code for statement-sequence S...
CloseFor
```

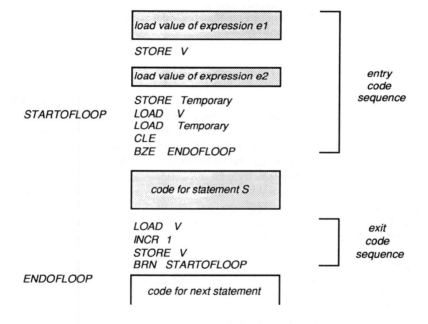

Figure 18.17 *Target object code structure for a for-statement*

The corresponding Target code that must be generated is shown in Figure 18.17. This code is equivalent to implementing the for-statement above as

```
V := e1;
Temporary := e2;
WHILE V <= Temporary DO
    S;
    INC(V)
END
```

Note that a temporary variable must be introduced to record the value of the final expression *e2* upon entry to the for-statement since its value at that point determines the upper bound of the range of values to be assumed by the control-variable *V*.

The entry and exit code sequences indicated in Figure 18.17 are generated by the interface procedures *OpenFor* and *CloseFor*, respectively. The information created and used by both of these operations is embedded in the fields of a *ForRecord*—such records are once more organized into a stack since for-statements can, of course, be arbitrarily nested. The top of this stack is referenced by a variable *TopOfForStack*, thus

```
TYPE ForEntry = POINTER TO ForRecord;
     ForRecord = RECORD
                    ControlVariable: StackEntry;
                    StartOfLoop, EndOfLoop: CodeLabel;
                    Next: ForEntry;
                 END;

VAR  TopOfForStack: ForEntry;
```

When *OpenFor* is called, the compile-time evaluation stack (see the interface call sequence above) contains a variable reference for the associated control-variable, and expression trees for the initial and final expressions of the for-statement. It creates a new *ForRecord* and the stack record for the control-variable is referenced via the *ControlVariable* field. Following this, the entry sequence instructions are generated—the generator procedure *AddressFor* is used to allocate the temporary storage required to hold the final expression value within the run-time stack frame of the current procedure. Two code labels are also introduced—one to label the object code instruction which is the start of the code sequence which performs the loop-termination test *V < Temporary* and the other, a future label, to label the end of the for-statement. Thus we have

```
PROCEDURE OpenFor;
    VAR  ThisFor: ForEntry; InitialExpression, FinalExpression: StackEntry;
         Temporary: RunTimeAddress;
    BEGIN
      Host.New(ThisFor, SIZE(ForRecord));
      WITH ThisFor^ DO
        Stack.Pop(FinalExpression); Stack.Pop(InitialExpression);
        Stack.Pop(ControlVariable);
        Load(InitialExpression);
        AccessWord(ControlVariable^.RefAddress, STORE);
        Load(FinalExpression);
        AddressFor(1, Temporary); AccessWord(Temporary, STORE);
        Code.NewLabel(StartOfLoop); Code.FutureLabel(EndOfLoop);
        AccessWord(ControlVariable^.RefAddress, LOAD);
        AccessWord(Temporary, LOAD);
        Code.Ins0(CLE);
        Code.JumpIns(BZE, EndOfLoop);
        Stack.FreeNode(InitialExpression); Stack.FreeNode(FinalExpression);
        Next := TopOfForStack
      END;
```

```
        TopOfForStack := ThisFor
    END OpenFor;
```

CloseFor uses the information in the *ControlVariable* field in the topmost *ForRecord* to generate code to increment the control-variable and also to jump to the exit test code (labelled by the *StartOfLoop* code label field). Finally it sites the code label denoted by the field *EndOfLoop*, and deallocates both the control-variable reference and the topmost *ForRecord*.

```
PROCEDURE CloseFor;
    BEGIN
        WITH TopOfForStack^ DO
            AccessWord(ControlVariable^.RefAddress, LOAD);
            Code.InsD(INCR, 1); AccessWord(ControlVariable^.RefAddress, STORE);
            Code.JumpIns(BRN, StartOfLoop);
            Code.ExpectedLabel(EndOfLoop);
            Stack.FreeNode(ControlVariable)
        END;
        pop and deallocate top record of ForRecord stack
    END CloseFor;
```

18.9 The complete compiler

The development of the code generator and the local modules on which it depends is almost complete. All that remains to be done is to include suitable object code in the final program to enable its correct entry and initialization for execution at run-time. We adopt the convention that the first three words of each object program will initialize the processor status word and stack register (SP) of the Target machine and then transfer control to the start of the main program, as shown in Figure 18.18.

The *Code* module is given the responsibility of generating these initial instructions and provides two more exported procedures to enable the required information for their generation to be supplied to it, viz.

```
PROCEDURE EnterHere;
PROCEDURE GenerationComplete;
```

EnterHere is called by the interface procedure *EnterProgram* to indicate that the next instruction generated is the first instruction of the main program block. *GenerationComplete* is called by the main program exit operation *LeaveProgram* to indicate that code generation is complete and the next available location in the object program will serve as the base of the run-time stack when the program is executed. The processor status word is set to zero by *GenerationComplete* to indicate that the object program is not to terminate if an arithmetic overflow or subscript range error occurs (see Chapter 2). In the next chapter we describe how the compiler can generate code to handle such errors at run-time.

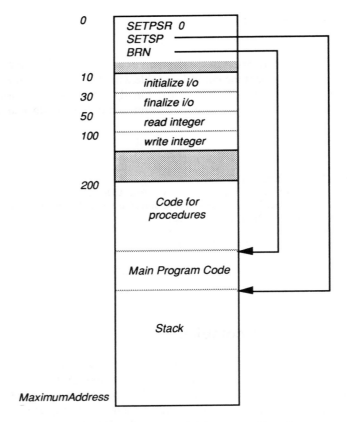

Figure 18.18 *Model object program format*

We must also decide how to implement the code generator interface procedure

```
PROCEDURE NoFurtherCode;
```

which is called by the analyzer following detection of any compile-time error to signal that further code generation is unnecessary now that an error has been detected in the program being compiled. In order to turn off the code generation a variable

```
VAR SuppressCodeGeneration: BOOLEAN;
```

is introduced into the code generator module and initialized to the value *FALSE*. The action of *NoFurtherCode* is simply

```
PROCEDURE NoFurtherCode;
  BEGIN SuppressCodeGeneration := TRUE END NoFurtherCode;
```

and all of the various generator interface procedures must be amended so that they carry out their generative actions only if code generation is not to be suppressed, thus

```
PROCEDURE ...;
  BEGIN
    IF NOT SuppressCodeGeneration THEN
      normal actions as defined before
    END
  END ...;
```

With the generator module complete (as listed in Appendix 13) it remains only to provide a suitable *CodeHandler* module which files the object code produced by the generator, and then to assemble the various modules which we have constructed, to produce a complete compiler for Model.

The implementation of the *CodeHandler* module used in the final version of the compiler will depend on the conventions for storing object programs in the environment of its use. However, during compiler development and testing, the compiler writer might use a substitute *CodeHandler* module which collects the object code generated and prints it out at the end of compilation in a form suitable for inspection. Appendix 14 contains a *CodeHandler* module which operates in this manner.

The final compiler module commences analysis of an input program by calling *Analyzer.Programme*—this will cause the compilation to be carried out, after which the *SourceHandler* module is informed that the program listing is to be completed and the *CodeHandler* module is invoked to list the object code generated.

```
MODULE ModelCompiler;
  IMPORT SourceHandler, CodeHandler, Analyzer;
  BEGIN
    Analyzer.Programme;
    SourceHandler.FinalizeIO;
    CodeHandler.ListCode
  END ModelCompiler.
```

Appendix 15 also shows a sample of the output which the final compiler produces using a code-printing module such as that suggested above. The output should be examined in conjunction with the object program layout diagram given as Figure 18.18.

The final compiler is a program of over 6000 lines. It was developed as a set of modules, each of which deals with a particular aspect of the overall compilation process. As we have demonstrated, each module was programmed in isolation from the other modules, so simplifying the programming task at each stage. Although we have not shown the testing details (end of chapter exercises have challenged the reader to provide suitable testing), whenever possible each module was tested in isolation, or by its addition to a set of modules already tested, thus simplifying the identification of errors within and between the modules concerned.

Again we have shown how, within each module, a similar structured approach was used to simplify the programming task. The stepwise refinement of the code and data structures required hopefully has led to a final program which is easy to understand, to debug and to maintain.

Although the modular structure of the compiler and the logical structure of the code and data within each module are significantly reinforced by the notations of Modula-2, it is the perception of this structure which is the vital factor in achieving a clear and reliable program, not the precise notation used to express it. This is a vital characteristic of effective program design and implementation and, hopefully, the Model compiler demonstrates to its readers that the same approach can be used on other comparable programming projects.

18.10 Further reading

Barron (1981) contains a number of papers which describe the code generation process within various Pascal compilers for different target machines. A description of the generation of object code for a register-based machine is described in Welsh and McKeag (1980). Aho, Sethi and Ullman (1986) give a thorough treatment of the problems and techniques of code generation for such machines. In his three-pass compiler, Watt (1993) develops code generation algorithms which choose appropriate *object code templates* for the various declaration, statement and expression forms in the source language.

Further details of the traversal of expression trees can be found in Knuth (1973). The use of binary decision trees in the generation of an alternative form of object code for case-statements is described in Welsh and Hay (1986). The Model compiler's code generator uses a numerical representation for Boolean values and manipulates them using the Target computer's logical *AND* and *OR* operations. The approach in both Welsh and McKeag's and Welsh and Hay's compilers is to generate code using conditional jump instructions to evaluate sequences of *AND* and *OR* operators.

Although the Model compiler employs a certain amount of compile-time folding of operands within expressions, other object code optimizations are possible. Watt (1993) and Watson (1989) examine various machine-dependent techniques such as *peephole optimization* (examination of the object code generated to detect redundancies such as popping an operand from the stack and immediately reloading it back onto the stack), *elimination of common sub-expressions* occurring within an expression such as

(a+b) * (3 / (a +b))

and *optimization of loop structures* such as

FOR I := 1 TO N DO I := I * (J+K/4) END

in which the sub-expression can be evaluated before entry to the for-statement object code rather than on each iteration.

Much recent and current research has been carried out into the automatic production of code generators (*compiler-compilers*). The PQCC system described by Leverett

(1980) and Tremblay and Sorenson (1985) produces an optimized code generator using a formal description of the target machine expressed in a description language ISP.

Exercises 18

18.1 How might the technique described in this chapter for generation of efficient sequences of object code instructions for arithmetic expressions be generalized to generate code for machines with more than one computation register? Illustrate the stages in the generation of efficient code for the assignment-statement

y := a * c − (b + (e + d) * f)

assuming that *four* computation registers are available.

18.2 Assuming the following variable-declarations

```
VAR   a, b, c, d: INTEGER;
        W: ARRAY [2..22] OF CHAR;
```

what hypothetical machine stack records and expression trees would the Model code generator construct for each of the following expressions and statements?

```
(a < b) and (c = d)
−a
(a + 3) * (4 + 7)
W[a} + 4
W[3] + b
READ(d)
```

18.3 Assuming the following variable-declarations appear within a procedure *P*

```
VAR   I, J: INTEGER;
        B: BOOLEAN;
        Ch: CHAR;
        A: ARRAY [10..20] OF INTEGER;
```

what would be the object code generated by the Model compiler for the following statements appearing within the statement-part of *P?*

```
REPEAT I := I − 2 UNTIL I <= 0;
FOR I := 4 TO J + 3 DO READ(Ch) END;
CASE I+1 OF
| 1, 5:  J := 0
| 2, 6, 0:   B := FALSE OR (I = J)
| 3, 4:  A[I−1] := I + 3 * 3
| 6: WRITE(J * 1)
END
```

18.4 Suggest how the object code generated for each of the following statements might be optimized:

```
X := (Y * Y) + Z DIV (Y * Y)
FOR I := 1 TO 100 DO T := T * (X + Y) END
FOR J := 1 TO N DO A[I, J] := A[I, J] + K END
```

Chapter 19

Run-time error checks and diagnostics

Not all violations of the rules of a programming language can be detected during compilation of a source program—some can only be detected at run-time during its execution. Detection of *run-time errors* normally requires additional instructions to be included in the object program. In this chapter we consider the various categories of run-time errors that may occur in programs wriiten in languages such as Modula-2, and then investigate the requirements and problems of generating such additional object code.

The treatment of run-time errors within a programming system is, as one would expect, subject to criteria similar to those for compile-time error handling:

(a) the system should (optionally) guarantee detection of all violations of the programming language rules and implementation-defined restrictions during the execution of the object program;
(b) the diagnostic messages generated to describe any such violation should be explicit, source related and complete.

That the first requirement above should be optional is a direct result of the overriding conflict which arises in error handling—that correct programs should be economical in the amount of storage they use and should execute efficiently, while incorrect programs should have full error protection. The incorporation of error protection into a machine code object program inevitably degrades its storage economy and execution speed (sometimes by an alarming amount). The usual solution, whatever its wisdom, is for the compiler to make run-time error protection optional so that the programmer may request it or exclude it as he or she sees fit.

Most compilers provide a number of error detection options which the programmer may select by means of *pragmas* or *directives* embedded within the source program, or by selecting them when the compiler is invoked. A pragma or directive is a non-executable statement or declaration which conveys a programmer's requirements to the compiler. Often these options can be selected and de-selected at various points in the source program.

19.1   Detecting run-time errors

The following are typical of the range of errors which may be detected at run-time in Modula-2 programs:

- the value of an *array index is out of range*, i.e. given a reference to an array element *A[e]*, the value of the index-expression *e* does not lie within the range of values defined by the index-type of the array *A*;
- *arithmetic overflow* or *division by zero*, i.e. an arithmetic computation produces a result which lies outside the machine-defined range of integer or real values;
- a *subrange violation*, i.e. assigning to a variable declared to be of a subrange-type a value which does not belong to that type;
- a *case selection error*, i.e. the value of a case-statement selector expression does not correspond to any case label specified within the case-statement;
- the *construction of an illegal set*, i.e. constructing a set value *T{e1..e2}* where the value of either of the expressions *e1* or *e2* does not belong to the base-type *T*;
- *illegal membership testing*, i.e. performing a set membership test *I IN S*, where the value of the expression *I* does not lie within the range of values of the base-type of the set *S*;
- an access to the value of an *unassigned variable*, i.e. one which has not previously been assigned a value in the program;
- accessing a so called *dangling reference*, i.e. a pointer-variable which references a dynamically allocated variable on the heap which has subsequently been de-allocated;
- a *NIL pointer access*, i.e. attempting to reference a variable via a pointer-variable whose value is *NIL*;
- a *variant record error*, i.e. accessing a field within a variant-part of a record for which the tag field value currently defines a different variant.

The range of actual errors that may occur is much greater but the above represent the most common run-time errors. The first six categories listed above are examples of *range-sensitive errors*.

19.1.1   Detecting range-sensitive errors

Array index checks can always be implemented, although at some cost. For example, suppose that a source program contains a declaration of an array-variable

    VAR A: ARRAY [b..c] OF INTEGER

and a subsequent assignment-statement

    A[I] := 0

Without array index checks the Target machine code generated for the assignment is

```
LOADL   0
LOADA   address of A[0]
LOAD    address of I
STOREI  1
```

If index checks are to be included then the checking code might take the form

```
LOADL   0
LOADA   address of A[0]
LOAD    address of I
LOADL   b
SUB
BNG     error
LOADL   c–b+1
SUB
BPZ     error
LOADL   c+1
ADD
STOREI  1
```

where *error* is an error handling routine within the run-time support package for the object program which causes some diagnostic information (see the next sub-section) to be generated before halting the program.

The above code sequences illustrate how an object program dominated by such array accesses will be slowed down by a factor of about three following the incorporation of array index checking instructions. However, the Target computer, in common with many real machines, provides some support for the generation of such checking operations. The Target *CHECK* instruction checks that the value located two words below the top of the run-time evaluation stack lies in the range defined by the topmost two values on the stack, and then pops the top values from the stack. If the value does not lie in the required range then the *E* bit in the processor status word is set to *1*. Hence the above assignment-statement object code sequence may be reduced to

```
LOADL   0
LOADA   address of A[0]
LOAD    address of I
LOADL   b
LOADL   c
CHECK
BES     error
STOREI  1
```

where the *BES* instruction is used to switch control to the diagnostic routine *error* if an array index violation has occurred.

Similar code, with similar overheads, is required for other range-sensitive operations such as assignment to variables of subrange-types, case selection, and set construction and membership testing. It is worth noting, however, that the language features of Modula-2 create many opportunities for the folding, i.e. elimination, of these run-time checks and, instead, their verification at compile-time. For example, given Modula-2 declarations

```
TYPE    IndexType = [b..c];
VAR     A: ARRAY IndexType OF ...;
        I: IndexType;
```

and assuming all previous assignments to the variable *I* within the object program have been checked at run-time, then no run-time check of an indexed-variable *A[I]* is necessary. Likewise, a for-statement such as

```
FOR J := b TO c DO ... A[J] ...END
```

requires no run-time checks to be performed on the indexed-variable *A[J]*.

A special case of a range violation error is the occurrence of *arithmetic overflow*. Its detection depends on the hardware on which the object program is executed. Three cases commonly arise:

(a) Where the occurrence of overflow during arithmetic operations causes a *hardware interrupt*, protection against overflow is available without any overhead on the object program's normal size and execution speed.

(b) On some machines a previous occurrence of overflow is detectable by execution of a special machine instruction. For example, most machines provide conditional jump instructions which inspect an *overflow flag* or register, in which case overflow detection can always be provided by generating such an instruction after each arithmetic operation. This of course places a corresponding overhead on the object program's size and running speed. The Target, for instance, sets the *V* flag within the processor status word following any arithmetic computation which causes overflow to occur. Provided the *C* flag is not set, the object program can then proceed to test for possible overflow using the *BVS* instruction. Hence, the code for a Model operation *I*100*, where *I* is a variable of type *INTEGER*, might take the form

```
LOAD     address of I
LOADL    100
MUL
BVS      error
```

(c) Some machines provide no specific means of detecting arithmetic overflow. On these machines it is either impossible, or prohibitively expensive, to implement any adequate detection of overflow within the object code generated for arithmetic operations.

In case (b) it should again be noted that, in languages such as Modula-2, compile-time analysis of the declared ranges of operands may enable the folding of many run-time overflow checks. For example, the expression

50*I+J

needs no overflow check if *I* and *J* have been declared, say, as

VAR I, J: [0..100];

and all previous assignments to *I* and *J* at run-time have been checked, and the *INTEGER* range of the machine concerned includes the range of the possible values of the expression *50*I+J*, i.e. *0..5100*.

Range analysis and the generation of object code for range and overflow checks in Model may be incorporated in the code generator operations which construct expression trees and also in the procedure *Load*. The generation of object code to perform array index checking can be incorporated within the code generator procedure *LoadAddress*.

The checking of the validity of the selector expression value in a case-statement involves generating additional code to check that the value lies within the range c_{min}.. c_{max}, where c_{min} is the minimum case label value occurring in the case-statement, and c_{max} is the maximum case label value. Hence, the case selection object code generated for the Target (see Figure 18.15) should use the *CHECK* instruction, viz.

```
     code to evaluate selector expression
     LOADL     c_min
     LOADL     c_max
     CHECK
     SUB       c_min
     BIDX      2
```

For case label values in the range c_{min}.. c_{max} which do not occur in the case-statement, the code generator procedure *GenerateJumpTable* should generate entries in the jump table which cause a branch to the run-time error routine (see Figure 18.15).

19.1.2   Detecting unassigned variable accesses

Detecting *unassigned variable accesses*, i.e. expressions containing variables which have not yet been assigned a value, is often one of the most difficult (and hence one of the most rarely implemented) forms of error protection. Essentially it requires that the representation of each variable should carry with it a tag indicating whether it has yet been assigned a value. Since common variable types such as *INTEGER* and *REAL* usually use a full computer word, or number of words, for their representation, representing this tag usually involves a significant storage overhead for the tag itself, as well as the additional object code to test or set it at each reference to the variable.

A cheaper (but not entirely satisfactory) solution is to initialize each variable to an *undefined* value which, though valid, is expected rarely to occur and then to check at each access for this value. This means of course that, if the chosen value does genuinely occur, an erroneous error message will be output.

However, this value could be chosen so that it is not part of the implementation-defined range of values for integers and reals, e.g. on the Target machine we might exclude the most negative integer value (whose binary representation is $100...000_2$) from the type *Target.Integer* and use this as the undefined value. Hence the *Target* module defines this value as the exported constant-identifier *Target.Undefined*. The compiler would then have to generate main program and procedure prelude code sequences which set all the variable storage within each stack frame to this initial value.

This particular undefined value could also be used for set variables by excluding the use of the left-most bit in a word from the representation of sets (see 16.5).

A different strategy needs to be used for variables which may occupy less than one word (e.g. fields of packed records, where the field is of an enumerated-type, a subrange-type or the type *CHAR*). In such cases the undefined value is chosen such that its ordinal value is 2^n, where n is the smallest integer such that

$$2^n > cardinality(T)$$

and T is the type concerned. Hence, for the subrange-type

    TYPE SomeType = [0..7];

the default value is chosen to be *8*. This means that a packed representation of a value of such a type may require an extra bit—in the absence of the undefined value, values of *SomeType* could be represented in 3 bits, but the introduction of the undefined value requires the minimum storage requirement to be extended to 4 bits. Since variables of such types use their own undefined values they must be individually initialized to the required value by special object code sequences.

A pointer value may be any valid memory address. If the memory address space spans the entire range of values that may be represented in a single word, it is necessary to use a two-word representation for pointer values, in which one of the words acts as a tag word, indicating whether the pointer value in the other word is currently defined. This tag word can use the same undefined representation as described above for integer values; a pointer-variable assignment or dynamic storage allocation operation thus involves an assignment to the word which holds the pointer value and an assignment of a value other than the undefined value (say, zero) to the tag word. Dynamic de-allocation of the storage referenced by a pointer-variable must then reset the tag word to the undefined value.

The folding of run-time checks for access to unassigned variables is also more difficult since it involves analyzing the actual sequence of assignment operations which the program will carry out. A complete analysis of the flow of control which may arise in a program is beyond the capability of compilers for most languages. However, even a one-pass compiler can perform a partial *flow analysis* which can split variables into three classes at any point:

(1) Those variables which have definitely been assigned values, e.g.

```
PROCEDURE P;
  VAR I: INTEGER;
  BEGIN
    I := 0;
    ...
    WRITE(I+1);                    no check required
    ...
```

In this case there is no run-time check required.

(2) Those variables which are definitely unassigned, e.g.

```
PROCEDURE P;
  VAR I: INTEGER;
  BEGIN
      WRITE(I+1);                  compile-time error
    ...
```

In this case the compiler can predict that, at run-time, the value of the variable *I* will not be defined, and hence it can report the error at compile-time.

(3) Those whose assignment depends on the control path or data values occurring before this point is reached, e.g.

```
PROCEDURE P;
  VAR I: INTEGER;
  BEGIN
    IF e THEN I := 0 END;
    WRITE(I+1);                    run-time check required
    ...
```

In this case it is not possible to predict whether the value of *I* will be defined or not when the *WRITE* statement is executed as the state of *I* depends on the previous value of *e*.

Object code to perform run-time assignment checks need only be generated for those variables in class (3). Unfortunately, in most programs a very high proportion of variable accesses fall into this class!

19.2 Reporting run-time errors

The requirement for run-time storage and execution efficiency also conflicts with meeting criterion (b) given on page 293, i.e. that all diagnostic messages reporting run-time errors should be explicit, source related and complete. In particular, source relation is extremely limited unless the compile-time semantic table, or some modified form of it, is retained through to run-time—an expense which some programming systems are not prepared to carry. For example, some programming systems will simply report the occurrence of a run-time error together with some rudimentary information relating to the object program, such as

Execution error at program location 16745

and (possibly) supply the contents of the registers at the point of execution. This is of very limited use to the programmer, to say the least!

However, it is possible for the compiler to generate information that enables the nature and point of occurrence of a run-time error to be indicated in terms of source program line numbers, statement numbers or some other compiler-generated frame of reference for the object program. We have already seen how the object program checking code can determine the nature of a run-time error and pass control to an error reporting routine which can report the particular error. One way of relating the point of occurrence of the error to the corresponding point in the source program is for the compiler to generate a *code map* file.

A code map file relates the structure of the object program to the line structure of the original source program. The code generator interface within the compiler may be augmented with an additional procedure

    PROCEDURE NoteFlowPoint;

which can be called by the analyzer each time it begins compilation of a statement. The code generator can then record the current source program line number (as provided by the *SourceHandler* module) together with the current address in the object program being generated. These (source program, object program) address pairs are then written to the code map file. When a run-time error occurs, the error reporting routine can then scan through this file to relate the object program address at which the error occurred to the corresponding source program line.

19.3   Run-time diagnostic aids

A correct error diagnostic message, even one meeting the ideal criteria we have defined, does not necessarily enable the programmer to find the underlying cause of the error condition—this may lie at some much earlier point in the program and may not be due to any direct violation of the programming language rules as such, but to some logical error in the algorithm which the program implements. For this reason it is desirable that a programming system should provide further run-time diagnostic facilities other than simply a terminal error message. Two such possible facilities are *program traces* and *postmortem dumps*.

Program tracing involves outputting a history of the events occurring during execution (of selected parts) of the program. An event description might consist of

- the *source program location* at which it occurs;
- the *event type* (e.g. an assignment, a Boolean expression evaluation within an if-statement, a case selection within a case-statement, a for-statement iteration, etc.);
- any *relevant value* involved in the event (e.g. the assigned value, the value of the Boolean expression, the value of the case selector expression, the for-statement control-variable's value, etc).

The incorporation of tracing code in an object program is not difficult to generate although the resultant degradation of the execution speed of the object program is enormous. However, the major disadvantage of tracing is that, even when used selectively, it may produce far too much output to be economically acceptable. Nonetheless, a restricted form of trace which can prove extremely useful in many error situations is one which traces each statement the first N times it is executed (typically $N = 2$). This reflects the fact that most run-time errors occur during the first one or two executions of the offending operation.

An alternative restricted form of trace is the pre-termination event history or *retro-trace*. In this the running object program maintains, within a cyclic buffer in the main memory, a record of the last N events which occurred, with each new event overwriting the Nth previous one. On program failure the last N events immediately preceding the occurrence of the error can then be reported. Some language implementations provide such a facility, and a typical value of N might be *100*.

Another limited form of trace which is extremely useful both for debugging and for program improvement is an *execution profile*. This is simply a tabulation of the program statements executed in any run with the frequency of execution for each.

A *postmortem dump* is a display of the current values of all the variables in existence at the point of termination of execution, preferably with a control history, i.e. the set of uncompleted procedure calls which led to the failure point. In principle a postmortem dump is easily provided—e.g. in a block-structured language it involves unwinding the run-time storage stack displaying the values in each stack frame as it is unwound. In practice such postmortem information is conveniently usable only if it is source related. For instance, some (unhelpful) language systems simply provide a hexadecimal display of the contents of selected memory locations in a form such as

Memory address	Contents
...	...
1000	1230
1001	2A45
1002	34CD
1003	5FFF
...	...

Such information is obviously very difficult to interpret. For instance, is the value stored in memory location *1000* an instruction or a data value—and, if it is a data value, is it an *INTEGER* value, a set value, a record field value, or a pointer value, ...? The unfortunate user is thus forced to decode this machine-oriented display of the program data areas with, sometimes, the help of a compiler-generated memory map which indicates which areas of memory contain instructions and which contain data.

The need for source relation of such information is essential but its generation involves the retention of some form of the compile-time semantic table. This is usually in the form of a *data map* file which contains details of the nature and representation of each variable in each program block. The compiler generates this file by traversing the identifier and type entries in the semantic table and writing out the necessary source relation information (e.g. spelling, run-time address, type, etc., in the case of variable-identifiers) within the entries to the file. One problem is that the semantic table may contain pointers which, being memory references, are meaningless when written to a file stored on some secondary storage medium. Instead, the compiler allocates unique serial numbers to each identifier and type entry in the semantic table and, when the data map file is created, pointers within the semantic table are replaced by the serial numbers of the entries which they reference.

Thus, following the reporting of a run-time error, the error handling procedure can invoke a *postmortem dump generator program* which takes the data map and code map files and examines the *corpse* of the program. The corpse is simply the state of the machine at the point at which the error occurred. Typically the output from this process might take the form shown below.

Arithmetic overflow at line 45 in procedure Multiply

Local variables:
   I   4567
   J   7895
   Initial "S"
   IsMale   FALSE

Multiply was called by procedure TestAllCases

Local variables:
   Person
      Name   ["S", "M", "I", "T", "H"];
      Age 4
      IdNumber   24684679
      Sex Male
   Number 4567

TestAllCases was called by ...

Economic arguments are sometimes used to preclude the provision of adequate run-time diagnostic facilities within high-level language implementations. Given the relatively low costs of machine time as compared with the costs of programmer time such arguments have little basis. Few people would doubt the paramount importance of the availability of high-quality error diagnostic facilities in any program development environment.

19.4   Further reading

A paper by Welsh (1978) discusses the provision and efficient implementation of run-time error checking. The Pascal compiler of Welsh and Hay (1986) illustrates the implementation of such checks. This compiler illustrates the implementation of checks for dangling references using a technique developed by Fischer and Leblanc. It also demonstrates the complexities of checking accesses to fields of variant records.

The source language diagnostics system that is used in the Welsh and Hay Pascal compiler provides a comprehensive source related postmortem dump and is an extension of an earlier Pascal system developed by Watt and Findlay (1981). The Pascal-S system of Wirth (1981) illustrates the ease of provision of source-related diagnostics within an interpretive object code system.

Exercises 19

19.1 Investigate the nature and quality of the run-time error reporting performed by the compiler that you use most often. How is run-time error checking invoked? Is the detection and reporting of run-time errors satisfactory? Are any additional error diagnostic aids provided? Are they provided in source-related form?

19.2 Extend the Model code generator as necessary to incorporate run-time checks on array index references and run the modified compiler on a suitable test program to demonstrate the correctness of the code generated for array index references.

19.3 Extend the Model code generator to incorporate run-time checks for arithmetic overflow, using the Target computer's *BVS* instruction. Again use a suitable test program to demonstrate the correctness of the code generated.

19.4 Extend the Model code generator to incorporate run-time checks for case-statement selection. Again use a suitable test program to demonstrate the correctness of the code generated.

19.5 Extend the Model code generator as necessary to incorporate run-time checks for references to the values of unassigned variables. Use the value *Target.Undefined* as the default undefined value. The main program and procedure prelude object code sequences should be modified to initialize all variable storage to this value and the generator procedure *Load* should generate the necessary checking code. Run the modified compiler on a suitable test program to demonstrate the correctness of the code generated.

Bibliography

Aho, A.H., Hopcroft, J.E., and Ullman, J.D. (1983) *Data Structures and Algorithms*, Addison-Wesley, Reading, Massachusetts, USA.

Aho, A.H., Sethi, R., and Ullman, J.D. (1986) *Compilers – Principles, Techniques, and Tools*, Addison-Wesley, Reading, Massachusetts, USA.

American National Standards Institute (1983) *The Programming Language Ada Reference Manual*, ANSI/MIL–STD–1815A–1983, Springer, New York, USA.

Backhouse, R. (1979) *The Syntax of Programming Languages*, Prentice Hall International, Hemel Hempstead, United Kingdom.

Barron, D.W., editor (1981) *Pascal – the Language and its Implementation*, Wiley, Chichester, United Kingdom.

Ben-Ari, M. (1982) *Principles of Concurrent Programming*, Prentice Hall International, Hemel Hempstead, United Kingdom.

Bornat, R. (1979) *Understanding and Writing Compilers*, Macmillan, London, United Kingdom.

Brinch Hansen, P. (1985) *Brinch Hansen on Pascal Compilers*, Prentice Hall International, Hemel Hempstead, United Kingdom.

Chomsky, N. (1959) 'On certain formal properties of grammars', *Information and Control* 2, 137–167.

Davie, F.J.T., and Morrison, R. (1981) *Recursive Descent Compiling*, Ellis Horwood, Chichester, United Kingdom.

Dijkstra, E.W. (1960) 'Recursive programming', in *Programming Systems and Languages* (S. Rosen, editor), McGraw-Hill, New York, USA, pp. 221–227.

Earley, J., and Sturgis, H. (1970) 'A formalism for translator interactions', *Communications of the ACM* 13, 607–617.

302

Ghezzi, C., and Jazayeri, M. (1987) *Programming Language Concepts*, 2nd edition, Wiley, New York, USA.

Hartmann, A.C. (1977) *A Concurrent Pascal Compiler,* Springer, Berlin, Germany.

Hoare, C.A.R. (1972) 'Notes on data structuring', in *Structured Programming* (O.J. Dahl, E.W. Dijkstra, and C.A.R. Hoare, editors), Academic Press, London, United Kingdom, pp. 83–174.

Hoare, C.A.R. (1975) 'Recursive data structures', *International Journal of Computer and Information Sciences* 4, 105–132.

Hoare, C.A.R., and Wirth, N. (1973) 'An axiomatic definition of the programming language Pascal', *Acta Informatica* 2, 335–355.

Hopcroft, J.E., and Ullman, J.D. (1979) *Introduction to Automata Theory, Languages, and Computation*, Addison-Wesley, Reading, Massachusetts, USA.

Horning, J.J. (1976a) 'What the compiler should tell the user', in *Compiler Construction: An Advanced Course* (F.L. Bauer and J. Eickel, editors), 2nd edition, Springer, Berlin, Germany.

Horning, J.J. (1976b) 'Structuring compiler development', in *Compiler Construction: An Advanced Course* (F.L. Bauer and J. Eickel, editors), 2nd edition, Springer, Berlin, Germany.

Hunter, R.B. (1981) *The Design and Construction of Compilers*, Wiley, New York, USA.

Knuth, D.E. (1973) *The Art of Computer Programming*, Volume 1, *Fundamental Algorithms*, Addison-Wesley, Reading, Massachusetts, USA.

Kowaltowski, T. (1981) 'Parameter passing mechanisms and run-time data structures', *Software Practice and Experience* 11, 757–765.

Leverett, B. W. *et al.* (1980) 'An overview of the Production-Quality Compiler-Compiler Projects', *IEEE Computer* 13, 38–49.

Lewis, P.M., and Stearns, R.E. (1968) 'Syntax-directed transduction', *Journal of the ACM* 15, 465–488.

McGettrick, A.D. (1980) *The Definition of Programming Languages*, Cambridge University Press, Cambridge, United Kingdom.

McKeeman, W.M. (1976a) 'Compiler construction', in *Compiler Construction: An Advanced Course* (F.L. Bauer and J. Eickel, editors), 2nd edition, Springer, Berlin, Germany.

McKeeman, W.M. (1976b) 'Symbol table access', in *Compiler Construction: An Advanced Course* (F.L. Bauer and J. Eickel, editors), 2nd edition, Springer, Berlin, Germany.

MacLennan, B.J. (1983) *Principles of Programming Languages: Design, Evaluation and Implementation*, Holt Saunders, New York, USA.

Morris, R. (1968) 'Scatter storage techniques', *Communications of the ACM* 11, 38–43.

Naur, P. (1963) 'Revised report on the algorithmic language ALGOL 60', *Communications of the ACM* 6, 1–17.

Nori, K.V. *et al.* (1981) 'Pascal-P implementation notes', in *Pascal – the Language and its Implementation* (D.W. Barron, editor), Wiley, Chichester, United Kingdom, pp. 125–170.

Pemberton, S., and Daniels, M.C. (1982) *Pascal Implementation – The P4 Compiler*, Ellis Horwood, Chichester, United Kingdom.

Rees, M., and Robson, D. (1987) *Practical Compiling with Pascal-S*, Addison-Wesley, Wokingham, United Kingdom.

Rosenkrantz, D.J., and Stearns, R.E. (1970) 'Properties of deterministic top-down grammars', *Information and Control* 17, 226–256.

Tennent, R.D. (1981) *Principles of Programming Languages*, Prentice Hall International, Hemel Hempstead, United Kingdom.

Terry, P.D. (1986) *Programming Language Translation*, Addison-Wesley, Wokingham, United Kingdom.

Tremblay, J.P., and Sorenson, P.G. (1982) *An Implementation Guide to Compiler Writing*, McGraw-Hill, New York, USA.

Tremblay, J.P., and Sorenson, P.G. (1985) *The Theory and Practice of Compiler Writing*, McGraw-Hill, New York, USA.

Watson, D. (1989) *High-level Languages and their Compilers*, Addison-Wesley, Wokingham, United Kingdom.

Watt, D.A. (1991) *Programming Language Syntax and Semantics*, Prentice Hall International, Hemel Hempstead, United Kingdom.

Watt, D.A. (1993) *Programming Language Processors*, Prentice Hall International, Hemel Hempstead, United Kingdom.

Watt, D.A., and Findlay, W. (1981) 'A Pascal diagnostic system', in *Pascal – the Language and its Implementation* (D.W. Barron, editor), Wiley, Chichester, United Kingdom, pp. 181–198.

Welsh, J., (1978) 'Economic range checks in Pascal', *Software Practice and Experience* 8, 85–97.

Welsh, J., and Bustard, D. (1979) 'Pascal Plus: another language for modular multiprogramming', *Software Practice and Experience* 9, 947–957.

Welsh, J., and Elder, J. (1987) *Introduction to Modula-2*, Prentice Hall International, Hemel Hempstead, United Kingdom.

Welsh, J., Elder, J., and Bustard, D. (1984) *Sequential Program Structures*, Prentice Hall International, Hemel Hempstead, United Kingdom.

Welsh, J., and Hay, A. (1986) *A Model Implementation of Standard Pascal*, Prentice Hall International, Hemel Hempstead, United Kingdom.

Welsh, J., and McKeag, R.M. (1980) *Structured System Programming*, Prentice Hall International, Hemel Hempstead, United Kingdom.

Welsh, J., Sneeringer, M.J., and Hoare, C.A.R. (1977) 'Ambiguities and insecurities in Pascal', *Software Practice and Experience* 7, 675–696.

Wirth, N. (1976) *Algorithms + Data Structures = Programs*, Prentice Hall, Englewood Cliffs, New Jersey, USA.

Wirth, N. (1981) 'Pascal-S: A subset and its implementation', in *Pascal – the Language and its Implementation* (D.W. Barron, editor), Wiley, Chichester, United Kingdom, pp. 199–259.

Wirth, N. (1982) *Programming in Modula-2*, 3rd edition, Springer, Berlin, Germany.

Appendix 1

Definition of Model

1 Summary of the language

A Model program consists of two essential parts, a description of *actions* which are to be performed, and a description of the *data* which are to be manipulated by these actions. Actions are described by *statements*, and data are described by *declarations*.

The data are represented by values of *variables*. Every variable occurring in a statement must be introduced by a *variable-declaration* which associates an *identifier* and a *data-type* with that variable. The data-type defines the set of values which may be assumed by that variable.

The basic data-types (known as *simple-types*) are the three types denoted by the standard identifiers *BOOLEAN*, *INTEGER*, *CHAR*. Values of the type *BOOLEAN* are the logical truth values denoted by identifiers *TRUE* and *FALSE*, values of type *INTEGER* are denoted by numbers and *CHAR* values are denoted by character values from the ASCII character set enclosed in quotation marks.

The only data structuring mechanism in Model type is provided by *array-types*; each value of an array-type comprises a number of components all of the same *component-type*. The component-type must be one of the above three *simple-types*. The number of components is defined by an *index-type* (a subrange of the type *INTEGER*) associated with the array-type. A component (known as an *indexed-variable*) is selected by computation of its index, i.e. a value of the index-type.

The actions of a program are described by a *statement-sequence*, each *statement* of which defines an executable action. The statements of a statement-sequence are executed sequentially.

The most fundamental statement is the *assignment-statement*. It enables a newly computed value to be assigned to a variable or indexed-variable. The value is obtained by evaluating an *expression*. An expression consists of variables, constants, and (possibly) operators which generate new values from the values of variables and constants. Model defines a fixed set of operators, each of which can be regarded as describing a mapping from its operand types onto its result type. The set of operators is subdivided into three groups as follows:

306

(a) *arithmetic* operators of addition, subtraction, inversion, multiplication and division;
(b) *Boolean* operators of negation, union, and conjunction;
(c) *relational* operators of equality, inequality, ordering.

A Model program has access to an *input stream* and an *output stream*. The input stream is capable of supplying information to the program in the form of a continuous character stream. The output stream is capable of receiving information from the program in the form of a continuous character stream. Transfer of information from the input stream, or to the output stream, is effected by *read-statements* or *write-statements*, respectively, within the program.

A *procedure-statement* causes the execution of the designated *procedure* (see below). An *exit-statement* causes termination of an enclosing *loop-statement* (see below). *Structured-statements* specify selective, or repeated, execution of sequences of statements. Conditional or selective execution is specified by the *if-statement* and *case-statement*, repeated execution by the *loop-statement* and *for-statement*.

A sequence of statements can be given a name (identifier), and be referenced through that identifier. The statement is then called a *procedure*, and its declaration is a *procedure-declaration*. Such a declaration may additionally contain a set of variable-declarations, or further procedure-declarations, to form a *block*. Since procedures may thus be declared within the blocks defining other procedures, blocks may be *nested*. This nested block structure determines the range of use, or *scope*, of the identifiers denoting variables, procedures, types and constant values, and also determines the lifetime of variables.

2 Notation, terminology and vocabulary

The syntactic definition of Model given here is defined using extended Backus–Naur form. Syntactic constructs are thus denoted by (hyphenated) English words. These words are chosen so as to describe the nature or meaning of the construct, and are then used in the accompanying description of semantics.

The vocabulary of Model consists of basic symbols classified into *letters*, *digits*, and *special-symbols*:

letter   = "A" | "B" | "C" | "D" | "E" | "F" | "G" | "H" | "I" | "J" |
                    "K" | "L" | "M" | "N" | "O" | "P" | "Q" | "R" | "S" |
                    "T" | "U" | "V" | "W" | "X" | "Y" | "Z" |
                    "a" | "b" | "c" | "d" | "e" | "f" | "g" | "h" | "i" | "j" |
                    "k" | "l" | "m" | "n" | "o" | "p" | "q" | "r" | "s" |
                    "t" | "u" | "v" | "w" | "x" | "y" | "z".

digit   = "0" | "1" | "2" | "3" | "4" | "5" | "6" | "7" | "8" | "9".

special-symbol = "+" | "–" | "*" | "=" | "<>" | "<" | "<=" | ">" | ">=" | "(" |
                    ")" | "[" | "]" | ":=" | "." | "," | ":" | ";" | ".." |

"MODULE" | "VAR" | "ARRAY" | "OF" | "PROCEDURE" |
"BEGIN" | "END" | "READ" | "WRITE" | "EXIT" | "LOOP" |
"FOR" | "TO" | "DO" | "IF" | "THEN" | "ELSE" | "CASE" |
"DIV" | "OR" | "AND" | "NOT".

Words used to represent *special-symbols* are reserved words which may not be used for any other purpose.

A Model program is expressed as a sequence of identifiers, numbers, character-constants and special-symbols, as described in this and following sections. In general an arbitrary number of blank characters, tabs or ends of line may occur between the identifiers, numbers and symbols. However, blanks, tabs or ends of lines may not occur within any identifier, number or special-symbol, and at least one blank, tab or end of line must occur between those identifiers, numbers and reserved word symbols which would otherwise be indistinguishable.

3   Identifiers

Identifiers denote constants, types, variables, and procedures. Their association must be unique within the block in which they are declared (see Sections 9 and 10 below). Upper- and lower-case letters within an identifier are considered to be distinct and only the first 12 characters of an identifier are significant.

> *identifier   =   letter { letter | digit }.*

4   Constants

Constants are the particular values which variables of the basic types, *INTEGER, CHAR* and *BOOLEAN*, may take.

> *constant   =   integer-number | character-constant | constant-identifier.*
> *constant-identifier   =   identifier.*

The usual decimal notation is used for those natural numbers which are constants of the type *INTEGER*.

> *integer-number   =   digit { digit }.*

Examples:

> 0   1   100

A constant of the type *CHAR* is denoted by the ASCII character concerned enclosed in either a pair of single quotes or a pair of apostrophes. If the character is itself a quote then it should be enclosed in apostrophes; if it is an apostrophe it should be enclosed in quotes.

character-constant   =   *""" any-character-other-than-apostrophe """* |
""" any-character-other-than-quote """.

Examples:

'A'   "'"   ';'   ' '   ""

The constants of the type *BOOLEAN* are denoted by the constant-identifiers *TRUE* and *FALSE*, which are the only constant-identifiers in Model.

5   Data-types

A data-type determines the set of values which variables of that type may assume and the range of operations which may be applied to those variables.

type   =   *simple-type* | *array-type*.

5.1   Simple-types

simple-type   =   *type-identifier*.
type-identifier   =   *identifier*.

The syntax category *type-identifier* denotes one of the three standard types in Model:

INTEGER   The values are a subset of the whole numbers defined by the particular implementation. Its values are as described in Section 4 above.

BOOLEAN   Its values are the logical truth values denoted by the identifiers *FALSE* and *TRUE*. By convention these values are assumed to be ordered such that *FALSE* < *TRUE*.

CHAR   Its values are the ASCII character set and are denoted by the characters themselves enclosed within quotes or apostrophes. Their ordering is determined by the ordering of the ASCII character set, in which characters which are letters or digits are ordered in a manner consistent with alphabetic and numeric ordering. Thus

$$'a' < 'b' < 'c' \ldots < 'z'$$
$$'A' < 'B' < 'C' \ldots < 'Z'$$
$$'0' < '1' < '2' \ldots < '9'$$

5.2   Array-types

An *array* is a data structure consisting of a fixed number of *components* which are all of the same type, called the *component-type*. An array-type consists of a definition of an *index-type* and an indication of the *component-type*. The index-type defines a subrange of the non-negative whole numbers and the *component-type* must be a simple-type. A variable of an array-type consists of one component for each value in the index-type.

A component of an array is known as an *indexed-variable* and is designated by a *subscript*, i.e. a value belonging to the index-type.

array-type	=	"ARRAY" *index-type* "OF" *component-type*.
index-type	=	"[" *integer-number* ".." *integer-number* "]".
component-type	=	*simple-type*.

Examples:

```
ARRAY [1..100] OF INTEGER
ARRAY [10..80] OF CHAR
```

6   Declarations and denotations of variables

Variables are those data items whose values are changed by execution of the program. They are denoted by identifiers. Each *variable-identifier* is introduced by a *variable-declaration*, which also specifies the type of the values which the variable may take. Variable-declarations are grouped in one or more *variable-declaration-parts*, which have the following form:

variable-declaration-part	=	"VAR" { *variable-declaration* ";" }.
variable-declaration	=	*identifier-list* ":" *type*.
identifier-list	=	*identifier* { "," *identifier* }.

Example of a variable-declaration-part:

```
VAR   NextCharacter: CHAR;
      OnLeave, ValidValue: BOOLEAN;
      I, J, K: INTEGER;
      MonthlySunshineHours: ARRAY [1..12] OF INTEGER;
```

Variables occurring in the examples in subsequent sections are assumed to have been declared as indicated above.

Denotations of variables designate either an *entire-variable* or an *indexed-variable*.

variable	=	*entire-variable*	*indexed-variable*.

6.1   Entire-variables

An *entire-variable* is denoted by its identifier.

entire-variable   =   *variable-identifier.*
variable-identifier   =   *identifier.*

Examples:

NextCharacter   MonthlySunshineHours;

The syntax category *variable-identifier* is used to denote the class of identifiers introduced by means of variable-declarations.

6.2   Indexed-variables

An individual component of an *array-variable* is denoted, as an *indexed-variable*, by writing the name of the array-variable followed (in square brackets) by an *expression* which denotes a value of the associated *index-type*.

indexed-variable   =   *array-variable* "[" *expression* "]".
array-variable   =   *entire-variable.*

Examples:

MonthlySunshineHours[12]
MonthlySunshineHours[I+J]

7   Expressions

Expressions are rules for the computation of new values. They consist of one or more *operands* (i.e. values of variables and constants) combined by means of *operators*.

A Model expression is evaluated according to the notion of *operator precedence*. Each operator has a precedence—*NOT* has the highest precedence, followed by the multiplication operators, then the addition operators, and finally, with the lowest precedence, the relational operators. The rules of evaluation of an expression are as follows:

(1) if all the operators in an expression have the same precedence the evaluation of the operations proceeds strictly left to right;

(2) when operators of different precedence are present then the highest-precedence operations are evaluated first, on a left-to-right basis, then the next highest-precedence operations are evaluated, and so on;

(3) rules (1) and (2) can be overridden by the inclusion of parentheses within an

expression—in which case those operations within the parentheses are evaluated first, with the above rules being applied within the parentheses.

The rules of precedence are reflected by the syntax rules for an *expression*:

expression	=	*simple-expression* [*relational-operator simple-expression*].
simple-expression	=	*sign term* { *addition-operator term* }.
term	=	*factor* { *multiplication-operator factor* }.
factor	=	*variable* I *constant* I "(" *expression* ")" I "NOT" *factor*.
relational-operator	=	"=" I "<>" I "<" I "<=" I ">" I ">=".
sign	=	["+" I "-"].
addition-operator	=	"+" I "-" I "OR".
multiplication-operator	=	"*" I "DIV" I "AND".

Examples:

```
NextCharacter
15
NOT ValidValue
3*K-193 MOD J
(NextCharacter <> "?") AND (I < 10)
-J+K
MonthlySunshineHours[10]+1
```

7.1   Operators

The order of evaluation of operands of a diadic operator is not defined.

7.1.1   The operator *NOT*

The operator *NOT* denotes negation of its *BOOLEAN* operand.

7.1.2   Multiplication and addition operators

operator	operation	type of operands	type of result
*	multiplication	both *INTEGER*	*INTEGER*
DIV	division with truncation	both *INTEGER*	*INTEGER*
AND	logical *and*	both *BOOLEAN*	*BOOLEAN*
+	addition	both *INTEGER*	*INTEGER*
-	subtraction	both *INTEGER*	*INTEGER*
OR	logical *or*	both *BOOLEAN*	*BOOLEAN*

When used as a prefix operator with one (*INTEGER*) operand only, the operator –

denotes sign inversion, and the operator + denotes the identity operation.

7.1.3 Relational operators

operator	type of operands	type of result
= <> < <= > >=	both *INTEGER*	*BOOLEAN*
= <> < <= > >=	both *CHAR*	*BOOLEAN*
= <> < <= > >=	both *BOOLEAN*	*BOOLEAN*

The operators =, <>, <, <=, >, >= stand for *equal, unequal, less than, less than or equal, greater than, greater than or equal*, respectively. The result of the operation is determined by the usual numeric ordering in the case of *INTEGER* operands, by the ordering of the ASCII character set in the case of *CHAR* operands, or by the conventional ordering defined previously for *BOOLEAN* operands.

8   Statements

A *statement-sequence* specifies a sequence of *statements*, each of which specifies a corresponding action to be carried out by the program. Execution of a statement-sequence involves the execution of its component statements in the order in which they are written.

> *statement-sequence* = *statement* { ";" *statement* }.

A statement may be a *simple-statement* or a *structured-statement*.

> *statement*   = *simple-statement* | *structured-statement*.

8.1   Simple-statements

A *simple-statement* is a statement which does not contain another statement as a component. It can take any of five forms:

> *simple-statement*   = *assignment-statement* | *exit-statement* |
>   *procedure-statement* | *read-statement* | *write-statement*.

8.1.1   Assignment-statements

An *assignment-statement* replaces the current value of a *variable* by a new value denoted by an *expression*.

> *assignment-statement*   = *variable* ":=" *expression*.

The effect of executing an assignment-statement is to evaluate the expression on the right of the assignment operator ":=" and to assign the value to the variable on the left.

The *variable* and the *expression* must be of identical type, i.e. of the same simple-type or of array-types with the same index-type and component-type.

Examples:

```
I := J+K−1
ValidValue := (1<=I) and (I<=100)
```

8.1.2   Procedure-statements

A *procedure-statement* specifies the execution (*invocation*) of the procedure denoted by the given procedure-identifier.

procedure-statement   =   *procedure-identifier.*
procedure-identifier   =   *identifier.*

The syntax category *procedure-identifier* is used to denote the class of identifiers introduced by means of *procedure-declarations* (see Section 10).

Examples:

```
GetNextCharacter
ExchangeValues
```

8.1.3   Exit-statements

An *exit-statement* specifies the termination of the execution of its immediately enclosing *loop-statement* (see 9.2.3) and execution continues at the statement following that loop-statement.

exit-statement   =   "EXIT".

Example:

```
EXIT
```

8.1.4   Read-statements

A *read-statement* specifies the transfer of a value from the input stream to a specified variable of the program.

read-statement   =   "READ" "(" *input-variable* ")".
input-variable   =   *variable.*

The *input-variable* must be of type *INTEGER* or of type *CHAR*. For a variable of type *CHAR* the value transferred is the next character from the input stream. For a variable of type *INTEGER* the value transferred is that denoted by a sequence of characters from the input stream. This sequence of characters must conform to the syntax for *integer-number* given in Section 5, preceded by a "+" or "–" sign and/or an arbitrary number of blanks. Successive *INTEGER* values must be separated by at least one blank character.

Examples:

```
READ(NextCharacter)
READ(MonthlySunshineHours[K])
```

8.1.5   Write-statements

A *write-statement* specifies the transfer of a value from the program to the output stream.

write-statement	=	"WRITE" "(" *output-value*")".
output-value	=	*expression.*

The *output-value* must be an expression of type *CHAR*, or of type *INTEGER*. A value of type *CHAR* is transferred as the single character denoted. A value of type *INTEGER* is transferred as the sequence of decimal digits denoting its value, preceded by a "–" sign when appropriate, and possibly some blanks. The length of the sequence of characters transferred is a constant sufficiently large to accommodate all integers representable on the target machine.

Examples:

```
WRITE (3*3*3*3);
WRITE(NextCharacter)
WRITE(MonthlySunshineHours[J]+1)
```

8.2   Structured-statements

Structured-statements are used to describe composite actions in terms of other component statements which have to be executed either conditionally (if-statements and case-statements), or repeatedly (loop-statements and for-statements).

structured-statement	=	*if-statement*	*case-statement*	
		loop-statement	*for-statement.*

8.2.1   If-statements

An *if-statement* specifies the conditional execution of one statement-sequence, or the choice between execution of two statement-sequences, depending upon the value of an expression which must produce a *BOOLEAN* value. It takes one of two corresponding forms

if-statement	=	"IF" *expression* "THEN" *statement-sequence*
		["ELSE" *statement-sequence*] "END".

In its shorter form (i.e. without an *ELSE* clause), thus

    IF E THEN S1 END

the action of the if-statement is to evaluate the expression *E* and, if and only if its value is *TRUE*, to execute the statement-sequence *S1*. In either case execution then continues at the statement following the if-statement.

If an *ELSE* clause is present, thus

    IF E THEN S1 ELSE S2 END

the *BOOLEAN* expression *E* is evaluated and if its value is *TRUE* then the statement-sequence *S1* is executed, otherwise the statement-sequence *S2* is executed. In either case execution then continues at the statement following the if-statement.

Examples:

    IF X < 0 THEN ValidValue := TRUE END
    IF I < J THEN K := I; I := J; J := K ELSE I := I+2 END

8.2.2   Case-statements

A *case-statement* specifies the selection for execution of one of a set of statement-sequences according to the value of some expression.

case-statement	=	"CASE" *expression* "OF" *case-limb* { *case-limb* } "END".
case-limb	=	"|" *case-label-list* ":" *statement-sequence*.
case-label-list	=	*constant* { "," *constant* }.

The expression following *CASE* is known as the *selector* and must yield a value of type *CHAR*, *INTEGER* or *BOOLEAN*. The constants which prefix the *statement-sequence* in each *case-limb* are known as *case-labels* and must be of the same type as the selector.

The action of a case-statement is to evaluate the selector expression and then execute the statement-sequence labelled by the resulting value. After this, execution proceeds to the statement following the case-statement. If there is no case label corresponding to the selector value then an error (*exception*) occurs.

A value of the type of the selector expression may appear as a case label at most once in any case-statement.

Example:

```
(* adjust value of K to next higher power of 2 *)
CASE K OF
| 1:       K := 2;
| 3:       K := 4;
| 5, 6, 7:   K := 8;
| 2, 4, 8:    (* do nothing *)
END
```

8.2.3   Loop-statements

A *loop-statement* specifies the repeated execution of a sequence of statements.

loop-statement   =   "LOOP" *statement-sequence* "END".

Termination of the loop-statement is achieved by execution of an *exit-statement* (see 9.1.3) within the statement-sequence.

Example:

```
LOOP
   GetNextCharacter;
   IF Character = "?" THEN EXIT END;
   I := I+1
END
```

8.2.4   For-statements

A *for-statement* specifies that execution of a statement-sequence is to be repeated a predetermined number of times.

for-statement   =   "FOR" *variable-identifier* ":=" *initial-expression*
                             "TO" *final-expression* "DO" *statement-sequence* "END".
initial-expression   =   *expression.*
final-expression   =   *expression.*

The *variable-identifier* must denote an entire-variable of type *CHAR*, *INTEGER* or *BOOLEAN* and is known as the *control-variable*. The *initial-expression* and *final-expression* must yield values of the same type as the control-variable.
The general form of a for-statement is thus

```
FOR V := I TO F DO SS END
```

where *I* and *F* are the values of the initial-expression and final-expression, respectively.

These values determine an ascending sequence of values to be taken by the control-variable as the statement-sequence *SS* is executed.

The action of a for-statement is to assign each of the values in the ascending sequence to the control-variable in turn and execute the statement-sequence *SS* after each assignment.

Examples:

```
FOR NextCharacter := "A" TO "Z" DO WRITE(NextCharacter) END
FOR I := 1 TO 10 DO WRITE(I); WRITE(I*I); WRITE(I*I*I) END
```

Notes:
(a) The initial and final values determined by the initial-expression and final-expression are evaluated once only, on entry to the for-statement.
(b) The value of the control-variable is changed implicitly by each cycle of the repetition and no action to change its value should appear within the statement-sequence of the for-statement, or within any procedure (see Section 10) that is invoked from within that statement-sequence.
(c) After completion of the execution of a for-statement the value of the control-variable is not defined, and programs should not make any assumption as to its value.

9   Procedure-declarations

Procedure-declarations define parts of a program and associate identifiers with them so that they can be invoked by means of *procedure-statements* (see Section 8.1.2).

procedure-declaration   =   procedure-heading block identifier.

The *procedure-heading* associates an identifier with the procedure being declared.

procedure-heading   =   "PROCEDURE" identifier ";".

The *identifier* following the *block* must be the same as the procedure-identifier appearing in the *procedure-heading*.

A *block* consists of a *declaration-part* followed by the *statement-part*. A *declaration-part* is a (possibly empty) sequence of *variable-declaration-parts* and *procedure-declarations*.

block   =   declaration-part statement-part.
declaration-part   =   {variable-declaration-part | procedure-declaration ";" }.

The variables of a block are declared in one or more *variable-declaration-parts* (see 6 above).

The *statement-part* specifies the sequence of statements to be executed upon activation of the procedure by a procedure-statement.

statement-part   = "BEGIN" *statement-sequence* "END"

Example of a *procedure-declaration*:

```
PROCEDURE WriteLineOfAsterisks;
    VAR Count: INTEGER;
    BEGIN
        FOR Count := 1 TO 50 DO Write("*") END
    END WriteLineOfAsterisks
```

Identifiers introduced in the *declaration-part* are local to the *block*, which is called the *scope* of these identifiers. More precisely the scope of an identifier declaration is defined by the following rules:

(1) The scope of an identifier declaration is the block in which the declaration occurs, and all blocks enclosed by that block, subject to rule 2.
(2) When an identifier declared in a block *A* is redeclared in some block *B* enclosed by *A*, block *B* and all blocks enclosed by *B* are excluded from the scope of the identifier's declaration in *A*.

An identifier may have at most one declaration in any block, and may be used only within the scope of such a declaration.

Variables declared in a block are created at the beginning of each execution of that block, and cease to exist when its execution is complete. Their values are undefined at the beginning of each execution of the block.

10   Programs

A Model program has the form of a procedure-declaration, except that its heading uses the word *MODULE* instead of *PROCEDURE*, and the program is terminated with a period.

program   = *program-heading block identifier* ".".
program-heading   = "MODULE" *identifier* ";".

The identifier following the symbol *MODULE* is the *program-identifier*; it has no further significance inside the program.

Identifiers declared within the program block are said to be global, since their scope comprises the program block and all enclosed procedure blocks, except those in which they are redeclared.

The standard identifiers *INTEGER, BOOLEAN, CHAR, TRUE* and *FALSE* have a scope which encloses the program block, and are thus usable throughout the program, except in blocks where they are redeclared.

Target machine definition

Definition module

```
DEFINITION MODULE Target;
  IMPORT Host;

  (* This module defines those characteristics of the Target computer's       *)
  (* architecture and instruction set that are required within the other modules *)
  (* of the compiler.                                                          *)
  (* It also defines the locations of the run-time support routines within the  *)
  (* object programs generated by the compiler.                                *)

               (* ------- Word Structure ------- *)

  CONST WordLength = 16; (* bits per word *)

  CONST MaxInteger = 77777B-1; (* i.e. 2**15 - 1 *)
        Undefined = -MaxInteger-1;

  TYPE  Integer = LONGINT[-MaxInteger..MaxInteger-1];

               (* ------- Character Set  ------- *)

  TYPE Ordinal = [0..255]; (* Target uses ASCII *)

    (* The following procedure provides a mapping from ASCII ordinal values to  *)
    (* Target ordinal values.                                                   *)

  PROCEDURE OrdinalOf(C: Host.ASCIIOrdinal): Ordinal;

               (* ----   Memory Dimensions   --- *)

  CONST MaximumAddress = 177777B;
  TYPE  AddressRange = [0..MaximumAddress];

               (* ---- Register Organization --- *)

  TYPE  Register = (BP, FP, MP, SP, PC, PSR);
        AddressRegister = [BP..SP];

               (* ------ PSR Organization -------*)
```

```
CONST C = 0;                    (* Checks On bit             *)
      V = 1;                    (* Overflow  bit             *)
      E = 2;                    (* Range error bit           *)
      H = 3;                    (* Halted bit                *)
      M = 4;                    (* Memory violation bit      *)
      R = 5;                    (* Register violation  bit *)
      I = 6;                    (* Illegal instruction bit *)

               (* ----      Instruction Set    --- *)

TYPE  OrderCode = (NOOP, LOAD, LOADL, LOADR, LOADA, LOADI,
                   STORE, STORER, STOREI, STZ,
                   INCR, INCREG, MOVE, SLL, SRL,
                   ADD, SUB, MUL, DVD, DREM, LAND, LOR, INV, NEG,
                   CLT, CLE, CEQ, CNE,
                   BRN, BIDX, BZE, BNZ, BNG, BPZ, BVS, BES,
                   MARK, CALL, EXT, SETSP, SETPSR, CHECK, HLT,
                   CHIN, CHOUT);

              (* ----  Instruction Format   ---- *)

TYPE Level = [0..77B];
TYPE Instruction = RECORD
                    OpCode: OrderCode; R: AddressRegister; L: Level;
                    N: Integer
                    END;


             (* -- Object Program Addresses -- *)

TYPE  SystemRoutines = (InitializeIO, FinalizeIO, ReadInteger, WriteInteger);
PROCEDURE AddressOf(Routine: SystemRoutines): AddressRange;

CONST FirstAvailable = 200;

END Target.
```

Implementation module

```
IMPLEMENTATION MODULE Target;
  IMPORT Host;

  PROCEDURE OrdinalOf(C: Host.ASCIIOrdinal): Ordinal;
    BEGIN
      RETURN C
    END OrdinalOf;

  PROCEDURE AddressOf(Routine: SystemRoutines): AddressRange;
    BEGIN
      CASE Routine OF
      | InitializeIO: RETURN 10;
      | FinalizeIO:   RETURN 30;
      | ReadInteger:  RETURN 50;
      | WriteInteger: RETURN 100;
      END
    END AddressOf;

  END Target.
```

Appendix 3

Host environment interface

Definition module

```
DEFINITION MODULE Host;
  IMPORT SYSTEM;

  (* This module defines the operations which must be provided for the compiler  *)
  (* by the host environment.  These include:                                    *)

  (* (1) An operation for determining the ASCII ordinal value of any character   *)
  (*     in the the host machine's character set:                                *)

  TYPE ASCIIOrdinal = [0..255];

  PROCEDURE ASCIIOrdinalOf(C: CHAR): ASCIIOrdinal;

  CONST EOL = 15C;

  (* (2) operations for dynamic allocation and deallocation of storage:          *)

  (*     The type SYSTEM.ADDRESS is provided by all Modula-2 implementations &   *)
  (*     is compatible with all pointer types.                                   *)

  TYPE AnyPointerType = SYSTEM.ADDRESS;

  PROCEDURE New(VAR Pointer: AnyPointerType; ObjectSize: CARDINAL);
  PROCEDURE Dispose(VAR Pointer: AnyPointerType; ObjectSize: CARDINAL);

  (* (3) operations for performing text file input and output:                   *)

  TYPE FileAccessMode = (Input, Output);
       File;

  PROCEDURE OpenFile(OpenPrompt: ARRAY OF CHAR; Mode: FileAccessMode;
                     VAR F: File; VAR Opened: BOOLEAN);
  PROCEDURE ReadChar(F: File; VAR EndOfInput: BOOLEAN; VAR C: CHAR);
  PROCEDURE WriteChar(F: File; C: CHAR);
  PROCEDURE WriteCardinal(F: File; Number, FieldWidth: CARDINAL);
  PROCEDURE WriteInteger(F: File; Number: INTEGER; FieldWidth: CARDINAL);
  PROCEDURE WriteString(F: File; String: ARRAY OF CHAR);
  PROCEDURE WriteLine(F: File);
  PROCEDURE CloseFile(VAR F: File);
```

```
(* (4) properties of identifiers on the host implementation, and spelling    *)
(*     comparison operations.                                                 *)

CONST MaxSignificantIdLength = 12;
TYPE StandardIdentifiers = (Integer, Char, Boolean, False, True);

TYPE  Word = ARRAY [1..MaxSignificantIdLength] OF CHAR;
TYPE  WordRelation = (FirstIsLess, WordsEqual, SecondIsLess);
PROCEDURE ComparisonOf(W1, W2: Word): WordRelation;

VAR   BlankWord: Word;

PROCEDURE GetSpelling(Id: StandardIdentifiers; VAR Spelling: Word);

END Host.
```

Implementation module

```
IMPLEMENTATION MODULE Host;
  IMPORT SYSTEM, Storage, InOut;

  (* This environment is provided by the MetroWerks Modula-2 implementation for *)
  (* the MacIntosh, and uses the ASCII character set.                           *)

  PROCEDURE ASCIIOrdinalOf(C: CHAR): ASCIIOrdinal;
    BEGIN
      RETURN ORD(C)
    END ASCIIOrdinalOf;

  (* The operations for controlling dynamic allocation and deallocation of  *)
  (* storage are performed using operators defined by the MetroWerks library *)
  (* module Storage.                                                          *)

  PROCEDURE New(VAR Pointer: AnyPointerType; ObjectSize: CARDINAL);
    BEGIN
      Storage.ALLOCATE(Pointer, ObjectSize)
    END New;

  PROCEDURE Dispose(VAR Pointer: AnyPointerType; ObjectSize: CARDINAL);
    BEGIN
      Storage.DEALLOCATE(Pointer, ObjectSize); Pointer := NIL
    END Dispose;

  (* The operations for performing input and output of text files are  *)
  (* implemented using the standard InOut module.                       *)

  TYPE File = POINTER TO RECORD AccessMode: FileAccessMode END;

  PROCEDURE OpenFile(OpenPrompt: ARRAY OF CHAR; Mode: FileAccessMode;
                     VAR F: File; VAR Opened: BOOLEAN);
    BEGIN
      InOut.WriteString(OpenPrompt);
      New(F, SIZE(F^)); F^.AccessMode := Mode;
      CASE Mode OF
      | Input:  InOut.OpenInput("")
      | Output: InOut.OpenOutput("")
      END;
      Opened := InOut.Done
    END OpenFile;
```

```
PROCEDURE CloseFile(VAR F: File);
  BEGIN
    CASE F^.AccessMode OF
    | Input:  InOut.CloseInput
    | Output: InOut.CloseOutput
    END;
    Dispose(F, SIZE(F^))
  END CloseFile;

PROCEDURE ReadChar(F: File; VAR EndOfInput: BOOLEAN; VAR C: CHAR);
  BEGIN
    InOut.Read(C); EndOfInput := NOT InOut.Done
  END ReadChar;

PROCEDURE WriteChar(F: File; C: CHAR);
  BEGIN
    InOut.Write(C)
  END WriteChar;

PROCEDURE WriteCardinal(F: File; Number, FieldWidth: CARDINAL);
  BEGIN
    InOut.WriteCard(Number, FieldWidth)
  END WriteCardinal;

PROCEDURE WriteInteger(F: File; Number: INTEGER; FieldWidth: CARDINAL);
  BEGIN
    InOut.WriteInt(Number, FieldWidth)
  END WriteInteger;

PROCEDURE WriteString(F: File; String: ARRAY OF CHAR);
  BEGIN
    InOut.WriteString(String)
  END WriteString;

PROCEDURE WriteLine(F: File);
  BEGIN
    InOut.WriteLn
  END WriteLine;

PROCEDURE ComparisonOf(W1, W2: Word): WordRelation;
  VAR I: [1..MaxSignificantIdLength];
  BEGIN
    I := 1;
    LOOP
      IF W1[I] < W2[I] THEN RETURN FirstIsLess
      ELSIF W1[I] > W2[I] THEN RETURN SecondIsLess
      ELSIF I = MaxSignificantIdLength THEN RETURN WordsEqual
      ELSE INC(I)
      END
    END
  END ComparisonOf;

VAR StandardIdSpelling: ARRAY [Integer..True] OF Word;

PROCEDURE GetSpelling(S: StandardIdentifiers; VAR Spelling: Word);
  BEGIN
    Spelling := StandardIdSpelling[S]
  END GetSpelling;

BEGIN
  BlankWord := "        ";
  StandardIdSpelling[Integer] := "INTEGER ";
```

```
    StandardIdSpelling[Char]    := "CHAR    ";
    StandardIdSpelling[Boolean] := "BOOLEAN ";
    StandardIdSpelling[False]   := "FALSE   ";
    StandardIdSpelling[True]     := "TRUE    ";
END Host.
```

Appendix 4

Source handler

Definition module

```
DEFINITION MODULE SourceHandler;

(* Source text input and source listing generation are enabled through the      *)
(* following exported procedures:                                               *)
(*                                                                              *)
(* GetNextCharacter This procedure reads the next character from the input      *)
(*                  stream, copies it to the output stream, and leaves its value *)
(*                  in the exported variable CurrentCharacter.                  *)
(*                  The position of the character within the input text is      *)
(*                  maintained in the exported variable PositionNow.            *)
(*                  Ends of lines are transmitted as blanks.                    *)
(*                                                                              *)
(* Error            This procedure enables the analysis processes to record     *)
(*                  error code/text position pairs for output during listing    *)
(*                  generation.                                                 *)
(*                                                                              *)
(* FinalizeIO       This procedure handles printing of the compilation summary, *)
(*                  and closes the input and output streams.                    *)
(*                                                                              *)
(* The initialization of the source handler obtains the identity of each of the *)
(* source text file and listing file, and connects the compiler to both files.  *)
(* It also outputs a listing header.                                            *)

  CONST MaxCharsPerLine = 101;

  TYPE CharPosition = [1..MaxCharsPerLine];
       TextPosition = RECORD
                        LineNumber: CARDINAL; CharNumber: CharPosition
                      END;

  VAR CurrentCharacter: CHAR; PositionNow: TextPosition;

  PROCEDURE GetNextCharacter;

  PROCEDURE Error(Code: CARDINAL; Position: TextPosition);

  PROCEDURE FinalizeIO;

END SourceHandler.
```

Implementation module

```
IMPLEMENTATION MODULE SourceHandler;

  FROM Host IMPORT File, FileAccessMode, OpenFile, CloseFile, ReadChar, EOL,
                   WriteChar, WriteString, WriteLine, WriteCardinal;

  CONST MaxErrorsPerLine = 6;

  TYPE  TerminationStatus = (Normal, InputExhausted);

  VAR   SourceFile, ListingFile: File;
        Line: ARRAY CharPosition OF CHAR;
        FirstInLine, LastInLine: CharPosition;
        TotalNumberOfErrors: CARDINAL;
        ErrorsInThisLine: [0..MaxErrorsPerLine]; ErrorOverflow: BOOLEAN;
        ErrorList: ARRAY [1..MaxErrorsPerLine] OF
                        RECORD
                          ErrorPosition: TextPosition; ErrorCode: CARDINAL
                        END;

  PROCEDURE ListThisLine;

    PROCEDURE ListErrors;
      VAR K: [1..MaxErrorsPerLine]; J: CharPosition;
      BEGIN
        INC(TotalNumberOfErrors, ErrorsInThisLine);
        FOR K := 1 TO ErrorsInThisLine DO
          WITH ErrorList[K] DO
            WriteString(ListingFile, "*****   ");
            IF ErrorPosition.LineNumber <> PositionNow.LineNumber THEN
              WriteString(ListingFile, "ERROR ");
              WriteCardinal(ListingFile, ErrorCode, 1);
              WriteString(ListingFile, " AT CHARACTER ");
              WriteCardinal(ListingFile, ErrorPosition.CharNumber,1);
              WriteString(ListingFile, " OF LINE ");
              WriteCardinal(ListingFile, ErrorPosition.LineNumber, 1)
            ELSE
              FOR J := 1 TO ErrorPosition.CharNumber-1 DO
                WriteChar(ListingFile, " ")
              END;
              WriteString(ListingFile, "^ERROR ");
              WriteCardinal(ListingFile, ErrorCode, 1)
            END;
            WriteLine(ListingFile)
          END
        END;
        IF ErrorOverflow THEN
          WriteString(ListingFile,
                  "*****   FURTHER ERRORS ON THIS LINE SUPPRESSED");
          WriteLine(ListingFile)
        END;
        WriteLine(ListingFile);
        ErrorsInThisLine := 0; ErrorOverflow := FALSE
      END ListErrors;

    VAR I: CharPosition;
    BEGIN (* ListThisLine *)
      WriteCardinal(ListingFile, PositionNow.LineNumber, 5);
      WriteString(ListingFile, "   ");
      FOR I := 1 TO LastInLine DO WriteChar(ListingFile, Line[I]) END;
```

```
        WriteLine(ListingFile);
        IF ErrorsInThisLine > 0 THEN ListErrors END
    END ListThisLine;

  PROCEDURE Finalize(Reason: TerminationStatus);
    BEGIN
      IF Reason = Normal THEN ListThisLine END;
      WriteLine(ListingFile); WriteLine(ListingFile);
      IF Reason = Normal THEN WriteString(ListingFile, "COMPILATION COMPLETED: ")
      ELSE
        WriteString(ListingFile,
                  "COMPILATION ABORTED - PREMATURE END OF INPUT FILE");
        WriteLine(ListingFile)
      END;
      IF TotalNumberOfErrors = 0 THEN WriteString(ListingFile, "NO")
      ELSE WriteCardinal(ListingFile, TotalNumberOfErrors, 1)
      END;
      WriteString(ListingFile, " ERROR(S) REPORTED");
      WriteLine(ListingFile);
      CloseFile(ListingFile); CloseFile(SourceFile)
    END Finalize;

  PROCEDURE ReadNextLine;
    VAR I: CharPosition; NoInputRemains: BOOLEAN;
    BEGIN
      (* check if there is a next line in the input file *)
      ReadChar(SourceFile, NoInputRemains, Line[1]);
      IF NoInputRemains THEN Finalize(InputExhausted); HALT END;
      I := 1;
      (* read leading spaces and set FirstInLine *)
      WHILE Line[I] = " " DO
        INC(I); ReadChar(SourceFile, NoInputRemains, Line[I]);
      END;
      FirstInLine := I;
      (* read remainder of line *)
      WHILE Line[I] <> EOL DO
        INC(I); ReadChar(SourceFile, NoInputRemains, Line[I])
      END;
      Line[I] := " "; LastInLine := I;
      IF FirstInLine <> LastInLine THEN
        (* scan trailing spaces to set LastInLine *)
        REPEAT DEC(I) UNTIL Line[I] <> " ";
        LastInLine := I+1
      END
    END ReadNextLine;

  PROCEDURE GetNextCharacter;
    BEGIN
      WITH PositionNow DO
        IF CharNumber = LastInLine THEN
          ListThisLine; ReadNextLine;
          INC(LineNumber); CharNumber := FirstInLine
        ELSE INC(CharNumber)
        END;
        CurrentCharacter := Line[CharNumber]
      END
    END GetNextCharacter;

  PROCEDURE Error(Code: CARDINAL; Position: TextPosition);
    BEGIN
      IF ErrorsInThisLine = MaxErrorsPerLine THEN ErrorOverflow := TRUE
      ELSE
```

```
      INC(ErrorsInThisLine);
      WITH ErrorList[ErrorsInThisLine] DO
        ErrorCode := Code; ErrorPosition := Position
      END
    END
  END Error;

PROCEDURE FinalizeIO;
  BEGIN
    Finalize(Normal)
  END FinalizeIO;

VAR OK: BOOLEAN;
BEGIN
  OpenFile("Enter name of source text file: ", Input, SourceFile, OK);
  IF OK THEN
    OpenFile("Enter name of listing file: ", Output, ListingFile, OK);
    IF OK THEN
      WriteString(ListingFile, "LISTING PRODUCED BY Model COMPILER 1/93");
      WriteLine(ListingFile); WriteLine(ListingFile);
      ReadNextLine;
      WITH PositionNow DO
        LineNumber := 0; CharNumber := FirstInLine;
        CurrentCharacter := Line[CharNumber]
      END;
      TotalNumberOfErrors := 0; ErrorsInThisLine := 0; ErrorOverflow := FALSE
    END
  END
END SourceHandler.
```

Appendix 5

Lexical analyzer

Definition module

```
DEFINITION MODULE LexicalAnalyzer;

  IMPORT SourceHandler, Host, Target;

  TYPE SymbolType =   (Identifier, IntegerNumber, CharConstant, Module, Var,
                       Procedure, Array, Of, Begin, End, If, Then, Else, Case, Loop,
                       Exit, For, To, Do, Read, Write, Not, And, Or, Div, Times,
                       Plus, Minus, LessThan, LessThanOrEqual, GreaterThanOrEqual,
                       GreaterThan, NotEquals, Equals, RightParenthesis,
                       LeftParenthesis, RightBracket, LeftBracket, Comma, Semicolon,
                       Period, Colon, Becomes, Thru, Separator, OtherSymbol);

  (* The Lexical analyzer module enables the lexical scanning of symbols in the  *)
  (* source stream through the exported procedure GetNextSymbol.                 *)
  (* When called, GetNextSymbol scans the next language symbol in the input      *)
  (* stream and returns a representation of it in the exported variable          *)
  (* SymbolDescription which has the following fields:                           *)
  (* Symbol     In all cases Symbol represents the symbol scanned as defined by  *)
  (*            the type SymbolType                                              *)
  (* Spelling   When Symbol = Identifier, Spelling holds the (significant)       *)
  (*            characters of the identifier scanned                            *)
  (* IntValue   When Symbol = IntegerNumber, Value gives the integer            *)
  (*            representation of the constant on the target machine            *)
  (* CharValue  When Symbol = Charconstant, Value gives the ASCII ordinal value *)
  (*            of the constant on the target machine                          *)
  (* The starting position of the symbol scanned is left in the field Position.  *)
  (* The Lexical Analyzer reports errors with the following codes:               *)
  (*  1 .... integer constant too large                                         *)
  (*  2 .... illegal character constant                                         *)
  (*  3 .... character constant incomplete                                      *)

  VAR SymbolDescription: RECORD
                    CASE Symbol: SymbolType OF
                    | IntegerNumber: IntValue: Target.Integer;
                    | CharConstant:  CharValue: Target.Ordinal;
                    | Identifier:    Spelling: Host.Word
                    END;
                    Position: SourceHandler.TextPosition
                  END;
```

331

```
    PROCEDURE GetNextSymbol;

END LexicalAnalyzer.
```

Implementation module

```
IMPLEMENTATION MODULE LexicalAnalyzer;

  FROM SourceHandler IMPORT GetNextCharacter, CurrentCharacter, PositionNow, Error;
  IMPORT Target, Host;

  CONST MaxInteger = Target.MaxInteger; MaxIdLength = Host.MaxSignificantIdLength;

  CONST NumberOfWordSymbols = 22;
        WordSymbolTableSize = NumberOfWordSymbols + MaxIdLength;

  TYPE  WordSymbolTableRange = [1..WordSymbolTableSize];

  VAR   WordSymbols: ARRAY WordSymbolTableRange OF
                        RECORD
                          Spelling: Host.Word; Value: SymbolType
                        END;
        LastOfLength: ARRAY [0..MaxIdLength] OF [0..WordSymbolTableSize];

  PROCEDURE GetNextSymbol;
    VAR K: [0..MaxIdLength]; Digit: Target.Integer; Delimiter: CHAR;
        I: WordSymbolTableRange;

    PROCEDURE IsDigit(Ch: CHAR): BOOLEAN;
      BEGIN
        RETURN (Ch >= "0") AND (Ch <= "9")
      END IsDigit;

    PROCEDURE IsLetter(Ch: CHAR): BOOLEAN;
      BEGIN
        RETURN (Ch >= "A") AND (Ch <= "Z") OR (Ch >= "a") AND (Ch <= "z");
      END IsLetter;

    BEGIN
      WITH SymbolDescription DO
        (* Read characters until next significant character *)
        WHILE CurrentCharacter = " " DO GetNextCharacter END;
        Position := PositionNow;
        CASE CurrentCharacter OF
        | "A".."Z", "a".."z": (* Identifier or word symbol *)
            K := 0; Spelling := Host.BlankWord;
            REPEAT
              IF K < MaxIdLength THEN
                INC(K); Spelling[K] := CurrentCharacter
              END;
              GetNextCharacter
            UNTIL NOT IsDigit(CurrentCharacter) AND NOT IsLetter(CurrentCharacter);
            WordSymbols[LastOfLength[K]].Spelling := Spelling;
            I := LastOfLength[K-1]+1;
            WHILE Host.ComparisonOf(WordSymbols[I].Spelling, Spelling)
                    <> Host.WordsEqual DO INC(I) END;
            Symbol := WordSymbols[I].Value
        | "0".."9": (* Integer constant *)
            Symbol := IntegerNumber; IntValue := 0;
```

```
      REPEAT
        Digit := ORD(CurrentCharacter) - ORD("0");
        IF (IntValue < MaxInteger DIV 10) OR (IntValue = MaxInteger DIV 10)
           AND (Digit <= MaxInteger MOD 10) THEN
          IntValue := 10*IntValue + Digit
        ELSE Error(1, PositionNow); IntValue := 0
        END;
        GetNextCharacter
      UNTIL NOT IsDigit(CurrentCharacter);
  | "'", '"': (* Character constant *)
        Symbol := CharConstant; Delimiter := CurrentCharacter;
        GetNextCharacter;
        IF CurrentCharacter = Delimiter THEN Error(2, PositionNow) END;
        CharValue := Target.OrdinalOf(Host.ASCIIOrdinalOf(CurrentCharacter));
        GetNextCharacter;
        IF CurrentCharacter <> Delimiter THEN Error(3, PositionNow)
        ELSE GetNextCharacter
        END;

  (* 2-character operators and delimiters *)

  | ":":
        GetNextCharacter;
        IF CurrentCharacter = "=" THEN Symbol := Becomes; GetNextCharacter
        ELSE Symbol := Colon
        END
  | ".":
        GetNextCharacter;
        IF CurrentCharacter = "." THEN Symbol := Thru; GetNextCharacter
        ELSE Symbol := Period
        END
  | "<":
        GetNextCharacter;
        IF CurrentCharacter = "=" THEN
          Symbol := LessThanOrEqual; GetNextCharacter
        ELSIF CurrentCharacter = ">" THEN Symbol := NotEquals; GetNextCharacter
        ELSE Symbol := LessThan
        END
  | ">":
        GetNextCharacter;
        IF CurrentCharacter= "=" THEN
          Symbol := GreaterThanOrEqual; GetNextCharacter
        ELSE Symbol := GreaterThan
        END

  (* 1-character operators and delimiters *)
  | "+": Symbol := Plus; GetNextCharacter
  | "-": Symbol := Minus; GetNextCharacter
  | "*": Symbol := Times; GetNextCharacter
  | "=": Symbol := Equals; GetNextCharacter
  | "(": Symbol := LeftParenthesis; GetNextCharacter
  | ")": Symbol := RightParenthesis; GetNextCharacter
  | "[": Symbol := LeftBracket; GetNextCharacter
  | "]": Symbol := RightBracket; GetNextCharacter
  | ",": Symbol := Comma; GetNextCharacter
  | ";": Symbol := Semicolon; GetNextCharacter
  | "|": Symbol := Separator; GetNextCharacter

  ELSE (* illegal character *)
     Symbol := OtherSymbol; GetNextCharacter
  END (* Case *)
  END
END GetNextSymbol;
```

```
PROCEDURE InitializeLookUpTable;
  VAR I: WordSymbolTableRange;
  BEGIN
     LastOfLength[0]  := 0;   LastOfLength[1]  := 1;   LastOfLength[2]  := 7;
     LastOfLength[3]  := 14;  LastOfLength[4]  := 21;  LastOfLength[5]  := 25;
     LastOfLength[6]  := 27;  LastOfLength[7]  := 28;  LastOfLength[8]  := 29;
     LastOfLength[9]  := 31;  LastOfLength[10] := 32;  LastOfLength[11] := 33;
     LastOfLength[12] := 34;
     I := LastOfLength[1];
     WITH WordSymbols[I] DO Value := Identifier; Spelling := Host.BlankWord END;
     WITH WordSymbols[I+1] DO Value := Do; Spelling := "DO       " END;
     WITH WordSymbols[I+2] DO Value := If; Spelling := "IF       " END;
     WITH WordSymbols[I+3] DO Value := Of; Spelling := "OF       " END;
     WITH WordSymbols[I+4] DO Value := Or; Spelling := "OR       " END;
     WITH WordSymbols[I+5] DO Value := To; Spelling := "TO       " END;
     I := LastOfLength[2];
     WITH WordSymbols[I] DO Value := Identifier; Spelling := Host.BlankWord END;
     WITH WordSymbols[I+1] DO Value := And; Spelling := "AND      " END;
     WITH WordSymbols[I+2] DO Value := Div; Spelling := "DIV      " END;
     WITH WordSymbols[I+3] DO Value := End; Spelling := "END      " END;
     WITH WordSymbols[I+4] DO Value := For; Spelling := "FOR      " END;
     WITH WordSymbols[I+5] DO Value := Not; Spelling := "NOT      " END;
     WITH WordSymbols[I+6] DO Value := Var; Spelling := "VAR      " END;
     I := LastOfLength[3];
     WITH WordSymbols[I] DO Value := Identifier; Spelling := Host.BlankWord END;
     WITH WordSymbols[I+1] DO Value := Case; Spelling := "CASE     " END;
     WITH WordSymbols[I+2] DO Value := Else; Spelling := "ELSE     " END;
     WITH WordSymbols[I+3] DO Value := Exit; Spelling := "EXIT     " END;
     WITH WordSymbols[I+4] DO Value := Loop; Spelling := "LOOP     " END;
     WITH WordSymbols[I+5] DO Value := Read; Spelling := "READ     " END;
     WITH WordSymbols[I+6] DO Value := Then; Spelling := "THEN     " END;
     I := LastOfLength[4];
     WITH WordSymbols[I] DO Value := Identifier; Spelling := Host.BlankWord END;
     WITH WordSymbols[I+1] DO Value := Array; Spelling := "ARRAY    " END;
     WITH WordSymbols[I+2] DO Value := Begin; Spelling := "BEGIN    " END;
     WITH WordSymbols[I+3] DO Value := Write; Spelling := "WRITE    " END;
     I := LastOfLength[5];
     WITH WordSymbols[I] DO Value := Identifier; Spelling := Host.BlankWord END;
     WITH WordSymbols[I+1] DO Value := Module; Spelling := "MODULE   " END;
     I := LastOfLength[6];
     WITH WordSymbols[I] DO Value := Identifier; Spelling := Host.BlankWord END;
     I := LastOfLength[7];
     WITH WordSymbols[I] DO Value := Identifier; Spelling := Host.BlankWord END;
     I := LastOfLength[8];
     WITH WordSymbols[I] DO Value := Identifier; Spelling := Host.BlankWord END;
     WITH WordSymbols[I+1] DO Value := Procedure; Spelling := "PROCEDURE   " END;
     I := LastOfLength[9];
     WITH WordSymbols[I] DO Value := Identifier; Spelling := Host.BlankWord END;
     I := LastOfLength[10];
     WITH WordSymbols[I] DO Value := Identifier; Spelling := Host.BlankWord END;
     I := LastOfLength[11];
     WITH WordSymbols[I] DO Value := Identifier; Spelling := Host.BlankWord END;
     I := LastOfLength[12];
     WITH WordSymbols[I] DO Value := Identifier; Spelling := Host.BlankWord END;
  END InitializeLookUpTable;

BEGIN
  InitializeLookUpTable;
  GetNextSymbol   (* makes first symbol available *)
END LexicalAnalyzer.
```

Appendix 6

Syntax analyzer

Definition module

```
DEFINITION MODULE SyntaxAnalyzer;

    (* The Analyzer generates syntax error codes with the following meanings:    *)
    (*                                                                            *)
    (*  10 ... Symbol expected was Identifier                                     *)
    (*  11 ... Symbol expected was Integer Number                                 *)
    (*  12 ... Symbol expected was Character Constant                             *)
    (*  13 ... .......                                                            *)
    (*                                                                            *)
    (* i.e. one value for each of the values of SymbolType.                       *)
    (* The final value, ORD(OtherSymbol)+10, is used to mean                      *)
    (*                                                                            *)
    (*  NN ... Unexpected symbol                                                  *)

    PROCEDURE Programme;

END SyntaxAnalyzer.
```

Implementation module

```
IMPLEMENTATION MODULE SyntaxAnalyzer;

    FROM SourceHandler IMPORT Error;
    FROM LexicalAnalyzer IMPORT SymbolType, GetNextSymbol, SymbolDescription;

    (* SYNTAX ANALYSIS                                                             *)
    (*                                                                             *)
    (* Syntax analysis of Model programs is implemented as a set of recursive      *)
    (* descent procedures.  These procedures are based on the syntax rules given   *)
    (* in Appendix 1 and are nested as tightly as the mutual interaction permits.  *)
    (* The order, names, and nesting of the procedures are as follows:             *)
    (*                                                                             *)
    (*     Programme                                                               *)
    (*        Block                                                                *)
    (*            Declaration                                                      *)
    (*                VariableDeclarationPart                                      *)
    (*                    VariableDeclaration                                      *)
```

335

```
(*                    Type                                    *)
(*                        SimpleType                          *)
(*                        IndexRange                          *)
(*                ProcedureDeclaration                        *)
(*            StatementPart                                   *)
(*            StatementSequence                               *)
(*                Statement                                   *)
(*                    Variable                                *)
(*                    Expression                              *)
(*                        SimpleExpression                    *)
(*                            Term                            *)
(*                                Factor                      *)
(*                Assignment                                  *)
(*                ReadStatement                               *)
(*                    InputVariable                           *)
(*                WriteStatement                              *)
(*                    OutputValue                             *)
(*                IfStatement                                 *)
(*                CaseStatement                               *)
(*                LoopStatement                               *)
(*                ExitStatement                               *)
(*                ForStatement                                *)
(*                                                            *)
(* The syntax analyzers are written on the assumption that the next syntactic *)
(* goal can always be selected by inspection of (at most) the next incoming   *)
(* symbol (i.e. that the underlying grammar is LL(1)).  This is not so at the  *)
(* following points in the syntax rules actually used:                        *)
(*                                                                            *)
(* 1. A Statement beginning with an Identifier may be either an Assignment or *)
(*    a Procedure Call.                                                       *)
(* 2. A Factor beginning with an Identifier may be either a Variable or a     *)
(*    Constant.                                                               *)
(*                                                                            *)
(* In Case 1 to resolve the choice on a purely syntactic basis would require a *)
(* distortion of the syntax rules; choice 2 cannot be syntactically resolved  *)
(* in some cases.  However, if parallel semantic analysis is assumed (as in   *)
(* the case of this compiler) these choices can be resolved without syntax    *)
(* distortion, by inspection of the current semantic attributes of the        *)
(* Identifier involved.  For this reason syntactic resolution of these choices *)
(* is not used.                                                              *)


PROCEDURE SyntaxError(ExpectedSymbol: SymbolType);
  BEGIN
    Error(ORD(ExpectedSymbol)+10, SymbolDescription.Position)
  END SyntaxError;

PROCEDURE Accept(SymbolExpected: SymbolType);
  BEGIN
    IF SymbolDescription.Symbol = SymbolExpected THEN GetNextSymbol
    ELSE SyntaxError(SymbolExpected)
    END
  END Accept;

(* The module SymbolSets defines an abstract data-type SymbolSet denoting    *)
(* sets of symbols of type LexicalAnalyzer.SymbolType.                       *)

MODULE SymbolSets;
  IMPORT SymbolType;
  EXPORT SymbolSet, Clear, Include, Remove, Contains, Union;

  TYPE SymbolSet = ARRAY SymbolType OF BOOLEAN;
```

```
    PROCEDURE Clear(VAR S: SymbolSet);
      VAR B: SymbolType;
      BEGIN
        FOR B := MIN(SymbolType) TO MAX(SymbolType) DO S[B] := FALSE END
      END Clear;

    PROCEDURE Include(I: SymbolType; VAR S: SymbolSet);
      BEGIN
        S[I] := TRUE
      END Include;

    PROCEDURE Remove(I: SymbolType; VAR S: SymbolSet);
      BEGIN
        S[I] := FALSE
      END Remove;

    PROCEDURE Contains(VAR S: SymbolSet; I: SymbolType): BOOLEAN;
      BEGIN
        RETURN S[I]
      END Contains;

    PROCEDURE Union(VAR S1, S2, Result: SymbolSet);
      VAR B: SymbolType;
      BEGIN
        FOR B := MIN(SymbolType) TO MAX(SymbolType) DO
          Result[B] := S1[B] OR S2[B]
        END
      END Union;

  END SymbolSets;


PROCEDURE Programme;
  VAR DeclarationStarters, RelationalOps, AdditionOps,
      MultiplicationOps, Signs: SymbolSet;

  PROCEDURE InitializeSymbolSets;
    BEGIN
      (* DeclarationStarters := {Var, Procedure}                            *)
      Clear(DeclarationStarters);
      Include(Var, DeclarationStarters);
      Include(Procedure, DeclarationStarters);

      (* RelationalOps := {Equals, NotEquals, LessThan, LessThanOrEqual,    *)
      (*                   GreaterThanOrEqual, GreaterThan}                  *)
      Clear(RelationalOps); Include(Equals, RelationalOps);
      Include(NotEquals, RelationalOps); Include(LessThan, RelationalOps);
      Include(LessThanOrEqual, RelationalOps);
      Include(GreaterThan, RelationalOps);
      Include(GreaterThanOrEqual, RelationalOps);

      (* AdditionOps := {Plus, Minus, Or}                                   *)
      Clear(AdditionOps); Include(Plus, AdditionOps);
      Include(Minus, AdditionOps); Include(Or, AdditionOps);

      (* MultiplicationOps := {Times, Div, And}                             *)
      Clear(MultiplicationOps); Include(Times, MultiplicationOps);
      Include(Div, MultiplicationOps); Include(And, MultiplicationOps);

      (* Signs             := {Plus, Minus}                                 *)
      Clear(Signs); Include(Plus, Signs); Include(Minus, Signs);
    END InitializeSymbolSets;
```

```
PROCEDURE Block;

  PROCEDURE DeclarationPart;

    PROCEDURE VariableDeclarationPart;

      PROCEDURE VariableDeclaration;

        PROCEDURE Type;

          PROCEDURE SimpleType;
            BEGIN
              Accept(Identifier)
            END SimpleType;

          PROCEDURE IndexType;
            BEGIN
              WITH SymbolDescription DO
                Accept(LeftBracket);
                Accept(IntegerNumber);
                Accept(Thru);
                Accept(IntegerNumber);
                Accept(RightBracket)
              END
            END IndexType;

          BEGIN (* Type *)
            IF SymbolDescription.Symbol = Identifier THEN SimpleType
            ELSE
              Accept(Array);
              IndexType;
              Accept(Of);
              SimpleType
            END
          END Type;

        BEGIN (* VariableDeclaration *)
          Accept(Identifier);
          WHILE SymbolDescription.Symbol = Comma DO
            Accept(Comma);
            Accept(Identifier)
          END;
          Accept(Colon);
          Type
        END VariableDeclaration;

      BEGIN (* VariableDeclarationPart *)
        Accept(Var);
        WHILE SymbolDescription.Symbol = Identifier DO
          VariableDeclaration;
          Accept(Semicolon)
        END
      END VariableDeclarationPart;

    PROCEDURE ProcedureDeclaration;
      BEGIN
        Accept(Procedure);
        Accept(Identifier);
        Accept(Semicolon);
        Block;
        Accept(Identifier)
      END ProcedureDeclaration;
```

```
    BEGIN (* DeclarationPart *)
      WHILE Contains(DeclarationStarters, SymbolDescription.Symbol) DO
        CASE SymbolDescription.Symbol OF
        | Var:
            VariableDeclarationPart
        | Procedure:
            ProcedureDeclaration;
            Accept(Semicolon)
        END
      END
    END DeclarationPart;

PROCEDURE StatementPart;

  PROCEDURE StatementSequence;

    PROCEDURE Statement;

      PROCEDURE Expression; FORWARD;

      PROCEDURE Variable;
        BEGIN
          Accept(Identifier);
          IF SymbolDescription.Symbol = LeftBracket THEN
            Accept(LeftBracket);
            Expression;
            Accept(RightBracket)
          END
        END Variable;

      PROCEDURE Expression;

        PROCEDURE SimpleExpression;

          PROCEDURE Term;

            PROCEDURE Factor;
              BEGIN
                CASE SymbolDescription.Symbol OF
                | Identifier:
                    (* IF constant-identifier THEN *)
                    (*   accept as constant        *)
                    (*   ELSE                       *)
                        Variable
                    (*   END                        *)
                | IntegerNumber:
                    Accept(IntegerNumber)
                | CharConstant:
                    Accept(CharConstant)
                | LeftParenthesis:
                    Accept(LeftParenthesis);
                    Expression;
                    Accept(RightParenthesis)
                | Not:
                    Accept(Not);
                    Factor
                END
              END Factor;

            BEGIN (* Term *)
              Factor;
              WITH SymbolDescription DO
```

```
                    WHILE Contains(MultiplicationOps, Symbol) DO
                      GetNextSymbol; Factor
                    END
                  END
              END Term;

        BEGIN (* SimpleExpression *)
          WITH SymbolDescription DO
            IF Contains(Signs, Symbol) THEN GetNextSymbol END;
            Term;
            WHILE Contains(AdditionOps, Symbol) DO
              GetNextSymbol; Term
            END
          END
        END SimpleExpression;

      BEGIN (* Expression *)
        SimpleExpression;
        IF Contains(RelationalOps, SymbolDescription.Symbol) THEN
          GetNextSymbol; SimpleExpression;
        END
      END Expression;

    PROCEDURE Assignment;
      BEGIN
        Variable;
        Accept(Becomes);
        Expression;
      END Assignment;

    PROCEDURE ReadStatement;

      PROCEDURE InputVariable;
        BEGIN
          Variable
        END InputVariable;

      BEGIN (* ReadStatement *)
        Accept(Read);
        Accept(LeftParenthesis);
        InputVariable;
        Accept(RightParenthesis)
      END ReadStatement;

    PROCEDURE WriteStatement;

      PROCEDURE OutputValue;
        BEGIN
          Expression
        END OutputValue;

      BEGIN (* WriteStatement *)
        Accept(Write);
        Accept(LeftParenthesis);
        OutputValue;
        Accept(RightParenthesis)
      END WriteStatement;

    PROCEDURE IfStatement;
      BEGIN
        Accept(If);
        Expression;
```

```
      Accept(Then);
      StatementSequence;
      IF SymbolDescription.Symbol = Else THEN
        Accept(Else);
        StatementSequence
      END;
      Accept(End)
    END IfStatement;

  PROCEDURE ExitStatement;
    BEGIN
      Accept(Exit)
    END ExitStatement;

  PROCEDURE LoopStatement;
   BEGIN
      Accept(Loop);
      StatementSequence;
      Accept(End)
   END LoopStatement;

  PROCEDURE CaseStatement;

    PROCEDURE NewCaseLabel;
      BEGIN
        WITH SymbolDescription DO
          IF NOT (Symbol = IntegerNumber) AND
             NOT (Symbol = CharConstant) AND
             NOT (Symbol = Identifier) THEN
            SyntaxError(OtherSymbol)
          END
        END;
        GetNextSymbol
      END NewCaseLabel;

    BEGIN (* CaseStatement *)
      Accept(Case);
      Expression;
      Accept(Of);
      REPEAT
        Accept(Separator);
        LOOP
          NewCaseLabel;
          IF SymbolDescription.Symbol <> Comma THEN EXIT END;
          Accept(Comma)
        END;
        Accept(Colon);
        StatementSequence
      UNTIL SymbolDescription.Symbol = End;
      Accept(End)
    END CaseStatement;

  PROCEDURE ForStatement;
    BEGIN
      Accept(For);
      Accept(Identifier);
      Accept(Becomes);
      Expression;
      Accept(To);
      Expression;
      Accept(Do);
      StatementSequence;
```

```
              Accept (End)
            END ForStatement;

        BEGIN (* Statement *)
          CASE SymbolDescription.Symbol OF
          | Identifier:
                (* IF procedure-identifier THEN     *)
                (*   accept as procedure-statement  *)
                (* ELSE                             *)
                    Assignment
                (* END                              *)
          | If:    IfStatement
          | Exit:  ExitStatement
          | Loop:  LoopStatement
          | Case:  CaseStatement
          | For:   ForStatement
          | Read:  ReadStatement
          | Write: WriteStatement
          END
        END Statement;

      BEGIN (* StatementSequence *)
        Statement;
        WHILE SymbolDescription.Symbol = Semicolon DO
          Accept (Semicolon);
          Statement
        END
      END StatementSequence;

    BEGIN (* StatementPart *)
      Accept (Begin);
      StatementSequence;
      Accept (End)
    END StatementPart;

  BEGIN (* Block *)
    DeclarationPart;
    StatementPart
  END Block;

BEGIN (* Programme *)
  InitializeSymbolSets;
  Accept (Module);
  Accept (Identifier);
  Accept (Semicolon);
  Block;
  Accept (Identifier)
END Programme;

END SyntaxAnalyzer.
```

Appendix 7

Syntax analyzer with error recovery

Definition module

```
DEFINITION MODULE SyntaxAnalyzer;

  (* The Analyzer generates syntax error codes with the following meanings:   *)
  (*                                                                            *)
  (*  10 ... Symbol expected was Identifier                                     *)
  (*  11 ... Symbol expected was Integer Number                                 *)
  (*  12 ... Symbol expected was Character Constant                             *)
  (*  13 ... .......                                                            *)
  (*                                                                            *)
  (* i.e. one value for each of the values of SymbolType.                       *)
  (* The final value, ORD(OtherSymbol)+10, is used to mean                      *)
  (*                                                                            *)
  (*  NN ... Unexpected symbol                                                  *)

  PROCEDURE Programme;

END SyntaxAnalyzer.
```

Implementation module

```
IMPLEMENTATION MODULE SyntaxAnalyzer;

  FROM SourceHandler IMPORT Error;
  FROM LexicalAnalyzer IMPORT SymbolType, GetNextSymbol, SymbolDescription;

  (* For reasons of space and to avoid repetition commentary for the following *)
  (* areas of the Analyzer has been omitted since it has already appeared in the *)
  (* Appendix specified:                                                        *)
  (*                                                                            *)
  (*     Syntax analysis                     see Appendix 6                     *)
  (*                                                                            *)

  PROCEDURE SyntaxError(ExpectedSymbol: SymbolType);
    BEGIN
      Error(ORD(ExpectedSymbol)+10, SymbolDescription.Position)
    END SyntaxError;
```

```
PROCEDURE Accept (SymbolExpected: SymbolType);
  BEGIN
    IF SymbolDescription.Symbol = SymbolExpected THEN GetNextSymbol
    ELSE SyntaxError(SymbolExpected)
    END
  END Accept;

MODULE SymbolSets;
  IMPORT SymbolType;
  EXPORT SymbolSet, Clear, Include, Remove, Contains, Union;

  TYPE SymbolSet = ARRAY SymbolType OF BOOLEAN;

  PROCEDURE Clear(VAR S: SymbolSet);
    VAR B: SymbolType;
    BEGIN
      FOR B := MIN(SymbolType) TO MAX(SymbolType) DO S[B] := FALSE END
    END Clear;

  PROCEDURE Include(I: SymbolType; VAR S: SymbolSet);
    BEGIN
      S[I] := TRUE
    END Include;

  PROCEDURE Remove(I: SymbolType; VAR S: SymbolSet);
    BEGIN
      S[I] := FALSE
    END Remove;

  PROCEDURE Contains(VAR S: SymbolSet; I: SymbolType): BOOLEAN;
    BEGIN
      RETURN S[I]
    END Contains;

  PROCEDURE Union(VAR S1, S2, Result: SymbolSet);
    VAR B: SymbolType;
    BEGIN
      FOR B := MIN(SymbolType) TO MAX(SymbolType) DO
        Result[B] := S1[B] OR S2[B]
      END
    END Union;

  END SymbolSets;

(* SYNTACTIC ERROR RECOVERY                                                *)
(*                                                                         *)
(* Recovery in the syntax analysis process following the discovery of a syntax *)
(* error is incorporated into the syntax procedures on the following basis: *)
(* 1. Each procedure when called is passed an actual parameter which is a set *)
(*    of symbols which are possible followers of the string which it should *)
(*    scan. These followers normally include:                              *)
(*    (a) all symbols which may legitimately follow the string to be scanned; *)
(*    (b) such additional symbols as a superior (calling) procedure may wish *)
(*        to handle in the event of error recovery.                        *)
(*                                                                         *)
(* 2. When entered the procedure may ensure that the current symbol is an   *)
(*    acceptable starter for the string to be scanned and, if not, scan     *)
(*    forward (skip) until such a symbol is found (subject to 4, below). This *)
(*    check is performed by an initial call of the procedure CheckForStarter *)
(*    within each syntax procedure.                                        *)
(*                                                                         *)
(* 3. When calling a subsidiary syntax procedure the procedure passes on as *)
```

```
(*    followers its own followers plus those symbols, if any, which it may    *)
(*    determine as followers for the substring to be scanned.                 *)
(*                                                                            *)
(* 4. To recover from a syntax error the procedure may scan over any symbol   *)
(*    provided it is not contained in the followers passed to it.             *)
(*                                                                            *)
(* 5. On exit the syntax procedure ensures that the current symbol is         *)
(*    contained in the followers passed to it, flagging a terminal error and  *)
(*    skipping if this is not initially the case.  This action is performed by *)
(*    a final call of the procedure FindFollower within each syntax procedure. *)

PROCEDURE SkipTo(RelevantSymbols: SymbolSet);
  BEGIN
    WHILE NOT Contains(RelevantSymbols, SymbolDescription.Symbol) DO
      GetNextSymbol
    END
  END SkipTo;

PROCEDURE CheckForStarter(Starters, Followers: SymbolSet; VAR Found: BOOLEAN);
  VAR LocalSet: SymbolSet;
  BEGIN
    IF NOT Contains(Starters, SymbolDescription.Symbol) THEN
      SyntaxError(OtherSymbol);
      Union(Starters, Followers, LocalSet);
      SkipTo(LocalSet)
    END;
    Found := Contains(Starters, SymbolDescription.Symbol)
  END CheckForStarter;

PROCEDURE FindFollower(Followers: SymbolSet);
  BEGIN
    IF NOT Contains(Followers, SymbolDescription.Symbol) THEN
      SyntaxError(OtherSymbol); SkipTo(Followers)
    END
  END FindFollower;

PROCEDURE Programme;
  VAR DeclarationStarters, StatementStarters, FactorStarters,
      RelationalOps, AdditionOps, MultiplicationOps, Signs: SymbolSet;

  PROCEDURE InitializeSymbolSets;
    BEGIN
      (* DeclarationStarters := {Var, Procedure}                              *)
      Clear(DeclarationStarters);
      Include(Var, DeclarationStarters);
      Include(Procedure, DeclarationStarters);

      (* RelationalOps := {Equals, NotEquals, LessThan, LessThanOrEqual,      *)
      (*                  GreaterThanOrEqual, GreaterThan}                     *)
      Clear(RelationalOps); Include(Equals, RelationalOps);
      Include(NotEquals, RelationalOps); Include(LessThan, RelationalOps);
      Include(LessThanOrEqual, RelationalOps);
      Include(GreaterThan, RelationalOps);
      Include(GreaterThanOrEqual, RelationalOps);

      (* AdditionOps := {Plus, Minus, Or}                                     *)
      Clear(AdditionOps); Include(Plus, AdditionOps);
      Include(Minus, AdditionOps); Include(Or, AdditionOps);

      (* MultiplicationOps := {Times, Div, And}                               *)
      Clear(MultiplicationOps); Include(Times, MultiplicationOps);
      Include(Div, MultiplicationOps); Include(And, MultiplicationOps);
```

```
      (* Signs              := {Plus, Minus}                        *)
      Clear(Signs); Include(Plus, Signs); Include(Minus, Signs);

      (* StatementStarters := {Identifier, Read, Write, If, Case, Loop, Exit  *)
      (*                     For}                                     *)
      Clear(StatementStarters); Include(Identifier, StatementStarters);
      Include(Read, StatementStarters); Include(Write, StatementStarters);
      Include(If, StatementStarters); Include(Case, StatementStarters);
      Include(Loop, StatementStarters); Include(Exit, StatementStarters);
      Include(For, StatementStarters);

      (* FactorStarters := {Identifier, IntegerNumber, CharConstant, Not,   *)
      (*                    LeftParenthesis}                          *)
      Clear(FactorStarters); Include(Identifier, FactorStarters);
      Include(IntegerNumber, FactorStarters);
      Include(CharConstant, FactorStarters); Include(Not, FactorStarters);
      Include(LeftParenthesis, FactorStarters)
    END InitializeSymbolSets;

PROCEDURE Block(Followers: SymbolSet);

  PROCEDURE DeclarationPart(Followers: SymbolSet);

    PROCEDURE VariableDeclarationPart(Followers: SymbolSet);

      PROCEDURE VariableDeclaration(Followers: SymbolSet);

        PROCEDURE Type(Followers: SymbolSet);

          PROCEDURE SimpleType(Followers: SymbolSet);
            VAR Starters: SymbolSet; OK: BOOLEAN;
            BEGIN
              Clear(Starters); Include(Identifier, Starters);
              CheckForStarter(Starters, Followers, OK);
              IF OK THEN
                Accept(Identifier);
                FindFollower(Followers)
              END
            END SimpleType;

          PROCEDURE IndexType(Followers: SymbolSet);
            VAR Starters: SymbolSet; OK: BOOLEAN;
            BEGIN
              Clear(Starters); Include(LeftBracket, Starters);
              Include(IntegerNumber, Starters); Include(Thru, Starters);
              CheckForStarter(Starters, Followers, OK);
              IF OK THEN
                WITH SymbolDescription DO
                  Accept(LeftBracket);
                  Accept(IntegerNumber);
                  Accept(Thru);
                  Accept(IntegerNumber);
                  Accept(RightBracket);
                END;
                FindFollower(Followers)
              END
            END IndexType;

          VAR Starters, LocalSet: SymbolSet; OK: BOOLEAN;

          BEGIN (* Type *)
            Clear(Starters); Include(Identifier, Starters);
```

```
          Include(Array, Starters);
          CheckForStarter(Starters, Followers, OK);
          IF OK THEN
            IF SymbolDescription.Symbol = Identifier THEN
              SimpleType(Followers)
            ELSE
              Accept(Array);
              LocalSet := Followers; Include(Of, LocalSet);
              IndexType(LocalSet);
              Accept(Of);
              SimpleType(Followers)
            END;
            FindFollower(Followers)
          END
        END Type;


      VAR Starters: SymbolSet; OK: BOOLEAN;

      BEGIN (* VariableDeclaration *)
        Clear(Starters); Include(Identifier, Starters);
        Include(Comma, Starters); Include(Colon, Starters);
        CheckForStarter(Starters, Followers, OK);
        IF OK THEN
          Accept(Identifier);
          WHILE SymbolDescription.Symbol = Comma DO
            Accept(Comma);
            Accept(Identifier)
          END;
          Accept(Colon);
          Type(Followers);
          FindFollower(Followers)
        END
      END VariableDeclaration;


    VAR LocalSet: SymbolSet;

    BEGIN (* VariableDeclarationPart *)
      Accept(Var);
      LocalSet := Followers; Include(Semicolon, LocalSet);
      WHILE SymbolDescription.Symbol = Identifier DO
        VariableDeclaration(LocalSet);
        Accept(Semicolon)
      END;
      FindFollower(Followers)
    END VariableDeclarationPart;

  PROCEDURE ProcedureDeclaration(Followers: SymbolSet);
    VAR LocalSet: SymbolSet;
    BEGIN
      Accept(Procedure);
      Accept(Identifier);
      Accept(Semicolon);
      LocalSet := Followers; Include(Identifier, LocalSet);
      Block(LocalSet);
      Accept(Identifier);
      FindFollower(Followers)
    END ProcedureDeclaration;

  VAR Starters, VarDeclarationFollowers, ProcDeclarationFollowers: SymbolSet;
      OK: BOOLEAN;
```

```
    BEGIN (* DeclarationPart *)
      Union(DeclarationStarters, Followers, Starters);
      CheckForStarter(Starters, Followers, OK);
      IF OK THEN
        VarDeclarationFollowers := Starters;
        Include(Begin, VarDeclarationFollowers);
        ProcDeclarationFollowers := VarDeclarationFollowers;
        Include(Semicolon, ProcDeclarationFollowers);
        WHILE Contains(DeclarationStarters, SymbolDescription.Symbol) DO
          CASE SymbolDescription.Symbol OF
          | Var:
              VariableDeclarationPart(VarDeclarationFollowers)
          | Procedure:
              ProcedureDeclaration(ProcDeclarationFollowers);
              Accept(Semicolon)
          END
        END;
        FindFollower(Followers)
      END
  END DeclarationPart;

PROCEDURE StatementPart(Followers: SymbolSet);

  PROCEDURE StatementSequence(Followers: SymbolSet);

    PROCEDURE Statement(Followers: SymbolSet);

      PROCEDURE Expression(Followers: SymbolSet); FORWARD;

      PROCEDURE Variable(Followers: SymbolSet);
        VAR Starters, LocalSet: SymbolSet; OK: BOOLEAN;
        BEGIN
          Clear(Starters); Include(Identifier, Starters);
          CheckForStarter(Starters, Followers, OK);
          IF OK THEN
            Accept(Identifier);
            IF SymbolDescription.Symbol = LeftBracket THEN
              Accept(LeftBracket);
              LocalSet := Followers; Include(RightBracket, LocalSet);
              Expression(LocalSet);
              Accept(RightBracket)
            END;
            FindFollower(Followers)
          END
        END Variable;

      PROCEDURE Expression (Followers: SymbolSet);

        PROCEDURE SimpleExpression(Followers: SymbolSet);

          PROCEDURE Term(Followers: SymbolSet);

            PROCEDURE Factor(Followers: SymbolSet);
              VAR LocalSet: SymbolSet; OK: BOOLEAN;
              BEGIN
                CheckForStarter(FactorStarters, Followers, OK);
                IF OK THEN
                  WITH SymbolDescription DO
                    CASE Symbol OF
                    | Identifier:
                        (* IF constant-identifier THEN *)
                        (*   accept as constant       *)
```

```
                    (*   ELSE                        *)
                        Variable(Followers)
                    (*   END                         *)
                | IntegerNumber:
                    Accept(IntegerNumber)
                | CharConstant:
                    Accept(CharConstant)
                | LeftParenthesis:
                    Accept(LeftParenthesis);
                    LocalSet := Followers;
                    Include(RightParenthesis, LocalSet);
                    Expression(LocalSet);
                    Accept(RightParenthesis)
                | Not:
                    Accept(Not);
                    Factor(Followers)
              END
            END;
            FindFollower(Followers)
          END
        END Factor;

    VAR LocalSet, TempSet: SymbolSet;

    BEGIN (* Term *)
      Union(MultiplicationOps, FactorStarters, TempSet);
      Union(Followers, TempSet, LocalSet);
      Factor(LocalSet);
      WITH SymbolDescription DO
        WHILE Contains(TempSet, Symbol) DO
          IF Contains(MultiplicationOps, Symbol) THEN GetNextSymbol
          ELSE SyntaxError(Times)
          END;
          Factor(LocalSet);
        END
      END
    END Term;

  VAR Starters, LocalSet: SymbolSet; OK: BOOLEAN;

  BEGIN (* SimpleExpression *)
    Union(FactorStarters, Signs, Starters);
    CheckForStarter(Starters, Followers, OK);
    IF OK THEN
      WITH SymbolDescription DO
        IF Contains(Signs, Symbol) THEN GetNextSymbol END;
        Union(AdditionOps, Followers, LocalSet);
        Term(LocalSet);
        WHILE Contains(AdditionOps, Symbol) DO
          GetNextSymbol; Term(LocalSet)
        END;
        FindFollower(Followers)
      END
    END
  END SimpleExpression;

VAR LocalSet: SymbolSet;

BEGIN (* Expression *)
  Union(RelationalOps, Followers, LocalSet);
  SimpleExpression(LocalSet);
  IF Contains(RelationalOps, SymbolDescription.Symbol) THEN
```

```
            GetNextSymbol; SimpleExpression(Followers);
       END
    END Expression;

PROCEDURE Assignment;
  VAR LocalSet: SymbolSet;
  BEGIN
    LocalSet := Followers; Include(Becomes, LocalSet);
    Variable(LocalSet);
    Accept(Becomes);
    Expression(Followers);
  END Assignment;

PROCEDURE ReadStatement;

  PROCEDURE InputVariable;
    VAR LocalSet: SymbolSet;
    BEGIN
      LocalSet := Followers; Include(RightParenthesis, LocalSet);
      Variable(LocalSet);
    END InputVariable;

  BEGIN (* ReadStatement *)
    Accept(Read);
    Accept(LeftParenthesis);
    InputVariable;
    Accept(RightParenthesis)
  END ReadStatement;

PROCEDURE WriteStatement;

  PROCEDURE OutputValue;
    VAR LocalSet: SymbolSet;
    BEGIN
      LocalSet := Followers; Include(RightParenthesis, LocalSet);
      Expression(LocalSet);
    END OutputValue;

  BEGIN (* WriteStatement *)
    Accept(Write);
    Accept(LeftParenthesis);
    OutputValue;
    Accept(RightParenthesis)
  END WriteStatement;

PROCEDURE IfStatement;
  VAR LocalSet: SymbolSet;
  BEGIN
    Accept(If);
    LocalSet := Followers; Include(Then, LocalSet);
    Include(Else, LocalSet); Include(End, LocalSet);
    Expression(LocalSet);
    Accept(Then);
    Remove(Then, LocalSet);
    StatementSequence(LocalSet);
    IF SymbolDescription.Symbol = Else THEN
      Accept(Else);
      Remove(Else, LocalSet);
      StatementSequence(LocalSet)
    END;
    Accept(End)
  END IfStatement;
```

```
    PROCEDURE ExitStatement;
      BEGIN
        Accept(Exit)
      END ExitStatement;

  PROCEDURE LoopStatement;
   VAR LocalSet: SymbolSet;
    BEGIN
        Accept(Loop);
        LocalSet := Followers; Include(End, LocalSet);
        StatementSequence(LocalSet);
        Accept(End)
    END LoopStatement;

  PROCEDURE CaseStatement;

    PROCEDURE NewCaseLabel;
      BEGIN
        WITH SymbolDescription DO
          IF NOT (Symbol = IntegerNumber) AND
             NOT (Symbol = CharConstant) AND
             NOT (Symbol = Identifier) THEN
            SyntaxError(OtherSymbol)
          END
        END;
        GetNextSymbol
      END NewCaseLabel;

    VAR LocalSet, TempSet: SymbolSet;

    BEGIN (* CaseStatement *)
      Accept(Case);
      LocalSet := Followers; Include(Of, LocalSet);
      Include(Separator, LocalSet); Include(End, LocalSet);
      Expression(LocalSet);
      Accept(Of); Remove(Of, LocalSet);
      Clear(TempSet); Include(Comma, TempSet);
      Include(Identifier, TempSet); Include(IntegerNumber, TempSet);
      Include(CharConstant, TempSet);
      REPEAT
        Accept(Separator);
        LOOP
          NewCaseLabel;
          IF NOT Contains(TempSet, SymbolDescription.Symbol) THEN EXIT
          END;
          Accept(Comma)
        END;
        Accept(Colon);
        StatementSequence(LocalSet)
      UNTIL (SymbolDescription.Symbol = End) OR
            Contains(Followers, SymbolDescription.Symbol);
      Accept(End)
    END CaseStatement;

PROCEDURE ForStatement;
  VAR LocalSet: SymbolSet;
  BEGIN
    Accept(For);
    Accept(Identifier);
    Accept(Becomes);
    LocalSet := Followers; Include(To, LocalSet);
    Include(Do, LocalSet); Include(End, LocalSet);
```

```
        Expression(LocalSet);
        Accept(To); Remove(To, LocalSet);
        Expression(LocalSet);
        Accept(Do); Remove(Do, LocalSet);
        StatementSequence(LocalSet);
        Accept(End)
      END ForStatement;

  VAR OK: BOOLEAN;

  BEGIN (* Statement *)
    CheckForStarter(StatementStarters, Followers, OK);
    IF OK THEN
      CASE SymbolDescription.Symbol OF
      | Identifier:
          (* IF procedure-identifier THEN        *)
          (*    accept as procedure-statement    *)
          (*  ELSE                                *)
                Assignment
          (*  END                                 *)
      | If:    IfStatement
      | Exit:  ExitStatement
      | Loop:  LoopStatement
      | Case:  CaseStatement
      | For:   ForStatement
      | Read:  ReadStatement
      | Write: WriteStatement
      END;
      FindFollower(Followers)
    END
  END Statement;

VAR LocalSet, TempSet: SymbolSet; OK: BOOLEAN;

BEGIN (* StatementSequence *)
  CheckForStarter(StatementStarters, Followers, OK);
  IF OK THEN
    Union(StatementStarters, Followers, LocalSet);
    Include(Semicolon, LocalSet); Remove(Identifier, LocalSet);
    Statement(LocalSet);
    TempSet := StatementStarters;
    Include(Semicolon, TempSet); Remove(Identifier,TempSet);
    WHILE Contains(TempSet, SymbolDescription.Symbol) DO
      Accept(Semicolon); Statement(LocalSet)
    END;
    FindFollower(Followers)
  END
END StatementSequence;

VAR Starters, LocalSet: SymbolSet; OK: BOOLEAN;

BEGIN (* StatementPart *)
  Clear(Starters); Include(Begin, Starters);
  CheckForStarter(Starters, Followers, OK);
  IF OK THEN
    Accept(Begin);
    LocalSet := Followers; Include(End, LocalSet);
    StatementSequence(LocalSet);
    Accept(End);
    FindFollower(Followers)
  END
END StatementPart;
```

```
      VAR Starters, LocalSet: SymbolSet; OK: BOOLEAN;

    BEGIN (* Block *)
      Clear(Starters); Include(Var, Starters);
      Include(Procedure, Starters); Include(Begin, Starters);
      CheckForStarter(Starters, Followers, OK);
      IF OK THEN
        LocalSet := Followers; Include(Procedure, LocalSet);
        Include(Var, LocalSet); Include(Begin, LocalSet);
        DeclarationPart(LocalSet);
        StatementPart(Followers);
        FindFollower(Followers)
      END
    END Block;

  VAR LocalSet: SymbolSet;

  BEGIN (* Programme *)
    InitializeSymbolSets;
    Accept(Module);
    Accept(Identifier);
    Accept(Semicolon);
    Clear(LocalSet);
    Include(Identifier, LocalSet); Include(Period, LocalSet);
    Block(LocalSet);
    Accept(Identifier)
  END Programme;

END SyntaxAnalyzer.
```

Semantic table (1)

Definition module

```
DEFINITION MODULE Table;

  FROM Host IMPORT Word;
  IMPORT Target;

    (* The Table module organizes the creation of, location of, and storage    *)
    (* recovery from the identifier and type records which support semantic     *)
    (* analysis.                                                                *)
    (*                                                                          *)
    (* Scope housekeeping is carried out by calls of the procedures OpenScope   *)
    (* and CloseScope for each block. Between calls of these procedures,        *)
    (* insertion and look-up of identifiers within the table is provided by the *)
    (* two procedures NewId and SearchId.                                       *)
    (*                                                                          *)
    (* The creation of type entries is handled by the procedure NewType.        *)
    (*                                                                          *)
    (* The Table module reports errors with the following codes:                *)
    (*                                                                          *)
    (*  51 .... Identifier declared twice                                       *)
    (*  52 .... Identifier not declared                                         *)
    (*  53 .... Identifier of wrong class for this context                      *)


    (* TYPE ENTRIES                                                             *)
    (* All types underlying the data defined by the program being compiled are  *)
    (* represented by type entries whose form is determined by the 'form' of    *)
    (* the type so represented (i.e. scalars, arrays, etc.).                    *)
    (* Entries are constructed using a corresponding variant record-type        *)
    (* TypeRecord.  These type entries are accessed only via the identifier     *)
    (* table entries for type-identifiers, or via the representation of the     *)
    (* data objects (variables, constants, expressions) whose type they         *)
    (* describe.  Thus, for example, all identifier table entries have a common *)
    (* field IdType which points to an underlying type entry (with an obvious    *)
    (* interpretation for all classes of identifier other than a procedure-     *)
    (* identifier).                                                             *)

  TYPE TypeEntry = POINTER TO TypeRecord;
       TypeClass = (Scalars, Arrays);
       TypeRecord = RECORD
                       Next: TypeEntry;
```

```
                    CASE Form: TypeClass OF
                    | Arrays: IndexMin, IndexMax: Target.Integer;
                             ElementType: TypeEntry
                    | Scalars:
                    END
                 END;

(* IDENTIFIER ENTRIES                                                    *)
(* An entry is recorded for each identifier, standard or user defined,   *)
(* which may appear in the program being compiled.  The form of entry    *)
(* depends on the class of usage of the identifier and is represented by *)
(* the record-type IdRecord.                                             *)

TYPE IdentifierEntry = POINTER TO IdRecord;
     IdentifierClass = (Types, Constants, Variables, Procedures);
     IdClassSet = SET OF IdentifierClass;
     IdRecord = RECORD
                   Name: Word;
                   LeftLink, RightLink: IdentifierEntry;
                   IdType: TypeEntry;
                   Class: IdentifierClass
                END;

PROCEDURE OpenScope;

PROCEDURE CloseScope;

PROCEDURE NewId(Spelling: Word; VAR Entry: IdentifierEntry;
                ClassNeeded: IdentifierClass);

PROCEDURE SearchId(Spelling: Word; VAR Entry: IdentifierEntry;
                   AllowableClasses: IdClassSet);

PROCEDURE NewType(VAR Entry: TypeEntry; FormNeeded: TypeClass);
   (* Each type entry created by NewType is associated with the current  *)
   (* block.  All storage allocated to Table entries is recovered at final *)
   (* closure of a block scope.                                          *)

(* THE FUNCTION Compatible                                               *)
(* To facilitate type analysis within the semantic analyzer a general-  *)
(* purpose Boolean function Compatible is provided to test the          *)
(* compatibility of two types as represented by variables of the type   *)
(* Table.IdentifierEntry.  A result TRUE is returned if the types are   *)
(* identical (i.e. these variables point to the same type entry), or    *)
(* structurally equivalent (i.e. two distinct type entries of identical *)
(* form and content).                                                   *)
(* Compatible is defined to return TRUE if either of its parameters     *)
(* denotes an undefined type.  In this way normal type analysis can     *)
(* proceed without a preliminary screening for indeterminate types at   *)
(* every point at which they might arise.                               *)

PROCEDURE Compatible(Type1, Type2: TypeEntry): BOOLEAN;

PROCEDURE IsOrdinalType(Type: TypeEntry): BOOLEAN;
   (* Determines whether the parameter Type denotes a scalar type.      *)

PROCEDURE Undefined(Type: TypeEntry): BOOLEAN;

PROCEDURE SetUndefined(VAR Type: TypeEntry);

END Table.
```

Implementation module

```
IMPLEMENTATION MODULE Table;

  FROM Host IMPORT Word, WordRelation, ComparisonOf, BlankWord, New, Dispose;
  FROM SourceHandler IMPORT Error;
  FROM LexicalAnalyzer IMPORT SymbolDescription;

  (* The table is organized as a set of binary trees, one for each identifier *)
  (* scope currently open, the nesting of these scopes being represented by a *)
  (* stack of scope records.                                                  *)

  (* Recovery from semantic errors is accommodated within the Table data      *)
  (* structures and procedures as follows:                                    *)
  (*                                                                          *)
  (* (1) If NewId finds an entry for the identifier already in the current    *)
  (*     scope, an error is flagged but a second entry is still made (for     *)
  (*     possible selection by SearchId as below).                           *)
  (*                                                                          *)
  (* (2) SearchId when called is passed a parameter specifying the acceptable *)
  (*     classes of entry to be found.  If the first entry encountered for    *)
  (*     the identifier is not of an acceptable class searching continues     *)
  (*     within the current scope for a possible duplicate entry.  If no      *)
  (*     acceptable duplicate is found in the scope a Misuse error is         *)
  (*     reported and an anonymous default entry of acceptable class is       *)
  (*     returned.                                                            *)
  (*                                                                          *)
  (* (3) If SearchId fails to find an entry in any scope for the identifier   *)
  (*     sought, an Undeclared error is reported, and an entry of acceptable  *)
  (*     class is created for the identifier, with otherwise default          *)
  (*     attributes.                                                          *)

  TYPE Scope = POINTER TO ScopeRecord;
       ScopeRecord = RECORD
                          FirstLocal: IdentifierEntry;
                          TypeChain: TypeEntry;
                          EnclosingScope: Scope
                     END;

  VAR LocalScope: Scope;
      DefaultEntry: ARRAY[Types..Procedures] OF IdentifierEntry;

  PROCEDURE IdError(Code: CARDINAL);
    BEGIN
      Error(Code, SymbolDescription.Position)
    END IdError;

  PROCEDURE OpenScope;
    VAR NewScope: Scope;
    BEGIN
      New(NewScope, SIZE(ScopeRecord));
      WITH NewScope^ DO
        FirstLocal := NIL; TypeChain := NIL; EnclosingScope := LocalScope
      END;
      LocalScope := NewScope
    END OpenScope;

  PROCEDURE CloseScope;
    VAR OldScope: Scope;

    PROCEDURE DisposeIdRecords(Root: IdentifierEntry);
```

```
      BEGIN
        IF Root <> NIL THEN
          WITH Root^ DO
            DisposeIdRecords(LeftLink); DisposeIdRecords(RightLink);
            Dispose(Root, SIZE(IdRecord))
          END
        END
      END DisposeIdRecords;

    PROCEDURE DisposeTypeRecords(FirstType: TypeEntry);
      VAR ThisType, NextType: TypeEntry;
      BEGIN
        NextType := FirstType;
        WHILE NextType <> NIL DO
          ThisType := NextType; NextType := ThisType^.Next;
          Dispose(ThisType, SIZE(TypeRecord))
        END
      END DisposeTypeRecords;

    BEGIN (* CloseScope *)
      OldScope := LocalScope;
      LocalScope := LocalScope^.EnclosingScope;
      WITH OldScope^ DO
        DisposeIdRecords(FirstLocal); DisposeTypeRecords(TypeChain)
      END;
      Dispose(OldScope, SIZE(ScopeRecord))
    END CloseScope;

PROCEDURE NewId(Spelling: Word; VAR Entry: IdentifierEntry;
                ClassNeeded: IdentifierClass);
    VAR ThisScope: Scope; NewEntry, ThisEntry, LastEntry: IdentifierEntry;
        LeftTaken: BOOLEAN;
    BEGIN
      New(NewEntry, SIZE(IdRecord));
      (* Set Name, Class, and default attributes *)
      WITH NewEntry^ DO
        Name := Spelling; IdType := NIL; LeftLink := NIL; RightLink := NIL;
        Class := ClassNeeded
      END;
      (* Enter in current scope *)
      ThisScope := LocalScope; ThisEntry := ThisScope^.FirstLocal;
      IF ThisEntry = NIL THEN ThisScope^.FirstLocal := NewEntry
      ELSE
        REPEAT
          LastEntry := ThisEntry;
          IF ComparisonOf(Spelling, ThisEntry^.Name) = FirstIsLess THEN
            ThisEntry := ThisEntry^.LeftLink; LeftTaken := TRUE
          ELSIF ComparisonOf(Spelling, ThisEntry^.Name) = SecondIsLess THEN
            ThisEntry := ThisEntry^.RightLink; LeftTaken := FALSE
          ELSE
            IdError(51); ThisEntry := ThisEntry^.RightLink; LeftTaken := FALSE
          END
        UNTIL ThisEntry = NIL;
        IF LeftTaken THEN LastEntry^.LeftLink := NewEntry
        ELSE LastEntry^.RightLink := NewEntry
        END
      END;
      Entry := NewEntry
    END NewId;

PROCEDURE SearchId(Spelling: Word; VAR Entry: IdentifierEntry;
                AllowableClasses: IdClassSet);
```

```
    VAR ThisEntry, LastEntry: IdentifierEntry;
        MisUsed: BOOLEAN; ThisScope: Scope;

    PROCEDURE MostLikelyOf(Classes: IdClassSet): IdentifierClass;
      BEGIN
        IF Variables IN Classes THEN RETURN Variables
        ELSIF Procedures IN Classes THEN RETURN Procedures
        ELSIF Types IN Classes THEN RETURN Types
        ELSE RETURN Constants
        END
      END MostLikelyOf;

    BEGIN (* SearchId *)
      MisUsed := FALSE;
      ThisScope := LocalScope;
      REPEAT
        ThisEntry := ThisScope^.FirstLocal;
        WHILE ThisEntry <> NIL DO
          IF ComparisonOf(Spelling, ThisEntry^.Name) = FirstIsLess THEN
            ThisEntry := ThisEntry^.LeftLink
          ELSIF ComparisonOf(Spelling, ThisEntry^.Name) = SecondIsLess THEN
            ThisEntry := ThisEntry^.RightLink
          ELSIF ThisEntry^.Class IN AllowableClasses THEN
            Entry := ThisEntry; RETURN
          ELSE MisUsed := TRUE; ThisEntry := ThisEntry^.RightLink
          END
        END;
        IF MisUsed THEN
          IdError(53); Entry := DefaultEntry[MostLikelyOf(AllowableClasses)];
          RETURN
        END;
        ThisScope := ThisScope^.EnclosingScope
      UNTIL ThisScope = NIL;
      IdError(52);
      NewId(Spelling, Entry, MostLikelyOf(AllowableClasses))
    END SearchId;

  PROCEDURE NewType(VAR Entry: TypeEntry; FormNeeded: TypeClass);
    VAR ThisScope: Scope; NewEntry: TypeEntry;
    BEGIN
      New(NewEntry, SIZE(TypeRecord));
      CASE FormNeeded OF
      | Scalars:
          NewEntry^.Form := Scalars
      | Arrays:
          WITH NewEntry^ DO
            Form := Arrays; IndexMin := 0; IndexMax := 1; ElementType := NIL
          END
      END;
      ThisScope := LocalScope;
      WITH ThisScope^ DO
        NewEntry^.Next := TypeChain; TypeChain := NewEntry
      END;
      Entry := NewEntry
    END NewType;

  PROCEDURE Compatible(Type1, Type2: TypeEntry): BOOLEAN;
    (* Are types pointed to by Type1 and Type2 compatible? *)
    BEGIN
      IF Type1 = Type2 THEN RETURN TRUE
      ELSIF (Type1 = NIL) OR (Type2 = NIL) THEN RETURN TRUE
      ELSIF (Type1^.Form = Arrays) AND (Type2^.Form = Arrays) THEN
```

```
        RETURN (Type1^.IndexMin = Type2^.IndexMin) AND
               (Type1^.IndexMax = Type2^.IndexMax) AND
               Compatible(Type1^.ElementType, Type2^.ElementType)
      ELSE RETURN FALSE
      END
    END Compatible;

  PROCEDURE Undefined(Type: TypeEntry): BOOLEAN;
    BEGIN
      RETURN Type = NIL
    END Undefined;

  PROCEDURE SetUndefined(VAR Type: TypeEntry);
    BEGIN
      Type := NIL
    END SetUndefined;

  PROCEDURE IsOrdinalType(Type: TypeEntry): BOOLEAN;
    BEGIN
      IF Type = NIL THEN RETURN TRUE
      ELSE RETURN (Type^.Form = Scalars)
      END
    END IsOrdinalType;

VAR C: IdentifierClass;

BEGIN
  LocalScope := NIL;
  FOR C := MIN(IdentifierClass) TO MAX(IdentifierClass) DO
    New(DefaultEntry[C], SIZE(IdRecord));
    WITH DefaultEntry[C]^ DO
      Name := BlankWord; IdType := NIL; Class := C
    END
  END
END Table.
```

Appendix 9

Semantic analyzer

Definition module

```
DEFINITION MODULE SemanticAnalyzer;

    (* The Analyzer generates syntax error codes with the following meanings:   *)
    (*                                                                          *)
    (*  10 ... Symbol expected was Identifier                                   *)
    (*  11 ... Symbol expected was Integer Number                              *)
    (*  12 ... Symbol expected was Character Constant                          *)
    (*  13 ... .......                                                          *)
    (*                                                                          *)
    (*                                                                          *)
    (* i.e. one value for each of the values of SymbolType.                    *)
    (* The final value, ORD(OtherSymbol)+10, is used to mean                   *)
    (*                                                                          *)
    (*  NN ... Unexpected symbol                                               *)
    (*                                                                          *)
    (*                                                                          *)
    (* Semantic errors are reported with the following error codes:            *)
    (*                                                                          *)
    (*  61 ... Indexed-variable must be an array-variable                      *)
    (*  62 ... Index-expression must be of type INTEGER                        *)
    (*  63 ... Operand must be of type BOOLEAN                                 *)
    (*  64 ... Operand must be of type INTEGER                                 *)
    (*  65 ... Operands must both be INTEGER, CHAR or BOOLEAN                  *)
    (*  66 ... Expression must be of same type as Variable                    *)
    (*  67 ... Input variable must be of type INTEGER or CHAR                 *)
    (*  68 ... Expression must be of type INTEGER, CHAR or Boolean            *)
    (*  69 ... Expression must be of type Boolean                             *)
    (*  70 ... Identifiers at beginning and end of block must match           *)
    (*  71 ... For loop control-variable must be of type INTEGER, CHAR or BOOLEAN *)
    (*  72 ... An exit-statement must occur within a loop-statement           *)
    (*  73 ... Type of case label must be same as the selector type           *)
    (*  74 ... Case label must appear at most once in case-statement          *)
    (*  75 ... Case label must be of type INTEGER, CHAR or Boolean            *)


    PROCEDURE Programme;

END SemanticAnalyzer.
```

360

Implementation module

```
IMPLEMENTATION MODULE SemanticAnalyzer;

  IMPORT Target;
  FROM SourceHandler IMPORT Error;
  FROM LexicalAnalyzer IMPORT SymbolType, GetNextSymbol, SymbolDescription;
  FROM Host IMPORT StandardIdentifiers, GetSpelling, Word, WordRelation,
                   ComparisonOf, BlankWord, New, Dispose;
  FROM Table IMPORT OpenScope, CloseScope, NewId, SearchId, NewType,
                    IdentifierEntry, TypeEntry, IdentifierClass, IdClassSet,
                    TypeClass, Compatible, IsOrdinalType, Undefined, SetUndefined;

  (* For reasons of space and to avoid repetition commentary for the following   *)
  (* areas of the Analyzer has been omitted since it has already appeared in the *)
  (* Appendix specified:                                                         *)
  (*                                                                             *)
  (*                                                                             *)
  (*       Syntax analysis                    see Appendix 6                     *)
  (*       Syntax error recovery              see Appendix 7                     *)
  PROCEDURE SyntaxError(ExpectedSymbol: SymbolType);
    BEGIN
      Error(ORD(ExpectedSymbol)+10, SymbolDescription.Position)
    END SyntaxError;

  PROCEDURE Accept(SymbolExpected: SymbolType);
    BEGIN
      IF SymbolDescription.Symbol = SymbolExpected THEN GetNextSymbol
      ELSE SyntaxError(SymbolExpected)
      END
    END Accept;

MODULE SymbolSets;
  IMPORT SymbolType;
  EXPORT SymbolSet, Clear, Include, Remove, Contains, Union;

  TYPE SymbolSet = ARRAY SymbolType OF BOOLEAN;

  PROCEDURE Clear(VAR S: SymbolSet);
    VAR B: SymbolType;
    BEGIN
      FOR B := MIN(SymbolType) TO MAX(SymbolType) DO S[B] := FALSE END
    END Clear;

  PROCEDURE Include(I: SymbolType; VAR S: SymbolSet);
    BEGIN
      S[I] := TRUE
    END Include;

  PROCEDURE Remove(I: SymbolType; VAR S: SymbolSet);
    BEGIN
      S[I] := FALSE
    END Remove;

  PROCEDURE Contains(VAR S: SymbolSet; I: SymbolType): BOOLEAN;
    BEGIN
      RETURN S[I]
    END Contains;

  PROCEDURE Union(VAR S1, S2, Result: SymbolSet);
    VAR B: SymbolType;
```

```
    BEGIN
      FOR B := MIN(SymbolType) TO MAX(SymbolType) DO
        Result[B] := S1[B] OR S2[B]
      END
    END Union;

  END SymbolSets;

PROCEDURE SkipTo(RelevantSymbols: SymbolSet);
  BEGIN
    WHILE NOT Contains(RelevantSymbols, SymbolDescription.Symbol) DO
      GetNextSymbol
    END
  END SkipTo;

PROCEDURE CheckForStarter(Starters, Followers: SymbolSet; VAR Found: BOOLEAN);
  VAR LocalSet: SymbolSet;
  BEGIN
    IF NOT Contains(Starters, SymbolDescription.Symbol) THEN
      SyntaxError(OtherSymbol);
      Union(Starters, Followers, LocalSet);
      SkipTo(LocalSet)
    END;
    Found := Contains(Starters, SymbolDescription.Symbol)
  END CheckForStarter;

PROCEDURE FindFollower(Followers: SymbolSet);
  BEGIN
    IF NOT Contains(Followers, SymbolDescription.Symbol) THEN
      SyntaxError(OtherSymbol); SkipTo(Followers)
    END
  END FindFollower;

(* SEMANTIC ANALYSIS AND SEMANTIC ERROR RECOVERY                        *)
(*                                                                      *)
(* Semantic analysis and semantic error recovery are implemented by enrichment *)
(* of the syntax analyzer with semantic interludes. Creation, location and     *)
(* destruction of the necessary identifier and type records is handled by the  *)
(* Table module.  The semantic analysis depends on these Table data structures *)
(* and procedures.                                                      *)
(*                                                                      *)
(* Standard identifiers supported by the language are held within Table as if   *)
(* declared in a pseudo-block enclosing the main program. These entries are     *)
(* created in the initialization of the Analyzer module.                *)
(*                                                                      *)
(* The type entries representing the standard types supported by the language  *)
(* (INTEGER, CHAR, BOOLEAN) are created in the initialization of the Analyzer  *)
(* module. These entries are accessible via the pointer-variables IntegerType, *)
(* CharType, etc., as well as via the identifier entries for "INTEGER", "CHAR",*)
(* etc.                                                                 *)

VAR IntegerType, BooleanType, CharType: TypeEntry;

PROCEDURE SemanticError(Code: CARDINAL);
  BEGIN
    Error(Code, SymbolDescription.Position)
  END SemanticError;

PROCEDURE CheckIsSameAs(BlockIdentifier: Word);
  BEGIN
    IF ComparisonOf(BlockIdentifier, BlankWord) <> WordsEqual THEN
      IF ComparisonOf(SymbolDescription.Spelling, BlockIdentifier)
```

```
                <> WordsEqual THEN SemanticError(70)
        END
    END
  END CheckIsSameAs;


PROCEDURE Programme;
  VAR DeclarationStarters, StatementStarters, FactorStarters,
      RelationalOps, AdditionOps, MultiplicationOps, Signs: SymbolSet;
      NullIdentifier: IdentifierEntry;

  PROCEDURE InitializeSymbolSets;
    BEGIN
      Clear(DeclarationStarters);
      Include(Var, DeclarationStarters);
      Include(Procedure, DeclarationStarters);

      Clear(RelationalOps); Include(Equals, RelationalOps);
      Include(NotEquals, RelationalOps); Include(LessThan, RelationalOps);
      Include(LessThanOrEqual, RelationalOps);
      Include(GreaterThan, RelationalOps);
      Include(GreaterThanOrEqual, RelationalOps);

      Clear(AdditionOps); Include(Plus, AdditionOps);
      Include(Minus, AdditionOps); Include(Or, AdditionOps);

      Clear(MultiplicationOps); Include(Times, MultiplicationOps);
      Include(Div, MultiplicationOps); Include(And, MultiplicationOps);

      Clear(Signs); Include(Plus, Signs); Include(Minus, Signs);

      Clear(StatementStarters); Include(Identifier, StatementStarters);
      Include(Read, StatementStarters); Include(Write, StatementStarters);
      Include(If, StatementStarters); Include(Case, StatementStarters);
      Include(Loop, StatementStarters); Include(Exit, StatementStarters);
      Include(For, StatementStarters);

      Clear(FactorStarters); Include(Identifier, FactorStarters);
      Include(IntegerNumber, FactorStarters);
      Include(CharConstant, FactorStarters); Include(Not, FactorStarters);
      Include(LeftParenthesis, FactorStarters)
    END InitializeSymbolSets;

PROCEDURE Block(Followers: SymbolSet; BlockId: IdentifierEntry);

  PROCEDURE DeclarationPart(Followers: SymbolSet);

    PROCEDURE VariableDeclarationPart(Followers: SymbolSet);

      PROCEDURE VariableDeclaration(Followers: SymbolSet);
        TYPE IdList = POINTER TO ListRecord;
             ListRecord = RECORD
                            Id: IdentifierEntry; NextOnList: IdList
                          END;
        VAR VariableList: RECORD Head, Tail: IdList END;
            VariableType: TypeEntry;

        PROCEDURE NewVariable;
          VAR VariableEntry: IdentifierEntry; ListEntry: IdList;
          BEGIN
            IF SymbolDescription.Symbol = Identifier THEN
              NewId(SymbolDescription.Spelling, VariableEntry, Variables);
```

```
        New(ListEntry, SIZE(ListRecord));
        WITH ListEntry^ DO
          Id := VariableEntry; NextOnList := NIL
        END;
        WITH VariableList DO
          IF Head = NIL THEN Head := ListEntry
          ELSE Tail^.NextOnList := ListEntry
          END;
          Tail := ListEntry
        END
    END
  END NewVariable;

PROCEDURE AddAttributes;
  VAR ListEntry, OldEntry: IdList;
  BEGIN
    ListEntry := VariableList.Head;
      WHILE ListEntry <> NIL DO
        WITH ListEntry^ DO
          Id^.IdType := VariableType;
          OldEntry := ListEntry; ListEntry := NextOnList;
          Dispose(OldEntry, SIZE(ListRecord))
        END
      END
    END AddAttributes;

PROCEDURE Type(Followers: SymbolSet; VAR TypeFound: TypeEntry);

  PROCEDURE SimpleType(Followers: SymbolSet; VAR TypeNamed: TypeEntry);
    VAR Starters: SymbolSet; OK: BOOLEAN;
        TypeIdentifier: IdentifierEntry;
    BEGIN
      Clear(Starters); Include(Identifier, Starters);
      CheckForStarter(Starters, Followers, OK);
      IF OK THEN
        SearchId(SymbolDescription.Spelling,
                  TypeIdentifier, IdClassSet{Types});
        TypeNamed := TypeIdentifier^.IdType;
        Accept(Identifier);
        FindFollower(Followers)
      END
    END SimpleType;

  PROCEDURE IndexType(Followers: SymbolSet);
    VAR Starters: SymbolSet; OK: BOOLEAN;
    BEGIN
      Clear(Starters); Include(LeftBracket, Starters);
      Include(IntegerNumber, Starters); Include(Thru, Starters);
      CheckForStarter(Starters, Followers, OK);
      IF OK THEN
        WITH SymbolDescription DO
          Accept(LeftBracket);
          IF Symbol = IntegerNumber THEN
            TypeFound^.IndexMin := IntValue
          END;
          Accept(IntegerNumber);
          Accept(Thru);
          IF Symbol = IntegerNumber THEN
            TypeFound^.IndexMax := IntValue
          END;
          Accept(IntegerNumber); Accept(RightBracket);
        END;
```

```
              FindFollower(Followers)
            END
          END IndexType;

      VAR ElementType: TypeEntry;
          Starters, LocalSet: SymbolSet; OK: BOOLEAN;

      BEGIN (* Type *)
        Clear(Starters); Include(Identifier, Starters);
        Include(Array, Starters);
        CheckForStarter(Starters, Followers, OK);
        IF OK THEN
          IF SymbolDescription.Symbol = Identifier THEN
            SimpleType(Followers, TypeFound)
          ELSE
            NewType(TypeFound, Arrays);
            Accept(Array);
            LocalSet := Followers; Include(Of, LocalSet);
            IndexType(LocalSet);
            Accept(Of);
            SimpleType(Followers, ElementType);
            TypeFound^.ElementType := ElementType;
          END;
          FindFollower(Followers)
        END
      END Type;

  VAR Starters: SymbolSet; OK: BOOLEAN;

  BEGIN (* VariableDeclaration *)
    Clear(Starters); Include(Identifier, Starters);
    Include(Comma, Starters); Include(Colon, Starters);
    CheckForStarter(Starters, Followers, OK);
    IF OK THEN
      VariableList.Head := NIL;
      NewVariable; Accept(Identifier);
      WHILE SymbolDescription.Symbol = Comma DO
        Accept(Comma); NewVariable; Accept(Identifier)
      END;
      Accept(Colon);
      Type(Followers, VariableType);
      AddAttributes;
      FindFollower(Followers)
    END
  END VariableDeclaration;

VAR LocalSet: SymbolSet;

BEGIN (* VariableDeclarationPart *)
  Accept(Var);
  LocalSet := Followers; Include(Semicolon, LocalSet);
  WHILE SymbolDescription.Symbol = Identifier DO
    VariableDeclaration(LocalSet);
    Accept(Semicolon)
  END;
  FindFollower(Followers)
END VariableDeclarationPart;

PROCEDURE ProcedureDeclaration(Followers: SymbolSet);
  VAR ProcedureIdentifier: IdentifierEntry;
      ProcedureName: Word; LocalSet: SymbolSet;
  BEGIN
```

```
       Accept (Procedure);
       IF SymbolDescription.Symbol = Identifier THEN
         ProcedureName := SymbolDescription.Spelling
       ELSE ProcedureName := BlankWord
       END;
       NewId(ProcedureName, ProcedureIdentifier, Procedures);
       Accept (Identifier); Accept (Semicolon);
       LocalSet := Followers; Include(Identifier, LocalSet);
       Block(LocalSet, ProcedureIdentifier);
       IF SymbolDescription.Symbol = Identifier THEN
         CheckIsSameAs (ProcedureName)
       END;
       Accept (Identifier);
       FindFollower(Followers)
     END ProcedureDeclaration;

  VAR Starters, VarDeclarationFollowers, ProcDeclarationFollowers: SymbolSet;
      OK: BOOLEAN;

  BEGIN (* DeclarationPart *)
     Union(DeclarationStarters, Followers, Starters);
     CheckForStarter(Starters, Followers, OK);
     IF OK THEN
       VarDeclarationFollowers := Starters;
       Include(Begin, VarDeclarationFollowers);
       ProcDeclarationFollowers := VarDeclarationFollowers;
       Include(Semicolon, ProcDeclarationFollowers);
       WHILE Contains(DeclarationStarters, SymbolDescription.Symbol) DO
         CASE SymbolDescription.Symbol OF
         | Var:
             VariableDeclarationPart(VarDeclarationFollowers)
         | Procedure:
             ProcedureDeclaration(ProcDeclarationFollowers);
             Accept (Semicolon)
         END
       END;
       FindFollower(Followers)
     END
  END DeclarationPart;

PROCEDURE StatementPart(Followers: SymbolSet);

  VAR  CurrentLoopCount: CARDINAL;

  PROCEDURE StatementSequence(Followers: SymbolSet);

    PROCEDURE Statement(Followers: SymbolSet);

      PROCEDURE Expression(Followers: SymbolSet;
                           VAR ExpressionType: TypeEntry); FORWARD;

      PROCEDURE Variable(Followers: SymbolSet; VAR VariableType: TypeEntry);
        VAR Starters, LocalSet: SymbolSet; OK: BOOLEAN;
            VariableIdentifier: IdentifierEntry; IndexType: TypeEntry;
        BEGIN
          Clear(Starters); Include(Identifier, Starters);
          CheckForStarter(Starters, Followers, OK);
          IF OK THEN
            SearchId(SymbolDescription.Spelling,
                     VariableIdentifier, IdClassSet{Variables});
            VariableType := VariableIdentifier^.IdType;
            Accept (Identifier);
```

```
          IF SymbolDescription.Symbol = LeftBracket THEN
            IF NOT Undefined(VariableType) THEN
              IF VariableType^.Form <> Arrays THEN
                SemanticError(61); SetUndefined(VariableType)
              END
            END;
            Accept(LeftBracket);
            LocalSet := Followers; Include(RightBracket, LocalSet);
            Expression(LocalSet, IndexType);
            IF NOT Compatible(IndexType, IntegerType) THEN
              SemanticError(62)
            END;
            IF NOT Undefined(VariableType) THEN
              VariableType := VariableType^.ElementType
            END;
            Accept(RightBracket)
          END;
        FindFollower(Followers)
      END
    END Variable;

  PROCEDURE Expression (Followers: SymbolSet;
                        VAR ExpressionType: TypeEntry);

    PROCEDURE SimpleExpression(Followers: SymbolSet;
                               VAR SimpleExpressionType: TypeEntry);

      PROCEDURE Term(Followers: SymbolSet; VAR TermType: TypeEntry);

        PROCEDURE Factor(Followers: SymbolSet;
                         VAR FactorType: TypeEntry);
        VAR LocalSet: SymbolSet; OK: BOOLEAN;
            FirstIdentifier: IdentifierEntry;
        BEGIN
          CheckForStarter(FactorStarters, Followers, OK);
          IF OK THEN
            WITH SymbolDescription DO
              CASE Symbol OF
              | Identifier:
                  SearchId(Spelling, FirstIdentifier,
                           IdClassSet{Variables, Constants});
                  CASE FirstIdentifier^.Class OF
                  | Constants:
                      FactorType := FirstIdentifier^.IdType;
                      Accept(Identifier)
                  | Variables:
                      Variable(Followers, FactorType);
                  END
              | IntegerNumber:
                  FactorType := IntegerType;
                  Accept(IntegerNumber)
              | CharConstant:
                  FactorType := CharType;
                  Accept(CharConstant)
              | LeftParenthesis:
                  Accept(LeftParenthesis);
                  LocalSet := Followers;
                  Include(RightParenthesis, LocalSet);
                  Expression(LocalSet, FactorType);
                  Accept(RightParenthesis)
              | Not:
                  Accept(Not);
```

```
                       Factor(Followers, FactorType);
                       IF NOT Compatible(FactorType, BooleanType) THEN
                         SemanticError(63)
                       END;
                       FactorType := BooleanType
                   END
                 END;
                 FindFollower(Followers)
             ELSE
                 SetUndefined(FactorType)
             END
        END Factor;

    VAR LocalSet, TempSet: SymbolSet;
        FactorType: TypeEntry; Operator: SymbolType;

    BEGIN (* Term *)
      Union(MultiplicationOps, FactorStarters, TempSet);
      Union(Followers, TempSet, LocalSet);
      Factor(LocalSet, FactorType); TermType := FactorType;
      WITH SymbolDescription DO
        WHILE Contains(TempSet, Symbol) DO
          Operator := Symbol;
          IF Contains(MultiplicationOps, Symbol) THEN GetNextSymbol
          ELSE SyntaxError(Times)
          END;
          Factor(LocalSet, FactorType);
          IF Contains(MultiplicationOps, Operator) THEN
            CASE Operator OF
            | Times, Div:
                IF NOT (Compatible(TermType, IntegerType) AND
                          Compatible(FactorType, IntegerType)) THEN
                  SemanticError(64)
                END;
                TermType := IntegerType
            | And:
                IF NOT (Compatible(TermType, BooleanType) AND
                          Compatible(FactorType, BooleanType)) THEN
                  SemanticError(63)
                END;
                TermType := BooleanType
            END
          ELSE
            SetUndefined(TermType)
          END
        END
      END
    END Term;

  VAR Starters, LocalSet: SymbolSet; OK: BOOLEAN;
      Signed: BOOLEAN; TermType: TypeEntry; Operator: SymbolType;

  BEGIN (* SimpleExpression *)
    Union(FactorStarters, Signs, Starters);
    CheckForStarter(Starters, Followers, OK);
    IF OK THEN
      WITH SymbolDescription DO
        IF Contains(Signs, Symbol) THEN
          Signed := TRUE; GetNextSymbol
        ELSE Signed := FALSE
        END;
        Union(AdditionOps, Followers, LocalSet);
```

```
                Term(LocalSet, TermType); SimpleExpressionType := TermType;
                IF Signed THEN
                  IF NOT Compatible(ExpressionType, IntegerType) THEN
                    SemanticError(64)
                  END
                END;
                WHILE Contains(AdditionOps, Symbol) DO
                  Operator := Symbol; GetNextSymbol;
                  Term(LocalSet, TermType);
                  CASE Operator OF
                  | Plus, Minus:
                     IF NOT (Compatible(SimpleExpressionType,
                                        IntegerType) AND
                             Compatible(TermType, IntegerType)) THEN
                       SemanticError(64)
                     END;
                     SimpleExpressionType := IntegerType
                  | Or:
                     IF NOT (Compatible(SimpleExpressionType,
                                        BooleanType) AND
                             Compatible(TermType, BooleanType)) THEN
                       SemanticError(63)
                     END;
                     SimpleExpressionType := BooleanType
                  END
                END;
                FindFollower(Followers)
              END
            ELSE
              SetUndefined(SimpleExpressionType)
            END
          END SimpleExpression;

        VAR LocalSet: SymbolSet; SimpleExpressionType: TypeEntry;

        BEGIN (* Expression *)
          Union(RelationalOps, Followers, LocalSet);
          SimpleExpression(LocalSet, SimpleExpressionType);
          ExpressionType := SimpleExpressionType;
          IF Contains(RelationalOps, SymbolDescription.Symbol) THEN
            SimpleExpression(Followers, SimpleExpressionType);
            IF NOT (Compatible(SimpleExpressionType, IntegerType) OR
                    Compatible(SimpleExpressionType, CharType) OR
                    Compatible(SimpleExpressionType, BooleanType)) AND
                    Compatible(SimpleExpressionType, ExpressionType) THEN
              SemanticError(65)
            END;
            ExpressionType := BooleanType
          END
        END Expression;

      PROCEDURE Assignment;
        VAR LocalSet: SymbolSet; VariableType, ExpressionType: TypeEntry;
        BEGIN
          LocalSet := Followers; Include(Becomes, LocalSet);
          Variable(LocalSet, VariableType);
          Accept(Becomes); Expression(Followers, ExpressionType);
          IF NOT Compatible(VariableType, ExpressionType) THEN
            SemanticError(66)
          END
        END Assignment;
      PROCEDURE ReadStatement;
```

```
    PROCEDURE InputVariable;
      VAR LocalSet: SymbolSet; VariableType: TypeEntry;
      BEGIN
        LocalSet := Followers; Include(RightParenthesis, LocalSet);
        Variable(LocalSet, VariableType);
        IF NOT Compatible(VariableType, CharType) AND
           NOT Compatible(VariableType, IntegerType) THEN
          SemanticError(67)
        END;
      END InputVariable;

    BEGIN (* ReadStatement *)
      Accept(Read);
      Accept(LeftParenthesis);
      InputVariable;
      Accept(RightParenthesis)
    END ReadStatement;

  PROCEDURE WriteStatement;

    PROCEDURE OutputValue;
      VAR LocalSet: SymbolSet; ExpressionType: TypeEntry;
      BEGIN
        LocalSet := Followers; Include(RightParenthesis, LocalSet);
        Expression(LocalSet, ExpressionType);
        IF NOT Compatible(ExpressionType, CharType) AND
           NOT Compatible(ExpressionType, IntegerType) THEN
          SemanticError(68)
        END
      END OutputValue;

    BEGIN (* WriteStatement *)
      Accept(Write);
      Accept(LeftParenthesis);
      OutputValue;
      Accept(RightParenthesis)
    END WriteStatement;

  PROCEDURE IfStatement;
    VAR LocalSet: SymbolSet; ExpressionType: TypeEntry;
    BEGIN
      Accept(If);
      LocalSet := Followers; Include(Then, LocalSet);
      Include(Else, LocalSet); Include(End, LocalSet);
      Expression(LocalSet, ExpressionType);
      IF NOT Compatible(ExpressionType, BooleanType) THEN
        SemanticError(69)
      END;
      Accept(Then); Remove(Then, LocalSet);
      StatementSequence(LocalSet);
      IF SymbolDescription.Symbol = Else THEN
        Accept(Else); Remove(Else, LocalSet);
        StatementSequence(LocalSet)
      END;
      Accept(End)
    END IfStatement;

  PROCEDURE ExitStatement;
    BEGIN
      Accept(Exit);
      IF CurrentLoopCount = 0 THEN SemanticError(72) END
    END ExitStatement;
```

```
PROCEDURE LoopStatement;
 VAR LocalSet: SymbolSet;
 BEGIN
     INC(CurrentLoopCount);
     Accept(Loop);
     LocalSet := Followers; Include(End, LocalSet);
     StatementSequence(LocalSet);
     Accept(End);
     DEC(CurrentLoopCount)
   END LoopStatement;

PROCEDURE CaseStatement;
  TYPE CaseEntry = POINTER TO CaseRecord;
       CaseRecord = RECORD
                      CaseValue: Target.Integer; NextCase: CaseEntry
                    END;

  VAR CaseType: TypeEntry; FirstCase: CaseEntry;

  PROCEDURE CaseLabel(VAR CaseLabelType: TypeEntry;
                      VAR CaseLabelValue: Target.Integer);
    VAR ConstantIdentifier: IdentifierEntry;
        SpellingOfTRUE: Word;
    BEGIN
      WITH SymbolDescription DO
        IF Symbol = IntegerNumber THEN
          CaseLabelType := IntegerType; CaseLabelValue := IntValue
        ELSIF Symbol = CharConstant THEN
          CaseLabelType := CharType; CaseLabelValue := CharValue
        ELSIF Symbol = Identifier THEN
          SearchId(Spelling, ConstantIdentifier,
                   IdClassSet{Constants});
          CaseLabelType := ConstantIdentifier^.IdType;
          GetSpelling(True, SpellingOfTRUE);
          IF ComparisonOf(Spelling, SpellingOfTRUE) = WordsEqual THEN
            CaseLabelValue := 1
          ELSE CaseLabelValue := 0
          END
        ELSE
          SetUndefined(CaseLabelType)
        END
      END
    END CaseLabel;

  PROCEDURE NewCaseLabel;
    VAR LabelType: TypeEntry; LabelValue: Target.Integer;
        ThisCase, LastCase: CaseEntry;
    BEGIN
      CaseLabel(LabelType, LabelValue);
      IF NOT Undefined(LabelType) THEN
        IF Compatible(LabelType, CaseType) THEN
          ThisCase := FirstCase; LastCase := NIL;
          LOOP
            IF ThisCase = NIL THEN
              New(ThisCase, SIZE(CaseRecord));
              WITH ThisCase^ DO
                CaseValue := LabelValue; NextCase := NIL
              END;
              IF LastCase = NIL THEN FirstCase := ThisCase
              ELSE LastCase^.NextCase := ThisCase
              END;
              EXIT
```

```
              ELSIF ThisCase^.CaseValue = LabelValue THEN
                SemanticError(74); EXIT
              ELSE
                LastCase := ThisCase; ThisCase := ThisCase^.NextCase
              END;
            END
          ELSE SemanticError(73)
          END
        ELSE SyntaxError(OtherSymbol)
        END;
        GetNextSymbol
      END NewCaseLabel;

    PROCEDURE DisposeOfCaseList;
      VAR ThisCase, NextCase: CaseEntry;
      BEGIN
        NextCase := FirstCase;
        WHILE NextCase <> NIL DO
          ThisCase := NextCase; NextCase := ThisCase^.NextCase;
          Dispose(ThisCase, SIZE(CaseRecord))
        END
      END DisposeOfCaseList;

    VAR LocalSet, TempSet: SymbolSet;

    BEGIN (* CaseStatement *)
      Accept(Case); LocalSet := Followers; Include(Of, LocalSet);
      Include(Separator, LocalSet); Include(End, LocalSet);
      Expression(LocalSet, CaseType);
      IF NOT IsOrdinalType(CaseType) THEN
        SemanticError(68); SetUndefined(CaseType)
      END;
      Accept(Of); Remove(Of, LocalSet);
      FirstCase := NIL;
      Clear(TempSet); Include(Comma, TempSet);
      Include(Identifier, TempSet); Include(IntegerNumber, TempSet);
      Include(CharConstant, TempSet);
      REPEAT
        Accept(Separator);
        LOOP
          NewCaseLabel;
          IF NOT Contains(TempSet, SymbolDescription.Symbol) THEN EXIT
          END;
          Accept(Comma)
        END;
        Accept(Colon);
        StatementSequence(LocalSet)
      UNTIL (SymbolDescription.Symbol = End) OR
            Contains(Followers, SymbolDescription.Symbol);
      DisposeOfCaseList;
      Accept(End)
    END CaseStatement;

  PROCEDURE ForStatement;
    VAR LocalSet: SymbolSet; ControlVariableId: IdentifierEntry;
        ControlVariableType, ExpressionType: TypeEntry;
    BEGIN
      Accept(For);
      IF SymbolDescription.Symbol = Identifier THEN
        SearchId(SymbolDescription.Spelling, ControlVariableId,
              IdClassSet{Variables});
        ControlVariableType := ControlVariableId^.IdType;
```

```
        IF NOT IsOrdinalType(ControlVariableType) THEN
          SemanticError(71); SetUndefined(ControlVariableType)
        END
      ELSE SetUndefined(ControlVariableType)
      END;
      Accept(Identifier); Accept(Becomes);
      LocalSet := Followers; Include(To, LocalSet);
      Include(Do, LocalSet); Include(End, LocalSet);
      Expression(LocalSet, ExpressionType);
      IF NOT Compatible(ControlVariableType, ExpressionType) THEN
        SemanticError(66)
      END;
      Accept(To); Remove(To, LocalSet);
      Expression(LocalSet, ExpressionType);
      IF NOT Compatible(ControlVariableType, ExpressionType) THEN
        SemanticError(66)
      END;
      Accept(Do); Remove(Do, LocalSet);
      StatementSequence(LocalSet);
      Accept(End)
    END ForStatement;

  VAR OK: BOOLEAN; FirstIdentifier: IdentifierEntry;

  BEGIN (* Statement *)
    CheckForStarter(StatementStarters, Followers, OK);
    IF OK THEN
      CASE SymbolDescription.Symbol OF
      | Identifier:
          SearchId(SymbolDescription.Spelling, FirstIdentifier,
                   IdClassSet{Procedures, Variables});
          IF FirstIdentifier^.Class = Variables THEN Assignment
          ELSE Accept(Identifier)
          END
      | If:     IfStatement
      | Exit:   ExitStatement
      | Loop:   LoopStatement
      | Case:   CaseStatement
      | For:    ForStatement
      | Read:   ReadStatement
      | Write:  WriteStatement
      END;
      FindFollower(Followers)
    END
  END Statement;

VAR LocalSet, TempSet: SymbolSet; OK: BOOLEAN;

BEGIN (* StatementSequence *)
  CheckForStarter(StatementStarters, Followers, OK);
  IF OK THEN
    Union(StatementStarters, Followers, LocalSet);
    Include(Semicolon, LocalSet); Remove(Identifier, LocalSet);
    Statement(LocalSet);
    TempSet := StatementStarters;
    Include(Semicolon, TempSet); Remove(Identifier, TempSet);
    WHILE Contains(TempSet, SymbolDescription.Symbol) DO
      Accept(Semicolon); Statement(LocalSet)
    END;
    FindFollower(Followers)
  END
END StatementSequence;
```

```
        VAR Starters, LocalSet: SymbolSet; OK: BOOLEAN;
        BEGIN (* StatementPart *)
          Clear(Starters); Include(Begin, Starters);
          CheckForStarter(Starters, Followers, OK);
          IF OK THEN
            CurrentLoopCount := 0;
            Accept(Begin); LocalSet := Followers; Include(End, LocalSet);
            StatementSequence(LocalSet); Accept(End);
            FindFollower(Followers)
          END
        END StatementPart;

      VAR Starters, LocalSet: SymbolSet; OK: BOOLEAN;
      BEGIN (* Block *)
        Clear(Starters); Include(Var, Starters);
        Include(Procedure, Starters); Include(Begin, Starters);
        CheckForStarter(Starters, Followers, OK);
        IF OK THEN
          OpenScope;
          LocalSet := Followers; Include(Procedure, LocalSet);
          Include(Var, LocalSet); Include(Begin, LocalSet);
          DeclarationPart(LocalSet); StatementPart(Followers);
          CloseScope;
          FindFollower(Followers)
        END
      END Block;

  VAR ProgramName: Word; IdSpelling: Word;
      LocalSet: SymbolSet; Entry: IdentifierEntry;
  BEGIN (* Programme *)
    OpenScope;
    NewType(IntegerType, Scalars);
    NewType(CharType, Scalars);
    NewType(BooleanType, Scalars);
    GetSpelling(Integer, IdSpelling);
    NewId(IdSpelling, Entry, Types); Entry^.IdType := IntegerType;
    GetSpelling(Char, IdSpelling);
    NewId(IdSpelling, Entry, Types); Entry^.IdType := CharType;
    GetSpelling(Boolean, IdSpelling);
    NewId(IdSpelling, Entry, Types); Entry^.IdType := BooleanType;
    GetSpelling(False, IdSpelling);
    NewId(IdSpelling, Entry, Constants);
    WITH Entry^ DO IdType := BooleanType END;
    GetSpelling(True, IdSpelling);
    NewId(IdSpelling, Entry, Constants);
    WITH Entry^ DO IdType := BooleanType END;
    InitializeSymbolSets;
    Accept(Module);
    IF SymbolDescription.Symbol = Identifier THEN
      ProgramName := SymbolDescription.Spelling
    ELSE ProgramName := BlankWord
    END;
    Accept(Identifier); Accept(Semicolon);
    Clear(LocalSet); Include(Identifier, LocalSet); Include(Period, LocalSet);
    NullIdentifier := NIL; Block(LocalSet, NullIdentifier);
    IF SymbolDescription.Symbol = Identifier THEN CheckIsSameAs(ProgramName)
    END;
    Accept(Identifier);
    CloseScope
  END Programme;

END SemanticAnalyzer.
```

Appendix 10

Code generation interface

Definition module

```
DEFINITION MODULE Generator;

    FROM LexicalAnalyzer IMPORT SymbolType;
    IMPORT Target;

    (* The Generator provides a program generation interface for the syntactic/   *)
    (* semantic analyzer as a set of procedure calls.  These calls and the types  *)
    (* underlying their parameter lists provide a generation interface which is    *)
    (* independent of the precise object code to be generated.  Between calls the  *)
    (* analyzer stores and transmits data of these types but without any necessary *)
    (* knowledge of their internal nature.                                          *)

    (* (a) REPRESENTATION AND STORAGE OF DATA                                       *)
    (*      The representation and storage of data within the object program is     *)
    (*      described by the Generator as follows:                                  *)
    (*      (1) For each type the Generator creates a representation of             *)

    TYPE TypeRepresentation = Target.AddressRange;

    (*          which describes how such data are to be represented in the object   *)
    (*          program.                                                            *)
    (*      (2) For each variable the Generator creates an address of               *)

    TYPE RunTimeAddress = RECORD
                            TextualLevel: CARDINAL;
                            RelativeAddress: Target.AddressRange
                          END;

    (*          which holds the necessary address coordinates for the run-time      *)
    (*          access of those data.                                               *)
    (*      (3) These descriptors are generated as follows:                         *)
    (*          Representations for the built-in types are made available as        *)
    (*          accessible values:                                                  *)

    VAR BooleanRepresentation,
        CharRepresentation,
        IntegerRepresentation: TypeRepresentation;
```

```
PROCEDURE ArrayRepresentation(BoundMin, BoundMax: Target.Integer;
                              ElementRepresentation: TypeRepresentation;
                              VAR Representation: TypeRepresentation);

(*        generates a representation for each program-defined type.        *)

PROCEDURE AddressFor(Representation: TypeRepresentation;
                     VAR Address: RunTimeAddress);

(*        determines the run-time address coordinates for a variable.  Run-  *)
(*        time addresses are assumed to lie within storage frames, one frame *)
(*        for each active procedure instance, and so calls of                *)

PROCEDURE OpenFrame;
PROCEDURE CloseFrame;

(*        are used to delimit the static nesting of frames for the address   *)
(*        allocation.                                                        *)

(* (b) VARIABLES, EXPRESSIONS AND ASSIGNMENT                                 *)
(*     The code generation interface for variable access, expression        *)
(*     evaluation and assignment assumes a postfix code form (though the     *)
(*     generating procedures called may transform this code thereafter).     *)
(*     The generating calls represent operations on a hypothetical run-time  *)
(*     stack of operand references and values, as follows:                   *)
(*     (1) Variable access is realized by the following hypothetical         *)
(*         operations:                                                       *)

PROCEDURE StackReference(Location: RunTimeAddress);
PROCEDURE IndexedReference(BoundMin, BoundMax: Target.Integer;
                          ElementRepresentation: TypeRepresentation);

(*     (2) Expression evaluation is realized by the following additional stack *)
(*         operations:                                                        *)

PROCEDURE Dereference(Representation: TypeRepresentation);
PROCEDURE StackConstant(ConstantValue: Target.Integer;
                        ConstantRepresentation: TypeRepresentation);
PROCEDURE NegateInteger;
TYPE      OperatorType = [Not..Equals];
PROCEDURE BinaryIntegerOperation(Operator: OperatorType);
PROCEDURE Comparison(Operator: OperatorType);
PROCEDURE NegateBoolean;
PROCEDURE BinaryBooleanOperation(Operator: OperatorType);

(*        The operation BinaryBooleanOperation is defined and used in a way  *)
(*        which permits either infix or postfix evaluation of AND/OR         *)
(*        operations.                                                        *)
(*     (3) Assignment is realized by the single hypothetical stack operation *)

PROCEDURE Assign;

(* (c) INPUT-OUTPUT OPERATORS                                                *)
(*     The input and output operations are realized by the following        *)
(*     generative operations:                                               *)

TYPE IOMode = (CharMode, IntegerMode);
PROCEDURE ReadOperation (ReadMode: IOMode);
PROCEDURE WriteOperation(WriteMode: IOMode);

(* (d) CONTROL STATEMENTS AND SEQUENTIAL CODE GENERATION                     *)
(*     The code generated, whatever its form, is assumed to be for sequential *)
```

```
(*     execution.  Each code sequence which can be entered other than          *)
(*     sequentially is represented at compile-time by a value of a CodeLabel   *)
(*     type, defined thus:                                                     *)

CONST CodeMax = 1000;
TYPE  CodeRange = [0..CodeMax];
      CodeLabel = RECORD
                     CASE Expected: BOOLEAN OF
                     | FALSE: StartAddress: Target.AddressRange;
                     | TRUE:  LastCodeReference: CodeRange;
                     END
                  END;

(*     These values are bound to points in the object code by                  *)

PROCEDURE NewCodeLabel(VAR Sequence: CodeLabel);

(*     for a previously unreferenced label                                     *)

PROCEDURE FutureCodeLabel(VAR Sequence: CodeLabel);

(*     for a label which may be referenced before it is generated              *)

PROCEDURE ExpectedCodeLabel(VAR Sequence: CodeLabel);

(*     for a label previously expected.                                        *)

(*     All references (jumps, etc.) are generated by the control generating    *)
(*     procedures manipulating these label descriptors.  Control statement     *)
(*     code is realized by the following hypothetical operations:              *)

PROCEDURE JumpOnFalse(VAR Destination: CodeLabel);
PROCEDURE Jump(VAR Destination: CodeLabel);
(*                                                                             *)
(* (e) CASE-STATEMENTS AND FOR-STATEMENTS                                      *)
(*     Following evaluation of the case selector in a case-statement           *)

PROCEDURE OpenCase;

(*     is called.  Each label in case limb is signalled by a call of           *)

PROCEDURE NextIsCase(CaseLabel: Target.Integer);

(*     and the final case-limb is followed by a call of                        *)

PROCEDURE CloseCase;

(*     The object code of the statement-sequence controlled by a for-statement *)
(*     must be preceded by a call                                              *)

PROCEDURE OpenFor;

(*     and followed by a call of                                               *)

PROCEDURE CloseFor;

(* (f) PROCEDURE AND PROGRAM CONTROL                                           *)
(*     The necessary compile- and run-time housekeeping operations associated  *)
(*     with the object program are realized as follows:                        *)
(*     (1) A linkage record of                                                 *)

TYPE ProcedureLinkage = RECORD
```

```
                    TextualLevel: CARDINAL;
                    CodeBody: CodeLabel; EntryPoint: CodeRange;
                END;
```

(*   is generated for each procedure by a call of   *)

PROCEDURE NewLinkage(VAR Linkage : ProcedureLinkage);

(*   (2) Transfer of control to a procedure is realized by a call of   *)

PROCEDURE CallProcedure(VAR Linkage: ProcedureLinkage);

(*   with the appropriate linkage record supplied as an actual parameter.*)
(*   (3) The necessary prelude and postlude code for each procedure or   *)
(*   program block is realized by means of   *)

PROCEDURE EnterBody(VAR Linkage: ProcedureLinkage);
PROCEDURE LeaveBody(VAR Linkage: ProcedureLinkage);
PROCEDURE EnterProgram;
PROCEDURE LeaveProgram;

(*   The Analyzer may suppress further code generation at any point by a   *)
(*   call of   *)

PROCEDURE NoFurtherCode;

(*   The generator ignores all subsequent calls to its operations. This is   *)
(*   necessary if analysis of (any part of) an incorrect program causes   *)
(*   inconsistent sequences of interface calls.   *)

(* The generator reports violations of implementation restrictions with the   *)
(* following codes: *)
(*   91 ... block too long   *)
(*   92 ... too much non-local recursion   *)
(*   93 ... arithmetic overflow at compile-time   *)
(*   94 ... division by zero   *)

END Generator.
```
```

Semantic table (2)

Definition module

```
DEFINITION MODULE Table;

  FROM Host IMPORT Word;
  IMPORT Target, Generator;

  (* For reasons of space and to avoid repetition commentary for this version of *)
  (* the Table module has been omitted since it is exactly  as in Appendix 8.    *)

  TYPE TypeEntry = POINTER TO TypeRecord;
       TypeClass = (Scalars, Arrays);
       TypeRecord = RECORD
                     Next: TypeEntry;
                     Representation: Generator.TypeRepresentation;
                     CASE Form: TypeClass OF
                     | Arrays: IndexMin, IndexMax: Target.Integer;
                               ElementType: TypeEntry
                     | Scalars:
                     END
                   END;

  TYPE IdentifierEntry = POINTER TO IdRecord;
       IdentifierClass = (Types, Constants, Variables, Procedures);
       IdClassSet = SET OF IdentifierClass;
       IdRecord = RECORD
                    Name: Word;
                    LeftLink, RightLink: IdentifierEntry;
                    IdType: TypeEntry;
                    CASE Class: IdentifierClass OF
                    | Constants: ConstantValue: Target.Integer;
                    | Variables: VariableAddress: Generator.RunTimeAddress;
                    | Procedures: Linkage: Generator.ProcedureLinkage
                    END
                  END;

  PROCEDURE OpenScope;
  PROCEDURE CloseScope;

  PROCEDURE NewId(Spelling: Word; VAR Entry:
              IdentifierEntry; ClassNeeded: IdentifierClass);
```

379

```
    PROCEDURE SearchId(Spelling: Word; VAR Entry: IdentifierEntry;
                       AllowableClasses: IdClassSet);

    PROCEDURE NewType(VAR Entry: TypeEntry; FormNeeded: TypeClass);

    PROCEDURE Compatible(Type1, Type2: TypeEntry): BOOLEAN;
    PROCEDURE IsOrdinalType(Type: TypeEntry): BOOLEAN;

    PROCEDURE Undefined(Type: TypeEntry): BOOLEAN;
    PROCEDURE SetUndefined(VAR Type: TypeEntry);

END Table.
```

Implementation module

```
IMPLEMENTATION MODULE Table;

  FROM Host IMPORT Word, WordRelation, ComparisonOf, BlankWord, New, Dispose;
  FROM SourceHandler IMPORT Error;
  FROM LexicalAnalyzer IMPORT SymbolDescription;
  IMPORT Generator;

  TYPE Scope = POINTER TO ScopeRecord;
       ScopeRecord = RECORD
                       FirstLocal: IdentifierEntry;
                       TypeChain: TypeEntry;
                       EnclosingScope: Scope
                     END;

  VAR LocalScope: Scope;
      DefaultEntry: ARRAY[Types..Procedures] OF IdentifierEntry;

  PROCEDURE IdError(Code: CARDINAL);
    BEGIN
      Error(Code, SymbolDescription.Position);
      Generator.NoFurtherCode
    END IdError;

  PROCEDURE OpenScope;
    VAR NewScope: Scope;
    BEGIN
      New(NewScope, SIZE(ScopeRecord));
      WITH NewScope^ DO
        FirstLocal := NIL; TypeChain := NIL; EnclosingScope := LocalScope
      END;
      LocalScope := NewScope
    END OpenScope;

  PROCEDURE CloseScope;
    VAR OldScope: Scope;

    PROCEDURE DisposeIdRecords(Root: IdentifierEntry);
      BEGIN
        IF Root <> NIL THEN
          WITH Root^ DO
            DisposeIdRecords(LeftLink); DisposeIdRecords(RightLink);
            Dispose(Root, SIZE(IdRecord))
          END
        END
      END DisposeIdRecords;
```

```
    PROCEDURE DisposeTypeRecords(FirstType: TypeEntry);
      VAR ThisType, NextType: TypeEntry;
      BEGIN
        NextType := FirstType;
        WHILE NextType <> NIL DO
          ThisType := NextType; NextType := ThisType^.Next;
          Dispose(ThisType, SIZE(TypeRecord))
        END
      END DisposeTypeRecords;

  BEGIN (* CloseScope *)
    OldScope := LocalScope;
    LocalScope := LocalScope^.EnclosingScope;
    WITH OldScope^ DO
      DisposeIdRecords(FirstLocal); DisposeTypeRecords(TypeChain)
    END;
    Dispose(OldScope, SIZE(ScopeRecord))
  END CloseScope;

PROCEDURE NewId(Spelling: Word; VAR Entry: IdentifierEntry;
                ClassNeeded: IdentifierClass);
  VAR ThisScope: Scope;
      NewEntry, ThisEntry, LastEntry: IdentifierEntry;
      LeftTaken: BOOLEAN;
  BEGIN
    New(NewEntry, SIZE(IdRecord));
    (* Set Name, Class, and default attributes *)
    WITH NewEntry^ DO
      Name := Spelling; IdType := NIL; LeftLink := NIL; RightLink := NIL;
      Class := ClassNeeded
    END;
    (* Enter in current scope *)
    ThisScope := LocalScope;
    ThisEntry := ThisScope^.FirstLocal;
    IF ThisEntry = NIL THEN ThisScope^.FirstLocal := NewEntry
    ELSE
      REPEAT
        LastEntry := ThisEntry;
        IF ComparisonOf(Spelling, ThisEntry^.Name) = FirstIsLess THEN
          ThisEntry := ThisEntry^.LeftLink; LeftTaken := TRUE
        ELSIF ComparisonOf(Spelling, ThisEntry^.Name) = SecondIsLess THEN
          ThisEntry := ThisEntry^.RightLink; LeftTaken := FALSE
        ELSE
          IdError(51);
          ThisEntry := ThisEntry^.RightLink; LeftTaken := FALSE
        END
      UNTIL ThisEntry = NIL;
      IF LeftTaken THEN LastEntry^.LeftLink := NewEntry
      ELSE LastEntry^.RightLink := NewEntry
      END
    END;
    Entry := NewEntry
  END NewId;

PROCEDURE SearchId(Spelling: Word; VAR Entry: IdentifierEntry;
                   AllowableClasses: IdClassSet);
  VAR ThisEntry, LastEntry: IdentifierEntry;
      MisUsed: BOOLEAN; ThisScope: Scope;
  PROCEDURE MostLikelyOf(Classes: IdClassSet): IdentifierClass;
    BEGIN
      IF Variables IN Classes THEN RETURN Variables
      ELSIF Procedures IN Classes THEN RETURN Procedures
```

```
        ELSIF Types IN Classes THEN RETURN Types
        ELSE RETURN Constants
        END
      END MostLikelyOf;

  BEGIN (* SearchId *)
    MisUsed := FALSE;
    ThisScope := LocalScope;
    REPEAT
      ThisEntry := ThisScope^.FirstLocal;
      WHILE ThisEntry <> NIL DO
        IF ComparisonOf(Spelling, ThisEntry^.Name) = FirstIsLess THEN
          ThisEntry := ThisEntry^.LeftLink
        ELSIF ComparisonOf(Spelling, ThisEntry^.Name) = SecondIsLess THEN
          ThisEntry := ThisEntry^.RightLink
        ELSIF ThisEntry^.Class IN AllowableClasses THEN
          Entry := ThisEntry; RETURN
        ELSE
          MisUsed := TRUE; ThisEntry := ThisEntry^.RightLink
        END
      END;
      IF MisUsed THEN
        IdError(53); Entry := DefaultEntry[MostLikelyOf(AllowableClasses)];
        RETURN
      END;
      ThisScope := ThisScope^.EnclosingScope
    UNTIL ThisScope = NIL;
    IdError(52);
    NewId(Spelling, Entry, MostLikelyOf(AllowableClasses))
  END SearchId;

PROCEDURE NewType(VAR Entry: TypeEntry; FormNeeded: TypeClass);
  VAR ThisScope: Scope; NewEntry: TypeEntry;
  BEGIN
    New(NewEntry, SIZE(TypeRecord));
    CASE FormNeeded OF
    | Scalars:
        NewEntry^.Form := Scalars
    | Arrays:
        WITH NewEntry^ DO
          Form := Arrays; IndexMin := 0; IndexMax := 1; ElementType := NIL
        END
    END;
    ThisScope := LocalScope;
    WITH ThisScope^ DO
      NewEntry^.Next := TypeChain; TypeChain := NewEntry
    END;
    Entry := NewEntry
  END NewType;

PROCEDURE Compatible(Type1, Type2: TypeEntry): BOOLEAN;
  (* Are types pointed to by Type1 and Type2 compatible? *)
  BEGIN
    IF Type1 = Type2 THEN RETURN TRUE
    ELSIF (Type1 = NIL) OR (Type2 = NIL) THEN
      RETURN TRUE
    ELSIF (Type1^.Form = Arrays) AND (Type2^.Form = Arrays) THEN
      RETURN (Type1^.IndexMin = Type2^.IndexMin) AND
             (Type1^.IndexMax = Type2^.IndexMax) AND
              Compatible(Type1^.ElementType, Type2^.ElementType)
    ELSE
      RETURN FALSE
```

```
      END
    END Compatible;

  PROCEDURE Undefined(Type: TypeEntry): BOOLEAN;
    BEGIN
      RETURN Type = NIL
    END Undefined;

  PROCEDURE SetUndefined(VAR Type: TypeEntry);
    BEGIN
      Type := NIL
    END SetUndefined;

  PROCEDURE IsOrdinalType(Type: TypeEntry): BOOLEAN;
    BEGIN
      IF Type = NIL THEN RETURN TRUE
      ELSE RETURN (Type^.Form = Scalars)
      END
    END IsOrdinalType;

VAR C: IdentifierClass;

BEGIN
  LocalScope := NIL;
  FOR C := MIN(IdentifierClass) TO MAX(IdentifierClass) DO
    New(DefaultEntry[C], SIZE(IdRecord));
    WITH DefaultEntry[C]^ DO
      Name := BlankWord; IdType := NIL; Class := C
    END
  END
END Table.
```

Appendix 12

Complete analyzer

Definition module

```
DEFINITION MODULE Analyzer;

  (* The Analyzer generates syntax error codes with the following meanings:    *)
  (*                                                                            *)
  (*   10 ... Symbol expected was Identifier                                    *)
  (*   11 ... Symbol expected was Integer Number                               *)
  (*   12 ... Symbol expected was Character Constant                           *)
  (*   13 ... .......                                                          *)
  (*                                                                            *)
  (* i.e. one value for each of the values of SymbolType.                      *)
  (*                                                                            *)
  (* The final value, ORD(OtherSymbol)+10, is used to mean                     *)
  (*                                                                            *)
  (*   NN ... Unexpected symbol                                                 *)
  (*                                                                            *)
  (*                                                                            *)
  (* Semantic errors are reported with the following error codes:              *)
  (*                                                                            *)
  (*   61 ... Indexed-variable must be an array-variable                       *)
  (*   62 ... Index-expression must be of type INTEGER                         *)
  (*   63 ... Operand must be of type BOOLEAN                                   *)
  (*   64 ... Operand must be of type INTEGER                                   *)
  (*   65 ... Operands must both be INTEGER, CHAR or Boolean                   *)
  (*   66 ... Expression must be of same type as Variable                      *)
  (*   67 ... Input variable must be of type INTEGER or CHAR                   *)
  (*   68 ... Expression must be of type INTEGER, CHAR or BOOLEAN              *)
  (*   69 ... Expression must be of type Boolean                               *)
  (*   70 ... Identifiers at beginning and end of block must match             *)
  (*   71 ... For loop control-variable must be of type INTEGER, CHAR or BOOLEAN *)
  (*   72 ... An exit-statement must occur within a loop-statement             *)
  (*   73 ... Type of case label must be same as the selector type             *)
  (*   74 ... Case label must appear at most once in case-statement            *)
  (*   75 ... Case label must be of type INTEGER, CHAR or Boolean             *)

  PROCEDURE Programme;

END Analyzer.
```

384

Implementation module

```
IMPLEMENTATION MODULE Analyzer;

  IMPORT Target, Generator;
  FROM SourceHandler IMPORT Error;
  FROM LexicalAnalyzer IMPORT SymbolType, GetNextSymbol, SymbolDescription;
  FROM Host IMPORT StandardIdentifiers, GetSpelling, Word, WordRelation,
                   ComparisonOf, BlankWord, New, Dispose;
  FROM Table IMPORT OpenScope, CloseScope, NewId, SearchId, NewType,
                    IdentifierEntry, TypeEntry, IdentifierClass, IdClassSet,
                    TypeClass, Compatible, IsOrdinalType, Undefined, SetUndefined;

  (* For reasons of space and to avoid repetition commentary for the following  *)
  (* areas of the Analyzer has been omitted since it has already appeared in the *)
  (* Appendix specified:                                                         *)
  (*       Syntax analysis                        see Appendix 6                 *)
  (*       Syntax error recovery                  see Appendix 7                 *)
  (*       Semantic analysis                      see Appendix 9                 *)
  PROCEDURE SyntaxError(ExpectedSymbol: SymbolType);
    BEGIN
      Error(ORD(ExpectedSymbol)+10, SymbolDescription.Position);
      Generator.NoFurtherCode
    END SyntaxError;

  PROCEDURE Accept(SymbolExpected: SymbolType);
    BEGIN
      IF SymbolDescription.Symbol = SymbolExpected THEN GetNextSymbol
      ELSE SyntaxError(SymbolExpected)
      END
    END Accept;

MODULE SymbolSets;
  IMPORT SymbolType;
  EXPORT SymbolSet, Clear, Include, Remove, Contains, Union;

  TYPE SymbolSet = ARRAY SymbolType OF BOOLEAN;

  PROCEDURE Clear(VAR S: SymbolSet);
    VAR B: SymbolType;
    BEGIN
      FOR B := MIN(SymbolType) TO MAX(SymbolType) DO S[B] := FALSE END
    END Clear;

  PROCEDURE Include(I: SymbolType; VAR S: SymbolSet);
    BEGIN
      S[I] := TRUE
    END Include;

  PROCEDURE Remove(I: SymbolType; VAR S: SymbolSet);
    BEGIN
      S[I] := FALSE
    END Remove;

  PROCEDURE Contains(VAR S: SymbolSet; I: SymbolType): BOOLEAN;
    BEGIN
      RETURN S[I]
    END Contains;

  PROCEDURE Union(VAR S1, S2, Result: SymbolSet);
    VAR B: SymbolType;
```

```
        BEGIN
          FOR B := MIN(SymbolType) TO MAX(SymbolType) DO
            Result[B] := S1[B] OR S2[B]
          END
        END Union;

    END SymbolSets;

  PROCEDURE SkipTo(RelevantSymbols: SymbolSet);
    BEGIN
      WHILE NOT Contains(RelevantSymbols, SymbolDescription.Symbol) DO
        GetNextSymbol
      END
    END SkipTo;

  PROCEDURE CheckForStarter(Starters, Followers: SymbolSet; VAR Found: BOOLEAN);
    VAR LocalSet: SymbolSet;
    BEGIN
      IF NOT Contains(Starters, SymbolDescription.Symbol) THEN
        SyntaxError(OtherSymbol);
        Union(Starters, Followers, LocalSet);
        SkipTo(LocalSet)
      END;
      Found := Contains(Starters, SymbolDescription.Symbol)
    END CheckForStarter;

  PROCEDURE FindFollower(Followers: SymbolSet);
    BEGIN
      IF NOT Contains(Followers, SymbolDescription.Symbol) THEN
        SyntaxError(OtherSymbol); SkipTo(Followers)
      END
    END FindFollower;

  VAR IntegerType, BooleanType, CharType: TypeEntry;

  PROCEDURE SemanticError(Code: CARDINAL);
    BEGIN
      Error(Code, SymbolDescription.Position);
      Generator.NoFurtherCode
    END SemanticError;

  PROCEDURE CheckIsSameAs(BlockIdentifier: Word);
    BEGIN
      IF ComparisonOf(BlockIdentifier, BlankWord) <> WordsEqual THEN
        IF ComparisonOf(SymbolDescription.Spelling, BlockIdentifier)
              <> WordsEqual THEN SemanticError(70)
        END
      END
    END CheckIsSameAs;

  (* OBJECT CODE GENERATION                                                  *)
  (*                                                                         *)
  (* Object code generation is implemented by interfacing the Analyzer module to *)
  (* an object-code-dependent Generator module.  The interface itself, however, *)
  (* is independent of the object code to be produced.  The interface        *)
  (* specification is given in the Generator definition module.              *)


  PROCEDURE Programme;
    VAR DeclarationStarters, StatementStarters, FactorStarters,
        RelationalOps, AdditionOps, MultiplicationOps, Signs: SymbolSet;
        NullIdentifier: IdentifierEntry;
```

```
PROCEDURE InitializeSymbolSets;
  BEGIN
    Clear(DeclarationStarters);
    Include(Var, DeclarationStarters);
    Include(Procedure, DeclarationStarters);
    Clear(RelationalOps); Include(Equals, RelationalOps);
    Include(NotEquals, RelationalOps); Include(LessThan, RelationalOps);
    Include(LessThanOrEqual, RelationalOps);
    Include(GreaterThan, RelationalOps);
    Include(GreaterThanOrEqual, RelationalOps);
    Clear(AdditionOps); Include(Plus, AdditionOps);
    Include(Minus, AdditionOps); Include(Or, AdditionOps);
    Clear(MultiplicationOps); Include(Times, MultiplicationOps);
    Include(Div, MultiplicationOps); Include(And, MultiplicationOps);
    Clear(Signs); Include(Plus, Signs); Include(Minus, Signs);
    Clear(StatementStarters); Include(Identifier, StatementStarters);
    Include(Read, StatementStarters); Include(Write, StatementStarters);
    Include(If, StatementStarters); Include(Case, StatementStarters);
    Include(Loop, StatementStarters); Include(Exit, StatementStarters);
    Include(For, StatementStarters);
    Clear(FactorStarters); Include(Identifier, FactorStarters);
    Include(IntegerNumber, FactorStarters);
    Include(CharConstant, FactorStarters); Include(Not, FactorStarters);
    Include(LeftParenthesis, FactorStarters)
  END InitializeSymbolSets;

PROCEDURE Block(Followers: SymbolSet; BlockId: IdentifierEntry);

  PROCEDURE DeclarationPart(Followers: SymbolSet);

    PROCEDURE VariableDeclarationPart(Followers: SymbolSet);

      PROCEDURE VariableDeclaration(Followers: SymbolSet);
        TYPE IdList = POINTER TO ListRecord;
             ListRecord = RECORD
                            Id: IdentifierEntry; NextOnList: IdList
                          END;
        VAR VariableList: RECORD Head, Tail: IdList END;
            VariableType: TypeEntry;

        PROCEDURE NewVariable;
          VAR VariableEntry: IdentifierEntry; ListEntry: IdList;
          BEGIN
            IF SymbolDescription.Symbol = Identifier THEN
              NewId(SymbolDescription.Spelling, VariableEntry, Variables);
              New(ListEntry, SIZE(ListRecord));
              WITH ListEntry^ DO
                Id := VariableEntry; NextOnList := NIL
              END;
              WITH VariableList DO
                IF Head = NIL THEN Head := ListEntry
                ELSE Tail^.NextOnList := ListEntry
                END;
                Tail := ListEntry
              END
            END
          END NewVariable;

        PROCEDURE AddAttributes;
          VAR ListEntry, OldEntry: IdList;
          BEGIN
            ListEntry := VariableList.Head;
```

```
      WHILE ListEntry <> NIL DO
        WITH ListEntry^ DO
          Id^.IdType := VariableType;
          IF NOT Undefined(VariableType) THEN
            Generator.AddressFor
              (VariableType^.Representation, Id^.VariableAddress)
          END;
          OldEntry := ListEntry; ListEntry := NextOnList;
          Dispose(OldEntry, SIZE(ListRecord))
        END
      END
    END AddAttributes;

  PROCEDURE Type(Followers: SymbolSet; VAR TypeFound: TypeEntry);

    PROCEDURE SimpleType(Followers: SymbolSet;
                           VAR TypeNamed: TypeEntry);
      VAR Starters: SymbolSet; OK: BOOLEAN;
          TypeIdentifier: IdentifierEntry;
      BEGIN
        Clear(Starters); Include(Identifier, Starters);
        CheckForStarter(Starters, Followers, OK);
        IF OK THEN
          SearchId(SymbolDescription.Spelling,
                    TypeIdentifier, IdClassSet{Types});
          TypeNamed := TypeIdentifier^.IdType;
          Accept(Identifier);
          FindFollower(Followers)
        END
      END SimpleType;

    PROCEDURE IndexType(Followers: SymbolSet);
      VAR Starters: SymbolSet; OK: BOOLEAN;
      BEGIN
        Clear(Starters); Include(LeftBracket, Starters);
        Include(IntegerNumber, Starters); Include(Thru, Starters);
        CheckForStarter(Starters, Followers, OK);
        IF OK THEN
          WITH SymbolDescription DO
            Accept(LeftBracket);
            IF Symbol = IntegerNumber THEN
              TypeFound^.IndexMin := IntValue
            END;
            Accept(IntegerNumber);
            Accept(Thru);
            IF Symbol = IntegerNumber THEN
              TypeFound^.IndexMax := IntValue
            END;
            Accept(IntegerNumber); Accept(RightBracket);
          END;
          FindFollower(Followers)
        END
      END IndexType;

    VAR ElementType: TypeEntry;
        Starters, LocalSet: SymbolSet; OK: BOOLEAN;

    BEGIN (* Type *)
      Clear(Starters); Include(Identifier, Starters);
      Include(Array, Starters);
      CheckForStarter(Starters, Followers, OK);
      IF OK THEN
```

```
              IF SymbolDescription.Symbol = Identifier THEN
                 SimpleType(Followers, TypeFound)
              ELSE
                 NewType(TypeFound, Arrays);
                 Accept(Array); LocalSet := Followers; Include(Of, LocalSet);
                 IndexType(LocalSet); Accept(Of);
                 SimpleType(Followers, ElementType);
                 TypeFound^.ElementType := ElementType;
                 IF NOT Undefined(ElementType) THEN
                    Generator.ArrayRepresentation
                       (TypeFound^.IndexMin, TypeFound^.IndexMax,
                        ElementType^.Representation, TypeFound^.Representation)
                 END;
              END;
              FindFollower(Followers)
           END
        END Type;

     VAR Starters: SymbolSet; OK: BOOLEAN;

     BEGIN (* VariableDeclaration *)
       Clear(Starters); Include(Identifier, Starters);
       Include(Comma, Starters); Include(Colon, Starters);
       CheckForStarter(Starters, Followers, OK);
       IF OK THEN
          VariableList.Head := NIL;
          NewVariable; Accept(Identifier);
          WHILE SymbolDescription.Symbol = Comma DO
             Accept(Comma); NewVariable; Accept(Identifier)
          END;
          Accept(Colon); Type(Followers, VariableType);
          AddAttributes;
          FindFollower(Followers)
       END
     END VariableDeclaration;

  VAR LocalSet: SymbolSet;

  BEGIN (* VariableDeclarationPart *)
     Accept(Var);
     LocalSet := Followers; Include(Semicolon, LocalSet);
     WHILE SymbolDescription.Symbol = Identifier DO
        VariableDeclaration(LocalSet); Accept(Semicolon)
     END;
     FindFollower(Followers)
  END VariableDeclarationPart;

PROCEDURE ProcedureDeclaration(Followers: SymbolSet);
  VAR ProcedureIdentifier: IdentifierEntry;
      ProcedureName: Word; LocalSet: SymbolSet;
  BEGIN
     Accept(Procedure);
     IF SymbolDescription.Symbol = Identifier THEN
        ProcedureName := SymbolDescription.Spelling
     ELSE ProcedureName := BlankWord
     END;
     NewId(ProcedureName, ProcedureIdentifier, Procedures);
     Generator.NewLinkage(ProcedureIdentifier^.Linkage);
     Accept(Identifier); Accept(Semicolon);
     LocalSet := Followers; Include(Identifier, LocalSet);
     Block(LocalSet, ProcedureIdentifier);
     IF SymbolDescription.Symbol = Identifier THEN
```

```
            CheckIsSameAs (ProcedureName)
      END;
      Accept (Identifier);
      FindFollower (Followers)
   END ProcedureDeclaration;

VAR Starters, VarDeclarationFollowers, ProcDeclarationFollowers: SymbolSet;
    OK: BOOLEAN;

BEGIN (* DeclarationPart *)
   Union (DeclarationStarters, Followers, Starters);
   CheckForStarter (Starters, Followers, OK);
   IF OK THEN
      VarDeclarationFollowers := Starters;
      Include (Begin, VarDeclarationFollowers);
      ProcDeclarationFollowers := VarDeclarationFollowers;
      Include (Semicolon, ProcDeclarationFollowers);
      WHILE Contains (DeclarationStarters, SymbolDescription.Symbol) DO
         CASE SymbolDescription.Symbol OF
         | Var:
               VariableDeclarationPart (VarDeclarationFollowers)
         | Procedure:
               ProcedureDeclaration (ProcDeclarationFollowers);
               Accept (Semicolon)
         END
      END;
      FindFollower (Followers)
   END
END DeclarationPart;

PROCEDURE StatementPart (Followers: SymbolSet);

   TYPE LoopEntry = POINTER TO LoopRecord;
        LoopRecord = RECORD
                       EndOfLoop: Generator.CodeLabel;
                       EnclosingLoop: LoopEntry
                     END;

   VAR  CurrentLoop: LoopEntry;

   PROCEDURE StatementSequence (Followers: SymbolSet);

      PROCEDURE Statement (Followers: SymbolSet);

         PROCEDURE Expression (Followers: SymbolSet;
                               VAR ExpressionType: TypeEntry); FORWARD;

         PROCEDURE Variable (Followers: SymbolSet; VAR VariableType: TypeEntry);
            VAR Starters, LocalSet: SymbolSet; OK: BOOLEAN;
                VariableIdentifier: IdentifierEntry;
                IndexType, ElementType: TypeEntry;
            BEGIN
               Clear (Starters); Include (Identifier, Starters);
               CheckForStarter (Starters, Followers, OK);
               IF OK THEN
                  SearchId (SymbolDescription.Spelling,
                            VariableIdentifier, IdClassSet{Variables});
                  VariableType := VariableIdentifier^.IdType;
                  Generator.StackReference (VariableIdentifier^.VariableAddress);
                  Accept (Identifier);
                  IF SymbolDescription.Symbol = LeftBracket THEN
                     IF NOT Undefined (VariableType) THEN
```

```
            IF VariableType^.Form <> Arrays THEN
                SemanticError(61); SetUndefined(VariableType)
            END
        END;
        Accept(LeftBracket);
        LocalSet := Followers; Include(RightBracket, LocalSet);
        Expression(LocalSet, IndexType);
        IF NOT Compatible(IndexType, IntegerType) THEN
            SemanticError(62)
        END;
        IF NOT Undefined(VariableType) THEN
            ElementType := VariableType^.ElementType;
            Generator.IndexedReference
                (VariableType^.IndexMin, VariableType^.IndexMax,
                ElementType^.Representation);
            VariableType := ElementType
        END;
        Accept(RightBracket)
    END;
        FindFollower(Followers)
    END
  END Variable;

PROCEDURE Expression (Followers: SymbolSet;
                    VAR ExpressionType: TypeEntry);

  PROCEDURE SimpleExpression(Followers: SymbolSet;
                        VAR SimpleExpressionType: TypeEntry);

    PROCEDURE Term(Followers: SymbolSet; VAR TermType: TypeEntry);

      PROCEDURE Factor(Followers: SymbolSet;
                    VAR FactorType: TypeEntry);
        VAR LocalSet: SymbolSet; OK: BOOLEAN;
            FirstIdentifier: IdentifierEntry;
      BEGIN
        CheckForStarter(FactorStarters, Followers, OK);
        IF OK THEN
          WITH SymbolDescription DO
            CASE Symbol OF
            | Identifier:
                SearchId(Spelling, FirstIdentifier,
                        IdClassSet{Variables, Constants});
                CASE FirstIdentifier^.Class OF
                | Constants:
                    FactorType := FirstIdentifier^.IdType;
                    Generator.StackConstant
                        (FirstIdentifier^.ConstantValue,
                        ExpressionType^.Representation);
                    Accept(Identifier)
                | Variables:
                    Variable(Followers, FactorType);
                    IF NOT Undefined(FactorType) THEN
                        Generator.Dereference
                            (FactorType^.Representation)
                    END;
                END
            | IntegerNumber:
                FactorType := IntegerType;
                Generator.StackConstant
                    (IntValue, IntegerType^.Representation);
                Accept(IntegerNumber)
```

```
                | CharConstant:
                    FactorType := CharType;
                    Generator.StackConstant
                       (CharValue, CharType^.Representation);
                    Accept(CharConstant)
                | LeftParenthesis:
                    Accept(LeftParenthesis);
                    LocalSet := Followers;
                    Include(RightParenthesis, LocalSet);
                    Expression(LocalSet, FactorType);
                    Accept(RightParenthesis)
                | Not:
                    Accept(Not); Factor(Followers, FactorType);
                    IF NOT Compatible(FactorType, BooleanType) THEN
                       SemanticError(63)
                    END;
                    Generator.NegateBoolean;
                    FactorType := BooleanType
              END
            END;
            FindFollower(Followers)
        ELSE SetUndefined(FactorType)
        END
    END Factor;

VAR LocalSet, TempSet: SymbolSet;
    FactorType: TypeEntry;
    Operator: SymbolType;

BEGIN (* Term *)
  Union(MultiplicationOps, FactorStarters, TempSet);
  Union(Followers, TempSet, LocalSet);
  Factor(LocalSet, FactorType); TermType := FactorType;
  WITH SymbolDescription DO
    WHILE Contains(TempSet, Symbol) DO
      Operator := Symbol;
      IF Contains(MultiplicationOps, Symbol) THEN GetNextSymbol
      ELSE SyntaxError(Times)
      END;
      Factor(LocalSet, FactorType);
      IF Contains(MultiplicationOps, Operator) THEN
        CASE Operator OF
        | Times, Div:
            IF NOT (Compatible(TermType, IntegerType) AND
                    Compatible(FactorType, IntegerType)) THEN
              SemanticError(64)
            END;
            Generator.BinaryIntegerOperation(Operator);
            TermType := IntegerType
        | And:
            IF NOT (Compatible(TermType, BooleanType) AND
                    Compatible(FactorType, BooleanType)) THEN
              SemanticError(63)
            END;
            Generator.BinaryBooleanOperation(And);
            TermType := BooleanType
        END
      ELSE SetUndefined(TermType)
      END
    END
  END
END Term;
```

```
      VAR Starters, LocalSet: SymbolSet; OK: BOOLEAN;
          Signed, Negated: BOOLEAN; TermType: TypeEntry;
          Operator: SymbolType;

      BEGIN (* SimpleExpression *)
        Union(FactorStarters, Signs, Starters);
        CheckForStarter(Starters, Followers, OK);
        IF OK THEN
          WITH SymbolDescription DO
            IF Contains(Signs, Symbol) THEN
              Signed := TRUE; Negated := (Symbol = Minus);
              GetNextSymbol
            ELSE Signed := FALSE
            END;
            Union(AdditionOps, Followers, LocalSet);
            Term(LocalSet, TermType); SimpleExpressionType := TermType;
            IF Signed THEN
              IF NOT Compatible(ExpressionType, IntegerType) THEN
                SemanticError(64)
              ELSIF Negated THEN Generator.NegateInteger
              END
            END;
            WHILE Contains(AdditionOps, Symbol) DO
              Operator := Symbol;
              GetNextSymbol; Term(LocalSet, TermType);
              CASE Operator OF
              | Plus, Minus:
                  IF NOT (Compatible(SimpleExpressionType,
                                        IntegerType) AND
                          Compatible(TermType, IntegerType)) THEN
                    SemanticError(64)
                  END;
                  Generator.BinaryIntegerOperation(Operator);
                  SimpleExpressionType := IntegerType
              | Or:
                  IF NOT (Compatible(SimpleExpressionType,
                                        BooleanType) AND
                          Compatible(TermType, BooleanType)) THEN
                    SemanticError(63)
                  END;
                  Generator.BinaryBooleanOperation(Or);
                  SimpleExpressionType := BooleanType
              END
            END;
            FindFollower(Followers)
          END
        ELSE SetUndefined(SimpleExpressionType)
        END
      END SimpleExpression;

    VAR LocalSet: SymbolSet; Operator: SymbolType;
        SimpleExpressionType: TypeEntry;

    BEGIN (* Expression *)
      Union(RelationalOps, Followers, LocalSet);
      SimpleExpression(LocalSet, SimpleExpressionType);
      ExpressionType := SimpleExpressionType;
      IF Contains(RelationalOps, SymbolDescription.Symbol) THEN
        Operator := SymbolDescription.Symbol; GetNextSymbol;
        SimpleExpression(Followers, SimpleExpressionType);
        IF NOT (Compatible(SimpleExpressionType, IntegerType) OR
                Compatible(SimpleExpressionType, CharType) OR
```

```
                    Compatible(SimpleExpressionType, BooleanType)) AND
                    Compatible(SimpleExpressionType, ExpressionType) THEN
          SemanticError(65)
      END;
      Generator.Comparison(Operator);
      ExpressionType := BooleanType
    END
  END Expression;

PROCEDURE Assignment;
  VAR LocalSet: SymbolSet; VariableType, ExpressionType: TypeEntry;
  BEGIN
    LocalSet := Followers; Include(Becomes, LocalSet);
    Variable(LocalSet, VariableType);
    Accept(Becomes);
    Expression(Followers, ExpressionType);
    IF NOT Compatible(VariableType, ExpressionType) THEN
       SemanticError(66)
    END;
    Generator.Assign
  END Assignment;

PROCEDURE ReadStatement;

  PROCEDURE InputVariable;
    VAR LocalSet: SymbolSet; VariableType: TypeEntry;
    BEGIN
      LocalSet := Followers; Include(RightParenthesis, LocalSet);
      Variable(LocalSet, VariableType);
      IF Compatible(VariableType, CharType) THEN
        Generator.ReadOperation(Generator.CharMode)
      ELSIF Compatible(VariableType, IntegerType) THEN
        Generator.ReadOperation(Generator.IntegerMode)
      ELSE SemanticError(67)
      END;
    END InputVariable;

  BEGIN (* ReadStatement *)
    Accept(Read); Accept(LeftParenthesis);
    InputVariable; Accept(RightParenthesis);
    Generator.Assign
  END ReadStatement;

PROCEDURE WriteStatement;

  PROCEDURE OutputValue;
    VAR LocalSet: SymbolSet; ExpressionType: TypeEntry;
    BEGIN
      LocalSet := Followers; Include(RightParenthesis, LocalSet);
      Expression(LocalSet, ExpressionType);
      IF Compatible(ExpressionType, CharType) THEN
        Generator.WriteOperation(Generator.CharMode)
      ELSIF Compatible(ExpressionType, IntegerType) THEN
        Generator.WriteOperation(Generator.IntegerMode)
      ELSE SemanticError(68)
      END
    END OutputValue;

  BEGIN (* WriteStatement *)
    Accept(Write); Accept(LeftParenthesis);
    OutputValue; Accept(RightParenthesis)
  END WriteStatement;
```

```
PROCEDURE IfStatement;
  VAR LocalSet: SymbolSet; ExpressionType: TypeEntry;
      AfterTrueAction, AfterFalseAction: Generator.CodeLabel;
  BEGIN
    Accept(If);
    LocalSet := Followers; Include(Then, LocalSet);
    Include(Else, LocalSet); Include(End, LocalSet);
    Expression(LocalSet, ExpressionType);
    IF NOT Compatible(ExpressionType, BooleanType) THEN
      SemanticError(69)
    END;
    Generator.FutureCodeLabel(AfterTrueAction);
    Generator.JumpOnFalse(AfterTrueAction);
    Accept(Then); Remove(Then, LocalSet);
    StatementSequence(LocalSet);
    IF SymbolDescription.Symbol = Else THEN
      Generator.FutureCodeLabel(AfterFalseAction);
      Generator.Jump(AfterFalseAction);
      Generator.ExpectedCodeLabel(AfterTrueAction);
      Accept(Else); Remove(Else, LocalSet);
      StatementSequence(LocalSet);
      Generator.ExpectedCodeLabel(AfterFalseAction)
    ELSE
      Generator.ExpectedCodeLabel(AfterTrueAction)
    END;
    Accept(End)
  END IfStatement;

PROCEDURE ExitStatement;
  BEGIN
    Accept(Exit);
    IF CurrentLoop <> NIL THEN Generator.Jump(CurrentLoop^.EndOfLoop)
    ELSE SemanticError(72)
    END
  END ExitStatement;

PROCEDURE LoopStatement;

  PROCEDURE CreateThisLoopRecord;
    VAR NewEntry: LoopEntry;
    BEGIN
      New(NewEntry, SIZE(LoopRecord));
      NewEntry^.EnclosingLoop := CurrentLoop; CurrentLoop := NewEntry
    END CreateThisLoopRecord;

  PROCEDURE DestroyThisLoopRecord;
    VAR OldEntry: LoopEntry;
    BEGIN
      OldEntry := CurrentLoop;
      CurrentLoop := CurrentLoop^.EnclosingLoop;
      Dispose(OldEntry, SIZE(LoopRecord))
    END DestroyThisLoopRecord;

  VAR StartOfThisLoop: Generator.CodeLabel; LocalSet: SymbolSet;

  BEGIN
    CreateThisLoopRecord;
    Generator.NewCodeLabel(StartOfThisLoop);
    Generator.FutureCodeLabel(CurrentLoop^.EndOfLoop);
    Accept(Loop); LocalSet := Followers; Include(End, LocalSet);
    StatementSequence(LocalSet); Accept(End);
    Generator.Jump(StartOfThisLoop);
```

```
      Generator.ExpectedCodeLabel(CurrentLoop^.EndOfLoop);
      DestroyThisLoopRecord
    END LoopStatement;

PROCEDURE CaseStatement;
  TYPE CaseEntry = POINTER TO CaseRecord;
       CaseRecord = RECORD
                        CaseValue: Target.Integer; NextCase: CaseEntry
                    END;

  VAR CaseType: TypeEntry; FirstCase: CaseEntry;

  PROCEDURE CaseLabel(VAR CaseLabelType: TypeEntry;
                      VAR CaseLabelValue: Target.Integer);
    VAR ConstantIdentifier: IdentifierEntry;
    BEGIN
      WITH SymbolDescription DO
        IF Symbol = IntegerNumber THEN
          CaseLabelType := IntegerType; CaseLabelValue := IntValue
        ELSIF Symbol = CharConstant THEN
          CaseLabelType := CharType; CaseLabelValue := CharValue
        ELSIF Symbol = Identifier THEN
          SearchId(Spelling, ConstantIdentifier,
                   IdClassSet{Constants});
          WITH ConstantIdentifier^ DO
            CaseLabelType := IdType; CaseLabelValue := ConstantValue
          END
        ELSE SetUndefined(CaseLabelType)
        END
      END
    END CaseLabel;

  PROCEDURE NewCaseLabel;
    VAR LabelType: TypeEntry; LabelValue: Target.Integer;
        ThisCase, LastCase: CaseEntry;
    BEGIN
      CaseLabel(LabelType, LabelValue);
      IF NOT Undefined(LabelType) THEN
        IF Compatible(LabelType, CaseType) THEN
          ThisCase := FirstCase; LastCase := NIL;
          LOOP
            IF ThisCase = NIL THEN
              New(ThisCase, SIZE(CaseRecord));
              WITH ThisCase^ DO
                CaseValue := LabelValue;
                Generator.NextIsCase(LabelValue);
                NextCase := NIL
              END;
              IF LastCase = NIL THEN FirstCase := ThisCase
              ELSE LastCase^.NextCase := ThisCase
              END;
              EXIT
            ELSIF ThisCase^.CaseValue = LabelValue THEN
              SemanticError(74); EXIT
            ELSE
              LastCase := ThisCase; ThisCase := ThisCase^.NextCase
            END;
          END
        ELSE SemanticError(73)
        END
      ELSE SyntaxError(OtherSymbol)
      END;
```

```
        GetNextSymbol
      END NewCaseLabel;

  PROCEDURE DisposeOfCaseList;
    VAR ThisCase, NextCase: CaseEntry;
    BEGIN
      NextCase := FirstCase;
      WHILE NextCase <> NIL DO
        ThisCase := NextCase; NextCase := ThisCase^.NextCase;
        Dispose(ThisCase, SIZE(CaseRecord))
      END
    END DisposeOfCaseList;

  VAR LocalSet, TempSet: SymbolSet;
      FollowingStatement: Generator.CodeLabel;

  BEGIN (* CaseStatement *)
    Generator.FutureCodeLabel(FollowingStatement);
    Accept(Case); LocalSet := Followers; Include(Of, LocalSet);
    Include(Separator, LocalSet); Include(End, LocalSet);
    Expression(LocalSet, CaseType);
    IF NOT IsOrdinalType(CaseType) THEN
      SemanticError(68); SetUndefined(CaseType)
    END;
    Accept(Of); Remove(Of, LocalSet);
    FirstCase := NIL;
    Generator.OpenCase;
    Clear(TempSet); Include(Comma, TempSet);
    Include(Identifier, TempSet); Include(IntegerNumber, TempSet);
    Include(CharConstant, TempSet);
    REPEAT
      Accept(Separator);
      LOOP
        NewCaseLabel;
        IF NOT Contains(TempSet, SymbolDescription.Symbol) THEN EXIT
        END;
        Accept(Comma)
      END;
      Accept(Colon); StatementSequence(LocalSet);
      Generator.Jump(FollowingStatement)
    UNTIL (SymbolDescription.Symbol = End) OR
          Contains(Followers, SymbolDescription.Symbol);
    Generator.CloseCase;
    DisposeOfCaseList;
    Accept(End);
    Generator.ExpectedCodeLabel(FollowingStatement)
  END CaseStatement;

PROCEDURE ForStatement;
  VAR LocalSet: SymbolSet; ControlVariableId: IdentifierEntry;
      ControlVariableType, ExpressionType: TypeEntry;
  BEGIN
    Accept(For);
    IF SymbolDescription.Symbol = Identifier THEN
      SearchId(SymbolDescription.Spelling, ControlVariableId,
               IdClassSet{Variables});
      ControlVariableType := ControlVariableId^.IdType;
      IF NOT IsOrdinalType(ControlVariableType) THEN
        SemanticError(71); SetUndefined(ControlVariableType)
      END;
      Generator.StackReference(ControlVariableId^.VariableAddress)
    ELSE SetUndefined(ControlVariableType)
```

```
        END;
        Accept(Identifier); Accept(Becomes);
        LocalSet := Followers; Include(To, LocalSet);
        Include(Do, LocalSet); Include(End, LocalSet);
        Expression(LocalSet, ExpressionType);
        IF NOT Compatible(ControlVariableType, ExpressionType) THEN
          SemanticError(66)
        END;
        Accept(To); Remove(To, LocalSet);
        Expression(LocalSet, ExpressionType);
        IF NOT Compatible(ControlVariableType, ExpressionType) THEN
          SemanticError(66)
        END;
        Accept(Do); Remove(Do, LocalSet);
        Generator.OpenFor;
        StatementSequence(LocalSet);
        Generator.CloseFor;
        Accept(End)
      END ForStatement;


    VAR OK: BOOLEAN; FirstIdentifier: IdentifierEntry;

    BEGIN (* Statement *)
      CheckForStarter(StatementStarters, Followers, OK);
      IF OK THEN
        CASE SymbolDescription.Symbol OF
        | Identifier:
            SearchId(SymbolDescription.Spelling, FirstIdentifier,
                  IdClassSet{Procedures, Variables});
            IF FirstIdentifier^.Class = Variables THEN Assignment
            ELSE
              Generator.CallProcedure(FirstIdentifier^.Linkage);
              Accept(Identifier)
            END
        | If:    IfStatement
        | Exit:  ExitStatement
        | Loop:  LoopStatement
        | Case:  CaseStatement
        | For:   ForStatement
        | Read:  ReadStatement
        | Write: WriteStatement
        END;
        FindFollower(Followers)
      END
    END Statement;

  VAR LocalSet, TempSet: SymbolSet; OK: BOOLEAN;

  BEGIN (* StatementSequence *)
    CheckForStarter(StatementStarters, Followers, OK);
    IF OK THEN
      Union(StatementStarters, Followers, LocalSet);
      Include(Semicolon, LocalSet); Remove(Identifier, LocalSet);
      Statement(LocalSet); TempSet := StatementStarters;
      Include(Semicolon, TempSet); Remove(Identifier, TempSet);
      WHILE Contains(TempSet, SymbolDescription.Symbol) DO
        Accept(Semicolon); Statement(LocalSet)
      END;
      FindFollower(Followers)
    END
  END StatementSequence;
```

```
        VAR Starters, LocalSet: SymbolSet; OK: BOOLEAN;

        BEGIN (* StatementPart *)
          Clear(Starters); Include(Begin, Starters);
          CheckForStarter(Starters, Followers, OK);
          IF OK THEN
            IF BlockId = NullIdentifier THEN Generator.EnterProgram
            ELSE Generator.EnterBody(BlockId^.Linkage)
            END;
            CurrentLoop := NIL;
            Accept(Begin); LocalSet := Followers; Include(End, LocalSet);
            StatementSequence(LocalSet); Accept(End);
            IF BlockId = NullIdentifier THEN Generator.LeaveProgram
            ELSE Generator.LeaveBody(BlockId^.Linkage)
            END;
            FindFollower(Followers)
          END
        END StatementPart;

      VAR Starters, LocalSet: SymbolSet; OK: BOOLEAN;

      BEGIN (* Block *)
        Clear(Starters); Include(Var, Starters);
        Include(Procedure, Starters); Include(Begin, Starters);
        CheckForStarter(Starters, Followers, OK);
        IF OK THEN
          Generator.OpenFrame;
          OpenScope;
          LocalSet := Followers; Include(Procedure, LocalSet);
          Include(Var, LocalSet); Include(Begin, LocalSet);
          DeclarationPart(LocalSet); StatementPart(Followers);
          CloseScope;
          Generator.CloseFrame;
          FindFollower(Followers)
        END
      END Block;

VAR ProgramName: Word; IdSpelling: Word;
    LocalSet: SymbolSet; Entry: IdentifierEntry;

BEGIN (* Programme *)
  Generator.OpenFrame;
  OpenScope;
  NewType(IntegerType, Scalars);
  IntegerType^.Representation := Generator.IntegerRepresentation;
  NewType(CharType, Scalars);
  CharType^.Representation := Generator.CharRepresentation;
  NewType(BooleanType, Scalars);
  BooleanType^.Representation := Generator.BooleanRepresentation;
  GetSpelling(Integer, IdSpelling);
  NewId(IdSpelling, Entry, Types); Entry^.IdType := IntegerType;
  GetSpelling(Char, IdSpelling);
  NewId(IdSpelling, Entry, Types); Entry^.IdType := CharType;
  GetSpelling(Boolean, IdSpelling);
  NewId(IdSpelling, Entry, Types); Entry^.IdType := BooleanType;
  GetSpelling(False, IdSpelling);
  NewId(IdSpelling, Entry, Constants);
  WITH Entry^ DO IdType := BooleanType; ConstantValue := 0 END;
  GetSpelling(True, IdSpelling);
  NewId(IdSpelling, Entry, Constants);
  WITH Entry^ DO IdType := BooleanType; ConstantValue := 1 END;
  InitializeSymbolSets;
```

```
      Accept(Module);
      IF SymbolDescription.Symbol = Identifier THEN
        ProgramName := SymbolDescription.Spelling
      ELSE ProgramName := BlankWord
      END;
      Accept(Identifier); Accept(Semicolon);
      NullIdentifier := NIL;
      Clear(LocalSet);
      Include(Identifier, LocalSet); Include(Period, LocalSet);
      Block(LocalSet, NullIdentifier);
      IF SymbolDescription.Symbol = Identifier THEN CheckIsSameAs(ProgramName)
      END;
      Accept(Identifier);
      CloseScope;
      Generator.CloseFrame
   END Programme;

END Analyzer.
```

Appendix 13

Code generator

Implementation module

```
IMPLEMENTATION MODULE Generator;
  FROM Target IMPORT MaximumAddress, AddressRange, FirstAvailable, Integer,
                     AddressRegister, OrderCode, Level, Instruction,
                     SystemRoutines, AddressOf;
  FROM LexicalAnalyzer IMPORT SymbolType;
  FROM Host IMPORT New, Dispose;
  IMPORT SourceHandler, CodeHandler;

  VAR SuppressCodeGeneration: BOOLEAN;

  PROCEDURE NoFurtherCode;
    BEGIN
      SuppressCodeGeneration := TRUE
    END NoFurtherCode;

  PROCEDURE GeneratorError(Code: CARDINAL);
    BEGIN
      SourceHandler.Error(Code, SourceHandler.PositionNow)
    END GeneratorError;

  (*                    DATA REPRESENTATION AND STORAGE                    *)

  PROCEDURE SetScalarRepresentations;
    BEGIN;
      IntegerRepresentation := 1; BooleanRepresentation := 1;
      CharRepresentation := 1
    END SetScalarRepresentations;

  PROCEDURE ArrayRepresentation(BoundMin, BoundMax: Integer;
                                ElementRepresentation: TypeRepresentation;
                                VAR Representation: TypeRepresentation);
    BEGIN
      IF NOT SuppressCodeGeneration THEN
        Representation := (BoundMax - BoundMin + 1) * ElementRepresentation
      END
    END ArrayRepresentation;

  PROCEDURE InitializeRepresentations;
    BEGIN
      IntegerRepresentation := 1;  BooleanRepresentation := 1;
```

401

```
      CharRepresentation := 1
  END InitializeRepresentations;

CONST PseudoLevel = 0; GlobalLevel = 1;

VAR   FrameLevel: CARDINAL;

CONST FirstLocal = 3; (* Stack Frame Offsets *)

TYPE  FrameEntry = POINTER TO FrameRecord;
      FrameRecord = RECORD
                        NextLocal: AddressRange; NextFrame: FrameEntry
                    END;

VAR   LocalFrame: FrameEntry;

PROCEDURE InitializeFrames;
  BEGIN
    LocalFrame := NIL; FrameLevel := PseudoLevel
  END InitializeFrames;

PROCEDURE OpenFrame;
  VAR NewFrame: FrameEntry;
  BEGIN
    IF NOT SuppressCodeGeneration THEN
      INC(FrameLevel);
      New(NewFrame, SIZE(FrameRecord));
      WITH NewFrame^ DO
        NextLocal := FirstLocal; NextFrame := LocalFrame
      END;
      LocalFrame := NewFrame;
    END
  END OpenFrame;

PROCEDURE AddressFor(Representation: TypeRepresentation;
                     VAR Address: RunTimeAddress);
  BEGIN
    IF NOT SuppressCodeGeneration THEN
      Address.TextualLevel := FrameLevel;
      WITH LocalFrame^ DO
        Address.RelativeAddress := NextLocal;
        INC(NextLocal, Representation)
      END
    END
  END AddressFor;

PROCEDURE CloseFrame;
  VAR OldFrame: FrameEntry;
  BEGIN
    IF NOT SuppressCodeGeneration THEN
      OldFrame := LocalFrame; LocalFrame := LocalFrame^.NextFrame;
      Dispose(OldFrame, SIZE(FrameRecord));
      DEC(FrameLevel)
    END
  END CloseFrame;

(*                    INSTRUCTION ASSEMBLY & FILING                    *)

MODULE Code;
  (* Sequentially allocates object program locations from FirstAvailable   *)
  (* onwards.  Assembles and files Target machine instructions via procedures *)
  (* Ins and JumpIns.  Labelled points in the code may be represented by      *)
```

```
(* variables of type CodeLabel, which are bound to the code itself by      *)
(* procedures NewLabel, FutureLabel, and ExpectedLabel.                    *)
(* At run-time the first instruction of the program is a jump to the start *)
(* of the main program code.  Word 3 contains the address of base of the   *)
(* run-time stack.                                                         *)
IMPORT CodeHandler, AddressRange, OrderCode, AddressRegister, Integer, Level,
       Instruction, CodeLabel, CodeMax, CodeRange, SystemRoutines, AddressOf,
       FirstAvailable, GeneratorError;
EXPORT QUALIFIED NewCodeSpace, EndOfCodeSpace, Ins0, InsD, Ins, JumpIns,
                 ReserveInstruction, FixUp, NewLabel, FutureLabel,
                 ExpectedLabel, SystemCall, EnterHere, GenerationComplete;


VAR CurrentAddress: AddressRange;
    Code: ARRAY [1..CodeMax] OF Instruction;
    NextInstruction: [1..CodeMax+1]; NoCodeOverflow: BOOLEAN;

PROCEDURE NewCodeSpace;
  BEGIN
    NextInstruction := 1; NoCodeOverflow := TRUE
  END NewCodeSpace;

PROCEDURE EndOfCodeSpace;
  (* Outputs contents of code array to code file *)
  VAR NextLocation: AddressRange; I: CodeRange;
  BEGIN
    NextLocation := CurrentAddress - 2*(NextInstruction-1);
    FOR I := 1 TO NextInstruction - 1 DO
      CodeHandler.LocateInstruction(NextLocation, Code[I]);
      INC(NextLocation, 2)
    END
  END EndOfCodeSpace;

PROCEDURE CopyCode(CodeValue: Instruction);
  (* Copies CodeValue as next instruction in the Code array, pending *)
  (* possible fix-ups.                                               *)
  BEGIN
    IF NextInstruction > MAX(CodeRange) THEN
      IF NoCodeOverflow THEN
        GeneratorError(91); NoCodeOverflow := FALSE
      END;
      NextInstruction := 1
    END;
    Code[NextInstruction] := CodeValue; INC(NextInstruction);
    INC(CurrentAddress, 2)
  END CopyCode;

PROCEDURE Ins(Op: OrderCode; D: Integer; R: AddressRegister; L: Level);
  (*  Generates Target instruction Op D,[R, L]  *)
  VAR NewInstruction: Instruction;
  BEGIN
    NewInstruction.OpCode := Op; NewInstruction.N := D;
    NewInstruction.R := R; NewInstruction.L := L;
    CopyCode(NewInstruction)
  END Ins;

PROCEDURE Ins0(Op: OrderCode);
  (*  Generates Target instruction Op  *)
  VAR NewInstruction: Instruction;
  BEGIN
    WITH NewInstruction DO
      OpCode := Op; N := 0; R := MIN(AddressRegister); L := 0
    END;
```

```
      CopyCode (NewInstruction)
    END Ins0;

PROCEDURE InsD (Op: OrderCode; D: Integer);
  (*  Generates Target instruction Op D  *)
  VAR NewInstruction: Instruction;
  BEGIN
    WITH NewInstruction DO
      OpCode := Op; N := D; R := MIN(AddressRegister); L := 0
    END;
    CopyCode (NewInstruction)
  END InsD;

PROCEDURE ReserveInstruction (VAR CodeAddress: CodeRange);
  BEGIN
    CodeAddress :=  NextInstruction; Ins0 (NOOP)
  END ReserveInstruction;

PROCEDURE FixUp (FixUpAddress: CodeRange;
                Op: OrderCode; D: Integer; Reg: AddressRegister; Lev: Level);
  BEGIN
    WITH Code[FixUpAddress] DO
      OpCode := Op; N := D; R := Reg; L := Lev
    END;
  END FixUp;

PROCEDURE JumpIns (JumpType: OrderCode; VAR Sequence: CodeLabel);
  (* Generates jump instruction to the CodeLabel described by Sequence.  *)
  VAR Destination: Integer;
  BEGIN
    WITH Sequence DO
      IF Expected THEN
        Destination := LastCodeReference; LastCodeReference := NextInstruction;
      ELSE Destination := StartAddress
      END
    END;
    Ins (JumpType, Destination, BP, 0)
  END JumpIns;

PROCEDURE NewLabel (VAR Sequence: CodeLabel);
  BEGIN
    WITH Sequence DO
      Expected := FALSE; StartAddress := CurrentAddress
    END
  END NewLabel;

PROCEDURE FutureLabel (VAR Sequence: CodeLabel);
  BEGIN
    WITH Sequence DO
      Expected := TRUE; LastCodeReference := 0
    END
  END FutureLabel;

PROCEDURE ExpectedLabel (VAR Sequence: CodeLabel);
  VAR ThisFixUp, NextFixUp: [0..CodeMax];
  BEGIN
    WITH Sequence DO
      NextFixUp := LastCodeReference;
      WHILE NextFixUp <> 0 DO
        ThisFixUp := NextFixUp; NextFixUp := Code[ThisFixUp].N;
        Code[ThisFixUp].N := CurrentAddress
      END;
```

```
             Expected := FALSE; StartAddress := CurrentAddress
        END
      END ExpectedLabel;

  PROCEDURE SystemCall(RoutineNeeded: SystemRoutines);
    (* Generates call to specified system routine *)
    BEGIN
      Ins(CALL, AddressOf(RoutineNeeded), BP, 0)
    END SystemCall;

  PROCEDURE EnterHere;
    (* Sets third instruction as a jump to the start of the main program. *)
    VAR MainProgramJumpInstruction: Instruction;
    BEGIN
      WITH MainProgramJumpInstruction DO
        OpCode := BRN; N := CurrentAddress; R := BP; L := 0
      END;
      CodeHandler.LocateInstruction(4, MainProgramJumpInstruction)
    END EnterHere;

  PROCEDURE GenerationComplete;
    (* Sets first and second instructions of the object   *)
    (* program to set PSR and to set stack base address.  *)
    VAR ThisInstruction: Instruction;
    BEGIN
      WITH ThisInstruction DO
        OpCode := SETPSR; N := 0; R := BP; L := 0
      END;
      CodeHandler.LocateInstruction(0, ThisInstruction);
      WITH ThisInstruction DO
        OpCode := SETSP; N := CurrentAddress; R := BP; L := 0
      END;
      CodeHandler.LocateInstruction(2, ThisInstruction)
    END GenerationComplete;

BEGIN
  CurrentAddress := FirstAvailable;
  NextInstruction := 1; NoCodeOverflow := TRUE
END Code;


(*                 PROCEDURE, PROGRAM AND STORAGE HOUSEKEEPING                    *)

PROCEDURE NewLinkage(VAR Linkage : ProcedureLinkage);
  BEGIN
    IF NOT SuppressCodeGeneration THEN
      WITH Linkage DO
        TextualLevel := FrameLevel; Code.FutureLabel(CodeBody)
      END
    END
  END NewLinkage;

PROCEDURE CallProcedure(VAR Linkage: ProcedureLinkage);
  BEGIN
    IF NOT SuppressCodeGeneration THEN
      WITH Linkage DO
        Code.InsD(MARK, 3);
        Code.Ins(LOADA, 0, FP, FrameLevel - TextualLevel + 1);
        Code.JumpIns(CALL, CodeBody)
      END
    END
  END CallProcedure;
```

```
PROCEDURE EnterBody(VAR Linkage: ProcedureLinkage);
  BEGIN
    IF NOT SuppressCodeGeneration THEN
      WITH Linkage DO
        Code.NewCodeSpace; Code.ExpectedLabel(CodeBody);
        Code.Ins(STORE, 0, FP, 0);
        Code.ReserveInstruction(EntryPoint)
      END
    END
  END EnterBody;

PROCEDURE LeaveBody(VAR Linkage: ProcedureLinkage);
  BEGIN
    IF NOT SuppressCodeGeneration THEN
      WITH LocalFrame^ DO
        Code.FixUp(Linkage.EntryPoint, INCREG, NextLocal - FirstLocal, SP, 0)
      END;
      Code.Ins0(EXT); Code.EndOfCodeSpace
    END
  END LeaveBody;

VAR MainProgramFixUp: CodeRange;

PROCEDURE EnterProgram;
  BEGIN
    IF NOT SuppressCodeGeneration THEN
      Code.NewCodeSpace;
      Code.EnterHere;
      Code.InsD(MARK, 3);
      Code.ReserveInstruction(MainProgramFixUp);
      Code.SystemCall(InitializeIO)
    END
  END EnterProgram;

PROCEDURE LeaveProgram;
  BEGIN
    IF NOT SuppressCodeGeneration THEN
      WITH LocalFrame^ DO
        Code.FixUp(MainProgramFixUp, INCREG, NextLocal - FirstLocal, SP, 0)
      END;
      Code.SystemCall(FinalizeIO);
      Code.Ins0(HLT);
      Code.EndOfCodeSpace;
      Code.GenerationComplete
    END
  END LeaveProgram;

(*                  COMPILE-TIME EVALUATION STACK                    *)

TYPE StackEntry = POINTER TO StackNode;
     NodeKind = (Reference, Constant, Result, Operation, Address);
     OperatorKind = (Unary, Binary, ReadOp);
     StackNode = RECORD
                   NextNode: StackEntry;
                   Rep: TypeRepresentation;
                   CASE Kind: NodeKind OF
                   | Reference:
                       RefAddress: RunTimeAddress;
                       CASE Indexed: BOOLEAN OF
                       | TRUE:
                           Index: StackEntry; IndexMin, IndexMax: Integer;
                       | FALSE:
```

```
                                END
                     | Constant:
                          Value: Integer;
                     | Result:
                     | Address:
                     | Operation:
                          CASE OpKind: OperatorKind OF
                          | Unary:
                               UnaryOp: OperatorType; UnaryEntry: StackEntry;
                          | Binary:
                               BinaryOp: OperatorType;
                               LeftEntry, RightEntry: StackEntry
                          | ReadOp:
                               Mode: IOMode
                          END
                     END
                  END;

MODULE Stack;
   IMPORT StackEntry, StackNode, New, Dispose;
   EXPORT QUALIFIED Push, Pop, NewNode, FreeNode;

   VAR Top: StackEntry;

   PROCEDURE NewNode(VAR Entry: StackEntry);
     BEGIN
       New(Entry, SIZE(StackNode));
     END NewNode;

   PROCEDURE Push(Entry: StackEntry);
     BEGIN
       Entry^.NextNode := Top; Top := Entry
     END Push;

   PROCEDURE Pop(VAR Entry: StackEntry);
     BEGIN
       Entry := Top; Top := Top^.NextNode
     END Pop;

   PROCEDURE FreeNode(Entry: StackEntry);
     BEGIN
       Dispose(Entry, SIZE(StackNode))
     END FreeNode;

   BEGIN
     Top := NIL
   END Stack;


(*                          EXPRESSION EVALUATION                          *)

PROCEDURE StackReference(Location: RunTimeAddress);
   VAR NewEntry: StackEntry;
   BEGIN
     IF NOT SuppressCodeGeneration THEN
       Stack.NewNode(NewEntry);
       WITH NewEntry^ DO
         Kind := Reference; RefAddress := Location; Indexed := FALSE
       END;
       Stack.Push(NewEntry)
     END
   END StackReference;
```

```
PROCEDURE IndexedReference(BoundMin, BoundMax: Integer;
                          ElementRepresentation: TypeRepresentation);
  VAR ArrayVariableEntry, IndexEntry: StackEntry;
  BEGIN
    IF NOT SuppressCodeGeneration THEN
      Stack.Pop(IndexEntry); Stack.Pop(ArrayVariableEntry);
      WITH ArrayVariableEntry^ DO
      (* first adjust starting address of array as if lower bound = 0 *)
        DEC(RefAddress.RelativeAddress, BoundMin * ElementRepresentation);
        IF IndexEntry^.Kind = Constant THEN
          INC(RefAddress.RelativeAddress,
              IndexEntry^.Value * ElementRepresentation);
          Stack.FreeNode(IndexEntry)
        ELSE
          Indexed := TRUE; Index := IndexEntry;
          IndexMin := BoundMin; IndexMax := BoundMax
        END;
        Rep := ElementRepresentation;
      END;
      Stack.Push(ArrayVariableEntry)
    END
  END IndexedReference;

PROCEDURE Dereference(Representation: TypeRepresentation);
  VAR TopEntry: StackEntry;
  BEGIN
    IF NOT SuppressCodeGeneration THEN
      Stack.Pop(TopEntry); TopEntry^.Rep := Representation;
      Stack.Push(TopEntry)
    END
  END Dereference;

PROCEDURE StackConstant(ConstantValue: Integer;
                        ConstantRepresentation: TypeRepresentation);
  VAR ConstantEntry: StackEntry;
  BEGIN
    IF NOT SuppressCodeGeneration THEN
      Stack.NewNode(ConstantEntry);
      WITH ConstantEntry^ DO
        Rep := ConstantRepresentation; Kind := Constant;
        Value := ConstantValue
      END;
      Stack.Push(ConstantEntry)
    END
  END StackConstant;

PROCEDURE NegateInteger;
  VAR IntegerEntry, ResultEntry: StackEntry;
  BEGIN
    IF NOT SuppressCodeGeneration THEN
      Stack.Pop(IntegerEntry);
      IF IntegerEntry^.Kind = Constant THEN
        WITH IntegerEntry^ DO Value := -Value END;
        Stack.Push(IntegerEntry)
      ELSE
        Stack.NewNode(ResultEntry);
        WITH ResultEntry^ DO
          Rep := IntegerRepresentation; Kind := Operation;
          OpKind := Unary; UnaryOp := Minus; UnaryEntry := IntegerEntry
        END;
        Stack.Push(ResultEntry)
      END
```

```
        END
      END NegateInteger;

PROCEDURE BinaryIntegerOperation(Operator: OperatorType);

  PROCEDURE DoArithmetic(Operator: OperatorType; Left, Right: Integer;
                         VAR Result: Integer);
    VAR Overflow: BOOLEAN;
    BEGIN
      Overflow := FALSE;
      CASE Operator OF
      | Plus, Minus:
          IF Operator = Minus THEN Right := -Right END;
          IF (Left > 0) AND (Right > 0) THEN
            Overflow := (Left > MAX(INTEGER) - Right)
          ELSIF (Left < 0) AND (Right < 0) THEN
            Overflow := (Left < MIN(INTEGER) - Right)
          END;
          IF NOT Overflow THEN Result := Left + Right END
      | Times:
          IF Right = 0 THEN Result := 0
          ELSIF ABS(Left) > MAX(INTEGER) DIV ABS(Right) THEN Overflow := TRUE
          ELSE Result := Left * Right
          END
      | Div:
          IF Right = 0 THEN GeneratorError(94); Result := MAX(INTEGER)
          ELSE Result := Left DIV Right
          END
      END;
      IF Overflow THEN
        GeneratorError(93); Result := MAX(INTEGER)
      END
    END DoArithmetic;

  VAR LeftOperand, RightOperand, ResultEntry: StackEntry;
      ResultValue: Integer;

  BEGIN
    IF NOT SuppressCodeGeneration THEN
      Stack.Pop(RightOperand); Stack.Pop(LeftOperand);
      IF (LeftOperand^.Kind = Constant) AND (RightOperand^.Kind = Constant) THEN
        DoArithmetic(Operator, LeftOperand^.Value,
                     RightOperand^.Value, ResultValue);
        StackConstant(ResultValue, IntegerRepresentation);
        Stack.FreeNode(LeftOperand); Stack.FreeNode(RightOperand)
      ELSE
        Stack.NewNode(ResultEntry);
        WITH ResultEntry^ DO
          Rep := IntegerRepresentation; Kind := Operation;
          OpKind := Binary; BinaryOp := Operator;
          LeftEntry := LeftOperand; RightEntry := RightOperand
        END;
        Stack.Push(ResultEntry)
      END
    END
  END BinaryIntegerOperation;

PROCEDURE Comparison(Operator: OperatorType);
  VAR LeftOperand, RightOperand, ResultEntry: StackEntry;
      ResultValue: BOOLEAN;
  BEGIN
    IF NOT SuppressCodeGeneration THEN
```

```
        Stack.Pop(RightOperand); Stack.Pop(LeftOperand);
        IF (LeftOperand^.Kind = Constant) AND (RightOperand^.Kind = Constant) THEN
          WITH LeftOperand^ DO
            CASE Operator OF
            | LessThan:            ResultValue := Value < RightOperand^.Value
            | LessThanOrEqual:     ResultValue := Value <= RightOperand^.Value
            | GreaterThanOrEqual:  ResultValue := Value >= RightOperand^.Value
            | GreaterThan:         ResultValue := Value > RightOperand^.Value
            | NotEquals:           ResultValue := Value <> RightOperand^.Value
            | Equals:              ResultValue := Value = RightOperand^.Value
            END
          END;
          StackConstant(ORD(ResultValue), BooleanRepresentation);
          Stack.FreeNode(LeftOperand); Stack.FreeNode(RightOperand)
        ELSE
          Stack.NewNode(ResultEntry);
          WITH ResultEntry^ DO
            Rep := BooleanRepresentation; Kind := Operation;
            OpKind := Binary;
            IF (Operator = GreaterThan) OR (Operator = GreaterThanOrEqual) THEN
              IF Operator = GreaterThan THEN BinaryOp := LessThan
              ELSE BinaryOp := LessThanOrEqual
              END;
              LeftEntry := RightOperand; RightEntry := LeftOperand
            ELSE
              BinaryOp := Operator;
              LeftEntry := LeftOperand; RightEntry := RightOperand;
            END
          END;
          Stack.Push(ResultEntry)
        END
      END
  END Comparison;


PROCEDURE NegateBoolean;
  VAR BooleanEntry, ResultEntry: StackEntry;
  BEGIN
    IF NOT SuppressCodeGeneration THEN
      Stack.Pop(BooleanEntry);
      IF BooleanEntry^.Kind = Constant THEN
        WITH BooleanEntry^ DO Value := ABS(Value-1) END;
        Stack.Push(BooleanEntry)
      ELSE
        Stack.NewNode(ResultEntry);
        WITH ResultEntry^ DO
          Rep := BooleanRepresentation; Kind := Operation;
          OpKind := Unary;  UnaryOp := Not; UnaryEntry := BooleanEntry
        END;
        Stack.Push(ResultEntry)
      END
    END
  END NegateBoolean;


PROCEDURE BinaryBooleanOperation(Operator: OperatorType);
  VAR LeftOperand, RightOperand, ResultEntry: StackEntry;
      ResultValue: Integer;
  BEGIN
    IF NOT SuppressCodeGeneration THEN
      Stack.Pop(RightOperand); Stack.Pop(LeftOperand);
      IF (LeftOperand^.Kind = Constant) AND (RightOperand^.Kind = Constant) THEN
        CASE Operator OF
        | And: ResultValue := LeftOperand^.Value * RightOperand^.Value
```

```
        | Or:   ResultValue := ORD(LeftOperand^.Value + RightOperand^.Value > 0)
        END;
        StackConstant(ResultValue, BooleanRepresentation);
        Stack.FreeNode(LeftOperand); Stack.FreeNode(RightOperand)
      ELSE
        Stack.NewNode(ResultEntry);
        WITH ResultEntry^ DO
          Rep := BooleanRepresentation; Kind := Operation;
          OpKind := Binary; BinaryOp := Operator;
          LeftEntry := LeftOperand; RightEntry := RightOperand
        END;
        Stack.Push(ResultEntry)
      END
    END
  END BinaryBooleanOperation;

(*                       DATA ACCESS CODE GENERATION                        *)

VAR BinaryOpCode: ARRAY OperatorType OF OrderCode;

PROCEDURE InitializeBinaryOpCodes;
  BEGIN
    BinaryOpCode[Not] := NOOP;  BinaryOpCode[And] := LAND;
    BinaryOpCode[Or] := LOR;    BinaryOpCode[Div] := DVD;
    BinaryOpCode[Times] := MUL; BinaryOpCode[Plus] := ADD;
    BinaryOpCode[Minus] := SUB; BinaryOpCode[LessThan] := CLT;
    BinaryOpCode[LessThanOrEqual] := CLE;
    BinaryOpCode[GreaterThanOrEqual] := NOOP;
    BinaryOpCode[GreaterThan] := NOOP;
    BinaryOpCode[NotEquals] := CNE;
    BinaryOpCode[Equals] := CEQ;
  END InitializeBinaryOpCodes;

PROCEDURE AccessWord(WordAddress: RunTimeAddress; AccessOpCode: OrderCode);
  BEGIN
    WITH WordAddress DO
      Code.Ins(AccessOpCode, RelativeAddress, FP, FrameLevel-TextualLevel)
    END
  END AccessWord;

PROCEDURE Load(Entry: StackEntry); FORWARD;

PROCEDURE LoadAddress(Entry: StackEntry);
  BEGIN
    WITH Entry^ DO
      AccessWord(RefAddress, LOADA);
      IF Indexed THEN
        Load(Index);
        IF Rep > 1 THEN Code.InsD(LOADL, Rep); Code.Ins0(MUL) END;
        Code.Ins0(ADD);
        Stack.FreeNode(Index)
      END
    END;
    Entry^.Kind := Address
  END LoadAddress;

PROCEDURE Load(Entry: StackEntry);

  PROCEDURE DoUnaryOperation;
    VAR OpCode: OrderCode;
    BEGIN
      WITH Entry^ DO
```

```
        Load(UnaryEntry);
        IF UnaryOp = Minus THEN OpCode := NEG ELSE OpCode := INV END;
        Code.Ins0(OpCode);
        Stack.FreeNode(UnaryEntry)
      END
  END DoUnaryOperation;

PROCEDURE DoReadOperation;
  VAR OpCode: OrderCode;
  BEGIN
    WITH Entry^ DO
      CASE Mode OF
      | IntegerMode: Code.SystemCall(ReadInteger)
      | CharMode:    Code.Ins0(CHIN)
      END
    END
  END DoReadOperation;

PROCEDURE DoBinaryOperation;
  VAR Folded: BOOLEAN;
  BEGIN
    WITH Entry^ DO
      Folded := FALSE;
      IF RightEntry^.Kind = Constant THEN
        CASE BinaryOp OF
        | Plus, Minus:
            Load(LeftEntry);
            IF RightEntry^.Value <> 0 THEN
              IF BinaryOp = Plus THEN Code.InsD(INCR, RightEntry^.Value)
              ELSE Code.InsD(INCR, -RightEntry^.Value)
              END
            END;
            Folded := TRUE
        | Times, And:
            IF RightEntry^.Value = 0 THEN Code.InsD(LOADL, 0); Folded := TRUE
            ELSIF RightEntry^.Value = 1 THEN Load(LeftEntry); Folded := TRUE
            END
        | Div:
            IF RightEntry^.Value = 1 THEN Load(LeftEntry); Folded := TRUE END
        | Or:
            IF RightEntry^.Value = 0 THEN Load(LeftEntry); Folded := TRUE
            ELSIF RightEntry^.Value = 1 THEN
              Code.InsD(LOADL, 1); Folded := TRUE
            END
        ELSE (* cannot fold relational operations *)
        END
      END;
      IF LeftEntry^.Kind = Constant THEN
        CASE BinaryOp OF
        | Plus:
            Load(RightEntry);
            IF LeftEntry^.Value <> 0 THEN
              Code.InsD(INCR, LeftEntry^.Value)
            END;
            Folded := TRUE
        | Times, And:
            IF LeftEntry^.Value = 0 THEN Code.InsD(LOADL, 0); Folded := TRUE
            ELSIF LeftEntry^.Value = 1 THEN Load(RightEntry); Folded := TRUE
            END
        | Div:
            IF LeftEntry^.Value = 0 THEN
              Code.InsD(LOADL, 0); Folded := TRUE
```

```
                    END
             | Or:
                  IF LeftEntry^.Value = 0 THEN Load(RightEntry); Folded := TRUE
                  ELSIF LeftEntry^.Value = 1 THEN Code.InsD(LOADL, 1); Folded := TRUE
                  END
             ELSE (* cannot fold relational operations or minus *)
             END
          END;
          IF NOT Folded THEN
            Load(LeftEntry); Load(RightEntry);
            Code.Ins0(BinaryOpCode[BinaryOp])
          END;
          Stack.FreeNode(LeftEntry); Stack.FreeNode(RightEntry)
        END
    END DoBinaryOperation;

  BEGIN
    WITH Entry^ DO
      CASE Kind OF
      | Reference:
          IF Indexed THEN LoadAddress(Entry); Code.InsD(LOADI, 1)
          ELSE AccessWord(RefAddress, LOAD)
          END
      | Result: (* do nothing; already loaded on stack *)
      | Constant:
          Code.InsD(LOADL, Value)
      | Operation:
          CASE OpKind OF
          | Unary:  DoUnaryOperation
          | Binary: DoBinaryOperation
          | ReadOp: DoReadOperation
          END
      END
    END;
    Entry^.Kind := Result
  END Load;


PROCEDURE Assign;
  VAR ExpressionEntry, VariableEntry: StackEntry; Size: CARDINAL;
  BEGIN
    IF NOT SuppressCodeGeneration THEN
      Stack.Pop(ExpressionEntry); Stack.Pop(VariableEntry);
      Size := ExpressionEntry^.Rep;
      IF Size > 1 THEN
        LoadAddress(ExpressionEntry);
        LoadAddress(VariableEntry);
        Code.InsD(MOVE, Size)
      ELSIF VariableEntry^.Indexed THEN
        Load(ExpressionEntry);
        LoadAddress(VariableEntry);
        Code.InsD(STOREI, 1)
      ELSIF (ExpressionEntry^.Kind = Constant)
            AND (ExpressionEntry^.Value = 0) THEN
        AccessWord(VariableEntry^.RefAddress, STZ)
      ELSE
        Load(ExpressionEntry);
        AccessWord(VariableEntry^.RefAddress, STORE)
      END;
      Stack.FreeNode(ExpressionEntry); Stack.FreeNode(VariableEntry)
    END
  END Assign;
```

```
(*                               INPUT/OUTPUT OPERATIONS                          *)

PROCEDURE ReadOperation (ReadMode: IOMode);
  VAR ValueRead: StackEntry;
  BEGIN
    IF NOT SuppressCodeGeneration THEN
      Stack.NewNode(ValueRead);
      WITH ValueRead^ DO
        Kind := Operation; OpKind := ReadOp; Mode := ReadMode;
        CASE ReadMode OF
        | IntegerMode: Rep := IntegerRepresentation
        | CharMode:    Rep := CharRepresentation
        END
      END;
      Stack.Push(ValueRead)
    END
  END ReadOperation;

PROCEDURE WriteOperation(WriteMode: IOMode);
  VAR ExpressionValue: StackEntry;
  BEGIN
    IF NOT SuppressCodeGeneration THEN
      Stack.Pop(ExpressionValue);
      Load(ExpressionValue);
      CASE WriteMode OF
      | IntegerMode: Code.SystemCall(WriteInteger)
      | CharMode:    Code.Ins0(CHOUT)
      END;
      Stack.FreeNode(ExpressionValue)
    END
  END WriteOperation;

(*                               CONTROL STATEMENTS                               *)

PROCEDURE NewCodeLabel(VAR Sequence: CodeLabel);
  BEGIN
    IF NOT SuppressCodeGeneration THEN Code.NewLabel(Sequence) END
  END NewCodeLabel;

PROCEDURE FutureCodeLabel(VAR Sequence: CodeLabel);
  BEGIN
    IF NOT SuppressCodeGeneration THEN Code.FutureLabel(Sequence) END
  END FutureCodeLabel;

PROCEDURE ExpectedCodeLabel(VAR Sequence: CodeLabel);
  BEGIN
    IF NOT SuppressCodeGeneration THEN Code.ExpectedLabel(Sequence) END
  END ExpectedCodeLabel;

PROCEDURE Jump(VAR Destination: CodeLabel);
  BEGIN
    IF NOT SuppressCodeGeneration THEN Code.JumpIns(BRN, Destination) END
  END Jump;

PROCEDURE JumpOnFalse(VAR Destination: CodeLabel);
  VAR BooleanEntry: StackEntry;
  BEGIN
    IF NOT SuppressCodeGeneration THEN
      Stack.Pop(BooleanEntry);
      WITH BooleanEntry^ DO
        IF Kind = Constant THEN
          IF Value = 0 THEN Code.JumpIns(BRN, Destination) END
```

```
              ELSE Load(BooleanEntry); Code.JumpIns(BZE, Destination)
              END
          END;
          Stack.FreeNode(BooleanEntry)
      END
   END JumpOnFalse;

 TYPE CaseLabelEntry = POINTER TO CaseLabelRecord;
      CaseLabelRecord = RECORD
                             LabelValue: Integer; LimbAddress: CodeLabel;
                             Next: CaseLabelEntry
                        END;
      CaseEntry = POINTER TO CaseRecord;
      CaseRecord = RECORD
                       Selector: StackEntry;
                       CaseCode: CodeLabel;
                       MinLabel, MaxLabel: Integer; FirstLabel: CaseLabelEntry;
                       Next: CaseEntry
                   END;

 VAR  TopOfCaseStack: CaseEntry;

 PROCEDURE InitializeCaseStack;
   BEGIN
     TopOfCaseStack := NIL
   END InitializeCaseStack;

 PROCEDURE OpenCase;
   VAR ThisCase: CaseEntry;
   BEGIN
     IF NOT SuppressCodeGeneration THEN
       New(ThisCase, SIZE(CaseRecord));
       WITH ThisCase^ DO
         Stack.Pop(Selector);
         Code.FutureLabel(CaseCode); Code.JumpIns(BRN, CaseCode);
         FirstLabel := NIL;
         MinLabel := MAX(Integer); MaxLabel := MIN(Integer)
       END;
       TopOfCaseStack := ThisCase
     END
   END OpenCase;

 PROCEDURE NextIsCase(CaseLabel: Integer);
   VAR ThisLabel, PreviousLabel, NextLabel: CaseLabelEntry;
   BEGIN
     IF NOT SuppressCodeGeneration THEN
       New(ThisLabel, SIZE(CaseLabelRecord));
       WITH ThisLabel^ DO
         LabelValue := CaseLabel; Code.NewLabel(LimbAddress); Next := NIL
       END;
       WITH TopOfCaseStack^ DO
         PreviousLabel := NIL; NextLabel := FirstLabel;
         LOOP
           IF NextLabel = NIL THEN EXIT
           ELSIF NextLabel^.LabelValue > CaseLabel THEN EXIT
           ELSE PreviousLabel := NextLabel; NextLabel := NextLabel^.Next
           END
         END;
         IF PreviousLabel = NIL THEN
           ThisLabel^.Next := FirstLabel;
           FirstLabel := ThisLabel; MinLabel := CaseLabel
         ELSE
```

```
                    PreviousLabel^.Next := ThisLabel; ThisLabel^.Next := NextLabel;
                    IF NextLabel = NIL THEN MaxLabel := CaseLabel END
                END
            END
        END
    END NextIsCase;

PROCEDURE CloseCase;
  VAR ThisCase: CaseEntry;

    PROCEDURE GenerateJumpTable;
      VAR ThisLabel, PreviousLabel: CaseLabelEntry; L: Integer;
      BEGIN
        WITH TopOfCaseStack^ DO
          Code.InsD(LOADL, MinLabel); Code.Ins0(SUB);
          Code.InsD(BIDX, 2);
          ThisLabel := FirstLabel;
          FOR L := MinLabel TO MaxLabel DO
            IF L = ThisLabel^.LabelValue THEN
              Code.JumpIns(BRN, ThisLabel^.LimbAddress);
              PreviousLabel := ThisLabel; ThisLabel := ThisLabel^.Next;
              Dispose(PreviousLabel, SIZE(CaseLabelRecord))
            ELSE
              Code.Ins0(NOOP)
            END
          END
        END
      END GenerateJumpTable;

  BEGIN
    IF NOT SuppressCodeGeneration THEN
      WITH TopOfCaseStack^ DO
        Code.ExpectedLabel(CaseCode);
        Load(Selector);
        GenerateJumpTable;
        Stack.FreeNode(Selector)
      END;
      ThisCase := TopOfCaseStack; TopOfCaseStack := TopOfCaseStack^.Next;
      Dispose(ThisCase, SIZE(CaseRecord))
    END
  END CloseCase;

TYPE ForEntry = POINTER TO ForRecord;
     ForRecord = RECORD
                    ControlVariable: StackEntry;
                    StartOfLoop, EndOfLoop: CodeLabel;
                    Next: ForEntry;
                 END;

VAR  TopOfForStack: ForEntry;

PROCEDURE InitializeForStack;
  BEGIN
    TopOfForStack := NIL
  END InitializeForStack;

PROCEDURE OpenFor;
  VAR ThisFor: ForEntry; InitialExpression, FinalExpression: StackEntry;
      Temporary: RunTimeAddress;
  BEGIN
    IF NOT SuppressCodeGeneration THEN
      New(ThisFor, SIZE(ForRecord));
```

```
            WITH ThisFor^ DO
              Stack.Pop(FinalExpression); Stack.Pop(InitialExpression);
              Stack.Pop(ControlVariable);
              Load(InitialExpression); AccessWord(ControlVariable^.RefAddress, STORE);
              Load(FinalExpression);
              (* Save value of FinalExpression in a temporary location *)
              AddressFor(1, Temporary); AccessWord(Temporary, STORE);
              Code.NewLabel(StartOfLoop); Code.FutureLabel(EndOfLoop);
              AccessWord(ControlVariable^.RefAddress, LOAD);
              (* Load value of FinalExpression from temporary location *)
              AccessWord(Temporary, LOAD);
              Code.Ins0(CLE);
              Code.JumpIns(BZE, EndOfLoop);
              Stack.FreeNode(InitialExpression); Stack.FreeNode(FinalExpression);
              Next := TopOfForStack
            END;
            TopOfForStack := ThisFor
          END
      END OpenFor;

  PROCEDURE CloseFor;
    VAR ThisFor: ForEntry;
    BEGIN
      IF NOT SuppressCodeGeneration THEN
        WITH TopOfForStack^ DO
          AccessWord(ControlVariable^.RefAddress, LOAD);
          Code.InsD(INCR, 1); AccessWord(ControlVariable^.RefAddress, STORE);
          Code.JumpIns(BRN, StartOfLoop);
          Code.ExpectedLabel(EndOfLoop);
          Stack.FreeNode(ControlVariable)
        END;
        ThisFor := TopOfForStack; TopOfForStack := TopOfForStack^.Next;
        Dispose(ThisFor, SIZE(ForRecord))
      END
    END CloseFor;

BEGIN
  SetScalarRepresentations;
  InitializeBinaryOpCodes;
  SuppressCodeGeneration := FALSE;
  InitializeFrames;
  InitializeCaseStack;
  InitializeForStack
END Generator.
```

Code handler

Definition module

```
DEFINITION MODULE CodeHandler;

   FROM Target IMPORT AddressRange, Instruction;

   PROCEDURE LocateInstruction(At: AddressRange; Content: Instruction);

   PROCEDURE ListCode;

END CodeHandler.
```

Implementation module

```
IMPLEMENTATION MODULE CodeHandler;

   FROM Target IMPORT AddressRange, Instruction, OrderCode, Integer,
                      AddressRegister, Level;
   FROM Host IMPORT New, Dispose, File, FileAccessMode, OpenFile, CloseFile,
                    WriteChar, WriteString, WriteInteger, WriteCardinal, WriteLine;

   (* This module maintains a linked list of instructions transmitted from *)
   (* the code generator.                                                  *)

   VAR Mnemonic: ARRAY OrderCode OF ARRAY [1..6] OF CHAR;
       RegisterName: ARRAY AddressRegister OF ARRAY[1..2] OF CHAR;

   PROCEDURE InitializeMnemonicsTable;
     BEGIN
       Mnemonic[NOOP]   := "NOOP  ";  Mnemonic[LOAD]    := "LOAD  ";
       Mnemonic[LOADL]  := "LOADL ";  Mnemonic[LOADR]   := "LOADR ";
       Mnemonic[LOADA]  := "LOADA ";  Mnemonic[LOADI]   := "LOADI ";
       Mnemonic[STORE]  := "STORE ";  Mnemonic[STORER]  := "STORER";
       Mnemonic[STOREI] := "STOREI";  Mnemonic[STZ]     := "STZ   ";
       Mnemonic[INCR]   := "INCR  ";  Mnemonic[INCREG]  := "INCREG";
       Mnemonic[MOVE]   := "MOVE  ";  Mnemonic[SLL]     := "SLL   ";
       Mnemonic[SRL]    := "SRL   ";  Mnemonic[ADD]     := "ADD   ";
       Mnemonic[SUB]    := "SUB   ";  Mnemonic[MUL]     := "MUL   ";
       Mnemonic[DVD]    := "DVD   ";  Mnemonic[DREM]    := "DREM  ";
```

```
      Mnemonic[LAND]    := "LAND  ";  Mnemonic[LOR]   := "LOR   ";
      Mnemonic[INV]     := "INV   ";  Mnemonic[NEG]   := "NEG   ";
      Mnemonic[CLT]     := "CLT   ";  Mnemonic[CLE]   := "CLE   ";
      Mnemonic[CEQ]     := "CEQ   ";  Mnemonic[CNE]   := "CNE   ";
      Mnemonic[BRN]     := "BRN   ";  Mnemonic[BIDX]  := "BIDX  ";
      Mnemonic[BZE]     := "BZE   ";  Mnemonic[BNZ]   := "BNZ   ";
      Mnemonic[BNG]     := "BNG   ";  Mnemonic[BPZ]   := "BPZ   ";
      Mnemonic[BVS]     := "BVS   ";  Mnemonic[BES]   := "BBS   ";
      Mnemonic[MARK]    := "MARK  ";  Mnemonic[CALL]  := "CALL  ";
      Mnemonic[EXT]     := "EXIT  ";  Mnemonic[SETSP] := "SETSP ";
      Mnemonic[SETPSR]  := "SETPSR";  Mnemonic[HLT]   := "HALT  ";
      Mnemonic[CHECK]   := "CHECK ";  Mnemonic[CHIN]  := "CHIN  ";
      Mnemonic[CHOUT]   := "CHOUT ";
  END InitializeMnemonicsTable;

PROCEDURE InitializeRegisterNames;
  BEGIN
    RegisterName[BP] := "BP";  RegisterName[FP] := "FP";
    RegisterName[MP] := "MP";  RegisterName[SP] := "SP";
  END InitializeRegisterNames;

TYPE InstructionPointer = POINTER TO InstructionRecord;
     InstructionRecord = RECORD
                           Location: AddressRange; Inst: Instruction;
                           Next: InstructionPointer
                         END;

VAR InstructionList, LastInstruction: InstructionPointer;
    NextLocation: AddressRange;

PROCEDURE LocateInstruction(At: AddressRange; Content: Instruction);
  VAR NewEntry, ThisInstruction, PreviousInstruction: InstructionPointer;
  BEGIN
    IF At < NextLocation THEN (* search for insertion position *)
       ThisInstruction := InstructionList; PreviousInstruction := NIL;
       WHILE (ThisInstruction <> NIL) AND (ThisInstruction^.Location < At) DO
         PreviousInstruction := ThisInstruction;
         ThisInstruction := ThisInstruction^.Next
       END
    ELSE (* append to list *)
       PreviousInstruction := LastInstruction; ThisInstruction := NIL;
       NextLocation := At
    END;
    New(NewEntry, SIZE(InstructionRecord));
    WITH NewEntry^ DO
      Location := At; Inst := Content; Next := ThisInstruction
    END;
    IF PreviousInstruction = NIL THEN InstructionList := NewEntry
    ELSE PreviousInstruction^.Next := NewEntry
    END;
    IF ThisInstruction = NIL THEN LastInstruction := NewEntry END
  END LocateInstruction;

PROCEDURE ListCode;
  VAR CodeFile: File;

  PROCEDURE WriteInstruction(ThisInstruction: Instruction);
    BEGIN
      WITH ThisInstruction DO
        WriteString(CodeFile, Mnemonic[OpCode]); WriteString(CodeFile, "   ");
        CASE OpCode OF
        | LOAD, LOADA, STORE, STZ, BRN, BZE, BNZ, BNG, BPZ,
```

```
                    BVS, BES, CALL, SETSP:
                      WriteInteger(CodeFile, N, 6); WriteString(CodeFile, ",[");
                      WriteString(CodeFile, RegisterName[R]);
                      WriteChar(CodeFile, ",");
                      WriteCardinal(CodeFile, L, 2); WriteChar(CodeFile, "]")
                  | LOADL, LOADI, STOREI, INCR, MOVE, SLL, SRL, BIDX, MARK, SETPSR:
                      WriteInteger(CodeFile, N, 6)
                  | LOADR, STORER:
                      WriteString(CodeFile, "     ");
                      WriteString(CodeFile, RegisterName[R])
                  | INCREG:
                      WriteString(CodeFile, "     ");
                      WriteString(CodeFile, RegisterName[R]);
                      WriteChar(CodeFile, ","); WriteInteger(CodeFile, N, 2)
                ELSE (* no other fields *)
                END
              END
            END WriteInstruction;

        VAR ThisInstruction, NextInstruction: InstructionPointer;
            LastLocation: AddressRange; OK: BOOLEAN;

        BEGIN
          OpenFile("Enter name of object code listing file: ",
                    Output, CodeFile, OK);
          IF OK THEN
            WriteString(CodeFile, "*** OBJECT CODE GENERATED ***");
            WriteLine(CodeFile);
            ThisInstruction := InstructionList; LastLocation := 0;
            WHILE ThisInstruction <> NIL DO
              IF ThisInstruction^.Location <> LastLocation + 2 THEN
                WriteLine(CodeFile)
              END;
              WITH ThisInstruction^ DO
                WriteCardinal(CodeFile, Location, 8);
                WriteString(CodeFile, "   ");
                WriteInstruction(Inst); WriteLine(CodeFile);
                LastLocation := Location
              END;
              NextInstruction := ThisInstruction^.Next;
              Dispose(ThisInstruction, SIZE(InstructionRecord));
              ThisInstruction := NextInstruction
            END;
            WriteLine(CodeFile); WriteLine(CodeFile);
            WriteString(CodeFile, "*********** END ***********");
            WriteLine(CodeFile);
            CloseFile(CodeFile)
          END
        END ListCode;

BEGIN
  InitializeMnemonicsTable;
  InitializeRegisterNames;
  InstructionList := NIL; LastInstruction := NIL; NextLocation := 0
END CodeHandler.
```